MW00332287

Talks on the Parasha

Adin Even-Israel Steinsaltz

Talks on
the Parasha

Shefa
Maggid Books

Talks on the Parasha

First Edition, 2015

Maggid Books
An imprint of Koren Publishers Jerusalem Ltd.

POB 8531, New Milford, CT 06776-8531, USA
& POB 4044, Jerusalem 91040, Israel
www.korenpub.com

© Adin Even-Israel Steinsaltz 2015

The publication of this book was made possible through
the generous support of *Torah Education in Israel*.

ISBN 978-1-59264-418-6, *hardcover*

A CIP catalogue record for this title is
available from the British Library

Printed and bound in the United States

Contents

In early versions of the Talmud, the following inscription was added to the title page of each tractate: "Everything that is written here about non-Jews refers not to contemporary non-Jews but to the non-Jews who lived in past times."

In the title pages of Torah literature published today, similar disclaimers still appear – but they are invisible. They read, "Everything that is written here about Jews refers not to contemporary Jews but to Jews who lived in past times." For this reason, it is a relatively simple task to sit and study Bible, Talmud, or *musar* literature, since the information contained in these works does not apply to us or to our generation but to other people and other times.

This notion – that the book is addressing someone else, that it is practically irrelevant for us – must be erased from those invisible inscriptions. Whether it is the Bible, a *musar* text, or the Talmud, the inscription should be the exact converse: "Everything that is written here refers not to Jews who lived in past times but to contemporary Jews." In other words, the content of this book applies to me.

Editor's Introduction

This book is a collection drawn from Rabbi Adin Steinsaltz's oral discourses on the weekly *parashot*, the Torah portions that we read each Shabbat in the synagogue. As a rule, these discourses touch upon one point in each *parasha*, usually either exegetical or conceptual in nature. This point always illuminates a meaningful idea in the *parasha*, stimulating thought and introspection.

The book was not written as a discrete work. Most of the chapters are based on discourses that Rabbi Steinsaltz delivered over the years to students at his various institutions, including Yeshivat Mekor Chaim, the Bat Ayin Yeshiva, and Yeshivat Tekoa.

Some of the discourses were written especially for this collection. Naturally, the style of these discourses differs slightly from that of the oral discourses.

The book's origins can be traced to a weekly bulletin edited and published by students at Yeshivat Mekor Chaim in the year 5756 (1996). The discourses have now been re-edited, and many others have been added to complete the collection.

The discourses were edited with the intention of basically preserving the speaking style of Rabbi Steinsaltz. Hence, the book's language is conversational and reflective, not necessarily adhering to the formal style found in true written works.

I wish to thank all of the many associates who contributed to the work of collecting, editing, and proofreading throughout the lengthy and complex process of preparing this book. This includes those who worked at transcribing the recordings, finding the sources, editing the discourses, reading and commenting on the manuscript, and offering good advice. Their assistance was greatly appreciated.

Daniel Haberman translated the book into English, Daniel Landman skillfully edited it, and Sima Bozin proofread it with great care. Finally, our thanks to the staff at Maggid Books for their professionalism and dedication in bringing the book to print.

Yisrael Malkiel

Preface

The Torah contains within it many worlds. The themes, the language, all of the myriad ways in which to understand and interpret it – all of these are worlds that both exist independently and are connected to one another, inextricably linked from without and from within.

But from the totality of the Torah's manifold shades of meaning, what emerges is that the Torah is essentially "the book of the chronicles of man." The Torah – addressing, in particular, the Jewish people and the Jewish individual – helps the reader understand not only what happened in the past and what ought to happen in the future, but also the meaning of his own life. The Torah serves as a kind of wondrous looking glass in which we can simultaneously see the end of existence and our own reflection, and within that reflection not only are our outer facades visible, but the image of our true inner selves as well.

For this reason, it is no wonder that even today, new interpretations of the Torah are constantly being generated. In a telling account, the Rashbam wrote of a conversation with his eminent grandfather Rashi, regarding the interpretation of the Torah. Rashi told him that if it were within his power, he would continuously revise his commentary "according to the textual insights that are revealed each day." These new insights unfold not only because studying the Torah is like contemplating a gem that has countless facets, but also because we, too, renew ourselves daily.

This book is a collection and adaptation of oral discourses that were delivered over several years at Yeshivat Mekor Chaim and other places of learning. During those years, the audience changed, and the speaker changed as well, moving from perspective to perspective in response to the vagaries of his life and its events. At times the members of the audience were alert and lively, and at times they seemed drowsy, not necessarily because the content did not appeal to them. Rather, as we have stated, many new facets are revealed in the Torah each day, and not every facet is meant for every person.

Our sages say that when the Torah was given, God's voice split into 600,000 different voices – one voice for each person present at Sinai. They add that there were perhaps many more voices, each one individualized and personal, since the words were spoken not only for the people of that time but also for future generations. Sometimes a certain interpretation touches upon a meaningful point that a person will internalize and remember for years, and sometimes the emotional and spiritual experience will only last for a moment.

My hope is that these discourses, both as a whole and individually, will serve as a window into the inner and outer realms of the Torah, providing insights that will be meaningful not only for the Jewish people, but to each reader on a personal level as well.

Adin Even-Israel Steinsaltz

Genesis

Bereshit

With our warmest personal wishes to and great respect for Rav Adin and Sarah Steinsaltz, may they be blessed with good health and long life together, to continue their wonderful work. It is our honor to be able to dedicate this parasha for our children and grandchildren.

Families: Goldschlager, Slonim, Gerschman & Sable

Noaḥ

In honor of our parents and grandparents Greta and David Itescu
With love, respect, and gratitude from Silviu and Nicki, Isaac and Alex Itescu

Lekh Lekha

Dedicated to the memory of my father, Robert S. Brill, z"l, who, together with my mother Marian M. Brill, encouraged us to go out into the world, to love nature, to work hard, be determined, to have dreams, to be an active family member, to serve others, and to have faith and connection to our heritage.

Peggy Brill, Jerusalem

Vayera

In honor of Yehudah Yisrael Ben Shlomo Zalman Moshe HaLevi's Bar Mitzva
Ruth & Conrad, z"l Morris

Ḥayei Sara

Dedicated to the memory of Isaiah Berlin ז"ל
Martine and Peter Halban

Toledot

In memory of Göran Nisell, z"l; Doris Nisell, z"l; Jan Nisell, z"l; Martin Kischinovsky, z"l

Vayetzeh

In honor of Nachshon Yitzhak Ben Shlomo Zalman Moshe HaLevi's Bar Mitzva
Ruth & Conrad, z"l Morris

Vayishlaḥ

In loving memory of our dear Fred Worms z"l 1920-2012 to mark his Bar Mitzva portion. A man who loved Torah and its traditions and found inspiration in the great works of Rabbi Steinsaltz.

Della Worms and Family

Vayeshev

With great appreciation for the complete humanity of Rav Steinsaltz on the occasion of the wedding of Gabe Turner and Lauren Gold.

David and Frances Turner

Miketz

In honor of our ever-growing family
Dedicated by Arthur and Gisela Garmais, Jerusalem

Vayigash

Dedicated in memory of our beloved parents Marcello David ben Joseph and Emilia Barda, z"l
and Doris bat Amos and Lisa Saada, z"l
Milly, Giuliana, Luciano and Miriam and their families.

Vayeḥi

Dedicated in memory of our beloved husband and father
Shalom Arbib ben Efraim and Rachel, z"l
His wife Misa with Efraim, Hai Vito, Joseph, Hanna, Rachel,
Vera, Nora, Luciana and their families

Bereshit

THE FUNDAMENTAL QUESTIONS OF GENESIS

One of Rashi's most well-known exegetical questions can be found in his first comment on the Torah, where he famously asks, "Why does the Torah begin with the account of the Creation?" However, according to Nahmanides, the very question is unwarranted. While it is true, as Rashi points out, that Genesis lacks the sheer quantity of mitzvot that can be found in the other books of the Torah, Genesis stands out as a source of all the basic principles of our faith. Genesis is preoccupied with fundamental questions, its narratives brimming with exemplary figures whose actions shape our lives today. Clearly, it would have been impossible to begin the Torah without them.

The protagonists of Genesis are *tzaddikim* – supremely righteous individuals – but they are not flawless, one-dimensional characters. These are real people with real failings. To be sure, this does not mean that Abraham, Isaac, and Jacob, or even Joseph and his brothers, should be regarded as sinners, but each of them encountered scenarios in which the correct path was not necessarily clear. Nevertheless, these are our *tzaddikim*, our "pillars of the world." Indeed, four of the "seven shepherds"[1] – the Jewish people's spiritual fathers – are characters from the book of Genesis.

---

1. Referenced in Micah 5:4, the Kabbalists interpreted the "seven shepherds" as the seven *Ushpizin* who attend our festive meals throughout the holiday of Sukkot, namely, Abraham, Isaac, Jacob, Joseph, Moses, Aaron, and David.

Parashat Bereshit itself addresses life's fundamental dilemmas in detail. Almost every important issue appears here, including ascent and descent, Creation, and the nature of man. *Parashat Bereshit* is also the single place where the Torah discusses the concept of sin directly: What is sin and what constitutes it? The *parasha* also deals with the more human challenges of life: relationships between people, between husband and wife, between a father and his sons; quarrels between brothers, even murder. These are the building blocks of life, and *Parashat Bereshit* is full of them.

THE NATURE OF CAIN

Shaar HaGilgulim, a kabbalistic work, identifies two different types of souls and elaborates on them: souls that possess the nature of Abel and souls that possess the nature of Cain. This is not a division between good souls and evil souls, for this source attributes the nature of Cain to the souls of many great Torah leaders. Rather, the division is one of character. The souls with the nature of Abel are milder and more pleasant, whereas those with the nature of Cain are stronger and more creative.

This distinction becomes apparent when one considers the Torah's portrayals of Adam's sons, Cain and Seth, and their descendants. Cain is remembered primarily for killing his brother Abel, but we are also told something else about him: He is the first person to build. Indeed, while Adam lived for many centuries and possessed abundant wisdom, Cain is the one who built the first city.

A look at the passage on Lemekh's sons, Cain's grandchildren, reveals that they are involved in creativity and progress. The first is a shepherd – not an ordinary shepherd, but "the father of all those who live in tents and keep herds." The second is the originator of music – "the father of all those who play the harp and flute." The third creates weapons – "who sharpened all implements of copper and iron."

It appears that, in a certain respect, Cain's descendants possess creativity the likes of which is not found among Seth's descendants. In this respect, Cain's legacy recalls Jacob's description of Reuben, his first-born: "Exceeding in eminence and exceeding in power" (Gen. 49:3). The "eminence" that Jacob speaks of here refers to innovation. This quality does not necessarily express itself positively; after all, Cain is also the first murderer. Nevertheless, Cain is man's first creation, Adam's firstborn son, of whom Eve says, "I have gained a man with God." In making this statement, Eve is actually exclaiming in wonderment, "I have created a human being in partnership with God!"

We don't know much about Seth's descendants, and the little information we do possess is often unclear. Regarding Enosh, one of Seth's sons, the Torah says, "It was then that men began to invoke the Lord by name," and it is not at all clear whether "to invoke the Lord by name" refers to something positive or negative. Regarding Enoch, another of Seth's descendants, it says, "Then he was no more, for God took him," and here, too, midrashic opinion is divided as to *why* God took him. According to one midrash, God took him so that he should not become corrupt (Genesis Rabba 5:24). In another midrash it says that Enoch transformed into the angel Metatron (Genesis Rabbati 5:24), and elsewhere it says that he is "prince of the world" (*Tosafot*, Ḥullin 60a).

At first glance, it seems that mankind survives through the line of Seth and Noah, since Cain's line was wiped out in the Flood. However, this is not necessarily the case. There is a difference of opinion regarding the role of Naama, Lemekh's daughter. According to the Zohar, she was "the mother of the demons" (*Bereshit* 55a). In contrast, Genesis Rabba states that she was the wife of Noah (23:3). If the latter opinion is true, Cain's line did not come to an end. Rather, Noah's children, who survived the Flood, represent a continuation of both Seth's line – through their father Noah – and Cain's line – through their mother Naama. This would explain the continued existence of the "nature of Cain" as an aspect of human nature and behavior.

CREATION FOR THE PURPOSE OF ACTION

The nature of Cain is part of our makeup as human beings. What is a person's purpose in this world? To put it simply – as the text hints, "There was no man to till the soil" (Gen. 2:5) – his task is "to till it and tend it" (2:15). Man is charged with preserving the world. He is the one who must water the trees and ensure that nothing is damaged.

But surely man's task cannot be summed up as being the Garden of Eden's caretaker, to tighten loose screws and clean up spills here and there. Man is charged with a greater mission, namely, "which God created to do (*laasot*)." Man was created to take dynamic action, not just to preserve the present state of things.

To be sure, at the conclusion of Creation it says, "And God saw all that He had made, and behold, it was very good" (Gen. 1:31) – the soil is "good," the trees are "good," the lights are "good" – but this does not mean that everything is perfect. When God creates the world, He intentionally leaves things in an incomplete state. It is as if He says, "Look, I made the pattern, but I left you several things to complete on your own." This introduces man's requirement "to do" – *laasot* – to take action, to become a partner, as it were, in the Creation. This is part of our essence as human beings.

Man, by his very nature, affects the world in a significant way. But it is not enough to simply maintain the world; he is also responsible for improving it. The very fact that man is capable of this demonstrates that he is also required to do so. Throughout history, our sages have disputed this subject, discussing the nature and scope of man's role in the world. Tineius Rufus,[2] a Roman governor of Judea, famously challenged Rabbi Akiva on the matter of *brit mila*, asking, "What right do I have to cut off part of an organ that a person was born with?" (Tanḥuma, *Tazria* 5). Rabbi Akiva pointed to the changes that man effects on the soil. Man does not leave it in its original state. He plows it, sows it, and constantly interferes with God's work. Man does not perform these actions merely to preserve the soil, but to improve on it as well, allowing it to yield crops that are greater in quantity and quality. Man is continually changing the order, improving nature – and this is exactly as it should be.

The same basic question arises in other contexts as well. Many have argued that seeking the services of a physician is a form of heresy. If God ordained that someone should be ill, how can you intervene and try to cure him? Likewise, if God ordained that someone should be poor, how dare you interfere with His doings? The answer is that although God indeed decides that some people should fall ill and some people should be poor, there is no requirement to preserve that reality. Man is permitted – even required – to intervene.

---

2. Known in the Talmud as Turnus Rufus.

Even Rabbi Nachman of Breslov, who denounced physicians in the strongest terms, saying that when the Angel of Death understood that he could not kill everyone by himself, he appointed the physicians to do it for him (*Siḥot HaRan* 50), did not oppose medicine per se. He himself claimed, on another occasion, that a father who does not vaccinate his son against smallpox is a murderer. Apparently, his opposition to physicians did not stem from a conception that it is forbidden to interfere with God's doings, but simply from his deep distrust of the physicians of his time. In a certain respect, he was truly justified in this distrust.

When the Torah says, "which God created to do," this means that the world is full of imperfect things. As the Midrash puts it, "Everything created during the six days of Creation requires rectification" (*Pesikta Rabbati* 23). One can always question whether the "imperfections" we encounter in life result from a defect in Creation or from the sins of human beings. But once it is clear that the thorns and thistles of life – for whatever reason – do exist, we must not abide them. We fight them, destroy them, and try to grow other things in their place.

Although none of these issues are discussed explicitly in *Parashat Bereshit*, they are present in the background of all the stories that concern Cain's line. Forging copper and iron entails a thorough transformation of the raw materials of nature – an act that only human beings are capable of undertaking. The process of refining iron and copper entails many stages, and once this is accomplished, one can then progress further, to steel and aluminum. This creativity is not limited to practical, technical areas such as mining, cutting, or chiseling. In spiritual areas as well, man acts within the world, advancing it toward perfection. Any man can sing with his own voice, but a man "who plays the harp and flute" uses the world's resources to develop aspects of humanity that extend beyond his basic existence.

THE TORAH'S ATTITUDE TO PROGRESS

Whether we like it or not, progress is always bubbling in the world. What is the proper attitude to these constant changes? There is a formula attributed to the *Ḥatam Sofer*: "Innovation is forbidden by the Torah." Indeed, there are many Jews who try to live by this mantra. Ultimately, however, it is notable that even Jews of the most conservative streams do not take this opposition to innovation as far as some non-Jews do. There are some non-Jews who truly believe that innovation is forbidden – the Amish in the United States, for example, whose dress resembles that of *ḥaredi* Jews, with black hats and black garments. They abstain from technology almost entirely, do not travel in cars, and use no mechanical tools. They work the land, build their own houses – all in the old-fashioned manner. They do this because they believe, simply, that all innovation is a product of the devil. Some object to airplanes, reasoning: If God had wanted human beings to fly, He would have created them with wings. This is an excellent rationale, but I do not know of any Jew – neither from the *Edah HaḤaredit* nor from the *Neturei Karta* – who refuses to fly because of it. Jews do not express their opposition to innovation in this way. In general, even those of us who claim to refuse innovation will not hesitate to benefit from the innovations of others. The permissibility of using electricity on Shabbat can be debated from various angles, but no one contests its use during the week.

A God-fearing individual need not necessarily fear the "new"; he need not necessarily feel that it is his duty to fight against new things and protest them. On the contrary, we believe that if "God created to do," then our duty is to improve and perfect the work of God in the world. God says, "I finished My work; now it is your turn."

Life is full of problems. This reality is an essential and built-in part of life. It is not merely a local problem, such as whether to wear leather belts or what to do on a rainy day; it is a question of approach: How should we deal with matters that require attention and rectification? Adam was told, "Thorns and thistles shall it sprout for you" (Gen. 3:18). If a person sows in the ground, and thorns and thistles grow instead of his desired crop, he must ask himself: What should I do with this problem? This is an essential question, one that is not connected to external conditions or to advantages that some people may have over others, but only to how each person decides to deal with the problems that arise in life.

FEAR OF SIN TAKES PRECEDENCE OVER WISDOM

Nowadays, when the power and the tools that man possesses are incomparably superior to those of the past, the question of how they should be utilized becomes critical. Our forebears never could have imagined what is available to us today. Once, for example, not everyone could be expected to know thousands of books by heart, whereas today we possess machines that put all these books at our fingertips, besides affording many other possibilities. This progress merely accentuates the imperative and the urgency of the question: What must be done with these tools? How can we exploit them to their fullest?

Here, however, a different side of progress presents itself. Many of the awful things in the world today exist as a result of technology. This is not because the tool itself is awful, but because its use was perverted. Today, everyone has more free time, but few people utilize this time properly. There are countless examples of things that once could not be done but now are possible. But what are we doing with all these possibilities? Are we improving the world with these new opportunities, or abusing them?

Deuteronomy 32:18 can be expounded as follows: "You neglected the Rock that begot you" – the Rock, God, created you with the capacity to forget, so that you should not remember everything that happens to you. We experience trouble, pain, and suffering. God was concerned that all this would weigh down on us, so He created in us the ability to forget. Yet what did people do? The verse concludes, "forgot the Lord who brought you forth." God created you with the capacity to forget things that you don't need to remember, but instead you forget God Himself.

Our sages say of David and Bathsheba, "She was intended for David…only that he took her before she was ripe" (Sanhedrin 107a). The same applies to the fruit of the Tree of Knowledge as well. Adam took it before it was given to him, before the proper time had come, like an unripe fig. According to this interpretation, the tree and its fruit were actually intended for Adam; it was only prohibited to eat from it because the proper time had not yet come: Either the man was not yet ready, or the fruit was not yet ripe. The assumption is that there was an order to the world, a plan as to how things were supposed to unfold, and it went awry. There are certain things that, when experienced at the right time, can be beneficial, but when experienced at the improper time can be damaging.

In light of this, we must ask today whether the world is running too fast. Is it progressing beyond all proportion? The human race now has tremendous power, primarily the power to destroy, on a scale that was unattainable to earlier generations. Do people today have more power than they require? Is it more than we can handle? Is our power greater than our ability to judge how to use that power? Is it possible that we are eating the fruit of the Tree of Knowledge when it is not yet ripe?

The Mishna in *Pirkei Avot* criticizes the person "whose wisdom is greater than his deeds" (3:17). This is not a repudiation of wisdom, but merely a safeguard: If a person does not want wisdom to affect him like a "deadly poison," he must always apply it. To be sure, no matter how much one applies his wisdom, it is never enough; one must always progress and improve. The Talmud in Ketubbot 50a advises teachers of young children that once a pupil has reached the age of six, "stuff him like an ox," i.e., feed him as much knowledge as possible. At the same time, however, a person's fear of sin should take precedence over his wisdom – his wisdom must never exceed his ability to use it.

Noaḥ

CRITICIZING NOAH

Rashi's comment on the first verse in the *parasha* – "Noah was a righteous man, pious in his generation" (Gen. 6:9) – is a bit puzzling: "Some interpret it to his credit ... while others interpret it to his discredit." If the verse can be interpreted to Noah's credit, why would Rashi, echoing our sages, interpret it to his discredit?

Noah appears at the end of *Parashat Bereshit* as the world's great hope. The world is rife with criminals and thieves, and only one man exists who stands out in his generation: "But Noah found favor in God's sight" (Gen. 6:8). Even Noah's name attests to this assessment: "This one will bring us relief (*yenaḥamenu*)" (5:29). This is a child who is born amidst great hope. But Noah – despite all the praise, and although he spoke with God and was close to Him – ultimately reaches a state in which his character is interpreted negatively.

It seems clear that this negative assessment of Noah cannot be completely negative, as it would be very difficult to claim that everything he did was bad. Rather, Noah can be seen as a negative character when held up to the standard of Abraham. In other words, when our sages interpreted Noah negatively, it was not so much to discredit him but to emphasize Abraham's worthiness.

LONELINESS

As we analyze Noah's narrative arc, familiar elements begin to arise that evoke the narratives of other characters throughout Tanakh. Noah starts out as a righteous and pious man, but the final episode of his narrative represents a radical departure from this image. To be sure, Noah is not entirely at fault in the ugly incident described in chapter 9, but some of the blame can certainly be placed on Noah and his drunkenness.

The character that immediately comes to mind when we read of Noah's fall from piety is Lot. Lot comes from a good family – he is Abraham's nephew – but his fall is similarly tragic. Lot did not personally commit any egregious sins; because of this it is difficult to blame him directly for the events that transpired as a result of his actions. However, the Torah conveys an air of unpleasantness surrounding Lot's poor decisions, and it is clear that our sages' variously negative assessment of Lot is merely an extension of a motif that already exists in the text.

There are additional points of resemblance between Noah and Lot. In both cases, their children were involved; both were enticed by wine, and their respective falls came about as a result of intoxication; and both were seemingly driven to drink in the wake of extraordinarily traumatic events. Noah and Lot are both survivors of bygone worlds, solitary individuals remaining from whole societies that disappeared in the blink of an eye. Everything that surrounded them is suddenly gone, and they are left isolated within themselves. Apparently, neither Noah nor Lot can bear the terrible loneliness, the feeling of being one of the only people left in the world. It should not be surprising that both of them, wallowing in loneliness, begin to drink.

The loneliness of Noah and Lot is a natural result of separation from the world. In fact, this is essentially the same loneliness that the *tzaddik* experiences, as one can only become a *tzaddik* if he is capable of being alone, able to countenance endless loneliness. A *tzaddik* must be willing to be like Abraham, of whom Ezekiel says, "Abraham was singular" (Ezek. 33:24).

Abraham wanted to change the world. But the moment he leaves his father's house, he also decides to be singular and alone, to be "Abram the Hebrew (*HaIvri*)" (Gen. 14:13) – that is, in a position where "the whole world stands on one side (*ever*) and he stands on the other side"

(Genesis Rabba 42:8).[1] Abraham's willingness to accept the loneliness of a *tzaddik's* task is part of what makes him the perfect *tzaddik*. Conversely, a person can be a truly exalted personality, but as long as he cannot exist without a community of supporters, he cannot be a true *tzaddik*.

In the book of Ezekiel, Daniel and Job appear together with Noah in the same verse (14:14). What the three have in common is that each of them had to begin his course by himself, all alone and without any support from others. An individual who follows such a path undertakes to be alone even where good company is available. He cannot truly connect with his father or mother, his brothers or sisters, or anyone else. Part of his essence is to be alone.

The *tzaddik* faces loneliness even when he is surrounded by his followers. Rabbi Nachman of Breslov (in a preface to *Likkutei Moharan* II) comments on the notion of "Abraham was singular" that the *tzaddik*, even when he is surrounded by good people, must be ready for the loneliness and singularity that Noah and Abraham experienced.

It is interesting to note that even people who lived in generations that, seemingly, were not at all sinful or degenerate still express the loneliness of one who longs to transcend his society. Take, for example, the book of Psalms. King David lives in neither a physical nor a cultural wilderness. Nor does he live in a place where everyone is wicked. But if we turn to chapter 69, we see that he speaks of terrible loneliness – everyone is mocking him, everyone is laughing. I imagine that a person in David's situation today, thirsting for spiritual growth, would be admonished by his peers, "There is a limit to the fear of God. Do you think you are better than the local rabbi? Do you think you are better than your friends? Know your place. Why do you have to be better than everyone else?"

This is what creates the sense of loneliness, and this is what David is complaining about. It is not about persecution but about a feeling of distance from his immediate circle or society. Even a fundamentally good society is not always interested in having a distinctive, exalted individual in its midst – even if that individual represents godliness and holiness.

---

1. The simple meaning of the epithet *"HaIvri"* is that Abraham came from the other side (*ever*) of the Euphrates; the Midrash adds another layer of meaning to this.

Many of the prophets experienced this same loneliness as well. That Jeremiah was wretched and persecuted is understandable. He came from a small village of Priests, who presumably did not possess great wealth. When a young man without noble ancestry stood up and criticized the people, it was no wonder that they beat him and tormented him. But the same phenomenon occurs to another prophet who was seemingly born into opposite circumstances. Isaiah was the King Uzziyahu's cousin, and from the style of his book it is evident that he did not speak like a commoner but like a member of the aristocracy. He was also the only prophet whom God did not have to push into accepting his mission; rather, Isaiah rushed to receive prophecy of his own accord – and yet even he says, "I did not hide my face from insult and spitting" (Is. 50:6).

A person can follow a righteous path and be considered one "who acts charitably at all times" (Ps. 106:3), as interpreted by our sages, "This refers to one who supports his sons and daughters" (Ketubbot 50a). One can also be a simple Jew, who plows in the plowing season, sows in the sowing season, and reaps in the reaping season, like an ordinary member of society. However, when one acts like a simple Jew, it becomes impossible to transcend this status, to ascend in holiness. There is an element of separation that is part of the essence of the *tzaddik*. For some, the justification for this separation is simple: I live in a hostile world, a world full of people who are totally different from me. In order to survive spiritually in such a world, it is necessary to separate from it to some extent. But even when a person lives in a world that he basically identifies with, a world that is populated by good, decent people, there, too, he must take care to incorporate an element of separation into his lifestyle and persona.

As we have stated, part of this problem is societal. Society does not like it when someone deviates from the norm – even if this deviation improves the society. It takes people a long time to accept someone who is better than they. Furthermore, some people harbor envy, hatred, and other emotions that act as obstacles to healthy relationships. But apart from dealing with the reaction of society, one must also face oneself. When an individual chooses to ascend toward God, he naturally isolates himself – not as a reaction to society but because he now devotes himself to a more sublime form of contact.

In order for an individual to follow the path of a *tzaddik*, he must, at least to a certain extent, be detached and devoted to God, and this is something that requires a kind of total dedication. One who is constantly enmeshed in his society can reach important achievements, but to reach the path of absolute truth requires the total disregard of other people's opinions. To be excessively cognizant of the opinions of others represents a defect in a person's willpower.

This concept applies to people living in any generation and, as we have seen, it is reflected in the Torah in the characters of Noah, Abraham, Moses, David, and many others.

"A TZADDIK IN PELTZ"

Ascending in holiness is not a simple matter. It involves an intrinsic danger, to which Noah fell prey. When one is occupied with a world that is entirely holy, he lives in it alone, and he is liable to forget that there are other people that exist in the world. When a person lives, grows, and develops alone, he may come to a point where he becomes unaware of the existence of others.

What does a *tzaddik* do when disaster strikes the world? He can respond in several ways. When Noah builds an ark, he opts for a very specific form of response. He explains to his neighbors that he is building an ark because God is about to bring retribution. Noah does not hate them, Heaven forbid. However, the essence of his work is to build a shelter in which he and his small group will be able to escape and survive, so that no matter what happens, he will not be harmed. Noah is certainly righteous and pious, but he lacks the ability to speak with his contemporaries, who consider him crazy. He has withstood 120 years of their mockery of both him and his promised flood, so it stands to reason that he is sick of these people and their jokes. When he builds an ark, he is building a shelter for himself. He is willing, perhaps, to let in another several people, but, tellingly, not enough to form a complete *minyan* of ten people. This fits perfectly with Noah's persona: Such a man, by his very nature, is incapable of making a *minyan*. Noah did allow a few relatives to board the ark, but even in this he did not go too far: Only his wife and his children were invited.

Noah lets into the ark only the very best, only those he deems deserving of survival. All the rest he rejects, and they all perish – and yet he does let into the ark at least one son whose worthiness is highly questionable. This phenomenon is not so rare. Sometimes a clique of *tzaddikim* forms – four, five, eight *tzaddikim* who sit by themselves – and they let into their group a Ham or a Japheth, saying, mistakenly, "We are family, so we will surely get along."

There is a well-known saying that Noah was the first example of the Yiddish expression, "a *tzaddik* in *peltz*" – a *tzaddik* wearing a fur coat. What is a *tzaddik* in *peltz*? When the cold weather comes, there are two ways of dealing with it. One way is to turn on a heater; the other way is to wear a fur coat. The result for the individual is the same: Whether one turns on the heater or wears a fur coat, he will be warm enough and can continue to function. The difference is only regarding others. When one turns on the heater, others will enjoy the warmth as well, whereas when one wears a fur coat, the individual becomes warm, but the others remain cold.

The problem with Noah's ark was not that there was no need for an ark. There was certainly a need for an ark, as otherwise it would have been impossible to escape the Flood. But when Noah closed his ark so that others could not enter, that was an exceedingly problematic course of action.

Strangely and paradoxically, the very fact that Noah saved only himself and his family was what caused his family to become no more than ordinary. Noah's descendants are ordinary people of all types and kinds. There are ten generations from Adam to Noah, and ten more from Noah to Abraham, but no notable descendants issue from Noah. Noah says, "Before I attempt to educate other people's children, before I try to influence others, I should concern myself with my own children." As a result of Noah's inward-facing perspective, his children do not achieve anything of consequence. By contrast, Abraham, who constantly concerns himself with the children of others, is blessed with a litany of notable descendants. His children, for better or for worse, are distinctive characters in our tradition.

LOVE OF GOD – A PASSION?

Anyone who worships God knows that there is an aspect of spiritual pleasure inherent in worship, as R. Sheshet says, "Rejoice, my soul, rejoice, my soul; for you have I read [the Torah], for you have I studied [the Mishna]" (Pesaḥim 68b). What could be better? We are not talking about contemptible people who derive physical benefits from their worship, but about pure spiritual pleasure.

Whether it is the act of getting up to pray or sitting down to study Torah, that moment has the potential to be the pinnacle of a person's worldly pleasure, unconnected to any concern about one's share in the World to Come. I was once the guest of a Jewish dairy farmer who lived on a kibbutz. He did physical labor for close to eight hours each day – and he was not a young man – and then he would bathe, have a small meal, and sit for between eight and nine hours studying Talmud. And whenever it was possible, he would study for another few hours after that. The fact that he studied bareheaded and that his home lacked a mezuza had nothing to do with the simple pleasure he derived from connecting with God through Torah study.

For the *tzaddik*, although solitude is one of his primary means of connection with God, it can also be a form of egoism. Within this solitude is an aspect of pure selfishness: This individual is concerned only with himself. There are various levels of excessive solitude. For some, it manifests itself in the desire to eat alone. For others, it means studying Talmud alone. For still others, it is a desire to claim the entire World to Come for themselves. All of these cases are problematic, which raises the extremely serious question about people who engage in the service of God: Could it be that the love of God is a passion like all other passions? Could there be a person who is so preoccupied with his Creator that he cannot see his fellow men?

THREE LEVELS OF *TZADDIKIM*

Needless to say, one does not necessarily have to isolate himself completely in order to be a *tzaddik*. The Torah mentions that on their journey to Canaan, Abram and Sarai took with them "the souls they had made in Ḥaran" (Gen. 12:5). What is the meaning of this expression – how does one "make souls"? The Midrash explains, "Abraham converted the men, and Sarah converted the women" (Genesis Rabba 39:14). Abraham and Sarah were only two people, but they were actively involved in redeeming the world, constantly engaging with and reaching out to others.

Broadly speaking, there are three levels of *tzaddikim*, each of which is considered praiseworthy in God's eyes: the level of Noah, the level of Abraham, and perhaps an even higher level – that of Moses. Noah represents the *tzaddik* who looks after himself alone. Abraham represents the *tzaddik* who cannot tolerate being totally self-centered, for he feels the need to look after the world. Moses represents the highest level of righteousness. When God wanted to isolate him from the People of Israel after they sinned, Moses refused. God turns to him after the sin of the Golden Calf and relays to him the same message that Noah received: "You are a *tzaddik*; the entire generation is unworthy of surviving. You should survive, and a new world shall arise from you." Moses responds, "Blot me out from Your book" (Ex. 32:32). Not only does Moses assume great responsibility and concern himself with the world around him, but he says that he does not want to be the only *tzaddik* among all these people. If God cannot forgive the entire generation, Moses will renounce even the personal relationship with God that he had cultivated until that point.

THE FLOOD IN EVERY GENERATION

The problem of the flood exists not just in the time of Noah. To be sure, God promised that there would never again be such a flood of water, but as any good lawyer would point out, He never promised to desist from other floods. God's promise is, in this respect, a carefully-termed legal clause, complete with limitations.

In fact, there is a flood in almost every generation. In some generations, the "flood" is physical; it may be a wildfire, a tsunami, an earthquake, or a volcanic eruption. In other generations, the flood is not physical but spiritual. Just as a physical flood may involve water falling down from heaven or surging up from the sea, in a spiritual flood the intellectuals inundate us with anti-religious messages from above, and from below, the masses initiate a deluge of dissatisfaction with the religious experience.

Hence, the need arises to build an ark. For this reason, people gather together and safeguard themselves; they build for themselves walls so as not to drown in the ocean of water. On the other hand, the story of Noah should remind us that even someone who is saved from the flood can end up like a drunkard, leading an insular life even in spiritual matters; and then the world will have to wait another ten generations until someone comes along to save it.

Today, our modern "arks" are sometimes much larger than that of Noah. The ark may be the size of a neighborhood or even a whole city – containing within it countless *tzaddikim*, perhaps one Canaan, one Ham, and even one Shem with his house of study. Beyond that, as far as the ark's inhabitants are concerned, no other world exists. This contemporary spiritual isolation is a problem that requires attention.

Noah's narrative begins with "Noah found favor" and ends on a note of defeat – he is an old and lonely man, with nothing to show for his life's achievements and struggles. Ultimately, the world's "second draft" ends in failure, just as the "first draft" did. God finished creating the world and beheld that "it was very good" (Gen. 1:31), but shortly thereafter *Parashat Bereshit* concludes, "and He grieved in his heart" (6:6).

Only later on comes the story of Abraham, the man who is capable of being entirely alone, and yet – in spite of everything – succeeds in his life's goal of fitting the entire world into his ark.

Lekh Lekha

TRIAL AND STRUGGLE

To a certain extent, the first two *parashot* in the Torah are tragic narratives, dealing with the fundamental failings of man. In contrast, *Parashat Lekh Lekha* begins a series of joyful *parashot*. From this *parasha* onward we enter a different reality, one that focuses on man's triumphs and achievements.

The central characters of these *parashot* – Adam, Noah, and Abraham – are more than individuals: They are symbols as well. Adam is a symbol of mankind's failed first trial, about which the Torah summarizes, "And God regretted" (Gen. 6:6). Noah is a symbol of failure as well – this time, of mankind's second trial – and his *parasha* concludes in a similar fashion, with the story of Noah's personal downfall and the story of the downfall of the generation that built the Tower of Babel.

Our sages comment briefly on these failures: "There were ten generations from Adam to Noah ... ten generations from Noah to Abraham" (Avot 5:2). All the generations in between are disregarded not because they are unimportant (if they were unimportant to us, we would not talk about them), but because, in the final analysis, they are failed generations. Only here, in *Parashat Lekh Lekha*, does a new story begin – the story of Abraham, of the triumph of man.

Abraham's story is not just the story of a perfect *tzaddik* who "walked with God," raised righteous children who learned in yeshivas, died peacefully, and all was well. The story does not end that way at all.

Abraham's children were not all *tzaddikim*, and certainly did not all attend yeshivas. In what sense, then, is Abraham's story about the triumph of man? The answer is that it is the story of a man who followed a path that included trials, struggles, and setbacks but, in the end, succeeded in achieving his goals. In light of this, we can confidently consider *Parashat Lekh Lekha* the first in a series of joyful *parashot*.

TRIALS

The *parasha* begins with a trial. Commenting on this trial and on similar trials throughout Genesis, our sages say, "The experiences of the patriarchs prefigure the history of their descendants" (Tanḥuma, *Lekh Lekha* 9; Nahmanides on Genesis 12:6). Because of this, it is important for us to understand what a trial is and what it means to withstand a trial. Although both Adam and Noah are our ancestors, the Torah never implies that we should follow their example in any regard. Abraham, by contrast, is our exemplar; we attempt to emulate his conduct, following his path in the process of building our character.

The Mishna states, "Abraham our patriarch was tested with ten trials, and he withstood them all" (Avot 5:3). Logic dictates that Abraham's trials became increasingly difficult, for a person who withstands a difficult trial will not then be tested with an easier one. Despite this, the trials did not necessarily increase in difficulty in terms of the physical suffering they entailed. After all, the very first trial – "Go forth (*lekh lekha*)" (Gen. 12:1), in which Abraham is told to pack his bags and move elsewhere – is much more difficult and complicated than the trial of "Whatever Sarah tells you, do as she says" (21:12), which does not entail physical strain. The increasing difficulty of the trials, then, is in terms of the spiritual effort required of Abraham: Each trial becomes more personal, more poignant, and more internally challenging than the preceding one. Each one of the trials cuts more deeply into Abraham's soul and demands a more profound inner and spiritual sacrifice.

A comprehensive view of all of the ten trials shows that Abraham is required to sever – albeit gradually and progressively – all of the ties between him and other people, between him and things that he is connected and close to. And he indeed does so, with all the difficulty that this entails.

First, he must leave his home and family, and separate from his friends and relatives and from everything with which he is familiar. Abraham is instructed to go forth "from your land" – i.e., his homeland, where he knows the language and the customs; "from your birthplace" – i.e., his own private sphere, not necessarily related to physical space; "and from your father's house" – i.e., his family. Abraham must detach himself from all the components of his life and personality.

Later on, there is a famine in Canaan, and Abraham is forced to leave his new home as well, even though he had arrived only recently. In Egypt, his wife is taken from him, and he does not know when she will return; Pharaoh does not give him an address or a date. He is told to cast out his eldest son Ishmael, and he does so.

The tenth trial – the *Akeda* – is the most difficult trial of them all. It is many times more difficult than the previous trials because it requires that Abraham do two things at once: First, he must kill his son Isaac, who is "your son, your only son, whom you love" (Gen. 22:2), and who is also the offspring promised him by God. Second, he must perform an act that is far more serious and difficult, beyond the private-personal crisis of losing his only son. It is the ultimate crisis of faith for Abraham – he must kill and sacrifice a human being, something that Abraham has stood against all his life.

NULLIFYING THE "WHY"

Upon examining the trial of *lekh lekha*, several puzzling questions immediately present themselves. God says to Abraham:

> Go forth from your land, from your birthplace and from your father's house to the land that I will show you. I will make of you a great nation. I will bless you and make your name great, and you will be a blessing. I will bless those who bless you and curse him that curses you, and through you all the families of the earth will be blessed. (Gen. 12:1–3)

At first glance, this command does not appear to be so terrible. God tells Abraham to go forth, promising to lavish blessings upon him if he does so. What could be better?

The question is only exacerbated when this trial is compared to that of the *Akeda*. It is interesting to note that the two trials share certain expressions ("go forth," "that I will show you," "that I will point out to you"), and they are stylistically similar in several practical details as well. Nevertheless, there is an essential difference between the trials. In the *Akeda*, there is no promise attached to the trial; there is only the command to perform the *Akeda*, without providing any reason, incentive, or assurance. Here, alongside the command to "go forth" there is a long list of blessings. Today, people frequently leave their home countries – whether it is the Land of Israel or another country with fewer problems – to pursue the mere possibility of finding prosperity elsewhere. Their explanations for their departure are characterized by uncertainty, by the words "perhaps," "possibly," and "maybe." People often move overseas even when they know that they will only find partial blessing, and not complete blessing. Here, however, God promises Abraham that he need only go away, and he will have all that is good. What more does he need?

Additionally, the trial of *lekh lekha* was not actually the first trial. It was preceded by another trial, which is not explicitly recounted in the Torah but which appears in the Midrash (*Pirkei DeRabbi Eliezer* 26). In that trial, Abraham had to cast himself into the fiery furnace in Ur Kasdim as a result of his refusal to worship idols. Abraham was willing to give his life rather than disavow his belief in one God. After such an experience, what is the difficulty of *lekh lekha*? It seems absurd: After Abraham was ready to sacrifice himself for the sake of his God, he is told, "I have seen that you are willing to die. Now I will put you to a greater test: Are you also willing to change your place of residence?"

The answer to these questions is twofold. First, as we have stated, the trials are in ascending order in terms of inner, spiritual difficulty, not in terms of their physical demands. It is true that suffering martyrdom for the glorification of God's name is incomparably more physically difficult than moving to a different land. Nevertheless, when a person dies for the glorification of His name, he knows why he is doing it. Granted, this kind of martyrdom is a great and praiseworthy act, a trial that not everyone has been able to withstand. Furthermore, over the course of history, those who elected to die as martyrs were always regarded as extraordinary examples. At the same time, martyrdom was never an entirely uncommon occurrence. As it says in the Midrash, recounting a dialogue between two Jews who were sentenced to death, "'For what are you going out to be stoned?' 'Because I circumcised my son.' 'For what are you going out to be burned?' 'Because I kept Shabbat'" (Leviticus Rabba 32). A person who is prepared to die for the glorification of God's name possesses an inner certainty; he knows that this is the absolute truth. He knows for whose sake he is about to die, and he knows for what purpose he is giving his life.

By contrast, the trial of *lekh lekha* lacks this element. Abraham receives an order, but no justification or reason is provided. If one wants to be a God-fearing individual, why can't this be accomplished in Brooklyn? Is it impossible to be a God-fearing person in Ḥaran, in Ur Kasdim, in Akkad, or in Shinar? Is there something wrong with those places? Why must Abraham, or anyone else, uproot himself from his home in the service of God?

Thus, the trial here pertains not to the physical strain but to the lack of inner justification, of a sense of meaning and purpose. In the trial of the fiery furnace, Abraham does not have to change what is in his heart. He has a clear purpose and absolute inner conviction. Here in *Parashat Lekh Lekha*, however, Abraham has no inner reason, and the question is to what extent he is willing to change himself, to renounce his personal beliefs, in order to accept upon himself God's kingship. Why should a person get up and leave – even if he is promised blessing and success – if there is seemingly no rhyme or reason for doing so? Nullifying the "why" is the challenge here, the true test of the trial of *lekh lekha*.

SETTING OUT WITH NO DESTINATION

There is also a second aspect to the trial of *lekh lekha*, which appears to be the essence of the difficulty, and which is found in the command's second part: "to the land that I will show you."

Abraham sets out without an address, without a destination. This is much more difficult than severing personal ties. When Noah builds an ark, he certainly knows why he is making it. Hence, his assignment is not referred to as "the trial of building the ark." It is a clearly defined assignment: He must build an ark over the course of 120 years and thereby save himself from the imminent worldwide catastrophe. But when Abraham leaves his home, he sets out for the endless horizon with no apparent goal or destination whatsoever.

It is very difficult to accept the idea that one must proceed without a destination. This is fundamentally different from the self-sacrifice that was required of Abraham earlier. When he is told to go to a place "that I will show you," then even if he has absolute faith in God, he is inevitably beset with a powerful personal question: "Where am I going?" "For what purpose?" If God had said to Abraham, "Go the land of Canaan," then even if he had not wanted to go specifically to the land of Canaan – which does not seem to have been a place of widespread piety – it would not have been the least bit difficult for him to have gone. He could have gone anywhere – even to Sodom. But to go without a destination, to "a land that I will show you," means to go without the anticipation of arriving at a certain place. Knowing where one is going lends a certain peace of mind, the particular location notwithstanding. God says to Abraham, "You are going." "Where to?" "You will find out; you will be told."

NO END

This trial is a personal dilemma faced not only by Abraham. It exists in many spheres, recalling the words of our sages cited above: "The experiences of the patriarchs prefigure the history of their descendants." Our lives are structured so that everything has a purpose, everything has a point where it begins and a point where it ends. Hence, doing something that has no known end can cause real anguish.

Thus, for example, one of the most frustrating things in the realm of Torah study is that there is no point at which one can say that he is finished learning. Because of this daunting infinite nature of Torah, students often create artificial end points for themselves. Throughout Israel, there are many batei midrash where students train to become rabbinical judges. Most of the students know that the program will not necessarily benefit them financially – they are not guaranteed a job after finishing the program. Why, then, do they enroll in such a program? In many cases, it serves to fill an emotional need: A student can feel that he is not going about aimlessly, getting nowhere. A person who dedicates his time to

Torah study for five years or ten years accomplishes nothing practically but the experience of having sat and learned. And if he decides to extend his learning for another year, what does he gain? Again, only the experience of having sat and learned for one more year. A person who studies at a university for far fewer years receives a diploma. To be sure, a university diploma is not always worth more than a yeshiva diploma; even an expert in ancient Roman literature cannot always use his degree to make a prosperous living. Nevertheless, a diploma or a degree gives a student a goal to strive for. The student proceeds systematically from one well-defined station to another on the way to the ultimate goal of achieving a degree. Upon reaching the first station, one continues on to the next, and one knows where one will arrive at the end. When there are no clear stations along the way to a distinct finish line, the lack of a goal becomes a pressing problem: What is the purpose of all of this? What will happen in the end?

When a person finishes a series of concerted actions with something tangible in his hand, he has the feeling that he has accomplished something real. In contrast, the lack of clearly defined objectives and goals inherent in the nature of Torah study makes it a very difficult world in which to thrive, and poses a real problem for proponents of intense, long-term Torah study.

WALK BEFORE ME

In truth, the act of setting out without a clear goal or destination evokes the Torah's dictate to "follow God your Lord" (Deut. 13:5). One may know one's starting point, but not where he will arrive. There is no assurance that if one sits for a certain period of time, then he will become wise, God-fearing, or pious. The only instruction is to "follow God" or, as we read in *Parashat Lekh Lekha*, "Walk before Me" (Gen. 17:1).

Others have discussed how the command "Walk before Me" is a greater test than "Follow God your Lord." The latter instruction is akin to saying to someone, "Follow me; I will go ahead and clear the way for you." But when God says to Abraham, "Walk before Me," in effect He is saying: "Clear your own path; find your own way. You have no assurances."

"Walk before Me" is a life problem. There is an aspect of Abraham in each one of us, and each one of us faces the same situation that Abraham faced. Sometimes, one stands to lose everything for the sake of walking on God's path – one's land, one's birthplace, and one's father's house; sometimes, it is not as difficult as that, but there is always an aspect of "I will go, and I will not receive anything for it." Naturally, one prefers that everything have some quantifiable end, at which one could state that he has become a little more holy. But God promises nothing of the sort; He just wants us to start walking – whether it is following Him or before Him.

Indeed, the Jewish people's excellence lies precisely in this quality:

> Israel demonstrated real greatness…For they did not say to Moses, "How can we go out into the wilderness without having provisions for the journey?" Rather, they had faith and followed Moses. Of them it is stated in the traditional sacred writings: "Go and cry in the ears of Jerusalem, saying, 'I remember for you the devotion of your youth, your love as a bride, how you followed me in the wilderness, in a land not sown'" (Jer. 2:2). (*Mekhilta DeRabbi Yishmael, Beshallaḥ*)

They simply went. The Jewish people traveled in the wilderness without a known destination, a fact that, in the end, drove them crazy. After all, they were eating manna, drinking well water and, outside of their internal quarrels, had no serious problems. So what was bothering them? The major trial over the course of forty years was the feeling that they were going around in circles: "And we circled Mount Seir for a long time" (Deut. 2:1). They were frustrated by the seemingly endless nature of their journey. They were driven mad by the lack of a point, an address, some kind of structure in their circuitous path.

The command to "go forth" is not only an instruction, but a description of how a person should go forward in life. We learn from Abraham that this is the way one must proceed, as Rabbi Judah HaLevi put it, "I will not question, I will not test" (*Reshuyot* 22). That is how one follows God: without a destination and without an aim. God's great call to man, the first call and the last, is a call without a destination. God says, "go forth," and one must get up and go, without knowing where one will arrive, without knowing one's objective, and without knowing one's aim. This path, with all its difficulties, is the proper path for the beginning of a person's life, for that is how Abraham's story begins. Despite all the blessings and promises, this is Abraham's first trial that appears explicitly in the Torah: to follow God and not to question; to go, without the comfort of physical space to call his home.

On this path, there is only one real request that Abraham makes throughout all the trials – and it is an eminently reasonable one: that he should know that it is God who is speaking with him, that it is He who is instructing him to go forth. Abraham needs only the assurance that God is always with him to justify his actions. Following God is the point; it justifies itself.

The truth is that, often, when a person follows God – whether through mitzvot, prayer, or diligent Torah study – something changes within him. The stone softens, the iron cracks, something happens. However, there is no assurance that a particular series of godly actions will lead to these formative changes. We know that if one follows God, this naturally leads to inner development – in one's self-purification, refinement, and connection to God – but there is no guarantee that this will happen.

If a person feels that he is not ready for this call, then perhaps he is not yet ready for *Parashat Lekh Lekha* as well. He is still languishing in *Parashat Noah*, sitting with Noah and his concerns – to drink or not to drink; to do or not to do. The story of Noah is completely different from that of Abraham. Noah, as his name implies, is the type of person who rests (*nah*); all he wants is to be at ease (*noah*).

In order to be like Abraham, one must be willing to depart "from your land, from your birthplace and from your father's house," each individual according to his capacity. Every person must undertake this departure, some in a very real way, and others for whom it is only a partial departure – but a departure nonetheless.

One who follows God, by his very nature, cannot be found in his land, in his birthplace, or in his father's house. Psalms 135 states: "O house of Israel, bless the Lord; O house of Aaron, bless the Lord; O house of Levi, bless the Lord; you who fear the Lord, bless the Lord" (19–20). There is a "house of Israel," a "house of Aaron," and a "house of Levi," but there is no "house of you who fear the Lord." Ultimately, those who fear God have no house. They follow God.

Vayera

"BEKHOL MEODEKHA"

The Mishna states, "Abraham our patriarch was tested with ten trials, and he withstood them all" (Avot 5:3). It stands to reason that these trials begin with "*lekh lekha*" (or, possibly even earlier, with the trial of the fiery furnace in Ur Kasdim) and with time become progressively more difficult. The trials include famine, domestic distress, and geopolitical crises, each trial more difficult than the preceding one.

It would have been fitting, then, for the series of trials to conclude with the trial of the *Akeda*. The trial of *lekh lekha* is certainly difficult, but "your son, your only son, whom you love" is the greatest trial that a person could face, and yet Abraham withstood even that.

However, at least according to Rabbi Jonah Gerondi, Abraham's final trial is not the *Akeda*. Rather, it is the story that appears at the beginning of *Parashat Ḥayei Sara*, namely, the search for a burial site for his wife Sarah and the difficulties that accompanied this search. After God had promised Abraham, "For all the land that you see, to you will I give it" (Gen. 13:15–17), he had to go to Efron the Hittite and bargain with him over the price of a parcel of land.

What is the point of testing a man like Abraham, who already withstood the *Akeda*, demonstrating his willingness to sacrifice his only son to God, with such a trial, which at first glance does not even approach the level of difficulty of the *Akeda*?

Our sages interpret the verse, "You shall love God your Lord with all your heart (*bekhol levavekha*), with all your soul (*bekhol nafshekha*), and with all your might (*bekhol meodekha*)" (Deut. 6:5) as follows: "'With all your heart' means with both your inclinations, with the good inclination and with the evil inclination; 'with all your soul' means even if He takes your life; and 'with all your might' means with all your money" (Berakhot 54a). Focusing on the third clause, our sages go on to explain, "There are people who value their lives more than their money... and there are people who value their money more than their lives" (61b). Indeed, there are people who would rather lose a limb than lose their money, including even great *tzaddikim*. The Talmud reports regarding Abba Ḥilkiya that when he would pass through thorns he would roll up his garment because, he said, a scratch on the body heals by itself, but if his garment were to be torn, he would not have the money to buy a new one (Taanit 23b).

From the order of the verse's wording, however, and from our sages' interpretation, it appears that "with all your soul" is a higher level of devotion to God than "with all your heart," and that "with all your might" – i.e., with all your money – is the highest of them all. How is this possible?

DROP BY DROP

In *Likkutei Torah*, a hasidic work by Rabbi Shneur Zalman of Liadi, "with all your might" is interpreted as follows: In everything that one does, one must do more, in the sense of "*meod*," which literally means "more" (*Shir HaShirim* 16:3). This understanding of "*meod*" makes "with all your might" an even higher level than giving up one's life; giving up one's life requires a moment's decision, and with that the matter is settled, whereas "with all your might," as the *Likkutei Torah* understands it, represents unending love of God.

An example of this level of devotion is found in the Talmud: "If Ḥanania, Mishael, and Azaria had been lashed, they would have worshiped the golden image" (Ketubbot 33b). They were threatened and even thrown into the fiery furnace because they refused to bow down and worship the idol, and it is true that they were willing to die. But if they had been lashed, says the Talmud, they would not have been able to bear it. There is suffering that is worse than death, and such suffering is much harder to bear.

In this respect, "with all your money," while seemingly unimpressive, is no less of a sacrifice than the other two levels of devotion. The meaning is not in the sense of "hand over your money or give up your life." Rather, the Torah commands us to love God even in the face of oppressive poverty, whose effects are cumulative, gradually piling up. These are not troubles that occur all at once, but troubles that drain the spirit drop by drop, each day drawing out another drop and yet another. In the process known as "Chinese water torture," water is slowly dripped onto a person's head, drop after drop. It turns out that this method of torture breaks even people who were not broken by any other method.

Even people who are capable of enduring major tribulations and who proved themselves willing to actually offer up their lives are not always capable of bearing the suffering of small troubles. There was once a Chabad Hasid who eventually apostatized, and toward the end of his life became the chief censor of Russia. It is said about him that even forty years after he apostatized, though he had long since ceased to keep the mitzvot, he would mention the name of the Baal HaTanya (Rabbi Shneur Zalman of Liadi) only with the greatest awe and reverence. This individual, once a pious man and a Torah scholar, was not broken by sudden, momentous tribulations but by smaller troubles. To earn a living, he had to work in a large city, even though, as a Jew, this was prohibited by Russian law. He was repeatedly caught and evicted until the strain of this lifestyle finally broke him.

Thus, "with all your might" does not entail choosing between life and death; rather, it entails withstanding hardships that befall a person little by little. This was the nature of Abraham's tenth trial. Our sages say that Sarah died just as Abraham returned from the *Akeda* (Genesis Rabba 58:5). After the *Akeda*, during which Abraham truly offered up his entire soul, he now had to return to daily life, with all the picayune annoyances of everyday affairs. It is not just the distress of his wife's death and the need to arrange for her burial, but the very fact that he must deal with the petty process of the negotiations, the purchase, and the burial. After Abraham reached such a high level of intimacy with God, instead of being able to sit down and mourn his wife as people do, he must endure a different type of suffering: He must meet with Efron the Hittite and deal with the business of purchasing land, forcing himself to be polite and to repeatedly bow down before the people of the land.

To be sure, this still may not appear to be the ultimate trial for Abraham. Everyone experiences the slog of daily life, yet it can frustrate some people even more deeply than a life-threatening situation. For many people, it is precisely these small things, which are seemingly easier for a person to withstand, that can become the biggest stumbling block.

SELF-SACRIFICE

Broad generalities are not always perfectly accurate, and are often debatable. Despite this, I would like to attempt an overarching analysis of the ten trials of Abraham. Each of the trials of Abraham represents a different type of self-sacrifice. The trials are not about breaking the body or slaying the evil inclination. They are not about things that are intrinsically difficult to accomplish. The difficulty lies in the fact that self-sacrifice completely transcends the question of bodily limits; the challenge is to break the bounds of one's self. In each one of the trials, Abraham must prevail not over some external foe, but over himself.

Furthermore, in each of the trials, God presents Abraham with a choice whose different sides do not fall into simple categories of good and bad. In most trials, there is no moral dilemma: The individual knows that what he is doing is right. However, doing the right thing is often difficult, and it is this difficulty that constitutes the trial. In the trials of Abraham, however, God commands him to do things that are sometimes morally problematic, and therein lies the difficulty of the trials.

When a person fights an inclination with which he has no internal relationship, it is relatively easy for him to speak of "overcoming the inclination." In such a case, a person can stand up, laughing and proclaiming, "An arrow in the eye of Satan" (Sukka 38a). This may not be a simple task, but there is a clear moral path to success. However, when the evil inclination is close to one's heart, it becomes much more difficult to overcome it. One may know all the considerations that direct him to the proper course of action, and still fail to overcome one's inclination to act otherwise.

Still, even the most difficult struggle with one's inclinations and desires cannot compare to the level of inner difficulty that Abraham encountered in his trials. Abraham was tested by God with genuine moral-spiritual dilemmas, with real struggles between God's will and personal conviction.

SACRIFICING MORALITY

Abraham achieved great success through his spiritual work in Ḥaran, as our sages interpret, "'The souls they had made in Ḥaran' – they brought them under the wings of the *Shekhina*. Abraham converted the men, and Sarah converted the women" (Genesis Rabba 84:4). In Ḥaran, Abraham carries out his mission, proclaiming God's name in the world, and he is regarded as one of land's eminent and noble personalities. After all that, God tells him to go away to an unfamiliar place, where he does not know the people, and begin everything anew. Abraham was, after all, seventy-five years old – not a young man, even in those days. What was to become of all his life's work? What was to become of all the energy he had invested, all of his great accomplishments? God tells him to go and sever all ties with his former life.

Yet here, too, Abraham's trials continue. Even the war of the Canaanite kings is a trial. Spilling blood is out of character for Abraham; he may be courageous but he is certainly not a man of war. Nevertheless, he must go off with people he does not truly know to a war that barely concerns him. He is charged with saving Bera, Birsha, and all the other kings – characters with whom he has very little connection. Still, he must wage war, endanger himself and all that he has, in order to save a few despicable creatures: the kings of Sodom, Gomorrah, Adma, and Tzevoyim. When a man who fights for his country, homeland, and home puts his life in danger, he at least knows why he is fighting. Here, Abraham goes to save Lot, after Lot had parted ways with him in the wake of the shepherds' quarrel. Because of Abraham's lack of connection to the Canaanite conflict, he refuses to keep any of the spoils of war: This money is loathsome to him. Abraham does not want anything to do with these people, does not want to negotiate with them, and does not want their money. When the war is over, all Abraham wants is to go home. He did what he had to do, and now he must leave.

When Abraham has to cast out Hagar and his son Ishmael, he openly expresses his reluctance to do so. How can he bring himself to take human beings – his wife and his son no less – and cast them out into the wilderness? But God tells him that this is what he must do, and he obeys. When he obeys, his problem is not what to do with the child; it is how to come to grips with his own moral persona after such an act.

Not long before the story of Hagar and Ishmael, the Torah relates a different story – that of Abraham and the three angels – which perhaps serves to emphasize the poignancy of what is required of Abraham here. Despite Abraham's advanced age and frailty, when three people come his way he immediately runs toward them and does all that he can to help them. He does this for no reason other than "because you have passed by" (Gen. 18:5) – because they have come this way. By contrast, when it comes to his own wife and son, he must do the opposite: Not only does he not provide them with food, but he banishes them from his home. How should he view himself now? A man whose whole essence is kindness to others must now do something that is entirely anti-thetical to his character – like one who urges others to pursue one course of action and then himself does the opposite.

In the case of the *Akeda*, the worst thing from Abraham's point of view was that he had to slaughter a human being, let alone "your son, your only son, whom you love." The slaughter of children appears in the Torah itself as an example of the most abhorrent of all acts: "For even their sons and their daughters do they offer up in fire to their gods" (Deut. 12:31). And yet Abraham, who knows that it is abhorrent, is commanded: "Take your son, your only son" – and sacrifice him. Before facing the trial of love for his own child, Abraham was forced to ask, "Where is my whole world? Where is my whole concept of justice? Where is my morality?" At the *Akeda*, Abraham sacrifices not only his son's body but his own soul.

GIVING UP THE WORLD TO COME

Abraham's trials present us with an opportunity to discuss self-sacrifice in our own lives. When is self-sacrifice required of us? What is the challenge of self-sacrifice in today's world?

Throughout our lives, we must often give of ourselves for God's sake, but that is only a minor sacrifice. The prospect of giving up our portion in the World to Come, however, is a much weightier matter. It would be short-sighted and even animalistic to give up the World to Come for the sake of this world. But from Abraham's narrative we learn that for the sake of Heaven, we must sometimes renounce even the World to Come. Deciding not to go to a nightclub when one's ticket to the Garden of Eden is at stake is simple. It is much more difficult when one is required, for God's sake, to walk into Gehenna of one's own volition, into the fire.

The Talmud interprets Esther's statement to Mordekhai, "and if I perish, I perish" (Est. 4:16), as follows: "As I am lost to my father's house, so will I be lost to you" (Megilla 15a). But Rabbi Tzadok HaKohen of Lublin offers another interpretation: "As I am lost in my worldly existence, so will I lose the next world" (*Likkutei Amarim* 16). Until now Esther had associated with Ahashverosh under compulsion, but now she must continue their relationship of her own volition. To do such a thing, Esther must go beyond her ordinary limits. Until this stage, Esther had preserved her innocence, for her entire relationship with Ahashverosh had been under duress. The moment it ceases to be under duress, she forfeits her moral and spiritual high ground. Though all she does is for God's sake, she nevertheless seemingly loses her portion in the World to Come.

There are various stories that deal with this difficult subject. The Midrash relates that when Elisha b. Avuya died, Rabbi Meir thought that he died in a state of repentance. However, when Rabbi Meir was later told that a fire was burning in Elisha b. Avuya's grave, he visited the grave, covered it with his *tallit*, and gave the following interpretation of Ruth 3:13: "'Stay for the night' – in this world, which is like the night – 'and it shall be, in the morning' – regarding the world that is wholly good [i.e., the World to Come], 'if the Good One' – God – 'would redeem you, let Him redeem. But if He does not want to redeem you, I will do so myself'" (Ruth Rabba 6). Rabbi Meir avows that if God does not take Elisha b. Avuya out of Gehenna, then he will do so himself.

"IF YOU SEEK IT LIKE SILVER"

The stories that we have been discussing are not simply "deeds of the patriarchs," what people call "Bible stories"; rather, these are guidelines that teach us how to act. But where can we possibly find the strength to emulate Abraham and our other biblical role models? Children draw strength from their parents, and disciples from their masters. In the Talmud there are several stories that convey this notion. For example, a woman once came to Rabbi Meir's beit midrash and said, "Rabbi, one of you [i.e., one of your students] betrothed me by way of intercourse" – but she did not know the identity of the student.[1] In order to avoid embarrassing a student who may have engaged in the unseemly practice of betrothal through intercourse, Rabbi Meir rose and wrote out for her a bill of divorce. Thereupon, all the students stood up and did likewise, and as a result the woman was released from the betrothal. The Talmud then explains that Rabbi Meir learned this mode of conduct from Samuel the Small, who in turn learned it from a tradition going back to Joshua and Moses (Sanhedrin 11a).

In order to act in an ideal way, one must truly care with one's whole being. When a person is suffering from physical pain, he immediately goes to the nearest doctor. A person who suffers greater pain will rush all the more quickly to find a cure for his ailment. Similarly, one who suffers from hunger – real hunger, not the hunger one experiences after fasting on Yom Kippur – and wonders where he will find bread to eat and water to drink will not first organize a symposium to discuss the question of poverty and unemployment. The acute sensation of hunger creates in him the readiness and urgency to act. One who is not experiencing pain or hunger personally may be tempted not to come to the aid of those who are needy, thinking, "What can I do? I am only one insignificant person." This line of thinking, however, implies that the matter is not his concern – it does not truly affect him. Others may rationalize their actions, saying, "I agree that in principle I should help, but in practice it is difficult for me." If he can help without expending much of his time or resources, he will not object to doing so, but this person will never go out of his way to help others.

This phenomenon occurs in other areas as well. Someone who has a love for Torah will find a way to study it even if he does not know

---

1. She wanted the student to come forward and either marry her or release her from the betrothal by giving her a bill of divorce.

"how to learn" in the conventional sense. He may have to work ten times harder than someone who has more experience in the world of Torah study, but in the end he will succeed. Proverbs 2 states, "If you seek it like silver and search for it like hidden treasure, then you will grasp the fear of God and discover knowledge of God" (4–5). If you identify Torah as something that is missing in your life, and you search for it as one searches for treasure, you will undoubtedly find it.

At the beginning of the *parasha*, God shows kindness to Abraham, as it were. It is hot outside, and God arranges that no guests arrive at his tent, allowing Abraham to rest. But Abraham does not want to rest – he wants to perform acts of kindness for others, and he cannot be at peace until guests arrive. When the guests finally come, in the form of angels sent by God, Abraham must rush about and attend to them in order to put himself at ease. When one's soul yearns for something and it affects him on a deep, personal level, he will always find a way to achieve his goal.

Ḥayei Sara

TEMPEST AND TRANQUILITY

The transition from *Parashat Vayera* to *Parashat Ḥayei Sara* is very abrupt; the contrast between them is almost immeasurably stark.

Parashat Vayera is full of exciting events, which surely made headlines in those days. As early as *Parashat Lekh Lekha*, Abraham's war against the four kings was an international affair. The devastation of Sodom was likewise a tumultuous and geopolitically significant event. In the narrative of Abraham's family life, we read of the *Akeda*, which was certainly a profound and important event. The *parasha* is replete with angels and lofty matters, and it takes place entirely on a plane of great tension between momentous ascents and descents. The story of Sodom and Gomorrah, for example, is very complex and raises fundamental questions, such as to what extent God intervenes in the world and how a place can be condemned to complete eradication, despite God's promise after the Flood.

By contrast, *Parashat Ḥayei Sara* is very tranquil. It deals with Sarah's burial in *Maarat HaMakhpela*, the courtship of Isaac and Rebecca, and the latter part of Abraham's life.

Unlike the previous *parasha*, in which each event was an extraordinary occurrence, this *parasha* features events that can and do happen in every generation. Nowadays as well, people often argue over burial sites – if not with the Hittites then with the head of the burial society. Similarly, the match of Isaac and Rebecca is, all in all, not such a dramatic story. The story of Jacob and Rachel is at least somewhat romantic. There is a man and a woman, there is love – there is at least a story. Here, the match is arranged by Isaac's representative Eliezer, who returns to the family's place of origin and finds an appropriate wife for his master. Finally, after Abraham has finished caring for his son, he remarries and has children, who do not appear to interest us at all. These are commonplace occurrences which, were it not for the fact that they involve our esteemed patriarchs, would not even be reported in the newspapers, and perhaps would not even be reported to the neighbors.

The two *parashot* – *Parashat Vayera* and *Parashat Ḥayei Sara* – stand side by side as though for the sake of contrast. What is more, even the ancillary characters that appear in *Parashat Vayera* seem to remain constant in *Parashat Ḥayei Sara* to reinforce this contrast. Our sages explain (Yoma 28b) that "his servant, the elder of his house" (Gen. 24:2) – whom Abraham sent to find a wife for Isaac – is Eliezer; and when the Torah records that Abraham took with him 318 men to the war of the kings (14:14), this refers to Eliezer as well, whose name has a numerical value of 318 (Genesis Rabba 44:9). Abraham's chief military officer, who is victorious in war, is the same person who is sent to negotiate a match for Isaac.

Every person's life consists of two different modes. One mode is characterized by ascents and descents, while the other is characterized by calm and tranquility, without major events or great excitement. In a certain respect, this is also the difference between the summer season and the winter season in the Jewish calendar. Our entire summer – from Passover onward – is full of events. In the winter, even if we include all the rabbinically-ordained holidays – Ḥanukka, Purim, and Tu BiShevat – these months are still largely devoid of religious events.

In every person, there is a sort of inner debate as to whether he would prefer great excitement or calm and tranquility. There is a side, even in one's spiritual life, that despises the sense that nothing is happening, feeling bored and unstimulated. But the opposite side also exists, the aspect of "Jacob wished to live in tranquility" (Genesis Rabba 84:3). Jacob was not interested in unusual or dramatic events; he did not want to pursue romance or other developments. He wanted to settle down quietly for as long as his circumstances would permit.

Rabbi Nachman of Breslov uses similar categories to describe two forms of worship: There is calm, tranquil worship, generally characteristic of people who feel settled in society; and there is also ecstatic, frenzied worship, characteristic of people who do not feel settled in society. It is worth noting that the first form of worship is not limited to laypeople – to *balebatim* – and the latter form of worship is not limited to yeshiva students. How one approaches his relationship with God does not depend on what he does during the day, as many believe, but on something more personal, more innate.

THE PENDULUM

Sometimes, it is precisely those who generally operate in a state of calm who will seek out excitement in their lives, and it is those who lead tumultuous lifestyles who will seek out calm and tranquility. In any case, even those who seek out excitement often find it difficult to maintain such a lifestyle over a long period of time. One cannot expect to achieve great things without experiencing periods of stagnation and complacency. This reality is rooted in human nature itself. After all, we are not built as one harmonious unit, with body, soul, and various aspects of our personalities in complete harmony. If one tries to pull things in one direction, the law governing both the physical and the spiritual dictates that there will be an equal reaction in the opposite direction.

Rabbi Menaḥem Mendel of Vitebsk, in his work *Peri HaAretz*, describes this problem using the example of a pendulum. A pendulum cannot move to just one extreme. If it swings far to the left, it must also swing back to the right in equal measure. So it is in the service of God: It is impossible to constantly ascend. Everyone inevitably experiences descents and falls in his spiritual life, each person in his own way. Although there is a difference between the fall of the righteous and the fall of the wicked – the distance of the fall, where one lands after the fall, and in what condition one finds himself – nevertheless, a fall is a fall, and the resulting trauma is the same trauma.

Anyone who has experienced such a rise and fall, even on a small scale, knows that this is a problem. Look at our history. Our greatest spiritual disaster was the sin of the Golden Calf, and that story underscores precisely this point. The People of Israel were taken and suddenly elevated to the great height of the giving of the Torah at Mount Sinai. When they, quite naturally, do not undergo fundamental change all at once, they inevitably experience a great fall.

My purpose here is not to denigrate a stirring, stormy life. However, one cannot ignore the dark side inherent in a life of dramatic ascents and jumps: equally dramatic descents and falls. In the tranquil mode of life, while one does not make drastic changes or great leaps, nevertheless, in avoiding exposure to falling he has a better chance of persevering in his course.

TWO PATHS

There have been many discussions, in various forums, as to whether these two modes lead to the same place but each one is appropriate for different types of people, or whether there is actually a preferred path that can take a person farther and higher than the other. In the animal kingdom, some creatures advance in jumps, while others can only crawl. There certainly is a difference between a deer and a snail. While they both can travel from one place to another, the snail is much more limited than the deer, unable to reach the high places to which the deer can easily leap.

A similar question is that of the "shorter but riskier" path and the "longer but safer" path. The first path may be quicker, but may also contain dangers along the way. The second path allows one to reach his destination more securely, but only if he dedicates more time to the journey. Do they really reach the same place?

To a great extent, these differences in style depend on and are ingrained in a person's character. For example, one who feels "settled down" in his life need not necessarily be married with children; even a five-year-old boy can already act the part of a layperson – a *baal habayit*. He still may need nurturing care, but his character may be that of a *baal habayit* in every respect. Conversely, there can be a lively old man for whom the pace of a *baal habayit* is inappropriate, and who never "settled down" entirely despite his advanced age.

There are Jews who are outraged by the sight of a *baal habayit*; they cannot stand his readiness to accept a life of utter tranquility. On the other hand, there are people who naturally gravitate to that lifestyle. It is clear to them, by their nature, that in life one must settle down and work, on a regular and steady basis, as a matter of routine. One does not change the order of things; one follows the custom of one's predecessors. If his father was an ox, then he will be a calf, as it says, "For I am not better than my fathers" (1 Kings 19:4). This is life's structure and its framework; only within that framework does one effect changes. Similarly, the Midrash relates that "Abraham called [the place of divine revelation] a mountain, Isaac called it a field, and Jacob called it a home" (Midrash Psalms 81). In this version, the sons operate within the same framework as the fathers and follow the same pattern, reflecting basic continuity. There is much virtue in this. The strength of such a person is the ability to steadily persist and persevere, without needing to go to extremes or experience grand adventures.

BACK AND FORTH

Ultimately, despite the ingrained differences in our personalities, there is also an element that transcends personality, namely, freedom of choice. Ultimately, people choose their own path, the path by which to ascend God's mountain.

The Torah itself does not appear to decisively favor one side or the other. If, nonetheless, there is a message that the Torah conveys, it is that a person need not adhere to one mode exclusively. After a period of excitement, there can be a period of calm, and this calm is not necessarily a descent.

The point of *Parashat Ḥayei Sara* is not that Abraham has grown old and can no longer do everything that he used to do – wage war, circumcise himself, etc. What this teaches us is that there are different periods in life. The Torah does not present one mode of life as intrinsically preferable to the other. Rather, the Torah posits the reality that people need to learn to conduct themselves in both modes, because there is no one single way to live in which one can find continuous and lasting success. On the one hand, we live in a world where each day presents new situations that have never been experienced before. On the other hand, this same world is also built on routine, and life is often characterized more by its trivialities than by its drama.

Both modes are integral to the complete human being; like the fires in Ezekiel's chariot vision, they move "back and forth" (Ezek. 1:14) within each person's character. Man must be capable of great excitement, but he must also be prepared to live without it. There are periods in a person's life when he must move at a frenetic pace, without stopping once to rest. Even when this frenzy of activity causes pain and stress, he must not stop, or he will fall. But there are other times when he must be passive and reactive rather than take dynamic action or innovate. In order to straddle both modes, one must be able to maintain a state of constant flux: at certain times emulating a burning flame, and at other times remaining calm and tranquil.

To some extent, the course of Jewish life forces us to follow this path of constant duality and change. Once a week, on Shabbat, we are instructed to change the basic pace of our lives. Throughout the week one is immersed in his work, whether it is physical labor or other work that involves pressure and stress. Once a week, a day arrives during which the whole essential structure must change: One moves from a state of constant activity and movement to the pattern of Shabbat, whose whole essence is that man becomes a vessel for the holiness of the day – he must sit still, in peace and tranquility, calm and quiet. This is a true "back and forth," and one must develop the inner ability to operate in both of these modes.

EXPLOIT THE ENERGY

The relationships between these two modes of life are diverse and multifaceted. Sometimes, it is best to begin with a period of listening, study, and absorption, and only afterward switch to a period of creativity and breakthrough. Sometimes, the proper order in the working process is precisely the opposite: First one works at breaking things down and smashing them, so that afterward it will be possible to build new things. And sometimes it is precisely one who has experienced a period of calm and tranquility who feels a need to change gears and accelerate the pace of his life.

These two aspects present themselves in the various stages of a person's life, and one must learn to utilize them when opportunities for growth arise. Paradoxically, the perfect time to acquire Torah and good deeds is when one's evil inclination seems to be at its strongest. When everything is most volatile, that is the time in which one can ascend in spirituality and intimacy with God. If one does not exploit the natural energy that one has when young in order to run, then when he is older it will become much more difficult for him. If one wants to engage in the service of God, and this does not cause him to reach for the heavens, then perhaps he is not truly as young as he appears. If a person does not desire great things at a time in his life when he is naturally driven toward them, when will he desire them? Later in life, when a person declines, it becomes much more difficult to leap to great heights.

Nevertheless, it is important to remember that our forefathers never accepted age as an excuse. Perhaps that is one of the reasons that Abraham was circumcised when he was ninety-nine years old – so that no one would be able to claim advanced age as an excuse to avoid starting on a new path. That person would simply look at Abraham, who at ninety-nine made a new start from the same place where an eight-day-old baby begins.

Even someone who has seemingly reached the latter part of his life, generally a time of decline, can still grow. After all, all of *Parashat Vayera* transpires at a time when Abraham, one would think, should have been sitting calmly in his rocking chair – he was about one hundred years old, yet it was at this stage that he experienced many of the momentous and dramatic events of his life.

BETUEL OUR PATRIARCH?

The sequence of *Parashat Vayera* immediately followed by *Parashat Ḥayei Sara* teaches us an additional point. In order to live properly in the mode of calm and tranquility, one must know how to live in the other mode as well. One cannot maintain a state of constant, fast-paced activity throughout his entire life; but to ensure that the quiet life does not become a life of stagnation and decline, one must first experience great ascents and self-devotion. If someone has not first experienced a spiritually exciting world and all that it entails, he must not proceed to the routine of everyday life, for then the dangers of such a life will overshadow its benefits. There are two worlds – a world of fire and a world of water, a world of tempest and a world of tranquility – and not only does each world exist alongside its opposite, but each world actually builds the other. If one has never seen angels, he will not be able to sit and engage properly with merchants without sinking into this mundane lifestyle and remaining there.

Similarly, if Abraham had never experienced the *Akeda* and the events of *Parashat Vayera*, he would not have been able to spiritually survive the tranquil events of *Parashat Ḥayei Sara*. In Isaac's narrative, from the *Akeda* onward, major events are far and few between, especially compared to Abraham's narrative. This is a direct result of the fact that only one who experienced the *Akeda* can later settle down and successfully lead a quiet life.

Isaac digs wells and the Philistines dig wells. What is the difference between the two? Abraham buys a field and the Hittites sell a field. What is the difference between the two? There are two fathers involved in the match of Isaac and Rebecca. In a certain sense, both fathers are our patriarchs. The Jewish people is descended from Betuel, the father of Rebecca, just as much as it is descended from Abraham. However, at least for us as a nation, there is a fundamental difference between the father of the groom and the father of the bride. Betuel is a faded figure, lost in the tides of time. He remained an Aramean, the son of an Aramean, and nothing more than that. In contrast, Abraham, who traveled from the deepest depths to the highest heights, is known as Abraham our patriarch. Because of his incredible journey, Abraham can now walk on level ground as well without sacrificing his greatness.

Toledot

ABRAHAM AND ISAAC

Isaac uncovers the wells that his father Abraham had dug, an act that appears to be a fundamental part of his divine service. The Torah recounts the episode as follows:

> Now all the wells which his father's servants had dug in the days of Abraham his father, the Philistines had stopped them up, filling them with earth... And Isaac dug again the wells of water which had been dug in the days of Abraham his father and which the Philistines had stopped up after Abraham's death; and he gave them the same names that his father had given them. (Gen. 26:15–18)

Our sages elaborated on the matter of the wells as well; many midrashim exist on the subject, attributing to them great importance and significance.

Abraham's divine service is to go and dig into the earth, and to discover that it holds living waters. Broadly considered, his task is to find the meaning in things. Abraham is known for this quality: We learn that even at age three, he is constantly searching for meaning, recognizing his Creator. Thus, the Midrash (Genesis Rabba 39:1) compares Abraham to a man who, upon seeing a building on fire, asks: "Does this building have an owner? When the building is on fire, who watches over it?"

It is very simple for a person to ignore the realities of this world, passing them by all his life without paying attention to them. Abraham is not this way; he looks all around him and asks questions, digging wells and discovering water within.

Isaac's divine service, whose essence is encapsulated in the words, "And Isaac dug again the wells that Abraham his father had dug" (Gen. 26:18), is to pattern his actions after Abraham's, and in a certain respect this is the most difficult task that a person can undertake. Isaac emulates Abraham not just in one particular practice but in his entire life; he follows the same path, step after step. What happened to his father involving the king of the Philistines happens to him as well, and the same is true of many other incidents.

All that Isaac does is redig the wells that his father dug and give them the same names that his father gave. This creates a problem that anyone who grew up in a good Jewish home and chooses to continue the path of his forebears has faced. If someone has to dig new wells, he lives in a different world, with different sources of inspiration and a different dynamic. But for Isaac, and for everyone like Isaac, there is no point of revival and renewal in one's own right. These are the same names and the same places – everything is the same. The wells that he puts so much effort into digging are not truly new wells at all.

The problem of Isaac's divine service is part of a larger dilemma – the difficulty of renewal, the challenge of redigging the wells that one's father already dug. Can this really be considered an accomplishment? What does one achieve by simply retreading old ground?

The Midrash comments on the verse, "These words that I command you today" (Deut. 6:6), explaining, "'That I command you today' – they [Torah and mitzvot] should not be in your sight like an obsolete ordinance to which no one pays any attention, but like a new one in which everyone takes a keen interest" (*Sifrei*, Deuteronomy 33). In the same vein, Rashi comments on the verse, "Today God your Lord commands you to obey these laws" (Deut. 26:16), saying, "Each day they should be in your sight like something new, as though you had received these commands on that very day." The suggestion that our sages offer – to treat old mitzvot as if they are new and exciting – only seems to accentuate the problem. New tasks are relatively easy to muster excitement for. When it is only as though they were new – that is much more difficult.

THE ABILITY TO CONTINUE

According to the Midrash (Ecclesiastes Rabba 1:13), we should thank God for creating us with the attribute of forgetfulness, for as a result we can learn things more than once. If we were unable to forget, then whenever we would study some subject a second time, the experience would be identical to the first time. Now, thanks to forgetfulness, our learning always contains an aspect of renewal. Nevertheless, sometimes it is easier to learn three new pages than to review one page, for in new things there is power and rejuvenation. The process of review, of relearning old ideas – fascinating as they may be – will inevitably be deficient simply because it is not new.

The saying goes that all beginnings are difficult. As true as this may be, it is not nearly as difficult to begin as it is to continue – and that is the challenge faced by the second generation, the generation that cannot be innovative, that must not be innovative. It must only continue, and it can only succeed in this by marshaling the strength and the power of renewal. Compared to continuing, beginning is easy; reaching the finish line is easy as well. What is truly difficult is to continue after the enthusiasm of the beginning has passed. For some people, the excitement of the new lasts for five years; for others, it lasts only five months or five minutes. But no matter what, the excitement ultimately ends and a question presents itself: What happens next?

The ability to persist, to continue, is what distinguishes one person from another and, on a larger scale, between one people and another.

The true test is if the second generation has the ability to maintain the same energy, inspiration, and enthusiasm – or at least the same pace – as the first generation. For the first generation, it is easy to break the mold; to the second generation, however, monotony and decay pose a real danger.

In *Parashat Vayera*, God says, "Shall I hide from Abraham what I am about to do?... For I have known him, so that he will command his children and his household after him to keep the way of God" (Gen. 18:17–19). The man who holds the secret to the future is not merely one who gives his children instructions and orders; rather, he is the one who can successfully encourage his children and posterity to continue his direction.

A look at earlier and later generations shows that the personal ability of an individual does not guarantee his ability to transmit his greatness to his posterity. There are people who by their very nature cannot produce children and disciples like themselves, even though they may be great Jewish leaders. Moses, for example, did not produce a dynasty of great leaders. The dynasty that continued through the ages is that of the sons of Aaron, for Moses had no sons who could qualify as his successor. There cannot be a "Moses II," let alone a glorious Mosaic line.

Isaac's whole essence is his ability to carry God's cause to the next stage in history. In this sense, it can be said, literally, that "this is the story of Isaac, son of Abraham: Abraham begot Isaac" (Gen. 25:19), and in exactly the same sense: "This is the story of Jacob – Joseph" (37:2). The ability to raise a son who will be able to carry on the cause, to bring to fruition what he had begun, is Abraham's genius – his story. Without Isaac, without Isaac's ability to provide continuity, Abraham would not be Abraham at all. Rather, he would be like any of the eminent personalities that preceded him. Abraham was preceded by Enoch, but the two could not have been more different. While Enoch was an angel, his son was not an angel. There have been all sorts of people throughout history who were essentially "dead ends," whose legacies could not continue after their demise. Likewise, the difference between Saul and David was apparently rooted not only in the nature of their respective personalities but also in that Saul was incapable of fashioning for himself a successor of his own kind.

In this sense, just as Abraham begets Isaac, Isaac "makes" Abraham by giving him relevance and an enduring legacy. If Abraham's sons had been only Ishmael and the sons of Ketura, his narrative would have been only a passing episode. For it does not matter who these sons were, or what they did with their lives. To be sure, the Talmud records that Ishmael atoned for his sins, a claim that is supported by the fact that his children are given his name. Nevertheless, in spite of his later righteousness, Ishmael and his line do not constitute continuity for the legacy of Abraham.

The ability to create continuity is not only important in itself and significant for the future, but it even changes the significance of the past. Therefore, one must ultimately judge a person based on the larger picture: what he did and what is left after him. A person is judged according to the deeds that he performed during his lifetime and according to the events that he indirectly effects after his lifetime. The greater his influence, the more he retroactively changes the total image of his essence as an individual. There could be an individual who was only a minor figure during his lifetime but who ultimately succeeds in reaching major accomplishments – even if these are achieved a hundred years after his death. Even after a person's death, the actions of his children and grandchildren can change the image of the person himself. The Midrash often notes that there are wicked people whom one should not judge without taking into consideration the whole range and entire network of their descendants, and from that vantage point one is forced to judge them differently.

Rabbi Isaac Luria taught (*Peri Tzaddik, Toledot*) that the verse, "Isaac favored Esau because game was in his mouth" (Gen. 25:28), alludes to the soul of Rabbi Meir, who, as we know from other sources (Gittin 56a), was a descendant of Esau, and that is the "game" in Esau's mouth. When Isaac sees Esau, he sees not only Esau but also Rabbi Meir, and therefore is faced with a problem: What should be done with Esau? Should he reject Esau or accept him? When Esau asks, "How should salt be tithed?" (Genesis Rabba 63:10), he does not ask out of hypocrisy; there truly exists in him – if not in practice then in potential – an aspect that will one day manifest itself as the great *Tanna* Rabbi Meir. It is Rabbi Meir's tone that we hear in his question. If we view a person as a whole, including his past, present, and future, the aspect of Rabbi Meir within Esau cannot be discounted.

THE UNCIRCUMCISED PHILISTINES

Isaac redigs his father's wells, after "the Philistines had stopped them up (*sitemum*), filling them with earth" (Gen. 26:15). The use of the word "*sitemum*" implies that the Philistines made the wells ordinary or insignificant (*stam*). Many instances in Tanakh label the Philistines "uncircumcised" (see Judges 14:3, for example), and this designation is the root of what they are all about, not just esoterically. The Philistines create a reality where everything is covered, and everything is insignificant. A troubling passage in the Talmud relates (Sanhedrin 38b) that Adam reversed his circumcision; that is, he was created circumcised but then rendered himself uncircumcised. This is a type of person who makes a conscious and constant effort to become a man of *stam*, of utter insignificance.

The Philistines are not fundamentally evil. Although they are called "the uncircumcised Philistines," the Torah does not speak of their sinfulness or abominable behavior. By contrast, we find lists of sins and transgressions entitled, "the practices of the land of Egypt" and "the practices of the land of Canaan" (Lev. 18:3), but there are no "practices of the land of the Philistines." Similarly, a look at Israel's contact with the Philistines over the years shows that although the Philistine kings – Avimelekh and even Akhish – were not just and merciful, on the whole they were decent people, rational actors who followed accepted norms of behavior.

What reveals their fundamental character is the following: "The Philistines had stopped them up." The Philistines consistently follow accepted norms of behavior; they are not especially righteous or wicked. When an important question or moral dilemma arises, instead of taking one side or another, the Philistines "stop up" the entire issue at hand. Instead of denying the existence of God, the Philistines avoid the question altogether. When the Philistines commit sins, they never do so out of spite; they sin because, "That's just the way it is." The Philistines dull and deflate everything they encounter, refraining from lending any special significance to their actions. By following this path of least resistance, the Philistines create for themselves a world of randomness. Instead of fastening locks to the mouths of Abraham's wells, thus barring people from using them, they "stopped them up," essentially claiming that they never held any water to begin with. This course of action should not surprise us – the Philistines stop up all the "wells" that they find in life, refusing to come to grips with the water within them.

This attitude of *stam* – the modern Hebrew equivalent of a shrug – is extremely powerful. For one thing, it requires neither proof nor support, neither character nor meaning. If a person asks a question or presents a topic for consideration, it is the simplest thing to diminish it, responding with this verbal shrug. To be a Philistine means that when someone presents a meaningful or inspiring point, the response is to immediately fill it with earth. Philistines do not poison wells, God forbid; they merely stop them up. This is a contagious phenomenon, for after a while the person who posed the original question will no longer search for a life of meaning; he, in turn, will adopt the attitude of the Philistines, growing accustomed to life in a world of *stam*.

"THE PHILISTINES HAD STOPPED THEM UP"

How does this process, this attitude of *stam*, develop within a person? Let us answer this question with the following scenario: A person attends a Torah lesson for the first time, and he is greatly inspired. He meditates upon the ideas he has learned, becomes enthusiastic, and is preoccupied with them day and night. How can he sit quietly after hearing such brilliant words of Torah? After a while, he attends another lesson, but this new lesson has no effect on him at all. So he attends another and another, his interest and enthusiasm slowly but steadily fading after each lesson. A person who reads a joke book from cover to cover experiences this same phenomenon: He reads one joke after another, in stitches at first, but by the end barely able to crack a smile.

A person who is constantly steeped in the world of Torah and piety is liable to lose the power of rejuvenation, not because he does not understand, but precisely because he understands. After all, he has already heard everything; and if, by chance, he has never heard a particular idea, he has certainly heard something like it. And even if the idea itself is totally novel, he is still uninterested, as he is already familiar with the subject.

It can happen that someone, during Shaḥarit, is struck by the sudden epiphany that he loves God. This is a rare thing, which happens perhaps once a year. Will he then jump onto the table and shout, "I love God!"? Generally not. But why not? The answer is that there is a certain element of *stam* that dictates that – even when a point of inspiration comes to him – it would not be proper: One must follow the practice of the land of the Philistines. In Jerusalem's German Colony, there is a law that prohibits building above three stories. Similarly, there are people who have an inner law to that effect, not to build above three stories, and not to delve beyond a certain depth: It is against municipal regulations. This is the custom of the land of the Philistines.

How does this happen to a person? It happens because all the wells that he owns and that he has ever owned have been stopped up by Philistines and filled with earth. This happens not just to the elderly but to young people as well. One's inner life is simply stopped up. Like sand dunes on the seashore, even if I do nothing to stop up the wells, little by little, time covers up everything. Where once there was a well of living water, now there remains only a small hole in the wilderness.

Throughout history, our sages have addressed the question of what can be done to protect oneself against this danger. The danger here is not that one will fall all at once. Rather, it is a gradual, hardly noticeable fall. Life wastes away, and when one finally dies, no one can tell the difference, since he had already been a walking corpse long before then.

When does a person begin to die? In truth, the process of dying can begin at any time in a person's life. He can be sixteen years old, and yet in effect he is dying. He lacks only the final act of physical death, for a doctor to sign his death certificate, and then he can be buried. He does not know it yet, and his family does not know it yet, but for years he has been living without purpose, dragging himself along. In some cases this happens because people dry up; in other cases it is because they become frozen or stopped up with earth. But in all these cases, the attitude of *stam* is at work.

A similar phenomenon occurs in the case of people who freeze to death. Walking in extremely cold weather, they reach a stage where they are on the verge of falling asleep in the snow – and *that* is the great danger.

Why does this happen? The wear and tear of everyday life slowly affect the person so that he does not want to move or to grow; he becomes complacent, and he remains in the same spot.

This well had already been dug and excavated, but if it is not frequently redug anew so as to rediscover the water within, over the course of time it becomes stopped up, even without the involvement of Philistines. Even for the very individual who personally dug the well, after a while the earth penetrates his soul and the feeling of *stam* begins to pervade his life. What is required is constant attention to the task of spiritual revival and renewal.

SPIRITUAL DIGGING

The task of Isaac is to redig the wells and thus banish the infectious force of *stam*. On the one hand, this is easy work, for an opening has already been made, and Isaac already knows that there is something inside. On the other hand, this is a difficult assignment, for it involves no new discoveries. Despite the difficulty, Isaac pushes himself forward and redigs the wells.

Every morning, we recite the *Shema*. Some people recite the Ten Commandments daily as well. But in addition, one must also resolve to himself each and every morning that he is not a Philistine. That is to say, every day must be different from the previous one; every experience must be different from the next.

This is a very difficult task. After all, we are not talking about a sudden point of change and renewal, like a spontaneous decision to travel to the Amazon rainforest. Rather, it is the simple decision to make a change, even if one does not yet know how and where he will make it. It is a decision to stay in the same place, redigging the same wells. One will continue to read his prayers from the same siddur that he used yesterday, to recite the same blessings that he recited yesterday. Nevertheless, one must recite, over and over again, "I am not a Philistine."

In addition, redigging old wells involves the same amount of physical labor as digging new wells. In the framework of each person's life, whether he is leading a holy life or not, a conscious effort must be made to search for the meaning behind things, to open up wells and find the waters hiding within. To be sure, not everyone can reach the same level and the same achievements, but part of one's success is a result of the spiritual effort that one expends.

One of the main ways of accomplishing this spiritual work is by asking new questions, something that has almost become second nature for the Jewish people. Whether one is facing a page of Talmud or a section of the siddur, the best way to explore and dig into things is by asking questions. One cannot always find the answers, but through questions one can always uncover important ideas and meaning.

Likkutei Torah notes (*Shir HaShirim* 38d) that just as there is a mitzva to "be fruitful and multiply" in the physical realm, there is a similar mitzva in the spiritual realm: One must reach at least one new Torah insight each day. This is true in the wider sense of this obligation as well. For even if the new insight is not always a spectacular innovation, and sometimes it may not even make sense, the main thing is not to suffice oneself with the world of *stam*. Instead, one must fight the world's existing format and flux by raising questions.

One of the great hasidic rabbis (who was the rabbi of a small town in his youth and would often volunteer to serve as a merrymaker at weddings) would say that the essence of Hasidism is that one must constantly be asking, "Why?" about everything that one encounters in life. That is the way his life went, he said. One day, when he went to perform the ritual washing of the hands, this question of "Why?" occurred to him. He began to reflect on the ritual and stood there, towel on his shoulder, for two hours. He said that afterward, whenever he recited the blessing on the ritual, his level of devotion was higher than ever.

To reach the point where one feels the need to renew oneself – where one is able to consistently dig the well anew, asking "Why?", "For what purpose?", and "For what reason?" – requires much training and practice. One must train oneself to understand that "that's just the way it is" is only a satisfactory answer for the Philistines. A Jew is not like a Philistine; he must constantly dig wells.

Not everyone can break new ground, and not everyone can dig new wells. What everyone can and must do is to take the old wells and rediscover them for himself as an entirely new creation.

Vayetzeh

THE OUTSIDE WORLD

At the beginning of the *parasha*, Jacob uproots himself and goes to Ḥaran. All in all, even though his brother is not especially nice to him, Jacob lives in a place that is as good as could possibly be. His father is the outstanding spiritual personality of the generation, a respected and wealthy man. Presumably, Jacob has everything that he needs. Nevertheless, he leaves everything and departs for another country.

We can safely assume that, once he leaves, Jacob is immediately struck by the acute sense that the outside world is different from his former home. Home was full of holiness and all sorts of good things, whereas the world outside is bleak and spiritually barren.

One of the things that Jacob must learn to do upon recognizing this contrast is to make a new accounting of the world in which he lives: He now must struggle to maintain his inner spirituality. He could not have learned this lesson had he remained in the spiritual comfort of his home or the academy of Shem and Ever. The house of study is warm and pleasant; it is an insulated place, full of good Jews who are engaged in Torah and piety.

Jacob ventures outside and he sees that, in the outside world, things are not at all as they were in his old world. He must struggle to survive in a world where there are pitfalls, a world where he cannot continue in his old mode of life because he must live with the smarmy Laban in his pagan household.[1]

The question that arises here is how a person reacts when he leaves his comfort zone, his own small world, and is faced with a harsh, new reality. Ultimately, every Jew faces this problem, whether he is traveling to Ḥaran or to a different place. Often, the first meeting with the outside world is a profound shock. When one sits in the house of study, one comes in contact primarily with the other people therein. When one inevitably leaves its halls, one begins to meet people from the outside world, who may be quite different from one's former friends.

A person can go for years interacting only with the Jews who share his bubble, those who are in his close circle, in his place or in his group. There may be arguments and disagreements among these people over minor matters, but on a fundamental level, these people all live in the same world. When one goes outside, however, and meets people who have never spent time at the house of study of Shem and Ever, nor visited the home of Isaac and Rebecca, he finds a world that is completely foreign to him. It is a world that does not understand the first thing about what motivates him in life – what he wants, what he aspires to, what guides him, and what agitates him.

An additional element that Jacob must deal with is much more pointed. When he arrives in Ḥaran, he meets his uncle Laban, his uncle Elifaz, and the rest of his family. Upon meeting them for the first time, he is surely deeply shocked that these are his kin. This is how my relatives look, the people closest to me besides my parents?

What does one do when he meets his own flesh and blood and discovers that it is Laban? We must understand that Jacob was forced to cope with an extraordinary internal crisis. The "outside world" consists not of the heathens who are unrelated to him but, rather, of Jacob's own blood. Laban is not a distant person from another world; he is Jacob's uncle. Yet it turns out that, despite this, they do not belong to the same world at all; indeed, they have nothing in common with each other. These people are technically Jacob's family, but in actuality they are distant and

---

1. See Genesis 32:4 and Rashi's commentary there.

foreign. How can Jacob deal with this traumatic moment of crisis and contradiction? This is Jacob's essential struggle, which at times, on the most basic level, is a struggle for spiritual survival.

FROM JACOB TO ISRAEL

All things considered, Jacob's relationship with Laban posed a great danger to him. To live with Laban for twenty years is not a simple matter. On the other hand, Jacob had much to benefit from the relationship, as he states, "With only my staff I crossed this Jordan, and now I have become two camps" (Gen. 32:11). From this world, Jacob extracts something of major importance. He enters as Jacob, a single individual, and returns as Israel, leader of an impressive tribe. The difference is not just in the numerical increase of his family and camp. The Jacob who leaves Beersheba is a man who is incapable of engaging in a struggle. When faced with an obstacle, he tries to circumvent it rather than approaching it head-on. Even his name, "Jacob" – from the Hebrew "*akov*," meaning "crooked" or "twisted" – attests to his propensity to avoid any confrontation. When Esau enters Isaac's tent, Jacob exits through the other door; that is simply how he conducts himself. When Esau threatens him, Jacob's feet are already in Ḥaran.

While Jacob as "Jacob" may be able to live comfortably in the bubble of his father's household, he cannot survive in the reality of the outside world, and he certainly cannot become a leader, the basis for a nation. He can only be an individual – a *tzaddik*, to be sure, but an individual nonetheless.

Only after Jacob encounters the angel – "For you have struggled with a divine being and have prevailed" (Gen. 32:29) – can he survive, growing into the leader he was destined to be. Without passing this test, Jacob cannot become Israel. Only when he resolves not to flee from his problems but to stand up and face them can he cease being Jacob the individual and return home as Israel. This is the beginning of a nation, the beginning of our enduring existence.

STORY OF THE GENERATIONS

In our time especially, we have regularly faced problems of this type. Rashi (Gen. 33:4) cites our sages' statement that "it is well established that Esau hates Jacob" (*Sifrei*, Numbers 69).

Although Esau may have hated Jacob from the moment he was born, nevertheless, for a long while – maybe sixty years – a sort of status quo prevailed: They coexisted. One got the best of the other, one angered the other, who then struck back, but all in all they lived in the same home and could have continued that way. At a certain stage, there came the tragic turning point when Esau decided, "Soon the days of mourning for my father will be here, and then I will kill my brother Jacob" (Gen. 27:41). This was a drastic, fundamental change. Until now, although the two brothers did not love each other, they managed to coexist. Their hatred was silent – "the heart cannot reveal to the mouth" (Ecclesiastes Rabba 12:10) – they did not speak of it. Ultimately, Esau did not kill Jacob, but the reality had been changed nonetheless: The hatred was now legitimized.

Jacob was now forced – whether he liked it or not – to deal with this new reality and to assume the role of, "For you have struggled with a divine being and have prevailed" (Gen. 32:29).

Parashat Vayetzeh is not just the weekly Torah portion, and the problems that arise in it are not Jacob's alone. This is the *parasha* of our era, of our age. When we move on to next week's *parasha*, the story of Jacob's struggle will still linger with us. This is the *parasha* in which we have been living during the last few generations, in the sense that we have suddenly been thrust into the world around us, forced to deal with the ramifications of this new interaction. And the question is: What does present-day Jacob do when he faces this struggle?

A distinction is sometimes drawn between "Israel" and "Elder Israel." When we speak simply of "Israel," of Jacob our patriarch, this refers to the actual person who lived in history. But when we speak of "Elder Israel," this refers to the Jacob who still lives in our midst, who still lives within each and every one of us, and thus his spiritual work devolves upon all of us as well.

In the generations before ours, the world in many respects resembled Jacob's parental home or the house of study of Shem and Ever – a self-contained world that provided, more or less, an organic and insular life. Nowadays, we face a world that no longer allows us to remain within our own small sphere, in the company of people who are the same as us. We have already left our parental home, and we are beginning to see that the world is not only physically vast but also full of hatred, division, alienation, and self-destruction. Even Jacob himself long ago ceased to be unified – the Jewish people has split into several factions, each faction continuously fragmenting internally.

This is the face of the world in which we live. It is a world that is very intimidating and very frightening, and its demands upon us are only increasing and expanding.

"NONE OF YOU IS DISTRESSED ABOUT ME"

What does today's reality require of the individual Jew, the one who sits in the academy of Shem and Ever, the "Elder Israel" within each one of us?

When the world is as it should be, each person needs only to look after himself. He gets up in the morning, works for eight hours, completes whatever other tasks need to be done, and at the end of the day he checks the *Shulḥan Arukh* to make sure that he has not committed any transgressions. In this way, he lives according to the dynamic of his own life. But what if one feels more than his own distress, his personal pain; what if he feels that there is a sickness here that affects all of society? This feeling is described in Tanakh as follows: "Truly it was our sickness that he bore, our suffering that he endured" (Is. 53:4). If one can bear the pain and suffering of others as though he feels it himself, one's attitude toward the world will inevitably be affected.

When King Saul said to his courtiers, "None of you is distressed about me" (1 Sam. 22:8), he was not complaining to them about failing to follow orders. After all, ultimately they gave up their lives for him. What he was lamenting was the fact that while his desires concerned the courtiers, none of them was so pained that he could not carry on. What hurts Saul is not his people's performance (or lack thereof), but that they do not care; for when people care, things are done differently.

Aaron says to Moses, "Let her [Miriam] not be like one dead… It would be as though half of one's own flesh were being consumed" (Num. 12:12). We are one family. Hence, when death strikes one part, one cannot ignore it, saying, "Rot has set in on my hand, leprosy has broken out on my ear, but I continue to be well." When one becomes aware that leprosy has broken out on part of oneself, this produces an entirely different kind of response.

One must acquire and internalize a certain understanding, the sense that every fleeting moment that goes by is something that never returns. We are not talking here about a work ethic but about an inner understanding that despite everything that is being done, it is not nearly enough. The specter of lost time should agitate him. How can one allow himself to rest? How can one sleep at night if the world is in such a state? If a person is hanging by one foot on the edge of a tower, he would certainly not choose that moment to take a short nap.

We should remember that everything that is being done to correct the problems plaguing the Jewish people, to help the spiritually destitute among us, does not meet even a tiny part of the need. What most people do is barely sufficient for their own obligations, let alone for the needs of the Jewish people. Indeed, there is much that needs to be done on this front.

When a person has an urgent feeling that he must take action in a certain way, then – even if he is not a leader but an ordinary individual who truly believes in some cause – it is impossible for his actions not to have repercussions all around him. Even one seemingly insignificant person can create around himself a circle of faith, which then, in turn, creates another circle. In this sense, although it often takes a great leader to instigate change, there is always a question that the individual must ask himself as well: How should he act and how should he live in a way that is consistent with his beliefs and principles?

ASCENDING AND DESCENDING

In its commentary on Jacob's dream, the following midrash disputes whether the verse, "and angels of God were ascending and descending on it" (Gen. 28:12), is describing angels going up and down on the ladder or on Jacob himself:

> According to the interpretation that they were ascending and descending on Jacob, the meaning is that they were exalting him but also degrading him, surrounding him, leaping around

him, and maligning him. For it says, "Israel, in whom I will be glorified" (Is. 49:3). [Said the angels,] "Are you the one whose image is engraved on high?" They ascended on high and saw his [ideal] image, and they descended below and found him sleeping. (Genesis Rabba 68:12)

The angels stand beside Jacob, leap on him, pinch him, and abuse him, asking, "Is this you, Jacob, whose image is found up in heaven – and here you are, sleeping? Is this what you do down here in this world?" The angels ascend and descend, and Jacob turns over onto his other side and continues sleeping.

If his image were not under the Throne of Glory, if angels of God were not ascending and descending on Jacob, then it would be perfectly acceptable for Jacob to sleep. After all, Pharaoh slept, Nebuchadnezzar slept – let Jacob sleep peacefully as well. But Jacob cannot sleep peacefully, because angels of God are ascending and descending on him. He himself is the ladder that bridges the chasm between heaven and earth, on which all of existence ascends and descends.

Let us take this problem and apply it to the individual: A person sets out on a journey. After progressing for a while, he decides to rest for a bit. Suddenly, he has a vision: He sees a path connecting the upper worlds and the lower worlds passing through him. This is the path that passed through Jacob, and the path that passes through everyone who travels on the journey of life, no matter who he may be. This is the house of God, this is a gate to Heaven – and at the transition point stands Jacob.

This Jacob, no matter who and where he may be, must remember that his obligation reaches to the sky because his image is engraved on high. It could be that, as far as one is concerned, it suffices that his image appears on his driver's license or passport. But the reality is that his image is engraved under the Throne of Glory, and as a result, there is more that is demanded of him; there is a higher standard. The top of the ladder reaches all the way to God, and because of this, no person can pass himself off as insignificant. When Jacob understands this, he begins the process that creates Israel.

Jacob does not just represent the Jewish people. He is also just one man who leaves home and must now find his way in the world. And this

Jacob must recognize the pinnacle of existence, the uppermost limit that he must touch. Seeing oneself as the center of a whole world is precisely what puts one's obligation on the highest possible level.

If no angels of God are available to leap up and down on one's sleeping body, as they did to Jacob, then one must ask the angels' questions on his own. One must look in the mirror, saying, "Is this 'Israel, in whom I will be glorified'? Is this his image? That is all? Your image is engraved on high, and here you are, sleeping?" If even Jacob, who sat for twenty years in the beit midrash, is not permitted to sleep, certainly the same applies to the average Jew. The world turns continuously, without end, on this axis, on this issue, and the ever-recurring question is, "Your image is engraved on high, and here you are, sleeping?"

Parashat Vayetzeh is the story of our lives as human beings, our lives as Jacob's descendants. This problem of Jacob, the man who slept, is a problem that every person experiences. Jacob beholds a vision of a ladder, one end reaching to the sky and the other end set on the ground, and can only discern and recognize the meaning of the vision once he leaves his parental home. The vision of the ladder only makes sense in the context of the outside world. When he was studying in the beit midrash, he did not see angels of God ascending and descending on him, for he did not know the extent to which the entire world depends on one individual – Jacob. It seemed to him that he could remain inside his box, looking after himself alone. Let the world endure through Shem and Ever, and others of their ilk who dedicate their lives to improving the spiritual lot of their fellow man.

The Talmud states, "The entire world was created only as company for this person" (Berakhot 6b). Each person must see his life in this light – that he alone is the justification of the world's existence, of its direction, and of its meaning. "For this is the whole man" (Eccl. 12:13) – this is the person on whom the world's very existence depends. The world is the framework in which every person has the responsibility to live a meaningful life. When there are blemishes, this means that the ideal of "Israel, in whom I will be glorified" is not being realized.

What is required of man is that his image below should correspond to his image above, the image that is engraved on high. This is a very difficult, very demanding requirement, and even those who work on this with all their heart and soul, without stopping for even a moment – even they are asked, "Is this Israel, in whom I will be glorified?"

This matter depends neither on the luminaries of Israel nor on the *tzaddikim* of the generations, neither on our great sages nor on our national leaders. It depends on one man who, after years of spiritual work, steps outside for the first time. He begins to see how the whole world hangs in the balance over him, how all of existence hinges on him. Although, like the ladder in Jacob's dream, his feet stand on actual ground, perhaps even entrenched in the earth, his head reaches up toward heaven. There alone is the limit.

Vayishlaḥ

GIVE TRUTH TO JACOB?

It is widely accepted that Jacob our patriarch represents the attribute of truth, as the prophet says of him, "Give truth to Jacob" (Mic. 7:20). In practice, however, throughout many of the stories we read of him, it seems that Jacob acts evasively, often deviously. That is the case in *Parashat Toledot,* that is the case in *Parashat Vayetzeh,* and that is also the case in *Parashat Vayishlaḥ.*[1]

The problem is formulated most sharply in this week's *parasha,* in connection with Jacob's sons: "And Jacob's sons replied to Shekhem and Ḥamor his father with guile (*bemirma*)" (Gen. 34:13). Onkelos removes some of the negative overtones of "with guile" by translating "*bemirma*" as "with wisdom," but nonetheless, this is crooked wisdom, wisdom that is characterized by deception.

From all the narratives about Jacob, Micah's plea, "Give truth to Jacob," seems very difficult to understand.

Jacob's three Hebrew names – Yaakov, Yisrael, and Yeshurun – all express some element of truth. The almost inverse relationship between the name "Yeshurun" and the name "Yaakov" appears in clear contrast in a verse in Isaiah, "and the crooked (*he'akov*) shall be made straight

---

1. In *Parashat Vayeshev,* we will see how this element of deviousness backfires on Jacob.

(*lemishor*)" (40:4). Apparently, this transition from Yaakov to Yeshurun is integral to Jacob's essence.

A WORLD OF FALSEHOOD

Falsehood can be defined as the absence of an accurate relationship between the true inner part of an entity and its superficial outer part. Falsehood is the disparity between the actual and the appearance, between the thing itself and the outward impression that is formed. Often, when people are called "liars," "hypocrites," or "deceivers," these are people whose insides differ from their outsides.

One of the most basic falsehoods in the world is the falsehood inherent in social life. Social life is only possible when people refrain from expressing their true feelings and opinions regarding others. In practice, no society can exist at all without falsehoods.

Everyone understands the need for this type of falsehood: These are the structures by which society operates. One does not share one's every thought or opinion with everyone. The Hebrew expression "*derekh eretz*," literally, "the way of the land," refers to the concept of social politeness. What people call "*derekh eretz*" is this whole institution of social falsehoods, which society is unfortunately unable to do without. Such behavior includes showing respect even to those one does not respect, saying things that one does not mean when these are expected of him, and holding in things that one would like to say. A look at how young children express themselves reveals that, often, their problems stem from the fact that their speech is uninhibited. This is not to suggest that adults consciously and deliberately lie, but merely that they do not always tell the whole truth. This is part of the system of social conventions. In this sense, falsehood can be thought of as a kind of garment that people wear, whose function is to conceal aspects of one's self.

In society, some take this idea to the extreme. For example, there are people who believe that modesty should be shunned because it is a form of falsehood. Some of these people advocate nudism for this reason. After all, if a person appears this way on the inside, he ought to appear this way on the outside as well – indeed, why be false? To their mind, removing one's physical and spiritual garments makes the world much cleaner. The world's first garment was a result of the sin of Adam and Eve. If man had not sinned, he would not have needed a garment.

An additional level of falsehood, which likewise stems from a discrepancy between the internal and the external, lies in the gap between one's inner desires and what one expresses externally. Here, the connection (or lack thereof) between inside and outside runs much deeper. This kind of falsehood is, to a large degree, a social necessity as well. A person who is stranded on a deserted island can say or do whatever he wants without social repercussions. In society, however, there are many things that people would like to do but nevertheless refrain from doing, since many types of conduct are considered unacceptable.

Many philosophers built their entire world views on this question – what is the relationship between things themselves and their external appearance? Or formulated much more pointedly, can a genuine entity actually exist in the world? Is there such a thing as truth in the world? In a telling line, Rava avows that "there is no truth" in the world (Sanhedrin 97a), a depressing prospect for many of us to accept.

A person's existence is built on a system of restraints, from the falsehood of conventional social manners, to the falsehood of outer coverings of all kinds, to the gap between what one feels in his heart and what one reveals outwardly. This world innately and by necessity demands of us not to be truthful. It forces us to refrain from expressing the truth, the whole truth, and nothing but the truth, even when we would love nothing more than to do so.

The Mishna states that "The Holy One, Blessed Be He, will ultimately cause every *tzaddik* to inherit 310 worlds" (Uktzin 3:12). Why is each and every *tzaddik* given 310 worlds? Wouldn't it make more sense for the *tzaddikim* to share these worlds? What can a *tzaddik* do with so many worlds? It must be that the ultimate reward for *tzaddikim* will be that each *tzaddik* will be able to create his own complete world, a world that truly suits him, his desires, and his dreams. Presumably, once he accomplishes this, one world will not be enough. A person needs 310 worlds in order to be everything that he wishes simultaneously, each world containing a different, unique version of him.

In our worldly existence, where many more than 310 of us must coexist, we often get in each other's way, to the point where we must live in a reality where the internal and the external do not correspond. This world, by its very nature and structure, is full of falsehood, and in a world of falsehood, the choice between truth and falsehood does not exist. Hence, our recurring question in this world is not whether to be truthful or not; in actuality, the whole truth was never within our grasp in the first place.

The choice that we have in the reality of this world is a lot less dramatic than the abstract question of truth versus falsehood, but it is a much more nuanced question. In a world where only partial truths exist, how and to what extent should we accept the inevitability of falsehood? Should we be satisfied with half-truths, quarter-truths, or three-quarters truths? If we accept that a life of total truth is impossible, the least that we can do is set forth guidelines as to the manner in which we do not speak truth.

"'VERY GOOD' REFERS TO THE EVIL INCLINATION"

It may be surprising, but just as there is an evil inclination to falsehood, the desire to constantly adhere to the truth can be a type of evil inclination as well, one that at times is much worse than the inclination to falsehood. Indeed, it turns out that a person can experience a spiritual fall not only by pursuing things that are overtly evil, but also by going to the other extreme. There is a certain appeal to the notion that one must make an unequivocal decision to either be entirely good or entirely evil, but one must realize that this is a false dilemma: Neither of these choices is the proper path.

It is much more difficult to withstand this type of evil inclination than to withstand an ordinary evil inclination, not because being entirely good is an inherently undesirable thing – on the contrary, in an ideal world this approach would be recommended – but because it sets an unreasonable standard by which to live.

Our sages (Genesis Rabba 77:3) agree that the man whom Jacob encounters is Esau's guardian angel, who represents the evil inclination, the Angel of Death, and evil in general. They disagree, however, as to the form in which Esau's angel appeared to Jacob. According to one opinion, "he appeared to him in the guise of a heathen." According to another, "he appeared to him as a chief bandit." But there is also an opinion that "he appeared to him as one of the wise" (Ḥullin 91a; Genesis Rabba 77:2).

When Esau's angel appears as a bandit, we recognize him. He explicitly says, "Rejoice, O youth, while you are young! Let your heart cheer you in the days of your youth" (Eccl. 11:9). When one encounters pure evil, it does not attempt to hide its agenda. It does not sell a system of values; it does not sell wisdom and morality; it sells crude merchandise unabashedly. To be sure, the struggle against pure evil is not always easy, but it is a very clear type of struggle.

When, however, Esau's angel appears as "one of the wise," he presents arguments that can be very convincing. He does not sell you this world; he sells you the World to Come, a very tempting prospect. The obvious question is: If this entity is so good, if he is so wise, why is he the guardian angel of Esau?

There are people in this world whose deviation from all things holy came not as a result of their association with heathens or bandits, but as a result of their association with wise men. Their fall was a result of their attempt to set impossible standards. The evil inclination presents a type of world whose requirements cannot be met; in such a world, an inner crisis is inevitable. The evil inclination confronts every individual with an insidious false dilemma: Are you righteous or wicked? Are you a decent person or not? According to the evil inclination, every person must choose a side – he must be one or the other, and if he is neither, there is no place for him in this world.

Facing these questions, a person will likely identify in himself some element that is incompatible with his self-image as a *tzaddik* or as a person who follows a righteous path. As a result, he jumps to the conclusion that he is a liar and a hypocrite, deceiving both himself and others. This mindset is not sustainable; eventually he will feel the need, in the interest of avoiding "hypocrisy," to eschew righteousness altogether.

This portrayal is not merely theoretical. There are many people who are affected by this type of evil inclination and this type of thinking much more than they are by the "standard" evil inclination, which openly tempts and entices people to sin. People frequently fall to this warped moral reasoning precisely because their souls are pure, and it is hard for them to come to terms with deficiency and imperfection. For such people, the usual, straightforward temptation of the evil inclination is less dangerous than the presentation of life in black and white terms.

The downfall of Elisha b. Avuya, known as "*Aḥer*" ("Other"), was partially a result of his inability to come to terms with this predicament – the world's intrinsic imperfection. A person encounters such a reality, he falls, he descends, and there is no remedy for him, because he cannot reconcile himself with the imperfect reality.

On the verse, "And God saw all that He had made, and behold, it was very good (*tov meod*)" (Gen. 1:31), the Midrash expounds, "'Good' refers to life; 'very good' refers to the Angel of Death. 'Good' refers to the good inclination; 'very good' refers to the evil inclination" (*Yalkut Shimoni* 1:16). Elsewhere, the Midrash relates that Rabbi Meir had written in his personal Torah scroll that "'And behold, it was very (*meod*) good' means 'And behold, death (*mavet*) is good'" (Genesis Rabba 9). The evil inclination emphasizes "very good" so strongly that it negates all of existence. Ordinary existence is almost never "very good"; hence, "very good" refers to the Angel of Death. The Angel of Death espouses the philosophy of perfection because there is no reality in which absolute perfection can be realized, leading a person to frustration and despair.

The very same evil inclination that generally appears as a bandit appears here as a wise man. The same evil inclination that appeared in the Garden of Eden as a serpent (Bava Batra 15a) appears here as "very good," and in both instances it leads to the same death.

THE CHILDREN OF JACOB-ISRAEL

In every possible real-life situation, we encounter this imperfection, this flawed existence, and this holds true even for truly great people. In this world, we cannot attain absolute perfection, absolute truth, or absolute good. What is required of us is an incredibly difficult form of existence. We must live continually with partial truth, which stems from compromise.

In this world, pure truth exists only in theory, not in actual practice. No material in the world can be 100 percent pure. Man has never succeeded – and apparently never will succeed – in finding or creating such a material, for this world, by its very nature, is not suited for absolute purity.

In our spiritual work, the question we face is often not that of truth versus falsehood, but how much truth can we manage to introduce into things that we concede can never be completely true and pure. It is our struggle for the truth, not our achievement of absolute truth, that defines us.

In the reality of this world, the shortest distance between two points is not always a straight line. To leave a room via the shortest route, in most cases one would have to break through the nearest wall. In reality, however, it is more advisable to go through the door. The route that is theoretically the straightest and the simplest is usually practically unfeasible.

It is for this reason that we are called the People of Israel; we are children of Jacob in that he represents our spiritual path, reminding us of the problem of "Give truth to Jacob" that is built into our world. This is our struggle with life, just as Jacob must struggle with his path, which is fraught with danger on both sides – from both the bandit and the wise man.

Jacob sets out on his journey, and instead of forging straight ahead continuously, without any deviation, his path is full of twists and bends, an integral feature of his (and, by extension, every person's) progress through life. Straight lines exist only in geometry; the real world is full of curves. To a large degree, our challenge is to maintain an overarching sense of direction and purpose for the duration of life's journey, despite the twists along the way. We must find the way to maneuver between the bandit on one side and the wise man on the other – and to stick to it.

This "truth" of Jacob includes how he acts with Esau and with Laban, deceitful as those interactions may appear. Jacob's truth is not a pure, abstract truth, but the truth that can be achieved in the real world. Because of this, Jacob is a figure that the Torah charges us to emulate, not despite his "truth," but because of it.

No one can break through all of his limits and limitations, but one can certainly try to find a way around them, emerging from them somehow unscathed, by forgoing the unattainable perfect truth.

Jacob, the most truthful of the patriarchs, says of Laban, "I am his brother in deceit" (Bava Batra 123a). Jacob does not say this because he actually considers himself a deceitful person; he says it because in order to preserve his own truth in Laban's world, he must also take this approach.

The Talmud tells of a man who said the word "true" twice upon completing the *Shema*, saying of him, "'True, true' got hold of this person" (Berakhot 14b). Rashi explains, "A stream of truth seized this man" – in other words, the insanity of the truth killed him. The evil inclination of truth is the attempt to find a "stream of truth" in one's life, to maintain a lifestyle to whose standard it is impossible to adhere.

Jacob admits that all he can do is live within his reality. For this reason, Jacob is not straightforward. This world – "the world of division" (Zohar, *Vayetzeh* 155a) – does not allow things to proceed in an ideal and direct way. While Isaiah's hope for the future is that "the crooked shall be made straight, and the rough places shall become a plain" (Is. 40:4), until then, the road remains winding.

In passing through the various stages of life, when we pursue the truth as much as possible, we must endure many imperfections along the way. Only then will we be able to reach the highest level of truth within the reality of this world.

Vayeshev

TZADDIKIM HAVE NO REST

Rashi introduces this week's *parasha* with the words of the Midrash:

> Jacob wished to live in tranquility, but then the trouble of Joseph
> sprang upon him. When the *tzaddikim* wish to live in peace, The
> Holy One, Blessed Be He, says, "Is it not enough for the *tzaddikim*
> that so much is prepared for them in the next world, that they
> seek to live in peace in this world?" (Genesis Rabba 84:3)

Jacob consistently tries to settle down quietly, to live at ease, and each
time, some new trouble springs upon him. In all the stories about Jacob,
and in stories of many other *tzaddikim* as well, we are often struck with
the question of to what extent *tzaddikim* can attain peace of mind. The
question is not about physical wellbeing. In the course of his life, Jacob
is hardly harmed at all physically. Jacob's trials are in the sphere of sorrow
and grief, and the story of Jacob is a struggle for peace of mind.

When Rabbi Yannai says that "in our hands we have neither the
tranquility of the wicked nor the suffering of the righteous" (Avot 4:16),
he notes the seemingly counterintuitive reality that the wicked experience tranquility while the righteous experience suffering. The suffering of
the righteous is part of their world, part of the pattern of their existence.
The assurance to the righteous is that they will "have no rest, neither in

this world nor in the next" (Berakhot 64a). This is no coincidence; it is a basic philosophical tenet – God bestows many favors and gifts upon the righteous, both in this world and in the next, but tranquility is not one of them.

Correspondingly, the Talmud states, "For the wicked, sleep is good for them and good for the world, but for the righteous, it is bad for them and bad for the world" (Sanhedrin 72a). There is no rest for the righteous. When a *tzaddik* wants to rest, God does not let him, as if to say that the lack of tranquility is an essential part of being a *tzaddik*.

PEACE OF MIND

In our world, peace of mind is one of the most sought after commodities on the market. We are not speaking only of the fields of psychology and psychotherapy. Every person, according to his emotional makeup, is troubled by all kinds of doubts and insecurities. This is even truer today than in the past, in a world that is much more dynamic, driven, and harried than ever before. Because of this, every person searches for tranquility, in one way or another. Whether a person's solution involves therapy, drugs, or personal introspection, the search for peace of mind is often motivated by the desire to escape from a world full of anguish to a world of calm. Everyone wants to live in peace, and many are even willing to pay for this.

For many people, choosing a path of faith is perceived as choosing a path of tranquility and ease – a way of securing peace of mind for oneself. The search for tranquility is often what leads people to connect with Judaism, since a religious life is often perceived as calm and effortless, in contrast to other lifestyles where one is always on the run.

Actually, there is some truth in this perception. This can be observed in the case of smokers. Many people cannot go fifteen minutes without a cigarette during the week, but on Shabbat, completely abstaining from smoking does not trouble them at all. How is this possible? There are many things in this world that are only troubling when they are in the realm of the possible and the doable. But on Shabbat, when these things are in the realm of the forbidden – completely out of bounds – peace of mind can be achieved.

This is true of many things in the framework of Torah and mitzvot, by virtue of the Torah's nature as a highly structured world of prohibition and permissibility. People are often afflicted with lusts and desires because the object of their desire is within reach. But as soon as they know that it is unthinkable, that it is entirely impossible, there is no longer a reason to lust for it.

An interesting example of this is cited by Ibn Ezra, in his commentary on the verse, "Do not covet" (Ex. 20:14). He writes that just as it does not even occur to a simple peasant to covet the royal princess, that is how it should be regarding a married woman. The peasant is not beset with dreams about the beautiful princess; he does not even think about her. Perhaps there are princes who are interested in her, but the simple peasant is not. When something is entirely beyond a person's reach, he simply does not think about it, does not seriously consider it. Because of this, there is neither an element of temptation nor a need for a struggle. Similarly, "your neighbor's house," "your neighbor's wife," and similar objects of desire should be seen as outside the realm of the permitted, in the realm of the completely forbidden.

To be sure, the very transition to a life of Torah and mitzvot requires a momentous, fateful decision, but ultimately such a life provides, in certain respects, a great deal of calm. To put it more profoundly: A world where God exists is a world of peace of mind and security. A world where God does not exist is a world that is fraught with anxiety and insecurity; it is like an endless maze.

A WORLD OF QUESTIONS

When we speak of the tranquility of a world of Torah and mitzvot, we must ask if this tranquility, while certainly making for a clearer and more orderly world, truly makes for a *better* world. It does appear to be a more complete world than the world that is devoid of Torah, but is it truly more complete, or does it just appear to be so?

The answer to this question is that, as already noted, "*tzaddikim* have no rest." Although it is possible to view this lack of rest as secondary, we see that, according to our sages, there is no rest in the World to Come either. Apparently, lack of rest is an integral and fundamental part of being a *tzaddik*, perhaps even an ideal form of existence.

Anyone who is a part of the world of faith knows that it is not an easy world in which to live. Anguish and inner struggle are par for the course for the faithful. It has been said that the verse, "Seven times a *tzaddik* falls and gets up" (Prov. 24:16), is not a description of the *tzaddik*'s failures but of his natural progression. A sharper formulation would be that crisis is part of the process of the *tzaddik*'s revitalization and rejuvenation, and falling is part of the process of his growth.

Somewhat similarly, the Talmud states that "one does not fully understand the words of the Torah unless he has been tripped up over them" (Gittin 43a). The simple meaning of this is that, by its very nature, Torah study requires rising and falling; failure is part of the process.

People are often curious about the "ideal method" of studying Torah. The answer may be found on every page of Talmud, in the *Rishonim* and in the *Aḥaronim*. Our corpus of Torah literature is full of questions and objections, difficulties and contradictions. Clearly, the Talmud thrives on questions more than on answers. The ideal methodology for Torah study is clear: Keep asking questions.

In the language of our sages, there exist many different words for questions. This poses problems for translators, since this vast "question" terminology, with all the various shades of meaning, cannot always be rendered properly in other languages. No other language seems to have quite so many different words for "question" as we do.

It has been claimed that Eskimos have a remarkably large number of words for snow – and it is no wonder. They live in snow throughout their lives, causing them to develop fine distinctions between different kinds of snow – heavy, light, thin, etc. Each type of snow has its own term. In countries where snow falls not nearly as frequently, many fewer terms for snow exist. By the same token, Jewish people live in a world that is rife with questions; it is therefore understandable that so many terms have developed, each of which expresses a different aspect of questioning or a different type of question.

In this regard, Maimonides is exceptional in his attempt to arrange all of Torah such that the framework of questions and answers would be rendered unnecessary. At the end of his introduction to the *Mishneh Torah*, Maimonides writes that he wants to spare the Jewish people the trouble of asking questions. He claims that anyone who reads the Written Law and his book can skip everything in between. He does not advocate forgoing the Written Law or claim that the *Mishneh Torah* should take the place of the Tanakh, but he is willing to recommend skipping the Oral Law. Why should a person spend his life on questions, answers, and comparisons? Why go into all that if everything can be laid out clearly and cleanly in one solitary book?

The fact is that this attempt was not successful. Maimonides himself writes (*Iggerot HaRambam* 11, 444–445) that he decided not to cite his sources because he wanted to avoid confusion, but later, when he realized what happened, he regretted this decision. What the Jews did to Maimonides and his great work would probably have exasperated him. Instead of the *Mishneh Torah* becoming a haven of calm and tranquility, where the weary could find rest, it became one the best sources for new questions. This work, which was meant to lead us to tranquility, in practice became a source for, and the focus of, many more questions.

Why is it that we thrive on questions? Before we answer, it is important to stress that there is no shame in asking questions. Though it may seem that one who asks questions admits that he lacks knowledge or understanding, the truth is quite the opposite. In a sense, it is the scholar – the one with the most knowledge of all – who asks the most questions. A non-scholar has no questions to ask, not because he knows the most but because he knows the least. In giving us the Torah, God is not selling us tranquility. Tranquility is not part of the reward. Rather, one who reaches a state in which he has no more questions, difficulties, doubts, or problems, is not the ideal man but, on the contrary, is one who has left the world entirely.

Rabbi Simḥa Bunim of Peshisḥa is said to have suggested that a man should always imagine that his head is on the execution block, the evil inclination standing over him with a large axe, ready to decapitate him. One of his disciples asked, "What happens if a man does not imagine this?" Rabbi Simḥa Bunim answered that this would be a sure sign that the evil inclination has already cut off his head. If a person no longer feels any anguish and lives in tranquility and peace, then he must have already been decapitated, and that is why he has a good life, full of peace and tranquility.

This conclusion is not comforting and certainly is not calming. A life of tranquility is surely more pleasant than a life of anxiety and stressfulness, but it is not a better life. Choosing the right path does not mean choosing a life of ease, nor does it mean choosing a life that is devoid of problem. Rather, it means choosing a life that inevitably contains a certain degree of anguish.

FROM STRENGTH TO STRENGTH

"Jacob wished to live in tranquility." Jacob is an old man, over a hundred years old, and he finally decides that he is done. He studied Torah for several years, he worked for several years, and he married four women. Now, reasons Jacob, he certainly deserves the right to settle down and lead a quiet life. The truth is that when the incident with Esau concludes, it appears that Jacob thinks that the world has more or less reached a state of tranquility.

Just when Jacob is preparing to enjoy his hard-earned rest, God interrupts, saying, "Is it not enough for the *tzaddikim* that so much is prepared for them in the next world, that they seek to live in peace in this world?" The righteous do not live at ease, not as a punishment for sins, but because for them, to sleep in tranquility would be "bad for them and bad for the world." The complication, the anguish, the pain that exist in the world – if the *tzaddik* does not have all of these, then apparently something is wrong in his essential character.

While it is undoubtedly true that, in certain respects, one who lives within the world of Judaism gains the ability to solve his inner dilemmas and torments, the end goal is never to enable one to settle down in tranquility. If, at any point, a Jew believes that he has freed himself of the Esaus and the Labans of his life, and that he will now be able to enter a good and spacious land where he will live at ease and rest in peace, he is simply mistaken. Going deeper and deeper into Judaism does not mean that one solves all of one's problems and attains tranquility. That kind of empty tranquility only brings a person closer and closer to death, to the point where his existence is entirely superfluous. Once our questions have been answered, they do not go away; they simply change, becoming new questions altogether.

The draw of Judaism is not the prospect of attaining tranquility, as it is in some other religions. When a person draws closer to God and to the world of Judaism, he is rewarded not with rest but only with questions and more questions. If a person is especially successful in his spiritual journey, every day three of his small questions will die, and three large questions will be born in their place.

Even in the World to Come, there is no rest for the righteous. "They go from strength to strength" (Ps. 84:8), which is another way of conveying this notion. When a *tzaddik* "graduates" from one world, finishing his learning process in this world, he is promoted to another world. What does he gain in this whole process if he is constantly working? What he gains through his labor are new questions, ones that he has never previously considered. Although these are more difficult questions, they are also questions that relate to a loftier world. He can engage in more exalted matters, but he never stops asking questions: What is more important? What is more fitting? What is the proper path to take?

That is what is truly required – not to live in pursuit of tranquility, but to live in a world of questions, each one lifting a person higher and higher in his spiritual journey.

Miketz

Parashat Vayeshev concludes with a puzzling statement: "Yet the chief butler did not remember Joseph; he forgot him" (Gen. 40:23). How can this be? A person's memory can be good or bad, but it seems unlikely that a person like Joseph and an experience such as the one the chief butler had in prison could have been forgotten so quickly. What happened to the chief butler? Why did he have to wait until – as *Parashat Miketz* begins – "the end of two full years" (41:1)?

On the simplest level, even if the chief butler had wanted to take action on Joseph's behalf, the right opportunity to do so would have been elusive. It takes time for such an opportunity to present itself, for the king to seek the butler's counsel. In the meantime, it is not necessarily surprising that the butler forgot about the matter.

Nehemiah 2 relates a story about another butler – Nehemiah himself – who finds himself in a similar situation. Nehemiah had heard long before that Jerusalem lay in ruins, and while he wants to to something to help improve the situation, it is not within his power to do so. Nehemiah does not turn to the king and request to be sent to Jerusalem, because such a blunt request made at the wrong time may not only be rejected, but may jeopardize his relationship with the king as well. As in the case of Pharaoh's butler, the problem is one of timing. There, too, the moment arrives when "I did not meet with disfavor before him"

(Neh. 2:1; see Ibn Ezra) – the king is in a good mood; he is amenable to conversation – and it is then that Nehemiah can make the offer, with the chance that it will actually be accepted.

What underlies these two stories is that things can take time to crystallize, to unfold. The essence of the matter is that everything that occurs has a predestined time, a particular point when it is supposed to happen. This notion, found both in Rashi and in the Midrash, is an important key to understanding how things develop, not only in Tanakh but in other areas as well.

Thus, the moment of "at the end of two full years" depends on two factors: when one would expect an event to occur based on the natural development of things, and when the event is destined to occur. The first factor refers to the complex and multifaceted process of causality; every event has a unique way of unfolding, a system characterized by cause and effect. The second factor represents a different kind of reckoning, which likewise plays a role in determining the nature of events. We are speaking of the intent of an event, its inner purpose. These two factors do not contradict each other but work in tandem.

In Joseph's case, it took two years and an opportunity until the chief butler opened his mouth. In the grand scheme, all the chief butler must do is open his mouth in order to get the process of Joseph's rise to greatness underway. The chief butler certainly did not intend for Joseph to reach the high station that he eventually achieved; that was not the intention of anyone who was involved in the story. Yet the butler's words to Pharaoh suddenly give Joseph an opportunity to get out of prison and begin advancing to a higher status.

This is where the chief butler's role in Joseph's ascension comes to an end. From this point on, the story can progress in many different ways. After Joseph interprets his dream, Pharaoh could have easily said to him, "You are the best dream interpreter that I have, and as a reward I am entering you into the ranks of the magicians." In order for the narrative to avoid the random whims of causality, to move further on its destined course, it needs a push in the right direction.

From the standpoint of inner causality, Joseph's departure from prison occurred at a predetermined date and time. When this moment arrives, all sorts of things begin to transpire that cause this departure to actually come about. "At the end (*miketz*) of two full years" – the event that propels Joseph at the age of thirty to the height of his greatness is his "fixed time" (*ketz*), which is independent of the series of events that preceded it. It was just as likely for Joseph to have fallen into a pit before meeting with his brothers. In that scenario, he would have stood there screaming until those same Midianites would have found him and brought him to Egypt, and he would have come to "the end of two full years" via a different route.

In order to reach this *ketz*, events are pushed forward so as to occur at a certain, designated time: "And it came to pass at the end of two full years that Pharaoh dreamed." The time assigned for this event to occur has come. Pharaoh experiences his dream, and a process begins to unfold.

"LET ME KNOW, O GOD, MY END"

Within time, there are often markers or signs that point to events that must occur. This is true in the life of the individual, and it is true as well in the life of a community or a nation: Events occur in a certain pre-ordained order. These markers are the fixed times at which each event must come about. That is to say, there is a course of events that advances with the assistance of a variety of mechanisms, a series of causes and effects that operate on one side of causality. Then, a heavenly decree determines the exact moment that the event must come into effect, and with that, it occurs.

The verse, "Let me know, O God, my end, and the measure of my days, what it is" (Ps. 39:5), speaks of a predetermined measure to a person's life. Our sages, both in the Talmud and in the Midrash, deal extensively with this subject. The basic assumption is that there is a *ketz* to every person's life, even if certain events or deeds can change its precise duration, shortening or lengthening it. Even when Maimonides (*Iggerot HaRambam* I, 264–272) discusses the relationship between the events that a person experiences and his predetermined *ketz*, it is clear that some kind of *ketz* exists for every person. There is a *ketz* for a person's greatness, a *ketz* for his death, and a *ketz* for every other significant lifetime event. As a rule, we are not privy to these fixed times. A person may sense that a significant event is approaching, but even then he does not truly know when it will transpire.

One aspect of fixed times is that even when we know when an event will occur, we cannot always be certain. The Talmud tells of various cases where, because of a person's behavior, a certain number of years was added or subtracted from their predetermined allotment of years. For example, several years were added to the life of Benjamin the Righteous because he supported a poor woman (Bava Batra 11a). Similarly, Rabbi Akiva's daughter was destined to die at her wedding, but as a result of a charitable deed that she performed, she was allowed to live beyond her wedding day (Shabbat 156b).[1]

Apparently, no *ketz* remains absolutely fixed to its exact date, irrespective of other factors. Even when a fixed date for a particular event is decreed from on high, as we find in various prophecies, these dates can shift as well. For the individual as well, there are dynamic factors in life that can alter his fate in one way or another. This idea is found frequently in Tanakh, as it says of the redemption, "In its time, I will hasten it" (Is. 60:22). We see from this example that even when an event is assigned a specific time, like the redemption, it is always possible for this time to be moved forward.

In the same vein, the *ketz* of the Exodus from Egypt and the *ketz* of the Babylonian exile were not fixed absolutely. It says in Jeremiah 25:11–12 that the Babylonian exile must last seventy years. But in reality, attempts to establish an accurate chronology seem to indicate that fewer than seventy years transpired between the destruction of the First Temple and the construction of the Second Temple. Our sages (Megilla 11b) offer three possible explanations in an attempt to reconcile the number found in Jeremiah with the actual chronology. Whatever the case may be, it seems clear that the length of the exile did not necessarily amount to the seemingly preordained seventy years.

The *ketz* of the Egyptian exile also seems to change. The Torah says, "They will serve them, and they will oppress them – four hundred years" (Gen. 15:13). For this exile as well, it must be that "In its time, I will hasten it" applies. When the words of the Covenant between the Pieces are compared to the time the People of Israel actually spent in Egypt, it turns out that the Egyptian exile lasted for less than half of

---

1. From this incident, our sages learned the precept that "charity saves from death."

the period that it was supposed to last. In order to reconcile this reality with the verse, our sages derive (Tanḥuma, *Shemot* 4) from the beginning of the verse – "your offspring will be a stranger" – that the years are counted not from the time of the Covenant between the Pieces, but from the birth of Isaac. Even then, when the two chronologies do match up approximately, it is a difficult interpretation to accept.

Each of these is an example of a *ketz* that, despite its fixed nature, also included ups and downs.

Whenever we speak of designated times for redemption, it should be understood that while the time exists, it does not necessarily hinge on a specific date. There are many historical examples of this. Even Maimonides, who was certainly not the type to engage in calculations of the time of redemption, records one *ketz*. In his *Epistle to Yemen*, he writes that although we know that our sages have said, and for good reason, "May those who calculate the end come to grief" (Sanhedrin 97b), a tradition has been passed down to him from his ancestors as to when the time of redemption will be. He says that the redemption will occur in approximately four hundred years, a prospect that displeases Maimonides, as it means that he and his contemporaries will not live to see it.

HOW EVENTS UNFOLD

Just as there are junctions in the road, there are also junctures in time. In order to reach one's destination, it may be that one must pass a particular junction. However, there is not always only one way to reach that junction; it may be that one can reach it in several different ways. Similarly, one ultimately arrives at a predestined juncture in time, but what exactly will happen at that time and, more significantly, which developments will lead to that juncture, is yet undetermined.

When Jacob blesses his sons before his death and speaks with them about "what will befall you in the end of days" (Gen. 49:1), this is the kind of statement that, whether in its plain or its midrashic sense, certainly does not refer to a specific predetermined date. Nevertheless, Jacob is clearly speaking about specific events that are destined to occur and which will arrive, sooner or later, at their appropriate times. His blessing includes a prophecy about the Kingdom of Judah and a prophecy about Samson. The two events are not of the same era and do not refer to the same *ketz*. However, in both cases it is understood that before the final *ketz* arrives, a series of events have to occur, though not necessarily all at the same time or in a specific way. Samson's exploits are bound to occur as a result of Jacob's blessing; but at least some of the developments of Samson's narrative appear to be the results of his own, frequently misguided freedom of choice.

Moses' blessing leaves a similar impression: To reach the *ketz*, certain events must occur, but each of these necessary events can come about in very different ways.

There is a tradition that every year that is predicted to be the *ketz*, the year of the redemption, is a dangerous and problematic year. Such a year can truly be the time that the Messiah is destined to arrive, but this is not guaranteed to be true. Hence, it is a time that is marked by anxiety, when we are especially encouraged to engage in Torah study and good deeds. Maimonides' tradition, for example, was based on the verse, "In this (*hazot*) year of jubilee you shall return each man to his ancestral heritage" (Lev. 25:13), where the numerical value of the word "*hazot*" alludes to the year 5408. In precisely that year there were major pogroms against the Jews of Poland, Ukraine, and Lithuania, known as the Chmielnicki Massacres.

The times of the *ketz* are sensitive periods for the Jewish people. Just as the physical world contains plateaus and mountains, the same is true in the realm of time. When one walks on flat land, it may seem that all is well, but when one encounters a mountain, it is impossible to ignore it, even if it can ultimately be overcome – and the same can be said of the events in the life of a person or in the history of a nation. Occasionally, we encounter signs that indicate that, as we proclaim in the *Musaf* service on Rosh HaShana, "today the world is pregnant." This "pregnancy" can result in the birth of a Jacob, but it can also result in the birth of an Esau. Whatever the nature of this momentous "birth" – whether it heralds salvation and consolation or, Heaven forbid, the opposite – it is always a time of upheaval.

The *ketz* of the Messiah is a time of tremendous change throughout the world. Hence, any potential preordained time for this is a significant point, a deep fissure in the sequence of time, foreshadowing that certain important events are about to happen. How they will happen and what their nature will be apparently depends on other factors.

Our sages say that the Messiah may come in stillness and quiet, but may also come in storm and tempest (Sanhedrin 97b). Here, too, the destination is known, but the way there is not set. If one follows the good and straight path, he will not have to experience tribulations; but if he does not follow the proper path, God will appoint over him "a king whose decrees are as harsh as Haman's." When the time of the redemption comes, the world will undergo change. If one allows the change to come quietly, it will be quiet; if not, its arrival will be accompanied by loud noise and great anger.

According to our sages, "It would have been fitting for Jacob our patriarch to go down to Egypt in iron chains, only that his merit saved him" (Shabbat 89b), and God brought it about that he traveled to Egypt of his own volition. The People of Israel had to end up in Egypt; they could not escape this fate. But the route to Egypt was never set in stone: If not for Jacob's merit, he and his family could have been brought there against their will. In the end, though the final destination remained the same – enslavement in Egypt – Jacob was able to improve his lot for the duration of the journey.

"And it came to pass, at the end of two full years" signals that the time has come for something to occur. The "how" of the matter is trivial – Pharaoh has a dream, the chief butler happens to be present, other events align, and ultimately, they all cross the threshold simultaneously, reaching their *ketz* at precisely the right time.

Vayigash

Parashat Vayigash deals primarily with the events surrounding Jacob's arrival in Egypt. After many tribulations, Joseph reconciles with his brothers, Jacob arrives in Egypt and finally reunites with Joseph, and the story comes to a close. By the time we reach *Parashat Vayeḥi*, we are already dealing with Jacob's death and his final reckoning with his sons.

As a rule, the *haftara* traditionally associated with each *parasha* emphasizes the central elements of that *parasha* as understood by our sages, and in effect constitutes a form of interpretation of the entire *parasha*. Sometimes the connection between the *haftara* and *parasha* is clear and obvious, and sometimes it is so remote that, in order to understand why the sages paired a particular *haftara* with a particular *parasha*, one must sit down and think. In the case of the *haftara* associated with *Parashat Noaḥ*, for example, the only similarity to the *parasha* seems to be the appearance of the words "the waters of Noah" (Is. 54:9). When there are divergent opinions and customs regarding which *haftara* we read – as in the cases of *Parashat Vayishlaḥ* or *Parashat Vayetzeh*, for example – these disputes usually revolve around the question of what the *parasha*'s essential point is.

The essence of *Parashat Vayigash* would appear to be the descent to Egypt, but the *haftara* (Ezek. 37:15–28), which relates Ezekiel's prophecy of the stick of Judah and the stick of Ephraim, shifts the focus away from this subject to the meeting, or perhaps clash, of Joseph and Judah. This, according to the *haftara*, is the essence of the *parasha*; everything else is ancillary material.

JUDAH AND JOSEPH

The Joseph-Judah relationship and the points at which their paths converge continue throughout history. From the sale of Joseph onward, Judah and Joseph constantly interact with each other, and their relationship continues in various forms. Here, in *Parashat Vayigash*, their interaction is a confrontation, as the Midrash comments, "'Then Judah went up to him' (Gen. 44:18) – advancing to battle" (Genesis Rabba 93:6). The Midrash views this confrontation as a momentous event, adding, "'For lo, the kings converged' (Ps. 48:5) – this refers to Judah and Joseph; 'they grew angry together' (48:5) – this one was filled with anger for that one, and that one was filled with anger for this one" (Genesis Rabba 93:2). This is an epic clash between two kings, one that continues to occur in various forms throughout history.

There are times and places where the Joseph-Judah relationship is one of cooperation and even love. In the battle against Amalek, the leadership of the People of Israel consists of Moses, Aaron, and two other people: Ḥur, a member of the tribe of Judah, stands by Moses' side opposite Aaron, while Joshua, from the tribe of Joseph, leads the actual war. This connection appears again in the story of the spies, where Joshua and Caleb are the only two spies who refrain from "spreading calumnies about the land" (Num. 14:36). Moses himself is connected by blood to the tribe of Judah (Aaron married the sister of the tribe's prince, Naḥshon the son of Amminadav, and Miriam, Ḥur's mother, was married to Caleb the son of Yefuneh). On the other hand, Joshua – of the tribe of Joseph – is his close disciple.

This duality does not end there but continues through the generations. The Shiloh Tabernacle stood in the territory of Ephraim for over 300 years, whereas the Temple was built in Jerusalem, on the border of the territories of Judah and Benjamin (Yoma 12a). The dirges of Ezekiel (chap. 23) feature the sisters Ohola and Oholiva, who correspond to the kingdoms of Judah and Israel: "Ohola is Samaria, and Oholiva is Jerusalem" (23:4). In the royal house, although Saul is not from a tribe of

Joseph, he is a descendant of Joseph's mother Rachel, while David is from the tribe of Judah. The encounter between them is one of antagonism, but, as if to balance out that animosity, we read of a parallel and opposite relationship: the friendship and love between Jonathan and David. There is Joshua and there is Caleb; the tribe of Judah and the tribes of Joseph; the Kingdom of Judah and the Kingdom of Israel; David and Jonathan. We see that this duality is woven throughout our history, to the point that we ourselves are an example of it: The Jewish people today consists solely of descendants of Judah and Benjamin.

This complicated relationship between Joseph and Judah, in all its manifestations, continues to persist, and will continue until the end of days: Even our eschatological texts describe a division between the Messiah son of David and the Messiah son of Joseph.

GLORY AND ETERNITY

The meeting of Joseph and Judah in *Parashat Vayigash* illuminates one aspect of their relationship. On the larger historical plane, Joseph possesses an aspect of glory that Judah lacks, in the real sense and in the esoteric sense. At their first meeting, members of the tribe of Joseph almost always overshadow members of Judah. Even from birth, Joseph has an advantage: He is smarter, more handsome, more successful, and more loved. In this respect he lives up to his characterization as the sun in his famous dream, in that he is far more lustrous than his peers, while Judah appears inferior from the very beginning.

This paradigm follows here as well. How do they meet? Joseph, unofficially the king of Egypt, meets with Judah, a peasant shepherd from some remote place. Joseph stands there in all his glory, and facing him, "Judah went up to him."

What, in comparison to Joseph, does Judah have to offer? What is unique about him? It appears that Judah's unique point is continuity and endurance. Judah perseveres, as he did when he admitted his responsibility to Tamar, and this is a point that can be observed in the cases of many other members of his tribe. Joseph outshines Judah with respect to glory, but as for perseverance and staying power – "'and the eternity' (1 Chr. 29:11) refers to Jerusalem" (Berakhot 58a) – Joseph, for all his nobility, does not measure up.

Judah perseveres because he has the advantage of being able to fall, as it says, "Though he may fall, he is not utterly cast down" (Ps. 37:24). When Judah falls, he is able to get up again. This is Judah's special quality; it is part of his essence.

The point of "Judah went up to him" is that Judah, in spite of being a person of minor importance – the contrast between his and Joseph's appearance must have been striking – nevertheless dares to approach the king. To some extent, this evokes the way in which Saul meets with David. Saul is the king, and David is a youth brought in from tending the flock to entertain Saul.

Intrinsic to Joseph and his descendants is a sort of perfection, but this perfection is very fragile: When something breaks, they are unable to fix it. For Joseph, every situation is all or nothing, whereas Judah is adept at raising himself up again.

For an example of this dichotomy, one must look no further than Saul and David. Saul and David both sinned. The difference between them is the following: After Saul "breaks" once, he breaks again a second time and a third time. Though Saul came from a distinguished family and was considered "of greater stature than all the people" (1 Sam. 9:2) – a courageous warrior; a humble, modest, and worthy individual; a pure soul – when he falls, he is unable to get up. When Saul sins, he reaches a state in which he is ready to die and is also willing to accept the entire punishment he deserves. In contrast, when David sins, he draws new wisdom and maturity from the experience, penning the book of Psalms in its wake. This is quite an accomplishment! King David can sink low, but he can channel that low point in his life into real spiritual growth. This is something that Joseph, by his very nature, cannot do.

This difference surfaces again when the Kingdom of Israel is divided in two, with the House of Joseph and the House of Judah going separate ways. Upon reading the assessment of the midrashim of the characters involved, it is clear whom our sages favored.

Yerovam is an exalted and impressive figure, a man chosen by God to rule over the ten tribes of Israel. No matter what we think of him, he is certainly an extraordinary personality, as demonstrated by a series of talmudic anecdotes: He is capable of rebuking King Solomon when the latter is at the height of his glory (Sanhedrin 101b). When Yerovam is together with Aḥiyya the Shilonite, all the wise men are like the grass of the field in comparison with them (102a), and God says to Yerovam, "Repent, and then I and you and the son of Jesse will stroll together in the Garden of Eden" (102a).

Facing Yerovam is Reḥavam. Who is Reḥavam? On the whole, he is a man who is a bit confused, who does not know what to do exactly with the fairly large kingdom that he inherited and which, through ill-advised harshness and imprudent softness, he manages to lose. Besides this, we are told little of Reḥavam.

Nevertheless, Yerovam – who certainly was a great man and a far greater scholar than Reḥavam – is among those who have no share in the World to Come. He sinned and caused others to sin, and there is no way to atone for this. Reḥavam may not have been a righteous king or an especially significant king, but he carried on the line of the House of David. No royal line of the kings of Joseph manages to last more than a few generations. By contrast, the kings of the House of David – who certainly count some wicked men in their number – are able to build a stable dynasty, and are able, ultimately, to persevere.

Elisha b. Avuya, the tannaitic apostate known as "*Aḥer*" (literally, "Other"), was similar to Yerovam in this sense. He was perhaps the most brilliant man of his generation and was younger than all the other scholars with whom he would confer. According to his own account (Ruth Rabba 6:4), Rabbi Yehoshua and Rabbi Eliezer attended his circumcision; thus, they were already scholars when he was born. But Elisha b. Avuya could not tolerate a world that lacked perfection, and when he discovers that there are problems in the world, he begins to fall apart. And when he falls apart, he cannot recover from the fall.

This conception of perfection is reflected in a saying of his: "One who learns when young, to what may he be compared? To ink written on fresh paper. But one who learns when old, to what may he be compared? To ink written on paper that has been erased" (Avot 4:20). Elisha b. Avuya does not want to write on erased paper; he wants ink written on fresh paper. He is saying – and this is part of his personality – that since he has been erased once, he cannot rewrite himself. By contrast, Rabbi Akiva is like Judah, a peasant from an undistinguished family. Unlike Elisha b. Avuya, who came from one of the prominent families of Jerusalem, Rabbi Akiva was the son of converts. Throughout his life, Rabbi Akiva "broke" not just once but several times, including during difficult events in his personal life, yet he always overcame his setbacks.

THE *TZADDIK* AND THE *BAAL TESHUVA*

Joseph was a true *tzaddik*. Sometimes this identity is apparent in a person's character from birth, and it is immediately clear that this person is innately good. There is a type of personality for whom perfection is innate. Jonathan, Saul's son, seems to fit this characterization – he is a person with no apparent defects.

Let us note, however, that such a person – a man who bears an aspect of perfection by his very nature, who was born with all the great gifts and who exercises them in perfect fashion – must be judged by his ability to remain at this level. Possessing all the virtues is not enough if he is unable to rectify himself the moment he becomes flawed.

In nature, too, there are structures that do not reach perfection by way of development but, rather, emerge perfect from the outset. The Talmud (Beitza 3b) mentions the possibility of using an egg to support the leg of a bed. This talmudic statement is strange and surprising. After all, even if this were possible, who would use an egg to support the leg of a bed? But the truth is that from a physical standpoint, an egg is one of the most perfect structures in existence. The only problem is that an egg's strength depends on its complete integrity. It is like a dome: The moment one stone falls, the whole structure collapses. This is often the nature of this kind of perfection: It can last only as long as there is no flaw.

In this sense – as is evident from their interaction before and after this point – the relationship of Joseph and Judah is that of a *tzaddik* and a *baal teshuva*. The story of Judah and Tamar compared to the story of Joseph and Potifar's wife is a striking example of this relationship.

Judah's character seems to deteriorate. He sells Joseph, which is a particularly despicable act. His conduct with Tamar demonstrates a moral deficiency as well. Nevertheless, he is also capable of confronting Joseph – "Judah went up to him." Here is a person who has quite a few matters on his conscience and an unsavory past. We might have expected him to sit quietly on the sidelines, but as we see, he takes action instead.

Judah not only puts his life on the line but is also willing to face up to his past actions. The wide gulf between those actions and his present conduct is precisely what defines Judah's essence. The Midrash (Tanḥuma, *Vayigash* 4) comments that Joseph attempted – rightfully – to silence Judah, asking him, "Why are you speaking up? You are neither the eldest nor the firstborn. So what are you doing? Let your eldest brother Reuben speak. Why do you even have the right to open your mouth?" Yet Judah, despite all his baggage, rises anew, ready to come to grips with whatever he must face. That is Judah's strength. By contrast, Joseph – by nature and as a matter of principle – cannot change, cannot be flexible. He is a perfectionist, and this is precisely what breaks him.

The Talmud (Ḥagiga 15a) recounts an interesting conversation between Elisha b. Avuya and Rabbi Meir. Elisha b. Avuya asks Rabbi Meir to interpret the verse, "Gold and glass cannot match its value, nor can vessels of fine gold be exchanged for it" (Job 28:17). Rabbi Meir responds, "This refers to Torah matters, which, like vessels of gold, are hard to acquire, but like vessels of glass are easily lost." Elisha b. Avuya says to him, "Rabbi Akiva, your master, did not interpret that way, but, rather, 'Both vessels of gold and vessels of glass, if broken, can be repaired.'" One can melt them and form them anew. But there are vessels – such as those of clay, mother of pearl, or even diamond – that, after being broken, remain forever broken. One cannot do anything about it; the defect remains a defect.

We read in *Megillat Ester*, "But Mordekhai neither bowed down nor prostrated himself" (Est. 3:2). On the one hand, this conduct reflects his strength and glory; but on the other hand, it gets him into trouble: According to the Talmud (Megilla 12b), the Jews became furious with him for not acquiescing to Haman's demands. "Why did you get us into all of this trouble?" they cried. "Bow down!" Mordekhai is cast in the same mold as his ancestors Saul and Joseph before him. He is called "Mordekhai the *tzaddik*" (10b), and *tzaddikim* often cannot abide even the slightest flaw. Mordekhai's essential nature requires that he be perfect.

Before going out to his last battle, Saul knows that he and his sons are going to die, and he does not care. An aspect of strength and idealism accompanies this man throughout his life – even at his fall. Just like Elisha b. Avuya, Saul does not act in half measures; if his flaws cannot be corrected completely, then he does not want them corrected at all. He aims for the highest heights, but if he cannot achieve this, he will consign himself to the lowest depths. To go halfway is not an option.

By contrast, for someone like Judah – the true *baal teshuva* – the existence of flaws is intrinsic to him and to his personality. If he did not have flaws, he would not be who he is. The *baal teshuva* thrives on his ability to deconstruct his personality in order to reshape it in another form, to make changes within himself.

Judah begins entirely from below. Like David, he comes "from following the flock" (II Sam. 7:8); he begins from nothing. Judah is neither the firstborn nor the most physically imposing of Jacob's children. However, he "prevailed over his brothers" (I Chr. 5:2), and he continuously perseveres, generation after generation.

Joshua and Caleb seem similar, to a large degree. However, though the Talmud likens Joshua to Moses, saying, "Moses' countenance was like that of the sun; Joshua's countenance was like that of the moon" (Bava Batra 75a), Joshua had no children. Caleb had a son and a brother – he had successors, generation after generation. Not all of his descendants were important or significant people, and most certainly did not measure up to his eminence, but Caleb's essence lived on. When Joshua died, however, only a tombstone remained. After the tribes of Joseph were smashed and exiled, they did not return home. We – who are basically the Kingdom of Judah – had our first Temple destroyed, but we built the Second Temple. We were exiled again for a period of time, but once again, we are returning.

Wherever Judah and Joseph interact, it is a meeting between perfection and adaptability. Throughout history, Joseph represents splendor, even heroism. In contrast, Judah is flawed and beleaguered, beset with difficulties; but in the end, Judah always prevails.

RECTIFYING THE WORLD

At the end of the *parasha*, there is a section that the commentators discuss extensively, even though it seems to have little to do with the main theme of the *parasha*, and is connected to a different aspect of the relationship between Judah and Joseph.

The entire final section of *Parashat Vayigash* is the story of how Joseph handles Egyptian politics for Pharaoh and how he governs the

Egyptians. That Joseph was a powerful ruler over the entire land has already been stated, but here we find a whole story about how Joseph interacts with the Egyptians.

Shortly before this story, the Torah states, "And he [Jacob] sent Judah before him unto Joseph, to show the way before him unto Goshen" (Gen. 46:28). Where do Judah and Joseph stand at this juncture?

In contrast to Judah, Joseph is practically a king. He speaks seventy languages, while Judah no doubt stammers in the only language he knows. But that is not the point. Here we see that Joseph acts not only in his own interest; rather, he tries to rectify the world. Joseph endeavors on behalf of the entire country and puts it back on its feet. While Joseph is saving the country, Judah brings the family to the land of Goshen, where they organize themselves in their own matters. While Joseph is engaged in a great undertaking, Judah deals with the small matters: his flock, his herd, and the question of how to support the family.

The interpretation by our sages (Genesis Rabba 95:3) that Jacob sent Judah in order to establish a house of study does not affect the analysis. The same conclusion emerges: Joseph is not just the most successful son in his family. He is a man who concerns himself with the whole world, while Judah concerns himself with parochial Jewish pursuits. Whereas Joseph is universal, Judah is only a Jew, engaging in his own pursuits and his own matters.

On the surface it appears that Joseph, the man of the world, is the hero of this narrative, while Judah is of minor importance. Precisely here, the *haftara* plays a crucial role, presenting the differences in the nature and character of Judah and Joseph as fundamental distinctions between two parallel worlds. When the Judah-Joseph duality is viewed under a different light, as it is in the *haftara*, we see the world of Joseph – who transcends his own individuality and represents a whole way of being – and a world of Judah, whose essence is that he begins from below, from crisis, from distress, and from the minutiae of life.

What Joseph does almost instantly takes Judah several generations to accomplish. Even when Judah builds, the building is not straight; his progress is characterized by ups and downs. But which is the ideal path, the worldview that we should adopt and strive for? Neither the book of Genesis nor the Torah as a whole presents a clear answer to this question.

When Jacob blesses his sons before his death and gives Judah and Joseph the biggest and most significant blessings, they are on equal ground, one facing the other. Evident in the blessings to Joseph is not just greater love for this son; they are blessings of tremendous scope – Jacob grants him heaven and earth: "May your father's blessing add to the blessing of my parents, to the utmost bounds of the everlasting hills. May they rest on Joseph's head, on the brow of the elect of his brothers" (Gen. 49:26). He gives him everything that can possibly be given. Correspondingly, Judah receives eternity: "The scepter shall not depart from Judah, nor the ruler's staff from between his feet" (49:10). Joseph is given grandeur, while Judah is given eternity.

The conclusion is not found in this *parasha*, nor in the book of Genesis, nor anywhere in the entire Torah. The final reckoning is that of the Messiah: Who will be the true Messiah? Since this reckoning moves back and forth over the generations, it is clear that Joseph and Judah are equals: It is the ultimate conflict between the perfect and the imperfect, between those who begin with a stacked deck and those who forge themselves.

THE STICK OF JUDAH AND THE STICK OF JOSEPH

The *haftara* presents Judah and Joseph as two branches, and the conflict between them is not personal but, rather, a conflict between essential natures. It is very difficult for them to join together, because they are two different character types that cannot be integrated.

The *haftara* concludes that in this disagreement, although from time to time the scales tip to the stick of Judah or the stick of Joseph, it is impossible to truly favor one side or the other. According to the *haftara*, ideally the two aspects should be able to work together, as the *Likkutei Torah* writes (*Shir HaShirim* 13a) regarding the verse, "We will add circlets of gold to your points of silver" (Song. 1:11).

In all the texts that deal with this subject, it is clear that there will be no solution to this question until the end of days. This conflict, like the "dispute for the sake of Heaven" of Shammai and Hillel (Avot 5:17), will ultimately endure.

When we say that these two aspects should go together, the meaning is not that they should be joined together like two planks, forcing each to adapt to the nature of the other. When the stick of Judah and the stick of Joseph join together, they should each exist independently, but side by side, in the perfect harmony of a string quartet. Judah and Joseph represent two different elements, each of which retains its distinctness. The inevitable internal conflict in this coexistence is the very thing that creates the beauty.

In Joseph's case, there is an element of great tragedy. People who possess the character traits of Joseph are incomparable in their splendor and virtual perfection. They are radiant suns, but they have no way of recovering from a fall. Must it always be that those of us who approach closest to perfection are also the most fragile among us? Will the spiritual descendants of Joseph never be able to lift themselves up and repair themselves?

Apparently, until the end of time, these two types will remain: one who is characterized by wholeness and perfection, and one who is characterized by fault and repair; one who draws his strength from his perfection, and the other, from the power of renewal. These two will never completely unite, but together they comprise the tension that makes our lives so vibrant. We live between Judah and Joseph, and when the two elements work in perfect tandem, the symphony of life is formed.

Vayeḥi

THE VEILED *KETZ*

Jacob calls his sons and says to them, "Gather yourselves together, that I may tell you what will befall you in the end of days" (Gen. 49:1). But in practice, Jacob's prophecy merely relates to distant times and does not reach the actual end of days.

Rashi's comment on the subject is well known: "'Gather yourselves together, that I may tell you' – he wished to reveal the *ketz*, but the *Shekhina* departed from him, and he began to speak of other things." To be sure, after the departure of the *Shekhina*, Jacob does not suddenly become an ordinary person speaking of ordinary things. After all, his words here are still words of prophecy. Although those "other things" do not relate to the actual end of days, still, they refer to the distant future, hundreds and thousands of years ahead. Thus, the *Shekhina* does not depart completely; it is still with him to a certain extent.

Jacob attempts to cut through the veil that conceals the events of the future, but he is stopped at a certain stage. Why does this happen to him?

According to the *Yalkut Shimoni* (157) and other midrashim, a great dread falls upon Jacob, as he does not understand why this has happened. Concerned, he asks his sons, "Are you all believers?" They answer him, "Hear, O Israel: God our Lord, God is one." When the time of the Messiah's coming was concealed from Jacob, he was overcome with anxiety that perhaps not all the tribes were worthy of blessing. After hearing their answer, he is encouraged, and the *Shekhina* rests upon him once again.

What emerges from the midrash is that this concealment, the curtain that stands before Jacob, is neither a result of sin nor a result of a defect in his sons or in himself. Jacob faces something else, which does not let him see through to the end of days. This is a phenomenon that we all experience: At one point or another, every person wants to know what will happen in the distant future, but this is always denied him.

LIMITATIONS OF THE AUDIENCE

Why can't Jacob reveal the *ketz*? When a person describes things or situations that lie within the range of his perception, he has words, concepts, and modes of expression for this. But when Jacob must speak of a phenomenon that is beyond his audience's range of perception, it turns out that he lacks the vocabulary to express himself. How can we explain to someone who has been blind from birth what other people see in the world? How can we explain to someone who is colorblind the difference between green and purple? These are things of which the listener has an utter lack of understanding. In such a case, there is a block, a real barrier in communication.

In other words, there are some fundamental gulfs that are impossible to bridge. Nothing can be said to get one's ideas across; any attempts to do so would be meaningless. The problem of how to talk about the incomprehensible, how to describe what cannot be described, is a problem that has no solution. At the point of transmitting the essence, there is a curtain that blocks the audience's view. It is not a matter of finding the right words, because the right words simply do not exist.

Consider, for example, the *Maase Merkava*, Ezekiel's vision of the workings of the divine chariot. We take for granted that the angels, the *ofanim*, and the holy *ḥayot* are spiritual entities, or, as Maimonides put it, "separate intellects" (*Guide for the Perplexed*, 1:49). But when we read Ezekiel's account, he seems to be describing physical forms, as if these are creatures that one might see at some kind of bizarre zoo. What is happening here? Ezekiel sees the holy *ḥayot*, and for some reason he is compelled to describe them in words. Though he sees and feels the reality of his vision, he lacks the right words to describe it. Instead, he settles for the inaccurate language of physical descriptions.

This point is part of the reason that the *Shekina* departs when people begin to speak of the end of days. Jacob sees all the way to the true *ketz*; not just "until he arrives in Shiloh" (Gen. 49:10), but even afterward, after the end of the exile. When he tries to tell his sons about this, he discovers that this is a vision that cannot be communicated – not because he is not permitted to do so, but because any attempt to speak about it is irrelevant.

There is a recurring prophecy in Tanakh – "every man will sit under his grapevine or under his fig tree" (Mic. 4:4) – that is meant to describe a condition of wealth and tranquility. Yet there are many people today who, if promised a future in which all they do is sit under a tree, would be completely uninterested – they would rather attend a nightclub instead. The prophecy tries to describe a future of wealth and harmony, but this can only be communicated using the range of concepts that people have. We can make an effort to describe the future using the most beautiful words that exist, but my message will only be successful if it is couched in terms of what is presently meaningful to our audience. When we have to transcend these bounds, anything we say will be incomplete. We are unable to describe things that are not within the range of the human imagination; even if we are able to comprehend these things, the concepts turn out to be meaningless without the proper tools of expression.

NO EYE HAS SEEN

The ability to relate to the end of days is limited not only by shortcomings of human nature, but also by something more basic: limitations in the nature of reality. Reality allows us to relate only to things that belong to the plane of being, experience, and action in which we exist. Just as we cannot fit a large object into a small receptacle, we cannot fit anything into a vessel – a concept, a description, or a figment of our imagination – that cannot receive or contain it.

This idea is expressed in the following talmudic passage: "All the prophets prophesied only regarding the days of the Messiah, but regarding the World to Come, 'No eye has seen, O God, but You' (Is. 64:3)"

(Berakhot 34b). No prophet's eye has seen what God will do for those who wait for Him; it can be seen by God's eye alone. The Talmud then asks, "What is it that 'no eye has seen'? Rabbi Yehoshua b. Levi said, 'This refers to the wine preserved in its grapes since the six days of Creation.'"

Similarly, the Talmud states (Bava Batra 74b) that in the World to Come, the righteous will partake of the Leviathan's flesh. Both of these rewards for the righteous – the wine preserved in its grapes since the six days of Creation and the Leviathan preserved in salt by God even before the creation of man – are things that have never existed in the realm of human experience. These descriptions of the World to Come are beyond our limits as human beings. It is a promise of things that we have never seen and cannot hope to comprehend.

The end of days is a period that "no eye has seen" – it is beyond our perceptual range, beyond the human conceptual ability that exists in the reality of the present day.

When we speak of the ultimate *ketz*, we refer to what cannot be seen or understood. When we speak of what will happen in the future, we can reach a certain point until we are stopped by a thick curtain. Even those who can see through this curtain cannot bring back a report of what they have seen. They cannot relate what they have beheld, because there can be no point of comparison to it, nothing in their lexicon to describe it.

In our generation, because of the many technological advances we continuously witness, we have a better sense of the gulf between the reality of this world and the reality of the World to Come. Products are invented, the likes of which we could not have even dreamed beforehand, whose existence we could not have imagined.

This also explains a puzzling talmudic statement: "Three come unawares: the Messiah, a found article, and a scorpion" (Sanhedrin 97a). At first glance, this statement raises a question: What does it mean that the Messiah comes unawares? After all, there are always Jews who pray for, talk about, and concern themselves with his coming. The entire Jewish people mentions the Messiah, in one form or another, in its prayers. So how can it be that he will come unawares?

The answer is that the Messiah whom everyone talks about, and whose coming everyone prays for, is not the Messiah who will actually arrive. We have no way of knowing or imagining what will happen when the Messiah comes, because his coming is something that "no eye has seen." It is inevitable, then, that the Messiah will come unawares, because no one really knows what to expect.

An example of this problem can be seen in the *Or HaHayim*'s commentary on *Parashat Aharei Mot*. As a rule, the book is written as a standard commentary, each section according to its particular case. In *Parashat Aharei Mot*, however, something interesting happens: The author attempts to describe the experience of man's contact with what is beyond him. Some of the language in the commentary is confusing: It is evident that the author felt and understood certain things that he was unable to communicate with his readers. It is the same block that Jacob encountered when he sought to reveal the *ketz*, the same block that inherently exists in these matters, and there will be no full solution for it until the end of days.

DEVELOPING SENSITIVITY

The inability to define certain things has ramifications beyond esoteric discussions of the divine chariot and the end of days. The expression, "the heart cannot reveal to the mouth" (Ecclesiastes Rabba 12:10), appears in connection with all sorts of subjects, for not everything that a person thinks can be expressed easily in words. There also exists a much more complex and difficult situation, when "the heart cannot reveal to the heart," that is, that the heart cannot reveal even to itself. These are difficulties that every person experiences at one point or another in his lifetime.

The Talmud (Pesahim 54b) presents a list of things that are concealed from us: the day of a person's death; the day of consolation; the full depth of justice; that which is in another person's heart – and the list goes on. The connection between these things is that they are all impossible to determine.

Why is it impossible to know what is in another person's heart? Because everything that a person draws from deep inside him he must communicate through an intermediary mechanism, the translation from thoughts and feelings into words. The listener then transfers the matter from those words into his own heart. My contact with another person's heart is, at best, twice removed from the source; there is no possibility of direct contact, of one spirit truly connecting with another.

We constantly try to solve the difficulty of communicating what is in our heart to the best of our ability, since that is the only way that a person can have an impact on the world around him. We hope that the other person not only hears our words, but is able to translate them back in his own heart while maintaining some of the purity of the original emotion. To be sure, the content of a person's heart is difficult to formulate in words, but if there is true resonance between two people, between two beings who are otherwise entirely separate, then while perhaps it cannot be said that each person knows what is in the other's heart, at least they are on the same wavelength.

There are some skills that are not included in any course of study, yet everyone must learn them. Sometimes a person must dedicate much of his life to these skills. One of these skills is the ability to develop a keen sense for things that cannot be said. Every Jew has his own inner dilemmas, but everyone shares the universal problem of faith – whether it is faith in God, or in other things. In matters of faith, anything that can be studied or articulated in words is irrelevant and unhelpful. If only we had a kind of window that would give us a direct view of God's glory! But there is no such window. What remains is the responsibility to learn to sense, to intuit, that something exists that is beyond our comprehension, beyond the range of man's ordinary perception, and to learn to relate to it. We must reach a point where we have, in addition to the vague awareness that such a thing exists, the maturity to understand that there is more to explore on the other side of the curtain, a continuation of our path. There may be no way to reach it, see it, or explain it, but it is possible to sense what lies on the other side of existence.

Our task, in any form of faith, is to develop an awareness that beyond the place that I know lies a place that I do not know. If we can accomplish this task, we can truly claim to have experienced even that which "no eye has seen."

Exodus

Shemot

To our children, Sarah, Elisa, Livia and Tobia Tagliacozzo, with the hope that our united family, in light of tradition, may find its way to Eretz Israel.
Maurizio and Fiammetta Tagliacozzo, Rome, Tammuz 5773

Va'era

Anonymous

Bo

For the love of Hashem, our people and children, and in memory of beloved Rafaela Batia (Rafaela Bo) OBM ~ Moshiach now.
Amiel Shaul ben Gita Rochel v'Yisroel
Leora bat Sarah Leah v'Chaim

Beshallaḥ

In dedication to Marion and Jean-Pierre, Mor and Alain Ilai, Yaniv and Levi Kugelmann
Yves Kugelmann, Basel

Yitro

In loving and everlasting memory of my dear Mother, Gittel Baila Bas Avrohom
נפטרה ב' באדר ב' תשס"ח *and In celebration of my Grandmother Edith Freedman's*
100th birthday, 12 December 2012, may she live to be 120 years old.
Aron M. Freedman, UK

Mishpatim

In loving memory of משה הלוי בן חיאל ע"ה
Dedicated by his children, grandchildren, and great-grandchildren

Teruma

In honor of Eitan Yehuda Ben Michael Calev's Bar Mitzva
Ruth & Conrad, z"l Morris

Tetzaveh

To our mother and father, grandfather and grandmother, Reuven and Ruth: We dedicate this portion with love and gratitude in your beloved memory. Dearly missed by your daughter Nili, and son-in-law Zeev, and your grandsons Gidon and Eliyahu.
Nikki & William Silverman (Sydney) Tammuz 5773

Parashat Zakhor

In memory of our unforgettable husband and father, Cyril Stein a"h
Stein Family

Ki Tissa

In Loving Memory of Betsy Shapiro ז"ל
נפטרה בג' לפרשת כי תשא, ט"ז אדר תש"ע אלישבע בת מלך יצחק ושיינע טעלוע
Mendel Shapiro

Vayak'hel

לעילוי נשמת
משה אליעזר בן גרשון ויהודית ז"ל
הלך לעולמו בשטוקהולם ח' ניסן תשנ"ג
חוה בת אשר אנשל ושרה ז"ל
הלכה לעולמה בשטוקהולם י"א אדר תשס"א
Stephen Meisels

Pekudei

In loving memory of Holly Rofé, the most dedicated Mom and wife, we miss you each day more than the last.
André, Rachel and Sarina Rofé, 28 Adar 1, 5771

Shemot

The book of Genesis deals with the life stories of the nation's patriarchs and matriarchs, beginning with Abraham, continuing with Isaac, and ending with Jacob and his sons. Essentially, these are narratives about individuals. The book of Exodus puts the focus, for the first time, on the Jewish people, not as a list of individuals but as a whole nation. With this begins a new narrative in the Torah – the story of the Jewish people. To be sure, in the book of Exodus as well, much attention is focused on the life of Moses. However, his story is the story of the Jewish people's emergence, in which the story of Moses the individual occupies only a subordinate place.

The Genesis narratives are certainly important, and they, too, have national significance, as our sages say, "The experiences of the patriarchs prefigure the history of their descendants" (Tanḥuma, *Lekh Lekha* 9; Nahmanides on Genesis 12:6). Nevertheless, in and of themselves, they are still narratives on a small scale. From Exodus onward, however, the narrative is on a much larger scale; it is the narrative of the Jewish people as a whole. Hence, even the minor narratives in Exodus have greater significance for us than the Genesis narratives do.

THE EXODUS FROM EGYPT

The major and central narrative in the book of Exodus is undoubtedly the story of the Exodus from Egypt: the experience of exile and the process of leaving it. The Exodus is a central theme not only in the book of Exodus but in Jewish life in general. An examination of the siddur reveals that we mention the Exodus at every opportunity, both when there is a clear and obvious connection, such as on Pesaḥ, and when the connection is less obvious as well, such as on all the other festivals – Shavuot, Sukkot, Rosh HaShana, and Yom Kippur. Even in the text of the Kiddush that we recite each Shabbat, the Exodus features prominently.

The Egyptian exile and the Exodus are, for us, far more than the specific historical narrative that appears in the book of Exodus; they are basic elements within our being. The exile and the redemption in Exodus were not a one-time event, but merely the paradigm for an event that recurs again and again throughout our history – exile followed by redemption followed by exile again – and thus the metamorphosis of the Jewish people continues.

These processes of exile and redemption exist on an even larger plane, as the basis of the entire world. The Jewish people are not the only ones who experience these stages; all of humanity does so as well. This does not happen in the same way and on the same level for every person or every group of people, but these are basic stages in the life process of everyone, individuals and nations alike.

We go through this cycle in the course of our individual lives. Some people spend sixty years in Egypt and ten years in the wilderness, some spend forty years in Egypt and forty years in the wilderness, and some merit a more generous division: They spend a short period of time in exile followed by a longer time in the redemption stage. But on the whole, the human life cycle always adheres to this process: There is a stage of exile, of difficulties and problems, followed by a stage of redemption, of bursting through the difficulties and the problems, and the cycle continues.

Scientists often speak of basic structures of which everything that exists in the world is merely a copy. For example, almost all forms of matter share the same type of molecular bonds, which serve to join together the tiny particles present in any material. Whether the material is as simple as salt or as complex as a hormone, every form of matter has a basic structure that repeats itself in other instances throughout the universe. Correspondingly, the cycle of the Egyptian exile and the Exodus is the prototype for this central pattern that we continue to experience, both as a community and as individuals, in a variety of forms.

The simple reason for mentioning the Exodus daily is not just to recall the historical story; rather, it is because the life cycle and even the daily cycle always follow this pattern. The cycle of exile and redemption forms the basis of our lives, and in this respect the story of the Exodus exists on a different plane from the other stories in the Torah; it is the central story of existence.

The Torah relates two universal stories: the story of Creation and the story of the Exodus. The story of Creation is a pattern that begins with a perfect world – the world of the Garden of Eden – and reaches a crisis that necessitates a resolution – in this case, the expulsion of Adam and Eve from Eden. Although this is the story of all of existence, nevertheless, it is not exactly what we encounter every day. Our world is not built like the Garden of Eden – it is certainly not a perfect world. To be sure, it is important to know that such a world once existed, but in our individual experience and in human life in general, we do not encounter it. We start out in a different kind of world, one that is patterned after the Exodus. Our world is built on the reality of exile, a complex existence with problems and difficulties. In the midst of exile, we must endeavor to ultimately attain redemption.

THE MEANING OF EXILE

We see that exile is not an accidental state – neither in our own history nor in the world in general. Therefore, understanding exile is all the more important. It is clear that exile is not a pleasant existence and that it entails various difficulties. But what is the essence of the problem with exile? What is its fundamental difficulty?

Exile has inherent significance beyond the reality of being unable to live in one's desired geographic location – in our case, the Land of Israel. When we say that the Jewish people is in exile, this is more than a determination of place, for exile is a state that is intrinsically problematic, not just because of its geographic location.

The problem of exile as it has been described as follows: "Your descendants will be strangers in a land not theirs" (Gen. 15:13) is tolerable – it is just a stay in another country. Does the true exile begin when "they will be enslaved and oppressed"? Perhaps, in determining whether a certain country is considered "exile," one need only check whether he is subjected to oppression. If he is oppressed, this is indeed exile; if he is not oppressed, then it is merely another country outside the Land of Israel. Hence, people might argue today that while life in Syria was certainly exile, life in America does not qualify as exile, because in America neither "and they will be enslaved" nor "and oppressed" apply.

In truth, it appears that exilic existence involves a more fundamental problem. The essential point of exile is that something is not where it should be, in its appropriate place. In the normal course of things, it may be that a person temporarily resides outside his homeland. The new place may be uncomfortable for him, but that is not yet considered an exilic existence. Nowadays, when a Frenchman moves to Canada, he may feel like a "stranger," but this is not an essential problem that creates a life of exile for him. If a carp is transferred from a pool near Atlit to a pool near Nahariya, it may have difficulty adapting, but being in one pool or the other is not an essential difference for it. Regardless of the pool in which it ends up, it is in an appropriate place for a fish. But when a fish is taken out of water altogether, whether this occurs near Atlit or Nahariya, or whether it was treated properly or not is irrelevant; it is in a place that is fundamentally inappropriate and, for a fish, life threatening as well.

INDIVIDUAL OR COLLECTIVE?

There are several stages to the Egyptian exile. The People of Israel settle in Egypt over a long period, and not all of this period is considered exile, certainly not in the true sense. Jacob and his family travel to Egypt of their own volition, willingly and for their own good. When, then, does their existence become one of exile? Where is the dividing line?

It appears that the oppression of the Egyptian exile begins only when Pharaoh says to his people, "Behold, the People of Israel are too numerous and strong for us" (Ex. 1:9). The beginning of the Egyptian exile hinges on the Egyptians' perception that Israel is a foreign nation – they sense Israel's foreignness. As long as this awareness is lacking, and the Egyptians relate to the People of Israel as individuals, this is not yet exile; the People of Israel are merely strangers.

Exile hinges on whether the person is part of a collective or a separate individual. When individuals, even a large number of them, are in another country, they may be considered foreigners, strangers in a strange land; but when there is a whole collective, an entire nation, in a place that is inappropriate for it – that is exile. For this reason, one of the ways in which Diaspora Jews often seek to solve the problem of exile is by attempting to ignore their collective identity. They want their countrymen to relate to them as to individuals, not as parts of a whole. They avow that they are Jewish only by chance, just as a Turk happens to have been born in Turkey and an Italian happens to have been born in Italy – they do not belong to the Jewish collective. Once these individuals remove themselves from the collective, then although they are not in their true homeland, and they are different in many ways from their non-Jewish neighbors, this is an individualized problem and not one of exile.

Even in the reality of Egyptian bondage, there surely were Jews who took such an approach. Imagine a Jew living in Egypt who is suddenly forced into slavery and ordered to work with mortar and bricks. These decrees are certainly not pleasant for him, so what does he do? The first thing he thinks of is how to advance in rank – how to be appointed a foreman and not merely a regular worker. After becoming a foreman, he continues to rise in rank becoming a taskmaster, and then rises further in the ranks until he finds a more desirable position. This Jew sees the problem as a personal one – a problem connected to his place and his personal situation – and he relates to the problem correspondingly. From his standpoint, the general state of things is, on the whole, in order. Therefore, if he is not content with where he is, or if something is bothering him, he adapts by simply changing his position, shifting to a more personally comfortable place, but doing nothing to fundamentally change his situation.

AWARENESS OF EXILE AND REDEMPTION

One who relates to himself strictly as an individual will never leave Egypt. He manages to convince himself that he has it good – so things are good for him; why should he change? Only one who is aware of his situation, who understands that he is in exile, has a chance of leaving it for the "good and spacious land."

Awareness of exile begins the moment there is a sense, which sometimes comes from within and sometimes comes from without, that the problem is not just a personal problem but an overall problem of disharmony. When there is awareness of exile, the problem is no longer how to make small adjustments within the reality but how to get out of this place entirely.

Awareness of exile is the awareness of the need for a revolution – that is, for a fundamental change in the order of the existing reality. One who considers himself a stranger is likely to think, for example, that he gets the worst jobs only because he does not yet have citizenship in his resident country. So he will try to attain citizenship and suffice himself with that localized solution. Only a feeling of essentially not belonging to the place in which one resides can bring an individual or a nation to move out. Only such a feeling will lead to an awareness of the fundamental problem of exile and produce the need for a revolution.

Emergence from exile requires an essential change, because the whole essence of redemption is revolution, an essential change in the world order. This point bears on a simple question that commonly arises: Does everyone who moves to Israel necessarily emerge from exile? What happens, for instance, when someone moves from a Jewish city like Miami Beach to a Jewish city like Jerusalem? In such cases, what usually happens is that the person, for some reason, is not comfortable in his hometown. The seaside weather is too humid, perhaps, and he prefers to live in Jerusalem's drier climate. Or perhaps he wants to send his children to a Belz *ḥeder*, which is lacking in his hometown. In any case, he moves to Jerusalem, and all is well in the end. In all other respects, from his standpoint, there is no essential difference between the two places, and his life remains fundamentally unchanged. In such cases, there are two possibilities: either the exile was not really exile, or the redemption was not really redemption.

These two states – exile and redemption – go together; they are interconnected. It is precisely a person's awareness that he is in exile that creates the opening through which he may emerge from that exile and attain redemption. So long as one accepts as a given the framework of the existing reality, he will never be able to recognize the possibility of redemption. So long as one sees the problems as a handful of disagreeable details within a reality in which he basically feels at home, he has no reason to take action to change that reality. Only when a person comes to the realization that he lives in exile – that the situation is fundamentally out of order – only then can he begin to discuss redemption, an essential change in the reality.

The existence of exile and the possibility of attaining redemption are, thus, bound up with the fundamental question of how the individual views the reality of his life. The moment one comes to the awareness that his reality is not as it should be and that it must be changed on an essential level is the very moment when he can begin the process of redemption.

Va'era

PHARAOH'S CHARACTER

The narrative of the first third of the book of Exodus (through *Parashat Beshallaḥ*) features a protracted confrontation between God and Pharaoh. In this respect, it can be said that the central character of these *parashot* is not Moses but Pharaoh. Moses fulfills his role as God's emissary, conducting himself in a clear and consistent fashion. By contrast, Pharaoh's character is more complex, engaging our interest and raising various questions.

One of the basic questions about Pharaoh's character is why, after suffering blow after blow, does he not respond? Granted, the Torah states that "God hardened Pharaoh's heart" (Ex. 9:12); still, this raises the question of what underlies this whole situation.

The Kotzker Rebbe used to say that he respects Pharaoh. Here was a man who was struck by the plagues of Egypt and nevertheless stubbornly upheld his principles. This characterization not only explains the question of Pharaoh's surprising behavior, but sheds light generally on many of the other antagonists in the Torah as well.

In the confrontation between Moses and Pharaoh, certainly we would like to feel that we are on the side of Moses, but the truth is that most people would probably relate more to Pharaoh. Moses and Aaron are lofty characters who are in direct contact with God, whereas Pharaoh, in terms of his personality, is more or less an ordinary human being. To be sure, not everyone is capable of decreeing, as he did, "Every boy who is born you shall throw into the Nile" (Ex. 1:22), or of opposing God so stubbornly. Nevertheless, in terms of a person's basic inner tendencies, Pharaoh's decisions seem eminently understandable.

In this respect, the wicked characters in the Torah are no less – and perhaps even more – fascinating than the righteous ones. When we study the wicked characters, we can understand them much more fully than we can understand the *tzaddikim*. It may be that some who study the Bible feel as if they can relate to the prophets, but there is a big difference between feeling this way and fully comprehending what prophecy entails. In the case of the wicked, it is undoubtedly easier for us to understand the entirety of what motivates such a personality. Hence, Pharaoh's character and essential nature are much more significant for us, and it is important to try to understand his mode of conduct and his responses.

PHARAOH'S REMORSE

After the first plagues, Pharaoh already appears to be shaken, and he humbles himself when facing Moses, but the alarm that seizes him after the plague of hail is much more significant: "Pharaoh sent and called for Moses and Aaron, and said to them: I have sinned this time; God is righteous, and I and my people are wicked" (Ex. 9:27).

Pharaoh's alarm is understandable, considering that he lives in a land such as Egypt, where hail is a rare occurrence. When the hail falls, it is likely the first time in his life that he has seen such a thing, and it surely makes a great impression on him, all the more so when it is a heavy hail accompanied by thunder and lightning.

Nevertheless, his response on this occasion is essentially different from his previous responses. What does he mean when he says, "I have sinned this time; God is righteous, and I and my people are wicked"? What is he talking about?

When we follow the confrontation between Pharaoh and God, we see that, at least on the surface, it is conducted like a negotiation. At the start, Pharaoh receives a proposal to let the People of Israel have a three-day vacation in order to celebrate a festival in the wilderness. Pharaoh, of course, is not thrilled by the idea, and he flatly rejects the proposal. Clearly, this refusal creates a confrontation, but it is still limited, an obstacle the likes of which are found in every negotiation.

It is clear that part of the significance of the leave that Moses demands of Pharaoh is symbolic. Just as nowadays certain countries prohibit the waving of certain flags, the demand to leave Egypt and celebrate God's festival in the wilderness is not merely a demand for three days of vacation; it is a fundamental demand for recognition that the People of Israel has a certain degree of independence. It is a symbolic demand: Who is the one in charge? These symbolic actions can lead to strikes, wars, and revolutions to this very day. Pharaoh realizes this and, in the interest of preserving his sovereignty over the People of Israel, considers Moses' request a nonstarter.

Despite the fundamental significance of the proposal to go on leave, and although the confrontation is protracted, at this stage the confrontation clearly remains a normal feature of the negotiation process.

In any case, following this rejection, Moses and Aaron return to Pharaoh, this time conveying God's demand to let the people go. When Pharaoh refuses, God inflicts a plague on Egypt, until he finally relents. However, like anyone who has participated in a negotiation process knows, concessions are often followed by immediate regret. Indeed, Pharaoh reneges on his promise to free the People of Israel repeatedly, sometimes refusing outright and sometimes hedging his allowance with unreasonable conditions, but never agreeing completely to the terms he accepted earlier.

After the plague of hail, however, Pharaoh expresses remorse in a way that seems striking. What causes him to suddenly say, "God is righteous, and I and my people are wicked"? In a way, Pharaoh's remorse evokes that of the wicked king Ahab, after Elijah rebukes him: "He rent his clothes and put sackcloth on his body. He fasted, lay in sackcloth, and walked about subdued" (1 Kings 21:27). However, when Ahab shows remorse, it is for very specific sins, and he truly has reason to be remorseful. Ahab's admission of sin is truly justified, whereas here Moses says nothing to Pharaoh about the distress he has caused the People of Israel; all that he demands of Pharaoh is "Let my people go." Why does Pharaoh say here, "I have sinned this time"? What is this sin that he is referring to?

SHATTERING THE "I AM ALWAYS RIGHT" MENTALITY

Pharaoh does not grow up as an ordinary person but as the king of Egypt. Consequently, he grows up under the simple assumption that he is no less than a god. This assumption is not a matter of abstract theology; it is bound up with the fundamental premise of his life and with the basic way he views the world. When a person grows up under the impression that he is a god, this also colors his understanding of the nature of justice. Whatever he wants is by definition the embodiment of justice, and if there is anyone or anything in the world that is just, it is certainly he.

In the course of the ten plagues, Pharaoh goes through a process of change in his fundamental conception of his own life, a process that reaches its climax in the plague of hail. His confrontation with Moses leads him to discover, for the first time in his life, that he is not infallible, that perhaps he is the one who is acting improperly. He is exposed to this idea for the first time, and for someone like him this comes as a great shock, shattering the foundations of his life. When Pharaoh reaches this conclusion, it is not merely theoretical knowledge; he is now forced to adopt a new attitude to his whole life. He must now re-examine and reassess all of his past actions.

Before Pharaoh's epiphany, he was capable of saying, "Every boy who is born you shall throw into the Nile" (Ex. 1:22), without suffering any pangs of conscience. As far as he was concerned, if he wanted them to drown, they drowned; if he wanted them to be killed, they were killed. Everything that he wanted was automatically defined as just and good, with no qualms whatsoever. Only when Pharaoh's basic premise that "I am always right" is shattered does he gain the ability to evaluate and assess things as they are, and only then can his self-assessment change.

Because of this, Pharaoh's remorse does not end with a simple, "I did not act properly in this case"; this is a remorse that shatters his whole value system. That is why he includes in his confession something that seems out of place. He says, "I have sinned this time," and not only that but, "I and my people are wicked." Why "I and my people"? Because now Pharaoh's thoughts go back many years, and for the first time it occurs to him that perhaps his whole life has been a great lie. This remorse is not limited to what just transpired between him and Moses but, rather, returns to the root of the matter, hundreds of years back. It returns to the order to collect straw, to the order to drown the firstborn sons, and even to the very enslavement of Israel.

The basic feeling of "I am always right," which kept Pharaoh from any kind of soul-searching, is not a phenomenon that was limited to him alone. In this regard, Pharaoh is merely an extreme example of an ordinary person. Granted, an ordinary person does not grow up under the same circumstances as Pharaoh, does not commit the same sins, and does not think the way Pharaoh thinks; but despite all these distinctions, Pharaoh is still fundamentally an ordinary person. The real obstacle to remorse and the possibility of repentance is always the same, both in its extreme expression in the case of Pharaoh and in its more banal expression in the case of an ordinary person.

Ezekiel cites in the name of Pharaoh – not the Pharaoh of Exodus but a different Pharaoh – the saying, "Mine is my Nile; I have made myself great" (Ezek. 29:3), which essentially means, "I am the world's epitome of perfection." This is how Pharaoh formulates the idea, but it exists – albeit in subtler form – in the mind of every person. Only when one frees himself from this way of thinking does the gateway to remorse open for him.

Thus, Pharaoh's experience exists in other people's experiences as well when, as a result of repenting for a certain act, they suddenly discover an entirely new way of thinking in which everything has a completely different significance. In such a case, the repentance is not limited to the matter that prompted it; rather, it broadens and has implications for the person's whole life.

COMPLETE REMORSE

Pharaoh's remorse, both in its scope and in its attempt to get at the roots of the sin, should teach us a lesson. Remorse is never a simple matter; even when a person expresses regret and wants to repent, there are liable to be basic problems with the remorse and with the implementation of the desired repentance. In this respect, Pharaoh's case is a good example of complete remorse.

One basic problem with remorse is the question of its sincerity. There is a well-known saying that "the wicked are full of regrets."[1] The

---

1. See Tanya, chap. 11.

simple meaning of this is that even a completely wicked person is not at peace with his sins, and he, too, has moments when he feels regret and wants to repent. Why, though, does this saying read, "full of regrets," in the plural? One explanation is that the wicked are full of many "regrets" because no matter how many times they have regret, it is never true regret. There is a humorous quote sometimes attributed to Mark Twain: "To cease smoking is the easiest thing I ever did. I ought to know because I've done it a thousand times." Similarly, the wicked are full of regrets. The wicked person has remorse, but he knows that he will revert to his evil ways, and that in another week or two he will again have remorse over the same matter, but even stronger. Thus it turns out that his life is full of regrets. Between each instance of remorse, he reverts to the very behavior that caused the remorse in the first place.

The Talmud states that "if a person commits a sin and repeats it, it becomes to him as though it were permissible" (Yoma 86b). Regarding repentance as well, there can be an equally dangerous predicament where someone is caught in a cycle of remorse and *teshuva* followed by a return to the sin, followed by remorse once again. When a person does *teshuva* the first time, it makes an impression. But when he does *teshuva* twice or five times for the same sin, *teshuva* becomes a meaningless procedure, one that can be repeated over and over again, while nothing actually changes.

Another problem with remorse is that sometimes a person is truly penitent and does *teshuva* from the bottom of his heart, but the *teshuva* is misplaced – he focuses on the wrong part of the transgression.

There is a hasidic story about a woman who came to the *rebbe* to seek repentance for eating on *Asara BeTevet*, forgetting that it is a fast day. After listening to her talk about her transgression, the *rebbe* began to tell her the story of a Jew who took over for a Priest. A farmer came to confess before him and told him that he stole a piece of rope. The Jew asked him under what circumstances he stole the rope. The farmer answered that the rope was tied to a cow, and since he stole the cow, the rope was stolen together with it. When the Jew then asked him what else happened, the farmer continued, recounting that the owner of the cow noticed the theft and tried to resist. When the Jew then asked how the farmer responded, he answered, "I killed him." When the Jew heard this, he could no longer contain himself and cried, "You killed him!?" The *rebbe*, too, shouted at the woman, "You killed someone?!" and the woman fainted in shock. It turned out that she had given birth to a child outside of wedlock, strangled him, and covered up the incident. This woman came to the *rebbe* to seek repentance for having mistakenly eaten on *Asara BeTevet*, and ended up revealing her guilt in a far more egregious matter.

Though this anecdote is an extreme example, this is a problem that many people encounter in their lives. A person can work toward self-improvement and atonement, but if he does not get to the heart of the problem, he will think that it is sufficient to rectify only a specific point, while the essential problem still exists. In such a case, the benefit of repentance would be merely temporary and local.

A similar problem exists among those who undergo cancer operations. It is often simple for a surgeon to remove the cancerous growth itself, but it is far more complicated to determine whether that particular growth is a metastasis of another growth that still remains in the person's body. If any growths remain, the treatment will not succeed.

It can be a great accomplishment for a person to admit, "I have sinned this time." But there is a higher level, where a person's soul-searching moves him to such a degree that he declares, "God is righteous, and I and my people are wicked." His remorse reaches back three hundred years, because he understands that his sin does not begin from the present moment, from the present phenomenon – he had to return to the root of the matter.

PENETRATING TO THE ROOTS

The thoroughness of Pharaoh's remorse can be found also in the Torah's description of the process of confession and atonement in Leviticus. One of the central verses reads, "They will then confess their sins and the sins of their fathers" (Lev. 26:40). At first glance, it is difficult to understand why "the sins of their fathers" are relevant. Clearly, the sinner must confess his own sins, but why should he confess those of his fathers? This point is so essential to confession that it is even included in the confession formula of the *Aseret Yemei Teshuva* (Days of Awe) – "But we and our fathers have sinned." Here, too, the same question arises: What do we want from "our fathers"? Why drag our fathers into a confession of our own sins?

The point is that when remorse is sincere, it penetrates to the roots of things, reaching one's whole value system, in its full scope. When a person looks at himself, it is easy for him to reach the conclusion that on the whole, he is not a bad person, an outlook that eliminates the possibility of comprehensive remorse. Sometimes a person looks not at himself but at his father, rationalizing that since there are areas in which he is better than his father, it must be that he himself is sufficiently virtuous. The formula, "we and our fathers have sinned," expresses the idea that sometimes a person must confess not only his own sins but also those of his father, and sometimes even those of his ancestors before that. When a person engages in comprehensive soul-searching, he should consider the possibility that his whole life has been full of bad decisions. He must not only evaluate his actions within the framework of his value system, but also evaluate that value system itself. When a person goes back to the very roots, he sees a completely different picture, in which the whole system can take on a different character. This is what Pharaoh understands when he says, "I and my people are wicked."

It often does not occur to us to question the broader scheme of things. Sometimes a person feels something nagging at him, a sense that something is wrong in his life. But he cannot pinpoint what this trouble is, because he cannot look beyond what he sees in front of him. He does not even raise the question of whether the entire framework of his life might need to be overhauled.

Where does such an attitude spring from? When the big picture of a person's life, with its problems and deficiencies, is acceptable to him, true remorse is impossible. If a person presupposes that his current way of life is how things should be, then he can no longer have full remorse for anything, except for superficial, local problems.

This is not to say that it is unimportant to perfect even the minor details in one's life; indeed, there is a great deal of value in this. But if someone asks whether the point of the letter *yod* in his *tefillin* is perfectly precise when the text of the parchment itself has been erased, it is a sign that he does not see things in proper perspective.

In the story of the ten plagues, Pharaoh goes through a life-changing ordeal. He suddenly experiences thunder and lightning, the likes of which he has never experienced in his life. Strange things are falling from the heavens, and he is seized with terror. He begins to think, for the first time in his life, that perhaps he is not a god. At that moment, an abyss opens wide before him, and he asks himself: What have I done with my whole life?

Only when basic conceptions like these are shattered, and everything suddenly seems different, does it becomes possible to start again from the beginning.

Bo

Parashat Bo, whose climax is the plague of the firstborn, concludes with a law that is likewise connected to the firstborn: "Consecrate to Me every firstborn" (Ex. 13:2).

The firstborn once possessed a special status: The firstborn in each family received a double share of the inheritance and, as a group, almost became the Priests. Nowadays, not much of this special status remains. The last remnant of it is perhaps the custom that, when there are no Levites present in the synagogue, the firstborn wash the hands of the Priests prior to *Birkat Kohanim*.

But what is the point of this special status? Are the firstborn more successful? It is a known fact that in the case of animals, this is not so. In fact, scientific literature has shown just the opposite – that the firstborn in many animal species have a much lower survival rate than offspring born to their mothers thereafter. In the case of human beings, however, the matter is not so simple, and in the Torah as well the matter of the firstborn is multifaceted and variegated.

In the Torah's narratives, only little importance is assigned to the firstborn. Various sources, such as "Reuben, you are my firstborn" (Gen. 49:3) or "Israel is My son, My firstborn" (Ex. 4:22), do seem to indicate preference given to the firstborn, but more prominent in these narratives is the tension between the firstborn and the chosen son. The world's first firstborn, Cain, does not distinguish himself with noble character traits. (According to one opinion among our sages, humanity today is actually descended from Cain, a possibility that would explain much of our history.) The overwhelming majority of the Torah's great personalities, with the prominent exception of Abraham, are not first-born: Isaac, Joseph, Judah, Moses, David, Solomon – the list goes on and is quite impressive.

On the other hand, in the laws of the Torah, clear preference is given to the firstborn. Besides the laws regarding human firstborn, the Torah assigns sanctity to the firstlings of "pure" animals, designating them as *korbanot*, and to the firstlings of donkeys, instructing us to redeem them or perform *arifa*, killing them with a blow to the back of the neck. In other areas of Torah law as well, we find mitzvot that reflect an aspect of the firstling or firstborn laws; for example: an *omer* of the first of the harvest, the first fruits of the soil, *teruma* (which is called "*reshit*," meaning, "first"), the first shearing of the fleece, etc.

In the case of human firstborn, however, there is an unresolved question: How do we redeem the firstborn, and what happens if he is not redeemed? Obviously, he is neither subjected to *arifa* nor taken by the Priest. The truth is that nothing happens to him. What, then, is the point of the firstborn? What is his role? Why is he given a special status, with a position of greater privilege and sanctity?

"THE FIRST FRUITS OF HIS HARVEST"

The answer to these questions lies not in the firstborn's own essential worth but in the special feeling and affection that we have for things that are first. The first fruit is not necessarily the choicest, but our connection to it is the deepest, and it is different from our connection to the fruit that comes after it, even if the first is not always worthy and deserving of this affection.

This can be observed in actual life as well. Everything that a person creates gives him a feeling of amazement, but some of the most powerful feelings are bound up with one's first creation. When Cain, the first child in the world, is born, Eve proclaims, "I have acquired a man together with God!" (Gen. 4:1). The names of her second and third children are given but not explained, and thereafter the Torah suffices with the statement, "and he begot sons and daughters" (5:4). The first letter that a child writes is not necessarily the most beautiful letter that he will ever write, but it is the first; every letter that follows it will be just another letter. Similarly, the Talmud states, "A woman is [like] an unfinished vessel, and makes a covenant only with [her first husband] who fashions her into a [finished] vessel [when they are first together]" (Sanhedrin 22b). The same applies to difficult experiences, such as one's first encounter with death or other crises.

As we have stated, in all these areas the first creation or the first experience is not necessarily the best or most perfect. Its uniqueness is that we remember it in a special way; it is indelibly engraved in our memories. After all, there cannot be two firstborn children, and even if the first does not turn out to be successful – like Reuben, "exceeding in eminence and exceeding in power" (Gen. 49:3)[1] – he is still Jacob's firstborn. Likewise, according to halakha, a firstborn who is a bastard or the son of an unloved wife still receives a double share in the inheritance, even if a different son is legitimate or more beloved.

Herein also lies the superiority of childhood education. At first glance, this superiority appears to be counterintuitive, for children are often immature and easily confused, whereas adults possess a far greater degree of understanding. In reality, however, what is absorbed as a primary experience becomes ingrained in a more fundamental way, while what is learned later in life – even if it is deeper and more nuanced – does not retain the same character of primacy.

This is what our sages mean when they say, "One who learns when young, to what may he be compared? To ink written on fresh paper. But one who learns when old, to what may he be compared? To ink written on paper that has been erased" (Avot 4:20). It could be that what is written on the fresh paper is inaccurate, and what is written afterward is correct; but since the latter is not written on fresh paper, it is much less likely to be retained.

The issue of the firstborn's uniqueness is not a quantitative question of greater or lesser feeling. Just as it is always possible to find a greater number, there can always be a greater emotion as well. However, it is impossible to find a number that is "more first." The first possesses a certain quality that is immutable and ineradicable.

---

1. See Rashi's explanation.

The Talmud presents an interpretation that seems almost hasidic:

> [The community of Israel] said before [The Holy One, Blessed
> Be He]: "Master of the Universe, since there is no forgetfulness
> before the throne of Your glory, perhaps you will not forget the
> sin of the [Golden] Calf?" He replied: "'Even these will be forgot-
> ten' (Is. 49:15)." She said before Him: "Master of the Universe,
> since there is forgetfulness before the throne of Your glory, per-
> haps You will forget [what You said at] Sinai?"[2] He replied to her:
> "'For your sake, I will not forget *Anokhi*' (49:15)."[3] (Berakhot 32b)

To be sure, after responding, "We will do and obey" (Ex. 24:7), before
receiving the Torah at Sinai, the people made the Golden Calf and went
on to make all sorts of calves, for themselves and for the entire world.
Nevertheless, what they said first – "We will do and obey" – will never
be forgotten.

LOSS OF THE BEGINNING

The essence of the firstborn, then, teaches us what a person should do
in his life, how he should devote his primary energy and creativity: "I
therefore offer to God all male firstborn animals, and shall redeem all
the firstborn of my sons" (Ex. 13:15). The things to which we have the
deepest emotional attachment, which can never be replicated, are the
very things that should be given to God. In every matter, one must
scrutinize himself as to whether he truly gave "the choicest first fruits
of his land" to God.

Traditionally, one of the first things a Jewish child is taught to say
is "*Shema Yisrael.*" But why bother? Does the child understand what the
Shema is? He will surely understand it better when he grows up. Nonetheless, we try to arrange it so that his first sentence, the "first fruit," will
be "*Shema Yisrael,*" for that is what will be ingrained in his personality.

---

2. Namely, "I (*Anokhi*) am God your Lord" (Ex. 20:2).
3. This is a play on words; the simple meaning of the verse is "For your sake, I (*Anokhi*)
   will not forget."

Just as there are first fruits of the soil, there are also first deeds and first dreams. Here as well, people become more sophisticated as they mature, as do their aspirations and dreams. Nevertheless, there is a special significance to one's first dreams.

However, there is a fundamental problem: A person who is in the stage of a fresh beginning does not always understand the world around him, and by the time he does understand, he often can no longer return to his original state of youthful freshness. In our youth, we do not always know the significance of the things we do, the activities to which we dedicate ourselves. Only after passing this stage do we understand how many things could have been done so much better, but by then it is too late – we cannot go back and correct our mistakes.

Innocence, the moment it is lost, can never be recovered. An infant possesses a freshness that is totally pure, but with time it gradually fades. For youth in general, freshness springs from the very nature of that period of life. With time, though, this fades as well.

One of the interpretations of the verse, "Like arrows in the hand of a warrior, so are the children of youth" (Ps. 127:4), is that an arrow, the moment it is shot, cannot be called back. All the arrows that we shoot when we are still "children of youth" are like "arrows in the hand of a warrior," in that they cannot be repeated. To be sure, every day of one's life is unique and original, and even in old age it is still possible to continue growing; even death itself is a new experience. But new experiences no longer come with the same regularity and succession as in the days of one's childhood and youth.

Almost any mistake can be rectified, but to reinvent oneself, to become like a new being, is the most difficult rectification of all. Regarding the verse, "For how shall I go up to my father if the youth is not with me?" (Gen. 44:34), one explanation is that "the youth" refers to a person's youthful years, for many people leave these years behind when they ascend to heaven to meet their Creator.

"GIVE ME THE FIRSTBORN OF YOUR SONS"

What should be done with the firstborn, then, is "Give Me the firstborn of your sons" (Ex. 22:28); that is, dedicate the first thing to God. Since there is some aspect of renewal each and every day, this dedication can be fulfilled by devoting one's first thought each day to holy matters.

This is one of the reasons that we recite "*Modeh ani*" upon awakening in the morning, even before the morning ritual washing of the hands, before uttering any other words. Clearly, not everyone says "*Modeh ani*" with reverence; generally, it is muttered out of habit, when one is still half asleep. Nevertheless, we persist in saying "*Modeh ani*," so that no matter what follows throughout the day, we always dedicate the first moment to God. For this same reason there are many people who take care not to do anything before they pray in the morning. This is also the reason why Rosh HaShana is considered one of the holiest days in the Jewish calendar: It begins a new year.

Approaching every undertaking as if it were an entirely new beginning, even if the reality is otherwise, is an extraordinarily difficult spiritual endeavor. Even with the guidance of our extensive *teshuva* literature, it is still incredibly challenging to become a new being, the likes of which never existed before.

Cain offered to God "of the fruit of the soil" (Gen. 4:3), surely consisting of fine, good fruit. In contrast, Abel "also (*gam hu*) brought of the firstlings of his flock" (4:4). Abel brought not only "firstlings" but "*gam hu*" – he brought himself as well. One who succeeds in offering his inner self to God will be able to experience "your youth will be renewed like an eagle" (Ps. 103:5), to approach the world through the fresh eyes of a child once again.

Beshallaḥ

In *Parashat Beshallaḥ* and *Parashat Yitro*, two events occur that inform the Jewish experience throughout the ages: the splitting of the Red Sea and the giving of the Torah.

The splitting of the Red Sea was the ultimate overt miracle, but it is perceived not only as a miracle but also, more significantly, as a revelation of the future.

God's revelation at the sea is portrayed as the pinnacle of the Exodus and as the culmination of the process that began with the ten plagues and with the miracle of "God will make a distinction between Israel's cattle and Egypt's cattle" (Ex. 9:4) and continued until the parting of the sea. The People of Israel walk into the sea, a great salvation ensues, and the Egyptians drown. Every element of the narrative emphasizes that the event is "Your hand, O God," "Your right hand, O God" (15:6).

The splitting of the Red Sea is a momentous event with a profound spiritual dimension, and when viewed in light of the Song of the Sea and all the wonders, miracles, and marvels that it describes, we see that all these events created an extraordinary sense of momentous times. As the Talmud says, "Even the babes in their mothers' wombs chanted a song by the Red Sea" (Berakhot 50a).

When the sea is split, the process is essentially different from the miracles that have occurred thus far – whether the plague of blood, the plague of frogs, or the plague of the firstborn. When the plagues come, they are clearly miraculous occurrences, but they are local miracles, events that transpire in the external world. By contrast, when the sea becomes a place in which people are able to walk, the feeling is completely different. Suddenly, nature changes, the whole system is transformed, and everything that we know about reality is no longer valid. The sea is no longer a sea; the water is no longer water: The rules of physics do not apply.

When our sages say that "maidservants beheld at the sea what even Isaiah and Ezekiel never saw" (*Mekhilta DeRabbi Yishmael, Beshallaḥ* 3), this is because the maidservants see firsthand how all of physical nature is not actually fixed but can suddenly change from one extreme to the other. The whole conception that the world is a place with strict laws and a set order collapses. The splitting of the sea demonstrated to the maidservants and to the rest of the People of Israel that everything we see in the world is a mere theatrical performance, where the house on stage is not truly a house and the tree is not truly a tree – everything is made of cardboard. The entire world dissolved and melted before the eyes of Israel into new forms and patterns: Before, the sea was water; now it has become dry land. The people understood that the world is no longer governed by rigid laws; everything has become possible.

THE AFTERMATH

Great and wondrous things abound in *Parashat Beshallaḥ*. However, let us try to view these events from below; not from the perspective of Moses and Aaron, not from God's perspective, but from the perspective of an ordinary Jew. One can argue that such a perspective misses the main point; nevertheless, we, the ordinary Jews, are the ones who read the Torah, so this is a natural perspective for us to take.

A Jew goes forth from Egypt. He is not a great man, but merely one of the thousands of nameless Jews who picked himself up and went along with everyone else. What is he experiencing following the upheaval of the splitting of the sea? How does he proceed from there?

After the sea returns to its normal condition, suddenly everything is over, and the people begin their journey through the wilderness. A short time ago, this nameless Jew was sure that he was about to die. Immediately afterward, he experienced an incredible supernatural event.

And after all that, he must crash back down into the mundane reality of the world. What is going on in his mind? How can he deal with these conflicting states of consciousness?

Immediately after Israel's emergence from the sea and the ecstasy of the Song of the Sea, the Torah says that "Moses made Israel travel from the Red Sea" (Ex. 15:22). After this experience, Moses had to force his people to travel onward, because they themselves were dazed and disoriented. They simply stood there in a state of confusion. It was necessary to organize them and start going. This individual who just emerged from the Red Sea does not know whether he is in a dream or in the real world; the whole world seems different to him.

It appears that this transition is the major test of *Parashat Beshallaḥ*, recurring several times: at Mara regarding the manna and at Refidim with the war against Amalek. In all these accounts, we see the great difficulty of moving from a world where everything is perfect, where the rules of physics can be altered on a benevolent divine whim, to a world that unforgivingly follows the way of the world.

The miraculous splitting of the Red Sea can provide a person with spiritual sustenance for a long time, but there comes a stage where this simply does not work anymore. And when one crashes down from the heightened reality of the miracle, there is deep disappointment from the very discovery that the world still exists. This is not always a sudden fall from a high peak to a deep pit, and perhaps no devastating crash occurs at all, but the question remains: How can a person shift from the miraculous world of the Red Sea to the world of Mara, where the water is so bitter that it is undrinkable.

The story of the manna is likewise connected to the difficulty of dealing with dramatic changes in reality. The manna is a confusing combination of two aspects. On the one hand, its whole essence is miraculous: Bread that falls from the sky in large quantities is something that is entirely incompatible with the order of nature. On the other hand, it comes regularly, day after day, week after week, month after month. Eventually, the People of Israel likely ceased to consider the manna a miracle at all – it is difficult to imagine that they continued to be amazed by it throughout their travels in the desert. Under such circumstances, even if a person who experiences a miracle remains aware of its miraculous nature, he no longer feels its miraculousness. The miracle ceases to be a wonder and becomes routine. Just as a child knows that he can go each morning to the grocery store and buy a loaf of bread, a child born into a reality of manna knows that each morning one goes and collects manna – there is no wonder in it. Just as one can get used to anything, one can also get used to miracle bread from heaven, and take it for granted just like bread from the earth.

The duality of the manna is a perfect metaphor for the life of the People of Israel in the wilderness. Right after Mara, the People of Israel arrive in Elim, "where there were twelve springs of water and seventy date palms; and they encamped there by the water" (Ex. 15:27). It is unclear whether the seventy date palms are seventy palm trees or seventy kinds of dates, but either way, these are numbers that possess great significance. The Midrash explains, "Twelve springs corresponding to the twelve tribes of Jacob, and seventy palm trees corresponding to the seventy elders" (*Mekhilta DeRabbi Yishmael, Beshallaḥ, Masekhta DeVayassa* 1). Right after the disappointment of Mara, the People of Israel come to a new place, and the twelve springs of water and seventy date palms give them a sense of the familiar: They again witness God's hand in nature, that the world is once again customized to their needs. They then leave this place and go back to traveling in the wilderness, returning to the throes of hunger and thirst, and the pattern repeats itself.

Every person must face this combination of miracle and routine in his life. Even a simple person who has no time for or interest in philosophy must deal with the same questions: What is nature? What is the supernatural? How, in the midst of this uncertainty regarding the nature of the world, do I direct the course of my life as a human being?

A HUMAN BEING REMAINS A HUMAN BEING

We know about the tests that Abraham faced. We know about the tests faced by the other patriarchs and prophets as well. But what can we learn from this test?

The answer is that the nature of our experiences in this world does not matter; adversity will always exist. Jews frequently complain, claiming, "If we were to experience miracles like our ancestors experienced, we would return completely to God." But it turns out that this complaint is unfounded. Even that very Jew who lived through *Parashat Beshallah* with its tremendous revelations is still capable of complaining, of yelling, and of dancing around the Golden Calf. The complaints continue after the sin of the Golden Calf as well. All those miracles did not stop Korah, nor did they stop Zimri, even though they grew up eating bread from heaven.

Our sages say, "Whoever fulfills the Torah in the midst of poverty will ultimately fulfill it in the midst of riches; whoever neglects the Torah in the midst of riches will ultimately neglect it of the midst of poverty" (Avot 4:9). One who neglects the Torah will do so whether it is a time of trouble and sorrow or a time of overt miracles, and one who fulfills the Torah will continue to fulfill it even at a time of great difficulty and upheaval. By his very nature, man tends to fall. Because of this, we must constantly be engaged in spiritual work, with or without miracles; the test of faith never ends.

In a sense, when our sages say that "the Torah was given only to those who ate the manna" (*Mekhilta DeRabbi Yishmael, Beshallah, Masekhta DeVayassa* 2), they are referring to this point. Trust and stability can be expected only from those who are always ready to proceed, with or without miracles. The Torah is given to those who can carry on even when oppressed and downtrodden, not to those who need constant miracles throughout their forty years of travel in the wilderness to sustain them spiritually. The test determining who merited entering the Land of Israel ultimately hinged on this same distinction as well.

People like the patriarchs and like many of our other great and holy ancestors were able to bear this burden, to live through all kinds of troubles and distressful situations and still remain faithful to God. But for someone who is not built for this, no number of wondrous miracles will change his basic nature. It is possible to survive for a while, but eventually one's basic nature comes to the fore.

Ezekiel relates (Ezek. 11:19) that in the future God will operate on us, removing our heart of stone and replacing it with a heart of flesh. Until then, however, we will continue to be tested: "You tested him at Massa and contended with him at the waters of Meriva" (Deut. 33:8).

A STIFF-NECKED PEOPLE

Though this test of faith can be daunting, it can equally be seen in a positive light, as it emphasizes man's inherent stubbornness. Free will, the divine spark imbedded in man, figures prominently here, in the sense that ultimately man cannot be bribed. God, as it were, attempts to sway the people's loyalty to Him by providing for their every physical need. He feeds them manna – and later on, quail – morning and evening, every day. But the people remain stubborn and unchanged.

In this sense, when Moses calls Israel "a stiff-necked people" (Ex. 32:9), it is actually a form of praise, in a way. He takes pride in this attribute: We cannot be so easily moved, like those for whom hearing one sermon by a Christian preacher leads them to proclaim, "I am born again!" When attempting to move a Jew, every inch is an exhausting process.

Man's glory is his free will, for his ability to decide is a kind of act of God. Man can use his free will to his own detriment, or as an expression of glory and dignity.

The conclusion to be drawn is that man cannot be induced by external means to make a change in his essential nature. Neither miracles nor bread from heaven can, in and of themselves, change human nature. Human nature can change, but we must make these changes from within.

The nameless Jew who experienced both the high point of the splitting of the Red Sea and the low point of Mara remains a bit stubborn and rebellious, but his mind is not completely closed to change. The most effective path to this change is not clearly defined – perhaps miracles are necessary, and perhaps they are not. But when a person uses his free will, the hallmark of his humanity, to draw closer to God, then change is always possible.

Yitro

YITRO'S COUNSEL

When the celebrations in honor of Yitro's arrival come to a close, Moses returns to his regular work of judging the people. Upon seeing this, Yitro counsels him that his system is inefficient: It is impossible to continue managing the people if Moses alone judges every person individually. An orderly judicial system must be established.

That it was necessary for Yitro to offer this counsel is puzzling. Our ancestors were not desert-dwelling bedouins who knew nothing about administration and judicial systems. The People of Israel did not come from the desert; they spent many years in Egypt, an organized country with a good deal of bureaucracy and a government with hundreds of years of experience in state administration. When a primitive tribal people forms a state, it is unsurprising that they are unfamiliar with administration and judicial systems. Even when the State of Israel was established, only a few members of the first Knesset had parliamentary experience. Moses, however, grew up in Pharaoh's palace. Throughout his childhood, he wandered around the royal court. He knew how to run a state, and Yitro's advice was not new to him. Why, then, when he became the leader of the People of Israel, did Moses create a situation that was bound to fail? Why did he wait until Yitro came and gave him counsel to institute an organized legal system that was obviously necessary?

From a practical standpoint as well, it is not clear how Moses thought he would manage the people. After all, he had to lead an entire nation and guide millions of people in their individual lives, not to mention the special problems that inevitably arise. The reality of life is that people are bound to have difficulty sorting things out on their own, creating the need for an effective legal system. Yet under Moses' leadership, the people had only one address for all of their problems. Life without quarrels is an impossibility, then as now. People will always find a way to fight with one another, even for no special reason.

In addition, Moses served not only as the people's judge, but as their rabbi as well. Even without all the quarrels and disputes and even without all the monetary cases, it still would have been impossible for him to answer all of the people's halakhic questions. Almost everyone has something to ask: whether a pot can be used for meat or for milk; whether a certain activity is prohibited or permitted on Shabbat; whether the text of a mezuza was written properly, etc. Even if one were to sit down to answer these questions day and night, it would not suffice.

There is a story about the daughter of the rabbi of a small community who, upon getting married, requested that a condition be added to the *ketubba* stating that her husband would not serve as a rabbi. Why? Because in her father's home, from early in the morning until the middle of the night, there were always people around, and she did not want to go on living that way.

At the time of *Parashat Yitro*, the People of Israel numbered over 600,000 people. Even if each person only needed to ask a question once in a while, it would still add up to an enormous number of questions. Even if Moses were to answer each question with only a "yes" or a "no," when this is multiplied by thousands, it still becomes impossible. In light of this great task that Moses accepted upon himself, it is hard to understand how he found time for anything else; even to greet his father-in-law, as he did at the beginning of the *parasha*, would have taken away precious time from his busy schedule.

Needless to say, such a situation is intolerable from the standpoint of the people as well. One can easily imagine the long line of people standing before Moses, and the interminable waiting time that we often associate with municipal offices.

How, then, could Moses have run things in this way?

"WOULD THAT ALL OF GOD'S PEOPLE WERE PROPHETS"

Apparently, Moses was not motivated by practical considerations but by a consideration stemming from an essentially different outlook. This case reflected a matter of principle for Moses. Moses and Yitro do not differ on the practical question of which method is more effective. Rather, they differ on whether it is at all appropriate to build a kind of hierarchical system within the Jewish people.

The implication of Yitro's suggestion is the establishment of a system of ranks within the Jewish people: When a person has a question or problem, he must turn to the person who is in charge of him. This person, in turn, has his own superior in charge of him, and so forth through the hierarchy until the chain reaches Moses himself. Thus, a situation is created where there are people of higher rank and people of lower rank.

Moses, however, is not interested in such a structure – neither from the standpoint of his personal inclination nor in consideration of the matter itself.

We see Moses' opposition to dividing the people by class or rank in other cases as well, such as the revelation at Sinai, when the People of Israel beckon to Moses, "You speak to us, and we will listen; but let not God speak to us, lest we die" (Ex. 20:16). In Deuteronomy this episode is described in greater detail, and there we see that this request is not a simple matter at all for Moses. In order to accept this idea, he had to receive confirmation from God that indeed "they have spoken well" (Deut. 5:25). For Moses, every Jew should aspire to the highest level. Ideally, Moses believes, every member of Israel should receive the Torah directly from the Almighty, as perfectly as he himself received it.

Moses responds similarly when Joshua runs to tell him that Eldad and Medad were prophesying in the camp. Moses responds, "Would that all of God's people were prophets" (Num. 11:29). He responds this way not out of politeness or humility, but because this is the way he sees things. Just as Eldad and Medad prophesied, Moses would like for there to be 600,000 such prophets.

This is not just Moses' personal desire; the Torah itself describes the Jewish people as follows: "This great nation is certainly a wise and understanding people" (Deut. 4:6). The notion of an entire people that is "wise and understanding" is a basic tenet of our belief system. In almost every society and culture, a class distinction exists between the learned and the ignorant, and often is even considered an ideal social framework. The aspiration of the Jewish people, however, is quite the opposite. We believe that, ideally, everyone should be wise and understanding. Every member of Israel should reach the highest level possible. From this standpoint, there is a fundamental difference between the Jewish people and other societies. There is no point at which a Jew is told that he is no longer permitted to learn and understand more of the divine will. Even at Sinai, where God spoke with Israel face to face, all of Israel were present, without any distinctions.

This principle appears frequently in our traditional texts, in various forms. Thus, for example, in *Tanna DeVei Eliyahu*: "I call upon heaven and earth to witness that whether it be a man or a woman, a servant or a maidservant, the holy spirit will come to rest on each of them according to his or her deeds" (*Seder Eliyahu Rabba* 10). Every human being, according to his deeds, can merit to attain a level at which the holy spirit rests upon him.

Moses' policy is the principle that all the people are equal. In his view, a system of hierarchical rule would spell the ruin of the Jewish people's equality. If, as none other than Koraḥ proclaimed, "All the people in the community are holy, and God is in their midst" (Num. 16:3), how can the people be divided into different ranks? Moses insisted on judging the people by himself because he thought that no person should be barred from approaching him directly as a result of a perceived inferiority. Why should any person be relegated to the "leaders of fifties" or the "leaders of thousands" (Ex. 18:21)? Every person is important enough to go directly to Moses. Moses does not set up an organized structure not because it does not occur to him, but because he does not want one. His argument is that if ranks are formed among the people, then although some people would become newly exalted leaders, many others would be rendered insignificant commoners, lowered and debased. All this runs counter to the view that "all the people in the community are holy, and God is in their midst."

BELIEF IN THE SOUL

The idea of establishing ranks within the Jewish people is so problematic to Moses that he is willing to bear not only his own personal suffering – "you will surely wear yourself out" (Ex. 18:18) – but also the system's inevitable collapse. It is obvious that such a judicial and governmental system cannot endure; yet Moses tries to keep it going for as long as possible, because it is a matter of principle for him.

In practice, Yitro's suggestion is implemented. Yitro thinks much more practically, and he recognizes that what Moses is trying to do is impossible. Behind his view, there is a great deal of common sense: How is it possible to create a nation where everyone is on the same level? The whole idea of equality is impractical. Similarly, an examination of the concept of democracy, which is based on the notion of equality, reveals that in fact it is illogical.

This is an important point because in today's Western world, "democracy" is taken for granted as an ideal that is prized over anything else. Yet the truth is that democracy is an unrealistic system, an illogical ideology. When a person has a stomach ache, he does not ask three different people for their opinions or go to the Knesset and take a vote in order to determine what to do. There could be 120 people sitting in the Knesset, all of whom are wise and discerning, but if they are opposed by one doctor, one relies on the doctor, not on the Knesset members. Common sense dictates that the opinion of the expert should be valued over the opinion of the masses.

This is true not only of medical questions, but of much larger questions as well. The idea that any ordinary person can decide complicated questions of international diplomacy or economic policy is fundamentally illogical. The idea that people are equal to one another in wisdom or ability is clearly false. People are not alike, whether in their height, in their appearance, or in their intelligence.

Nevertheless, in Moses' case, the principle of equality springs from his belief in the soul, which is unconnected to the intellect or to reason. A soul is something abstract, spiritual, and above all, holy. On the plane of the soul there can be no criterion by which to determine who is higher and who is lower. As a result, it can truly be said that "all the people in the community are holy."

NO ONE IS IMMUNE FROM QUESTION

The delegation of authority that results from Yitro's counsel is basically technical, and the divisions between higher and lower judges are practical, not essential. It is true that the People of Israel are now arranged in different ranks. But when someone becomes a "leader of thousands," this does mean that he is a hundred times wiser than a "leader of tens"; it could be that he is not wiser at all. In practice, we must establish ranks, because otherwise there will be chaos – "you will surely wear yourself out, as well as this people."

One lesson we can learn from this is that, according to the Torah, there is no person who cannot be questioned; no one is immune. The Talmud says, "Even father and son, master and disciple – when they are engaged in Torah study, they become each other's enemies" (Kiddushin 30b). The Talmud could have cited a much simpler example of this – that of two friends who study Torah together and begin arguing until the roof shakes. Yet the example cited is precisely that of father and son, or master and disciple, to teach us that although the son is obligated to honor his father, and although the disciple is obligated to honor his master, he does not have to agree with him. A person's duty to honor his father and teachers means only that he must show them respect, not that he cannot question them.

Respect means that one must ask questions in a courteous manner, and if it is a public setting one must take care not to cause shame to the other. But this does not mean that there is anyone, in this generation or in any other generation, who is immune from question.

There is a famous dispute between Hillel and Shammai regarding the quantity of drawn water that renders a *mikve* unfit for use, a dispute that was resolved only when two weavers entered from the Dung Gate and testified that Shemaya and Avtalyon had prescribed yet a third quantity (Shabbat 15a). In this anecdote, the law was decided not in accordance with the views of the generation's two leading sages, but with the opinion cited by two lowly weavers who came from the Dung Gate, one of the most contemptible places in Jerusalem.

Thus, the verse, "This great nation is certainly a wise and understanding people," takes on a practical meaning. Everyone can ask questions, and no one is immune from them. Even if someone studies the Torah diligently, with understanding and in holiness for seventy years, this still does not mean that the Torah is in his hands and his hands alone.

In this respect, even after Yitro's counsel was adopted, it established only a practical framework, not an essential one. Ultimately, the principle that Moses advocated remained the true philosophical construct underlying the essential framework of our society. If only it were possible, Moses' original method of judging and answering questions would be implemented practically as well. All questions would come directly to Moses, whether it is a young child who found a piece of candy and wants to know if he must return it, or a tribal prince who seeks resolution for a territorial dispute. Reality has its limits and does not allow for such a system to survive. Nevertheless, this does not negate the intrinsic value of Moses' system, only its practical viability. Even after the dust settled and Yitro's system was put into place – and rightfully so – it is clear to us that, in truth, Moses' way was right all along.

Mishpatim

It has been said that the most puzzling thing about *Parashat Mishpatim* is the *parasha* itself. This is the first *parasha* after the revelation at Sinai, and we might have expected that after this revelation the Torah would concern itself with lofty, spiritual matters. Instead, the Torah immediately concerns itself with legalities, including laws of servants and maidservants, cases of one man striking another, and capital punishment.

To be sure, *Parashat Mishpatim* is of enormous halakhic value. It is the Torah's gift to the yeshiva world. The *parasha* contains a significant percentage of the major halakhic sources for large swaths of *Seder Nezikin* and quite a few other parts of the Talmud. What is more, the Talmud says of civil law, which the *parasha* deals with, that "no branch of the Torah surpasses them, for they are like a never-failing spring" (Berakhot 63b). Nevertheless, after all this praise for the *parasha* and its content, it is still surprising to find such content immediately following the spiritual climax of Sinai.

Toward the end of the *parasha*, the concern with legal matters ends, and the Torah once again returns to lofty matters. Moses and the nation's elders ascend the mountain, and the Torah describes an exalted scene: "They beheld a vision of the God of Israel, and under His feet was something like a sapphire brick" (Ex. 24:10).

The Torah continues in the same vein at the beginning of *Parashat Teruma*, in the command to build the Tabernacle – "They shall make Me a sanctuary, and I will dwell in their midst" (Ex. 25:8) – where the subject is the *Shekhina* dwelling among the People of Israel. The construction of the Tabernacle is related to the revelation at Sinai, another aspect of the same event that began to unfold there. In our first meeting with God at Sinai, we transcended the human level in preparation for the encounter with God outside, in the wide open expanse surrounding Mount Sinai. The section on the Tabernacle, then, is the natural continuation of this encounter. After God reveals Himself at Sinai, He then desires to reside among us. As a result, we build Him a house, a place for Him to dwell.

This relationship can also be seen in Solomon's prayer at the dedication of the First Temple. On the one hand, Solomon says, "God has chosen to dwell in a thick cloud" (I Kings 8:12) and "Even the heavens and highest reaches cannot contain You" (8:27); and on the other hand, "I have built for You a residence, a place for You to dwell in forever" (8:13). These two aspects – God's transcendence and His immanence, His presence with us in our world – are essentially connected, and the same kind of connection exists between the giving of the Torah and the building of the Tabernacle.

Thus, the end of *Parashat Mishpatim* and the beginning of the *parasha* that follows it are the natural continuation of the revelation at Sinai. By contrast, what we find throughout most of this *parasha* are earthly matters – laws and ordinances – which seem out of place.

To be sure, even after the exalted experience at Mount Sinai, there was a need to deal with various laws, a need that was perhaps quite pressing. It is reasonable to assume that even the day after the revelation at Sinai, various practical questions began to arise that had to be answered, even if they were relatively insignificant. However, an examination of *Parashat Mishpatim* reveals that it mostly deals with matters that, though practical, nevertheless do not generally come up in the reality of life in the wilderness. The simple fact that the People of Israel were nourished by the manna rendered many of the laws of *Parashat Mishpatim* irrelevant. The economic reality underlying the laws in the *parasha* became applicable only later, when the People of Israel entered the Land. The context of *Parashat Mishpatim* is obviously that of a people dwelling in its own land, leading a normal life, having servants and maidservants, cultivating fields and vineyards. *Parashat Mishpatim* seems like it was thrust into the middle of a continuous unit to which it is entirely unrelated.

Why, then, were these laws given such a prominent position, right after the revelation at Sinai?

THE FUNDAMENTAL IDEAS OF THE TORAH

The answer is implicit in the question, and the message is simple: After the exalted revelation at Sinai, the most important laws for the People of Israel to learn – before the laws of *korbanot*, before the laws of the Sanctuary, and even before "*Shema Yisrael*," – are the most detailed and earthly matters, like how to treat one's servant or one's donkey.

In this sense, when God says, "These are the ordinances that you shall set before them" (Ex. 21:1), this is a profound statement: It is precisely these things that are the fundamental ideas of the Torah. In the world order established by the Torah, the momentous experience of the giving of the Torah is followed by something that is no less important: *Parashat Mishpatim*. To put them on equal footing may seem radical, but the Torah does exactly this – overtly and deliberately.

The question that now remains is more pointed, and it focuses on the reason behind the matter: Why is such great importance attached to this *parasha*?

One answer is that our lives, for better or for worse, do not take place in the Temple and do not revolve around the various daily *korbanot*. We live at home and in the marketplace, in the field and in the vineyard, with all the small details and problems that this life entails. Because this is the reality of our lives, these are the issues that the *parasha* deals with.

It is no accident that the content of *Parashat Mishpatim* relates much more closely to the laws of Bava Kamma than to those of Bava Metzia. The *parasha* deals much more with man's failings than with the legal aspects of the ordinary course of life. The *parasha* does not describe a pastoral, tranquil existence but an existence fraught with all sorts of troubles and problems: theft, violent crime, arguments, and confrontations. These are all unfortunate aspects of our lives as human beings.

By their very nature, our lives entail all sorts of disturbances and problems, which is why the fundamental ideas of the Torah relate precisely to these aspects of life.

It says in the Talmud (Ḥagiga 6b) that the Torah was given with both general rules and specific details. Indeed, the Torah can usually be divided into parts that deal with broad pronouncements of legal principles and parts that deal with how these principles play out in practice. But the truth is that although the Torah does devote much of its attention to larger questions, the basic principles of our belief system lie in the small details, and not in the few explicit articulations of our major tenets.

If our sages – whether in our own time or in previous generations – were charged with writing the Torah from scratch, it would no doubt include much more information on spirituality and the larger questions of life. However, the Torah is not built that way. In saying, "These are the ordinances that you shall set before them" (Ex. 21:1), the Torah gives primacy to the details, leaving the exalted and lofty matters for certain special occasions and places. Why? Because the Torah itself is characterized by those same dry ordinances that deal with life's details.

This basic characterization has implications in other areas as well and is crucial for understanding the whole orientation of the Jewish world. In a nutshell, Judaism takes the slogan, "the end justifies the means," and turns it on its head. For us, the means justify the end. The detailed and minute laws are more important to us than the lofty aims.

All of Jewish life is built on the existence of finely delineated laws and instructions and with few clearly articulated lofty goals. The Torah repeatedly uses specific examples to emphasize the right thing to do in various situations, rarely including broad explanations of the theory behind the laws – those can be left for another time. As the Talmud says, "'This day [you are] to do them' (Deut. 7:11), but only tomorrow will you receive their reward" (Eiruvin 22a). If a person wants to know why a law is a certain way, he will have to wait. He may have to wait 120 years, or perhaps 6,000 years – it does not matter, because that is not what the Torah and Jewish life are about.

Put differently, the Torah's questions are "how" questions: How should one act in such a case? How does one fulfill this law? In contrast, questions of "why?" or "what for?" are not emphasized in the Torah and appear only rarely. The Torah deals with the method – the technique and the details by which things are done – but not nearly as much with the larger, teleological questions.

To be sure, from the Torah's overall framework, which includes detailed laws as well as theoretical elements, we ultimately try to move from the details to the general principles, to infer the answers to the questions of "why" and "what for" as well. But in the Torah itself, there is only a long list of laws: "These are the ordinances." The details, with all their subtleties and nuances, are the main focus of the Torah. Even when the laws are assigned a reason, an explicit rationale, this explanation appears only as an addendum to the main element, a mere afterthought.

Obviously, none of this is meant to criticize the Torah's methodology or to take away from its majesty, but only to explain that the Torah sees things in a way that is often different from our usual way of thinking. The Torah is not a philosophical text that finds grandeur in metaphysical treatises. Rather, the Torah finds majesty precisely in the worldliness and in the details. At Sinai, we look up, toward the heavens above, toward the lofty, uplifting things. But immediately thereafter our view tilts downward, to the earthly, crude matter and, perhaps surprisingly, we are able to see holiness there as well.

In this respect, the revelation at Sinai and *Parashat Mishpatim* are actually one unit with two interconnected parts that deal with the same basic question: Where is majesty? Is it found in heaven alone, or perhaps elsewhere as well?

WHERE CAN GOD BE FOUND?

In a certain respect, the contraction that manifests itself in *Parashat Mishpatim* exists in the nature of the world as well. In our lives, the most profound and uplifting things are found precisely in the mundane details of the daily routine.

However, in the Torah we find a more radical statement, one that is more extreme in its implications, regarding the profound question of where God can be found. The Talmud says that "The Holy One, Blessed Be He, has no [place] in this world but the four cubits of halakha" (Berakhot 8a). Leaving aside the question of whether "four cubits of halakha" refer to the beit midrash or if there is a broader meaning, this is still a radical statement. We are used to raising our eyes heavenward when speaking of God, but the truth is that He is found in the small, insignificant, and seemingly unimportant minutiae of halakha.

Our world, with its insignificance, with all its problems, contains within it the model that reflects the most exalted matters of all. This is what our sages meant when they said, "Wherever you find the majesty of The Holy One, Blessed Be He, there you find His humility" (Megilla 31a). God's majesty can be found precisely in the small, earthly matters. The Talmud (Sota 5a) discusses the verse, "I dwell with the broken and the lowly in spirit" (Is. 57:15), explaining that God does not raise up the broken person so that he may be with Him, but comes down to the broken person and resides together with him.

This explains not only the question of the "four cubits of halakha" but also the question of the Temple. King Solomon mentions this problem in his prayer: "Will God really dwell on earth? Even the heavens and highest heavens cannot contain You, how much less this House that I have built!" (I Kings 8:27). But this is the essence of the Temple, where God contracts Himself, as it were, into a limited space. God does not reveal Himself in the wide open expanses of the outdoors; He wants to enter this small house. He abandons the heavens and goes to reside in the Temple, to engage with His people in the four cubits of halakha, to discuss what the law is if a person knocks out a Hebrew servant's tooth, or if a person's ox gores his neighbor's cow.

All of this leads to only one conclusion: Contrary to our expectations, the most exalted things can be found not above, but below. As we read in Psalms, "God is exalted above all nations, His glory is upon the heavens. Who is like God our Lord, who is enthroned on high, who sees what is below, in heaven and on earth?" (113:4–6). The other nations believe in God as well, but they take the opposite perspective. They say that "God is exalted above all nations" only when "His glory is upon the heavens." For the other nations, God's dwelling place is in heaven, and He remains there. In contrast, Israel says, "Who is like God our Lord, who is enthroned on high?" God is higher than the nations think, higher than the heavens, and that is precisely why He "sees what is below, in heaven and on earth"; He can reveal Himself equally in heaven and on earth, even in the smallest earthly details.

After the exalted experience at Sinai, after the people look heavenward and see the thunder and the lightning and the smoke, comes the real revelation, the one that truly touches upon the most exalted of all. *Parashat Mishpatim* demonstrates that exaltedness may be found in all of its many esoteric details, details that transcend the generation of the wilderness to impact upon the most distant generations, even to this day.

Teruma

"AND I WILL DWELL IN THEIR MIDST"

There is a well-known interpretation of the Torah's instruction to erect the Tabernacle, cited by Alshekh: "'They shall make Me a sanctuary, and I will dwell in their midst' (Ex. 25:8) – it does not say 'in it' but 'in their midst.'" With this statement, the matter of the Tabernacle is reduced to its most significant, fundamental point. The Tabernacle is in the midst of the Jewish people – it is "the tent He had set among men" (Ps. 78:60) – and the people's presence is essential for its existence. The notion that God will dwell "in *their* midst" invests the physical Tabernacle with inner meaning. Its sanctity is not due to its structure or to the materials from which it is built, but to the fact that the Jewish people resides around it.

In essence, this is true of every sacred object. Every holy vessel presents an opportunity to establish a holy connection, but this does not happen automatically; the sanctity exists only when the object is used. The sanctity becomes meaningful only in connection with a member of the Jewish people; if that factor is missing, while the object must still be treated with respect, it has no sanctity.

There is a story that illustrates this point: A young rabbi was once imprisoned and tortured by the Russians. When, after a while, he was unexpectedly released, it was discovered that one of the reasons given for his release was that he was insane. The authorities had seen him putting on *tefillin*, and when they asked him what this was, he answered that it was a communication device through which he spoke with God. After examining the *tefillin* inside and out and not finding any batteries or antennas, and particularly after seeing him put this device on his head and begin to talk, they came to the conclusion that he was definitely insane.

Obviously, the *tefillin* themselves are not some kind of magical communication device. But the truth is that, like every sacred instrument, *tefillin* are instruments for connecting with God, but they only receive their inner essence when combined with one's performance of the mitzvot associated with them.

What is true of sacred objects is equally true of the Tabernacle. The real meaning of the Tabernacle, its inner essence, is God's presence in the midst of the Jewish people: "I will dwell in their midst." Therefore, while it is certainly important to deal with the construction of the physical Tabernacle, it is particularly critical to deal with its inner aspect as well: the human tabernacle.

ONE WHOSE HEART MOVES HIM

What is the Tabernacle made of? In the opening of the *parasha*, God commands the people to donate the materials for the Tabernacle – "Let them bring Me a donation" (Ex. 25:2). "Every person whose heart moves him" participates in the construction of the Tabernacle, the building of holiness; everyone gives as much as he wants.

The funds required for the Tabernacle could have been collected in a variety of ways, but God specified that they be donated – "one whose heart moves him." In parallel situations in the Torah, different methods are prescribed. In the case of the gifts given to the Priests and Levites, for example, the process of giving is defined and obligatory – one must give a certain percentage of one's produce. Another possible option was graduated taxation: One who has a certain amount of assets pays two percent, one who has more pays three percent, and so on. The collection of funds for the Tabernacle could have been done in any of these ways, yet God required that each person give not according to a specific prescribed measure but according to his generosity.

Even the money that was collected not by donation but by set measure, like that of the shekel dues, was used in the Tabernacle for specific purposes. None of the service vessels was made from the silver of those coins; rather, this silver was used only to form the bases for the wooden boards of the Tabernacle and the sockets and hooks for the pillars. The service vessels were made of copper and gold donated by the People of Israel, "every person whose heart moves him."

The distinction between silver and other materials is not essential. At the time of the Temple, for example, this distinction did not exist. The Mishna provides a detailed description of the bringing of the Pesaḥ offering in the Temple, of the rows of golden receptacles and the rows of silver receptacles (Pesaḥim 5:5). We see, then, that there is nothing precluding service vessels from being made of silver. Hence, the fact that none of the service vessels in the Tabernacle were made of the shekel silver constitutes an essential statement: There is a difference between money that a person donates out of generosity and a set sum of money that he is obligated to pay.

It appears that the reason for the difference between the shekel silver and the donated money is that there is a limit to how far money that is collected and not donated can reach in the realm of holiness. The problem is not that people were unwilling to make the obligatory payments; it is unlikely that the police had to collect the half-shekel against the people's will. Nevertheless, a service vessel cannot be made from this silver.

What is more, the use of the Tabernacle donations themselves was not arbitrary. Each donation was used for a specific purpose; each donation had its own destination. What the "one whose heart moves him" donated was assessed and sent to the proper destination, according to his particular case. "From every person whose heart moves him" dictated, for example, that the laver was made from the mirrors of the dedicated women,[1] and as a result, the laver itself actually assumed the character of those mirrors. According to our sages, it is no concidence that the *sota* (suspected adulteress) was made to drink from the water of this very laver: The laver was made by women who were dedicated to holiness, and it is therefore fitting that it was used to test women who deviated from holiness (Numbers Rabba 9:14).

---

1. See Rashi's commentary to Exodus 38:8.

The following humorous story can serve as an analogy for this idea: A *rebbe* was once asked why he conducts his court with such pomp and splendor, considering that his forebears, who were great men, lived frugally and in poverty. He answered: "There are people who give a *pidyon nefesh*[2] for the sake of Heaven and with great holiness, and their intention is that it should truly serve as redemption for their soul. When I receive such a gift, I use it only for actual mitzvot – Torah study and charity. There are also people whose giving is tinged with other intentions as well, and in that case the money goes toward food, drink, and clothing. However, there are donations that people give as a bribe – if not to bribe me then to bribe God – and such money can be used only for horses. My grandfather's Hasidim were, for the most part, holy people, and most of the money they gave was for the sake of Heaven. Hence, it went to charity. My Hasidim are mostly of the sort whose money can only be used to buy horses."

The same basic idea appears here. Every donation has a certain character that depends on the nature of the giver, and this character determines the donation's destination. In the plans for the Tabernacle's construction, a specific order had to be followed: Certain materials were meant for the roof, while others were meant for the floor. Some materials belonged inside the Sanctuary, while others remained outside. Each item was assigned a particular function, depending on the giver.

When it came to the donations for the Tabernacle, no one was approached and asked to give more than he desired. If a person's heart moved him to donate a piece of wood, then he was a man of a piece of wood, and apparently that is what he can and should give. Hence, each person was asked what he, according to his standards, wanted to give. A person could say, "I want to give gold," and he can also say, "I want to give a piece of wood." Another person might have given three simple copper coins, while still another person might have donated processed hides or precious stones.

THE WHOLE SPECTRUM BUILDS THE TABERNACLE

"This is the gift that you shall accept from them: gold, silver, and copper" (Ex. 25:3). Since this was a gift, there was no specific gift that could

---

2. Lit., "redemption of a soul," a sum of money donated by a Hasid to his *rebbe*.

be demanded of everyone equally. Each person had to evaluate himself, and as a result, each person gave a different donation. A glance at the list of donations indicates that the gifts ranged greatly in value. On the one hand, some gave precious stones, some of which – considering their required size – were no doubt priceless. On the other hand, some gave materials that were almost worthless, including dyed wool and goat's hair, the coarsest material that can still be considered a garment.

The difference between the gifts lies in the question of how much a person is willing to give, and apparently, the construction of the Tabernacle required the whole range of materials. It required not only the precious stones, but the goat hair as well. It required rare materials, for which one must search deep underground or travel all over the world, but it also required acacia wood, which can be found near one's home. For the construction of the Tabernacle, there was no one equal standard for measuring the value of a person's donation. The entire community of Israel participated in building it, and each person contributed his share, from the simplest materials to the most precious. It was impossible to make demands of anyone, because it was impossible to know what each person's share was in the building. This notion – that no one member of the Jewish people could claim a disproportionate role in the construction of the Tabernacle – is precisely what enabled God to truly "dwell in their midst."

The Talmud says regarding the seemingly excessive quantity of materials in the Tabernacle that "there should be no poverty in a place of wealth" (Shabbat 102b). Why, then, does God need goat's wool, from which sacks are made? We could instead have used three covers of scarlet wool, and over them another thirty processed hides.

Apparently, the Tabernacle was based precisely on the totality of what the people have inside them, on each person's generosity and capacity for giving: the small and the great, the rich and the generous. From the combination of all of them together, from top to bottom, a sanctuary is made, and in the entirety of what is built, God's glory resides.

Tetzaveh

W̲hile *Parashat Teruma* deals primarily with the Tabernacle's outer structure, *Parashat Tetzaveh* deals with what is inside, its inner workings and the daily routine within its confines.

For this reason, one section of the *parasha* deals with the priestly garments, in which the Torah emphasizes: "And they shall be upon Aaron, and upon his sons, when they enter the Tent of Meeting, or when they approach the Altar to minister in the holy place, so that they not bear iniquity and die" (Ex. 28:35). This is how they must comport themselves, and anyone who does otherwise puts his life at risk.

The other section deals with the Priests' investiture, describing all the tasks that must be performed inside the Tabernacle. Each part of the daily service that the Priests will later perform in the Tabernacle is already represented in the proceedings of the investiture days, although not necessarily in the same order.

ARE ALL SYSTEMS GO?

The section on the Tabernacle – the command, the order of the service, the construction, the dismantling, and the actual performance of the tasks – repeats itself many times, to the point where it becomes wearisome. In order to understand these numerous minutely detailed repetitions, we must first analyze the nature of the Tabernacle itself.

The Tabernacle is a type of instrument whose function is to connect the earth with heaven. To succeed in this task, it has to function properly, without any mishaps. This instrument's only test is whether it really works. If it was assembled incorrectly, even if the error was only in the minutest detail, it does not matter if one had the best intentions when assembling it – it will not work; it will simply malfunction.

The construction of the Tabernacle can be compared to the construction of a spacecraft. A spacecraft is an extremely complex structure made of a multitude of parts, each one of which must be perfectly precise. First of all, all the calculations must all be correct. Then all the parts must be manufactured, and when construction begins, everything must be done exactly according to plan. An entire team of experts pores over each stage. One team checks the accuracy of the calculations; another checks whether the work was done according to all the specifications of the plans. Then an attempt is made to assemble all the parts, and even then everything must be checked: Do the screws really fit? Are they in the right place? Did anything fall out? Have any cracks developed? Once everything is assembled, the whole apparatus must be dismantled to verify whether all is truly in order. At the end of the entire process, after the arduous preparatory process is finally complete, comes the moment when someone presses a button and the real question arises: Will the spacecraft lift off or not?

In 1988, the Soviets sent two satellites to study Mars and its moons. The satellites were operated by solar energy, and for that purpose, they occasionally had to change their wing angle according to instructions they received from Earth. A daily communication lasting a few seconds was sent to them containing thousands of commands in computer code. These commands had to be checked on a daily basis, line after line, and then rechecked, so that no error should creep in. One day, someone erred and entered one incorrect letter in one of the lines of the program. Two days later, it was discovered that the satellite had shut down, was unable to change its wing angle, had depleted its batteries, and all contact with it was lost.

Thus, an incredibly expensive spacecraft was lost, all because of an error in one word, in one line, which caused it to shut down. The device may still exist somewhere in space, but it doesn't do anything meaningful. It changed from an instrument that could have been of great benefit to a worthless, insignificant object.

Likewise, after the assembly and construction of the Tabernacle was finished, after the anointing, the sanctification, and all the preparation, the Tabernacle had to rise heavenward – its moment of truth. In this respect, the climax of the construction of the Tabernacle is not in its "launch," but precisely in the days of investiture (Lev. 8–9), which, at first glance, appears to have been devoid of any suspense. After all, the Torah merely describes the attiring of the Priests and the bringing of the *korbanot*. In truth, however, there is a tremendous feeling of suspense that mounts with each and every verse in the narrative.

The Midrash relates that on each of the seven days of investiture, Moses would erect and dismantle the Tabernacle twice. After months of building the Tabernacle, and even though all appeared to be in order and the boards fit together, the Tabernacle was dismantled and rebuilt again and again (Numbers Rabba 12). For Moses, the fact that the boards fit together was not sufficient; perhaps it does not stand securely. They checked everything, dismantling and assembling; everything is in its proper place. And yet the tension continues to mount: Does it work or not?

On each of the seven days of investiture, the Tabernacle was assembled, Aaron entered, bringing the *korban* and slaughtering it. Each time, nothing happened – so the Tabernacle was dismantled. It was impossible to know where an error might have crept in, so once again everything needed to be checked from the beginning to determine what might have been the problem. As Rashi and the other commentaries explain, it was only on the eighth day, when Aaron entered the Tent with Moses and they prayed together, that the heavenly fire finally descended upon the Altar. At that moment, everything suddenly happened at once: "God's glory was then revealed to all the people. Fire came forth from before God and consumed upon the Altar the whole offering and the fat parts. When the people saw this, they became ecstatic and threw themselves on their faces" (Lev. 9:23–24).

An entire nation – all 600,000 men, and all the women and children as well – waits with bated breath. The instructions for how to proceed are complex and detailed; the more progress that is made, the more the tension mounts. What will happen in the end? The Tabernacle is meant to be an instrument that connects the earth with heaven. Will it achieve this goal? Yet the final tasks that Moses, Aaron, and the Priests perform are precisely the least dramatic: Is the Menora in place? Was the ram offered at the right time? And then – "God's glory was revealed to all the people," fire descends from heaven, there is contact and a connection. The same picture appears at the dedication of the Temple as well, with all the suspense and the sigh of relief at the end.

The Tabernacle was an instrument whose every part was made with great precision. Everything had its own specifications: where it should stand, what its function is, etc. This is what makes the Tabernacle an instrument for receiving the Divine Presence. If it is made a little differently, if the Menora is placed even slightly to the side, it will not work. Every one of these details forms the greater whole.

IMPORTANCE OF THE DETAILS

The passages describing the Tabernacle proceedings are so full of details that they are often perceived as some of the most boring parts of the Torah. Yet these details are repeated over and over again. Why does the Torah need to say exactly how the pants should be and where exactly the bells should be attached to the robe? The Torah also elaborates on the breastplate: It should have two rings, to which something else is attached, and to this attachment another thing is attached.

Why must the Torah mention these things? To teach us how to attach one clasp to another, or how to create gold settings? Even if these were indeed important details for us to know, why repeat these details so many times and ensconce them in the text of the Torah for eternity?

In truth, however, this story is full of suspense, almost like a cinematic thriller. How will all the intricate plans for the Tabernacle play out in reality? Did Bezalel make everything precisely according to the instructions? Did he perhaps attach one piece at the wrong angle, causing the whole enterprise to fail?

When an ordinary garment is sewn, it makes no difference whether the seam is placed a little to the right or to the left of the proper design. But when a diving suit or space suit is produced, if it is not sewn properly and as a result a small tear develops, the result is catastrophic. This is not a children's game, where someone mistakenly moves a little out of position or three steps ahead without any major consequence. Here, it is like an untrained homeowner who tries his hand at complicated electrical repairs. Even if he has seen the electrician take a certain tool, put it in a certain place, screw it in and turn it three times with his hand, and successfully repair the problem, if the untrained individual tries to imitate these steps he will likely electrocute himself. Every detail in the *parasha* is intensely serious. To go too far is a fatal mistake. As Aaron was told, he should not enter the Sanctuary without wearing the robe, "so that he not die" (Ex. 28:35). In essence, the Torah is telling Aaron that this is not a test. He is dealing with a mighty flame, with the holy of holies. The story of the death of Aaron's two sons relates to this very point. Nadav and Avihu, sons of the High Priest, enter, thinking that they are dealing with a simple matter. But when they make one misstep, they die as a result.

The Talmud describes the terror surrounding the High Priest's entry into the Holy of Holies on Yom Kippur. He is forbidden to remain inside too long, so as not to frighten the people (Yoma 53b). The Zohar comments that they would tie a rope to the High Priest's foot, so that they could pull him out if he dies while inside (*Emor* 102a). This is not because the place itself is frightening. The fact is that when inspections occasionally had to be made, people used to look inside and artisans would go in to perform renovations. If an artisan can enter, why is everyone seized with such terror when the High Priest is inside?

The answer is that it is just like electricity; it depends on the situation. On an ordinary day, it is possible to go in and touch things without ill effect. On Yom Kippur, however, all the fuses are lit, the current is flowing, and those who enter risk their lives.

INSIDE THE TABERNACLE

The Tabernacle contains two vital components for forming the connection between heaven and earth. The first component is the vessels, and in *Parashat Teruma* we saw how they are made and what they are made of. The second component, the Tabernacle's inner dimension, is the person who uses it. The Tabernacle is not an empty instrument; it is an instrument that depends on the people who operate it. The staff can consist of several thousand Priests, as in Second Temple times, or – as in the case of the Tabernacle – it can be a limited staff of several individuals.

In *Parashat Tetzaveh* we see that there are functions that are indispensable for the Tabernacle's overall structure to work and achieve its purpose; without them, it simply does not respond. The entire *parasha* deals with service in the Sanctuary – the inner proceedings of the Tabernacle. What allows the system to operate is the inclusion of the human component, the people themselves, who are charged with ensuring that the walls do not remain merely walls but much more than that.

Parashat Zakhor

Parashat Zakhor is not a complete *parasha* but a passage (Deut. 25:17–19) that is read following the weekly Torah portion on the Shabbat immediately preceding Purim.

The reading of this segment is not linked to a particular Torah portion. Rather, the *parasha* to which it is added changes from year to year, depending on the calendar and on Purim's position within the regular order of Torah readings. Nonetheless, *Parashat Zakhor* is more than a particular commemoration within the Torah reading; it is considered an important matter unto itself, to such an extent that its name supersedes the name of the *parasha* that is read on that Shabbat – *Shabbat Zakhor*.

The mitzva of remembering what Amalek did to us and the mitzva of obliterating Amalek raise many questions, problems, and misgivings about the emphasis and severity of the matter, but it also raises objections about the importance of the matter itself.

Jewish history is replete with wars, conflicts, and troubles. We grieve over these incidents because they involved loss of life, defeat, humiliation, and sometimes even protracted suffering in their wake. However, the more of these tragedies that we experience, the more we feel a certain erosion in our ability to recognize the importance of these events.

The Talmud discusses the list of tragedies and joyful events in *Megillat Taanit*. Many of these events refer to minor incidents that were commemorated for the ages as festive days on which all customs of mourning are set aside. Our sages point out that since the time *Megillat Taanit* was written, many other events have occurred that would also have deserved to be recorded and commemorated, only that the abundance of the events weakened their evocative power to the extent that, as our sages say, "dead flesh does not feel the scalpel" (Shabbat 13b). That is to say, we became desensitized to tragedy; hence, even when such events caused great sorrow and grief in the past, these feelings have not endured the test of time.

This happens in people's personal lives as well. Past events may have been very painful, but their memory becomes increasingly dulled with the passage of time. It is a physiological fact that human beings are incapable of remembering pain, and this fact influences the whole course of one's life. Pain is felt when it occurs, but the memory of the pain cannot vividly reproduce the experience from the past. As a rule, people can recall superficially that something caused them great pain, but the pain itself cannot be re-experienced.

If that is the case in the personal life and consciousness of the individual, all the more is it so in the case of a nation, which is composed of thousands of individuals who do not feel or think all at once or in a uniform manner.

For all these reasons, the commemoration of the war with Amalek seems puzzling, and the review of it each year seems, to a great extent, like "the snows of yesteryear." It is merely a memory, which, even when we recall it and perhaps carry it out, cannot be re-experienced. As the Torah says in the first description of the war with Amalek, "Write this in the book as a reminder, and rehearse it in the ears of Joshua" (Ex. 17:14).

Although life continually produces new experiences and feelings that naturally supplant the former ones, in the life of the individual and the community there are events whose significance goes beyond remembering the past. These are formative events, events that originated in the past but have continuity, ramifications, and repercussions in the present because they open the door to long-term developments.

One's birthday is a significant event, at least for the person himself, despite the fact that it is a thing of the past. This is because every moment of one's life is connected with that point. Even one who does not celebrate birthdays, and even one who must strain to remember the date of his birth, is inevitably connected to it.

In the Torah there are two short sections that speak of remembering and obliterating Amalek: Exodus 17:8–16 and Deuteronomy 25:17–19. Although the description of the events there is not very detailed, it is clear enough. After the People of Israel left Egypt, while they were on the way to Mount Sinai, the Amalekites attacked them and apparently killed a number of people. After a battle that lasted for an entire day, the Amalekites were defeated and fled.

From a historical perspective, this war against the Amalekites seems puzzling. According to the Torah's account, the Amalekites did not actually succeed in penetrating into the Israelite camp. Rather, they struck only those who were "lagging to your rear" (Deut. 25:18); that is, people who were not in the camp itself but who, for various reasons, lagged behind.

This implies that the Amalekites were not a people with an especially large army. While the Israelites, who were not trained in warfare, had some difficulty in repulsing the Amalekites, in no way does this conflict appear to have been a major war. Rather, it appears to have been a minor incident, considering its impact and aftermath.

The Torah's account raises a basic question: Why did the Amalekites attack the Israelite camp? Not only had the People of Israel not invaded their territory, they had not even turned in their direction! The Amalekites did not figure at all in Israel's grand political plans and goals, nor did they reside in the territories that Israel intended to conquer.

From the Torah's accounts about the encounters between Israel and Amalek that occurred over the following centuries, it emerges that the Amalekites were a nomadic people that lived in the wide open spaces of Transjordan, around the land of Edom and perhaps in the southern Land of Israel as well; they did not live in permanent settlements. Desert nomads have always engaged in robbery to survive. For thousands of years, nomads – in the Middle East and elsewhere – have considered it their right to rob caravans or to attack and plunder settlements. But the People of Israel traveling in the wilderness were not some small caravan; they were so numerous that it was almost impossible to view the whole extent of their encampment (Num. 23:13), and the temptation or motivation of nomads to attack such a camp should have been quite small.

Hence, before we discuss the question of our attitude toward Amalek, we should ask a different question: What motive did the Amalekites have to attack Israel? What was the purpose of this attack? The fact that Amalek's attack has no rational justification presents only one possibility, which, though it may seem far-fetched, seems to be the only explanation: The Amalekites hated the People of Israel. The attack on Israel was not meant to gain anything in particular or to achieve any goal. It was purely an expression of hatred.

For generations, many people – Jews and non-Jews alike – have struggled to find an explanation for anti-Semitism, and they have offered a list of reasons for it: hatred of strangers, hatred for religious reasons, envy of the Jews' accomplishments, etc. All of these reasons, which are treated quite extensively in scholarly literature, while perhaps not completely rational, have a basis in human nature and in outlooks that often come to expression in cases of conflict and hatred between peoples. However, age-old anti-Semitism, which, in its overt forms, is distinct and well defined, has existed for well over two thousand years, long before the emergence of Christianity.

To be sure, even in the ancient manifestations of hatred toward Israel, such as Haman and Apion of Alexandria, we find all the known elements of hatred between nations and between individuals. Nevertheless, in the hatred of Jews that has manifested itself throughout our history, there is also a trace of an additional element that cannot be explained rationally – a mysterious, fundamental hatred.

This kernel of hatred is part of anti-Semitism in all its manifestations throughout the ages. This mysterious element has no better explanation than the other mystery: the continued existence of the Jewish people. This aspect of anti-Semitism is simply a reaction to the very existence of the Jews in the world.

The same applies to the war of Amalek. This war lacked all the elements that could explain such hatred. All it had is this deep-seated hatred toward Jews simply because they are Jews. This fundamental hatred does not derive from any reason whatsoever, nor does it end when the hater recognizes and is rationally aware of the Jews' virtues; a person or a people can recognize all these virtues and still continue to hate to the same degree. Amalek's hatred of Israel, then, can be characterized as pure, causeless hatred, hatred that lacks a goal or a purpose. It is unqualified hatred of the very essence or existence of Israel.

This point is emphasized in *Parashat Zakhor*. The People of Israel are attacked for no reason, without any justification, while they are on their way to their ancestral homeland. Indeed, that the attack achieves only the killing of stragglers who lagged behind the camp points to the fact that Amalek cannot and dares not attack the large Jewish camp itself but can only enjoy its success in killing a few Jews in the rear.

A key to this point of fundamental hatred can be found in the very next expression in the Torah: "And he [Amalek] did not fear God" (Deut. 25:18). This expression in itself sounds almost meaningless. It is obvious that one who attacks people whom he has no reason to attack does not fear God. Nevertheless, this simple expression reveals the inner root of Amalek's hatred.

When the People of Israel goes forth from Egypt, this is not just another migration of just another people. The plagues of Egypt and the parting of the Red Sea become known far and wide, including in the Land of Israel, frightening the peoples of Canaan. It was clear not only to Pharaoh and his people but to other nations as well that unique events were occurring, a historical debut. It was clearly evident that the People of Israel were under God's protection, which manifested itself in Egypt in the form of a series of very severe and frightening plagues.

One would have expected that, as a result of these events, no one in the world would dare to challenge the People of Israel, who are under God's special protection. Indeed, not even Balak, king of Moab, who had much better reasons to fear the Jews' presence on the border of his country, dared to fight them, because he feared this divine protection.

Amalek, however, "did not fear God"; Amalek paid no regard to the divine revelation, despite the fact that God clearly possessed real, frightening power and was not just an abstract theological subject. Not only does Amalek ignore God's existence as a supreme being, but they also disregard the fear and dread that fighting against His people should entail.

The Midrash describes Amalek's behavior and its effect with the following parable:

> To what may this be compared? To a boiling hot bath into which no one could descend. A good-for-nothing came and jumped into it. Although he was scalded, he made it cooler to others. Here, too, [in the case of Amalek], when Israel went forth from Egypt, The Holy One, Blessed Be He, split the sea before them and the Egyptians sunk into it, [and as a result,] the fear of Israel fell upon all the nations…When Amalek came and attacked them, even though he got what he deserved at their hands, he made them [appear] cooler to the nations of the world. (Tanḥuma, *Ki Tetzeh* 9)

The one who jumped into the boiling hot bath did so with the clear knowledge that he would be scalded, and that the only result of doing so would be to cool off the boiling heat. Indeed, the war with Amalek sent a message to the entire world: The People of Israel, despite its divine protection, is still vulnerable; it is possible to fight them. This message indeed made its way to the other nations. They were still afraid – "all the inhabitants of Canaan are melted away" (Ex. 15:15) – and yet they try to fight against Israel anyway.

There is another way to understand the Torah's expression that Amalek "did not fear God." The phrase "did not fear" can be understood not only as a negation but also as a positive designation. That is to say, not only does Amalek not fear God, but actually sets himself against God. They "did not fear" in a deeper sense; they are the antithesis of one who fears. Not only do they reject divine authority, but they blatantly oppose it.

Thus, the expression "did not fear God" can be understood as the explanation of Amalek's actions. Amalek fought against God, of whose presence in this world the People of Israel is merely the physical expression. Hence, Amalek is not only anti-Semitic; they are anti-divine, and they direct their hatred of the Creator to the symbol of the Divine Presence in the world – the People of Israel, the people with whom God's name is associated (Deut. 28:10), the people who are God's witnesses (Is. 43:12).

In addition to all of this, there is a unique halakha regarding the conversion of an Amalekite to Judaism. Although the Amalekites are Edomites in origin, halakhically they are not considered Edomites. Only the third generation of Edomite proselytes may be accepted into the Jewish people, and there it is a mitzva not to hate them, as they are our brothers. For the Amalekites, however, while we are commanded to obliterate them, if an Amalekite converts, he is accepted into the Jewish people immediately.

We see from this that the essence of being an Amalekite is not connected with one's ethnic origin but with one's personal orientation. When an Amalekite wants to convert, he stops being an Amalekite, unlike other peoples, whose essence does not disappear immediately upon their conversion. What emerges from this halakhic definition is that "Amalek" is a spiritual state of being, much more than a biological group.

Israel's response to Amalek, then, is not revenge for the wrong that was done to us or for the loss of life inflicted on us; it goes far beyond that. After all, there is a long list of nations that fought against Israel, and some of them caused us immeasurable injuries, yet we are not duty-bound to remember this or to take revenge on them in every generation. The war against Amalek is connected with Amalek's essential nature.

Amalek is a state of being that is defined by hatred of Israel. Israel and Amalek cannot coexist, for the essence of Amalek's existence is the negation of Israel. As long as there are Amalekites in the world, even if only in very small numbers, this means that there exists an element that is Israel's antithesis, its complete opposite.

The radical statement that "neither [God's] name will be complete nor will [His] throne be complete until the eradication of the memory of Amalek" (Midrash Psalms 9) essentially says the very same thing. Only with the complete eradication of "Amalek" will the People of Israel's existence be ensured for all time. For this reason, the war against Amalek continues "throughout the generations" – a "war for God against Amalek" (Ex. 17:16).

Ki Tissa

WHAT WAS THE SIN OF THE GOLDEN CALF?

Among the various explanations of the sin of the Golden Calf, Nahmanides' explanation appears to be the closest to the plain meaning of the text.

In essence, Nahmanides explains that the calf was not meant to replace God, but rather to replace Moses. This explanation appears to derive from a simple reading of the verse, "Up, make us a god who will go before us; for that man Moses who brought us up out of the land of Egypt – we do not know what has happened to him" (Ex. 32:23). This is also the simplest explanation of why, when Moses descends from the mountain, takes the calf, and crushes it in front of the entire people, everyone remains silent. If the people had truly felt that their god was taken from them, they would surely have protested! Clearly, then, the whole point of the calf was to replace Moses. Now that Moses had returned, they no longer needed the calf.

On a deeper level, the People of Israel made the calf because they wanted a physical dwelling place for the Divine Presence, some relatable, tangible object on which holiness could rest. In lieu of a Tabernacle, an Ark, and cherubim, they took a calf and designated it the dwelling place for God's glory. In this respect, the basic idea of the calf was not without merit; it was simply an inappropriate application of a legitimate desire.

Our need for tangibility is innate, as it is very difficult to focus on God in the abstract. To be devoted exclusively to God on the most abstract level is very difficult, and not everyone is capable of this task; it may not even be possible for anyone to do completely. This is because life is full of questions. There are big questions – whom do we serve; in whom do we believe? – and small questions – how should we live; how will we die? And how do we, as individuals or as a community, handle all sorts of potentially fateful decisions? To be sure, the rule in all these matters is to "follow none but God" (Deut. 13:5). But today, when we are not on the level of, "You will hear a command from behind you, saying: 'This is the way; follow it, whether you turn to the right or to the left'" (Is. 30:21), this becomes problematic.

If God would tell each and every one of us specifically what is expected of him, everything would be simple. But we do not hear this voice, neither from behind us nor in front of us. All that we receive is very general instruction; as a result, people are always searching for something to hold on to.

It is said that "the *Shekhina* speaks out of Moses' throat" (see *Raaya Meheimna, Pinḥas* 232a). This is because Moses himself is like the Ark and the Tablets. We receive the Torah not from the tablets upon which the Ten Commandments were written, but from Moses' throat. Moses is the channel through which God reveals Himself to us in this world. In light of this, when Moses did not come down from the mountain, the People of Israel feared that Aaron, not being on Moses' level, would not be able to replace him in this role. Because of this, they proceeded to make the calf.

Indeed, when Moses reproached Aaron, saying, "What did the people do to you, that you brought upon them such a great sin?" (Ex. 32:21), Aaron answers him, "You know that this people have bad tendencies" (32:22); that is to say, they pressured me, threatened me, and then "I cast it into the fire and out came this calf" (32:24). He does not deny having made the calf; he just claims that he had intended something else.

According to this approach, the sin is clear. It is not as grievous as we might have thought – that the people who had just heard "I am God your Lord" (Ex. 20:2) then proceeded to make an idol. Rather, they began with a legitimate desire for tangibility that grew and developed until it finally became idolatry. If that is the case, however, why is the sin of the Golden Calf mentioned so often and considered so serious?

To answer this question, we must look at the origins of the calf. The whole episode began with the people's request to celebrate "a festival unto God tomorrow" (Ex. 32:5). On the occasion of this festival, a symbolic religious object is made. This is how the calf came into being. But the calf does not remain symbolic; it gradually deteriorates, until it becomes actual idolatry.

Often, spiritual descent does not happen all at once, but in stages, as in the case of the copper serpent, about which the Mishna asks, "Does a serpent kill or does a serpent keep alive?" (Rosh HaShana 3:8). The Mishna answers that the serpent did neither; instead, it reminded the people to look to God for solutions to their problems. But was a serpent truly necessary for this? Let them turn their thoughts above without a serpent! Apparently, it is difficult to turn our thoughts heavenward without any prompting. We need a focal point to help us relate to God, and that is why in the first stage of approaching God we look for something tangible.

This is true of concentration on any subject. When we try to think about something, the more general the thought, the less we are able to focus, to the point that our thoughts become meaningless. Thought must be anchored in something tangible. Hence, when a person is told to think about something, even about something holy, it is always simpler to focus on and deal with something specific.

PATTERN OF DETERIORATION

The problem does not stem from a lack of concentration; it is simply part of human nature. Since it is so difficult to turn our thoughts heavenward for more than a moment, we need some kind of focus, a point that we can grasp. However, once this focus is achieved, it is very easy for it to deteriorate. Instead of using this tangible point simply as a means of looking heavenward, one is liable to begin ascribing religious significance to the thing itself. We tend, increasingly, to forget the goal and remember only the means. Wherever we employ a means to an end in religious life, we must be extremely cautious, or the means itself may become an object of worship.

Maimonides maintains that this is precisely how idolatry first developed. In his view, the starting point is always belief in God's unity, but at a certain stage we begin to relate to the intermediaries more than to God Himself, until finally the center point is completely forgotten and we focus exclusively on the intermediaries (*Laws of Idolatry* 1:1–2).

From the chain of events that led to the sin of the Golden Calf, we learn of another characteristic of idolatry. Aaron declares, "There will be a festival unto God tomorrow" (Ex. 32:5), and the people respond to this important announcement enthusiastically: "They got up early the next morning" (32:6). The next stage involves bringing burnt offerings. This kind of offering is burned in its entirety; those who bring them do not partake of them. Afterward, however, they bring peace offerings, some of which are burned but some of which are eaten by those who bring them. After bringing peace offerings, "the people sat down to eat" (32:6). Then they began to drink and so forth, until "they got up to revel" (32:6). This is a clear sequence of events: It begins with "a festival unto God," which already contains a certain element of personal dissolution, and at each successive stage things become more and more relaxed, until the whole framework deteriorates.

This is the essence of idolatry – taking a heavenly form and corrupting it, bringing it down to the physical realm. But idolatry takes this notion one step further. Not only is a divine construct brought low, the converse occurs as well: An earthly entity is elevated to a lofty position. Man himself, in various ways, becomes an exalted figure, an object of worship. When our sages say that "when someone becomes angry, it is as though he worships idols" (Zohar, *Bereshit* 27b), or that "anyone in whom there is haughtiness is as one who worships idols" (Sota 4b), they are making this same point – that a person can deify himself. A person deifies himself when he rejects bounds and limits and begins to consider himself, to a certain degree, the king of the world.

In the sin of the Golden Calf, "they got up to revel" as a result of the convergence of both factors: lowering the exalted and exalting the low. We are constantly beset with base drives, whether it is the drive to engage in forbidden sexual relations or the drive to commit acts of violence, and we can usually keep these desires in check. But the moment one invests a base drive with lofty meaning, it becomes, in one's own mind, not only permissible but a mitzva. Even if, ordinarily, one would be embarrassed to commit a certain act, once it is wrapped in a lofty mantle, that same act becomes exalted. When the two factors converge, the idolatry appears in its full force, to the point of "they got up to revel."

This calf was not Aaron's calf; it was a calf produced by the people, by the lowest individuals of Israel, and elevated to a position of holiness.

FROM A HIGH PEAK TO A DEEP PIT

Even after this explanation, a major question regarding the sin of the Golden Calf still remains. How could it be that the holy People of Israel, who just now received the Torah on Mount Sinai, and who, forty days earlier, heard the voice of God speaking directly to them, fall so far as to make the calf, dance around it, and "get up to revel"?!

To a certain degree, there is a causal connection between the receiving of the Torah and the sin of the Golden Calf. To explain this connection, let us examine the condition known as "baby blues," a mild form of depression that many women experience following childbirth. In most cases, this sense of depression passes after a short while without becoming serious. In other cases, it becomes more serious and develops into full-blown postpartum depression, and there are even rare cases where the woman does not recover from it.

What is the cause of this phenomenon? At the moment of birth, the mother's whole body is mobilized for a tremendous effort. Massive releases of adrenaline and other hormones advance the labor vigorously to enable the birth of the child. All of the body's systems speed up dramatically, so the birth is, in every respect, an incredibly intense experience. Shortly after the birth, all of this intensity subsides, and suddenly all that remains is a void. The disparity between the preceding emotional high and the new reality in which all of this has dissipated creates a subjective sense of having fallen from a high peak to a deep pit. Before, there was heightened tension; now, all of this has vanished.

This phenomenon can be explained in more spiritual terminology as well. The Talmud says that the key to the mother's womb remains in God's hand alone (Taanit 2a), and according to our early sages, this is what creates the *tuma* of childbirth. The fall from the high of childbirth, where God Himself is present, to the low of the emptiness that follows it creates the *tuma*.

The People of Israel experience the revelation at Sinai, and for a moment they ascend to a level so high that they hear God speaking. Without any preparations an entire nation ascends to this level, and immediately afterward everything disappears; even Moses is gone. So what remains? At first glance, it would appear that the situation has reverted to the pre-Sinai reality. However, the depression that followed the exaltation of the giving of the Torah was so deep that a serious crisis developed. In light of this, it is not at all surprising that the giving of the Torah was followed by the sin of the Golden Calf. For Moses, the Ten Commandments were followed by forty days and forty nights of Torah. For the People of Israel, the Ten Commandments were followed by a vacuum. When this vacuum was not filled with spiritual content, it became filled with *tuma* instead.

In this respect, the sin of the Golden Calf was a normal phenomenon; it was the natural reaction to the giving of the Torah. This is what often happens when someone attains spiritual exaltation that is not built progressively, stage by stage, and then experiences a sharp descent, where everything suddenly disappears. *Baalei teshuva* often experience this very problem. These individuals attain a certain level of exaltation that can often feel like a burning flame. When this flame inevitably goes out, the void that remains can be devastating.

DO NOT TARRY

High, uplifting points in one's life can thus be very dangerous times, because they present the latent danger of a serious fall – to the point of making a calf or worse. The proper way to deal with this danger is not to tarry but to immediately begin a process that will enable one to maintain the spiritual high. We engage in this kind of process each week, in the Havdala. During the Havdala at the end of Shabbat, we not only drink wine, as we do in the Kiddush at the beginning of Shabbat, but we also inhale the fragrance of spices. We do this because "woe, the soul is lost" (Beitza 16a) – the *neshama yeteira* (additional soul) of Shabbat departs from us. By inhaling the spices, we guard ourselves against the danger of a precipitous fall, to which we are vulnerable following the spiritual high of Shabbat.

The spiritual high of Yom Kippur is likewise often followed by a fall, not because we become worse than we were beforehand, but because the sense of the disparity between the holy day and the days that follow it leads to a feeling of lowliness and descent. For this reason, as soon as Yom Kippur ends, the custom is to immediately begin building the sukka. Similarly, on Simhat Torah, after the reading of the entire Torah has been completed and the celebration is finished, we immediately begin reading the Torah anew. For this reason as well, we always try to attach the beginning of one mitzva to the conclusion of another. By doing this, we allow ourselves to continuously serve as instruments for performing mitzvot, thus guarding ourselves against a great fall.

When a person experiences major changes in his life and does not have the capacity to absorb these changes, the effects of these changes can be ruinous. The story is told of a French millionaire who, when informed that almost his entire fortune had been lost and what remained was only 100,000 francs, had a heart attack and died. This millionaire had an heir, who was very poor his entire life, and when he heard that he had inherited 100,000 francs, he, too, had a heart attack and died. Neither of them had the capacity to absorb the news.

For this reason, it is precisely in times of ascent that one must always try to engage in activities that foster spiritual growth, even if it is for the sole purpose of avoiding the creation of an opening for the entry of *tuma*. As we read in Numbers Rabba, we have not yet removed ourselves from the sin of the Golden Calf (9:49).

The period between the giving of the Torah and Moses' return lasted only forty days, but that was all that was needed to ignite the entire situation. But let us imagine that Moses had communicated the messages of *Parashat Teruma* and *Parashat Tetzaveh* not after descending Mount Sinai but beforehand. If he had done this, all the silver and gold that people gave to make the calf would have been channeled to holiness. The problem was that right after Sinai, the people were forced to return to a normal course of life, and this transition is what led to their fall.

Times of transition are times of real trial, times of true mortal danger, and there is only one remedy for this: to take action. The saying goes that Satan accuses a person when he makes a *siyum*, meaning that he denounces a person who completes a unit of Torah study without beginning something new. The denunciation is not for having completed a unit of study but for failing to channel the points of ascent into some new action.

SINS LIKE *SHANIM*

This understanding of the sin of the Golden Calf allows us to judge our ancestors favorably, as we can argue that their sin was only a result of human nature. The Yerushalmi expounds upon the verse, "If your sins are like *shanim*,[1] they will be as white as snow" (Is. 1:18), explaining that God only grants atonement for certain kinds of sins: "If a person's sins are in accordance with his years, they will become as white as snow" (Y. Shabbat 9:3). When a young man commits adultery or an old man steals, God grants atonement; but when the opposite is the case, He does not grant atonement. There are ages at which a person is prone to certain sins but not to others. When a person commits a sin that befits his age, there is an explanation for it. While the explanation obviously does not justify the sin, it does provide the possibility for atonement.

It can indeed be said that the sin of the Golden Calf was in the category of "sins like years"; it has a natural explanation according to the chain of events that we outlined above. And in fact we see that, after the sin, God not only forgives Israel but also gives a new set of Tablets, instructs the People of Israel to build the Tabernacle, and eventually brings the nation into the Land of Israel.

Although the sin of the Golden Calf seems more serious than the sin of the spies, the People of Israel were forgiven for the former but not for the latter. The reason for this is that the sin of the spies is a different type of sin. When a person commits a sin that cannot be mitigated by appealing to human nature, there can be no atonement. By contrast, the sin of the Golden Calf can be explained: It is part of human nature and therefore can also be rectified.

---

1. According to the plain meaning of the verse, *shanim* means "scarlet." In this midrashic interpretation, however, *shanim* is understood to mean "years."

Vayak'hel

Parashat Vayak'hel is one of the *parashot* in which most of the content has already appeared earlier in the Torah – in this case, the way the Tabernacle was built and the actual construction of its various vessels. Since we have already discussed this subject, let us now concentrate on those few things in this *parasha* that have not been spelled out elsewhere.

The *parasha* begins with the assembly of the entire community and with the command to keep Shabbat, a mitzva that has already been mentioned several times in the Torah.

The most basic characteristic of Shabbat, in both the Torah and halakha, is the prohibition on *melakha* (work), as it says in this *parasha*, "The seventh day must be kept holy as a Shabbat of *Shabbatot* unto God. Whoever does work on [that day] shall be put to death" (Ex. 35:2)

But the mention here of Shabbat and the prohibition of *melakha* on that day as an introduction to all the work that went into the construction of the Tabernacle is extremely significant. The only simple explanation for this juxtaposition is that although the construction of the Tabernacle is an exceedingly important value in the eyes of God, nevertheless, the command to keep Shabbat is more important. The implication is that the command to rest on Shabbat pertains not only to ordinary matters ("your work," as it says in the Ten Commandments) but to sacred work as well.

The juxtaposition of the Shabbat prohibitions to the work performed in the construction of the Tabernacle has both technical and halakhic significance. It teaches us the central halakhic basis of all the laws of Shabbat. In and of itself, the concept of *melakha* can be expansive or limited according to one's reasoning; nevertheless, only acts performed in the same manner as they were performed in constructing the Tabernacle are prohibited on Shabbat. Tractate Shabbat's designation of the thirty-nine categories of *melakha* is based on the tradition concerning the number of *melakhot* performed in the Tabernacle. Thus, the work of the Tabernacle serves as a basic, though not exclusive, model for the forms of work prohibited on Shabbat.

WHAT IS *MELAKHA*?

A deeper look into the definition of *melakha* reveals that the problem is far from simple. Even someone with a thorough knowledge of the laws of Shabbat must grapple with the complicated question of what exactly is considered work by the Torah's definition.

On the one hand, one may carry heavy loads, and labor and sweat over any number of undertakings, without violating any *melakha* according to halakha. On the other hand, simple acts such as lighting a fire, writing two letters, or moving a pin from one place to another are considered *melakha*, and entail a serious penalty.

Moreover, the fine details that create the complex system of the laws of Shabbat become intertwined and together form a structure that is full of puzzling questions and, seemingly, contradictions and illogic as well.

The challenge of finding one all-inclusive and complete definition of *melakha* – a question complicated by the profusion of details in talmudic and post-talmudic halakha – is uniquely difficult. And even if we are able to find such a definition, there is a more basic question: What is the inner logic that informs this definition?

In order to clarify the problem of cessation from work on Shabbat, we must first consider a broader question: How do we define work and rest in general? The concept of work – and along with it, the parallel concept of rest – can be understood in various ways. But if we dismiss the various professional senses and scientific definitions, there are essentially two possibilities.

The first possible definition that comes to mind is largely responsible for the common misunderstanding of the Torah's concept of work:

the identification of work with effort. According to this understanding, work is any activity in which one invests effort, and which is characterized by labor, toil, and sweat. Accordingly, defining a particular act as work depends on the amount of effort invested in it. An endeavor in which a great deal of effort is invested is considered major work, whereas one that does not require much effort is hardly considered work at all.

Connected with this understanding of work is a parallel rationale. According to this understanding, the exact definition of work is not effort; rather, the effort must be a forced effort, an act that one is obliged to perform, and not an act of one's own free will and desire. Thus, an act that brings enjoyment to its performer is not considered work but play and delight.

This understanding would obviously bring into question the prohibition against performing certain forms of work on Shabbat. Take, for example, light, relaxing work that a person might perform in his garden. Since this is not unpleasant labor, one might think to consider it *oneg Shabbat* (Shabbat enjoyment) rather than *melakha*.

This view of work is clearly based on the physical feeling that the work brings. It is a conception that begins and ends with the feeling of the physical exertion that work provides, and has nothing to do with the act that is performed. This perspective is not unlike that of a horse that works the land. The horse does not understand the meaning or result of its actions, only the physical experience that accompanies its exertion. It does not consider the aspects of cause and purpose, value and benefit.

This understanding of work would then affect the meaning of rest. Rest is the opposite of work; hence, rest would mean the cessation of physical exertion, and its ideal form would be inactivity. Indeed, according to halakha, this understanding of work and rest does exist, within certain parameters. As the Torah expressly states, "so that your ox and your donkey may rest" (Ex. 23:12).

CREATIVE EFFORT

Let us suggest a different approach to the concept of work, one that is not at odds with the preceding one but that nevertheless is essentially different from it. Work can be viewed not primarily with respect to the effort involved but with respect to the result that is produced. One cannot determine what is work and what is not work by comparing the effort invested in each case, but by the results produced. No matter how much labor was involved, an unorganized effort that produces no results whatsoever, or that produces results that have no positive value, will not be classified as work.

This conception of work is essentially connected with the intention and thought that inform the effort. Hence, only a purposeful activity can be considered work. That is, the defining concept of work is not toil but creation. This conception of work is a characteristically human conception, since it is based on the existence and activity of a guiding intentional faculty.

In this conception of work, the existence and measure of work are defined by the quantity and value of the result. Furthermore, the creative act is not merely an act of organized, intentional effort; rather, it must essentially be an effort whose result is a positive act. Creativity has a strictly positive meaning, the essence of which is building and progress. An act of destruction can be considered *melakha* only when there is some purpose to this destructiveness, when it is not destruction for its own sake but for the sake of achieving some other purpose. In such a case, even destruction can be a creative act, since it serves as a preliminary step to an act of positive creation.

Correspondingly, rest need not be defined as cessation of all effort, because effort itself is not important in this context. Rather, rest is defined as cessation of *creative* effort.

It stands to reason that the Torah's definitions of work and rest would be based on this human conception, and in fact, almost all of the detailed and complex laws of Shabbat derive from the principle that *melakha* is a physical act performed with intention and thought. As our sages put it, "The Torah prohibits work entailing the fulfillment of one's intent" (Beitza 13b), and "One who does work without awareness is exempt" (Keritot 20a). *Melakha* is a creative act; hence, "all who engage in destructive action are exempt" (Shabbat 106a), but a destructive act that is intended as preparation for something creative, such as "erasing in order to write" (73a), is considered *melakha*.

WHY STOP CREATING?

The myriad of details in the laws of Shabbat are all essentially practical corollaries of this definition, from which all of the Shabbat prohibitions derive, whether directly or indirectly. In essence, Shabbat is the suspension of work, the silencing and cessation of all creative activity. Here, however, arises the central problem: What is the reason for this suspension of creation and for those long Shabbat hours of noncreative inactivity?

First of all, let us look at the rationale provided by the Torah for resting on Shabbat: "For in six days God made heaven and earth...and He rested on the seventh day. Therefore, God blessed the Shabbat day and made it holy" (Ex. 20:11). The simple meaning of this verse is that because God rested on the seventh day, we too must rest. What, however, is the reason for and meaning of this imitation? To be sure, Shabbat is an eternal testament to the creation of the world, one of the basic tenets of Judaism. But the cessation from work on Shabbat does not attest directly to the world's creation but, rather, to the cessation from its creation, which seems secondary in importance to the creation itself.

A comprehensive analysis of this question would entail a great deal of deep thinking, but the essence of it is the following: To a large degree, the imitation of God is man's task in this world. As our sages put it, "Try to emulate Him. As He is gracious and merciful, so you be gracious and merciful" (Masekhet Soferim 3:17). In this way, man becomes a vehicle for carrying out God's work in the world. Man was created in God's image and likeness, or as one of the greatest hasidic masters put it: Man's soul is "truly a part of God from on high" (*Tanya*, ch. 2). Thus, his whole essential purpose is to be like a spark of divinity in this world. "You have made him but little lower than the angels and crowned him with glory and majesty. You have made him master over the works of Your hands, placed all things at his feet" (Ps. 8:6–7). Man's distinction in this world is the channeling, imitation, and completion of God's work.

Creation – the work of creating the world – concluded on Shabbat. However, although the direct, manifest, and deliberate divine creation came to an end, and since then, the world has operated according to the laws and patterns originally established in it, nevertheless the act of purposive creation never stops. The task of deliberately rectifying the world by completing the divine creation now devolves upon man. As it says in the Torah at the end of the Creation, "The heaven and the earth were finished...And God blessed the seventh day and made it holy, because on it He ceased from all His work which God created to do (*laasot*)" (Gen. 2:1–3). The Midrash expounds on the last word of the verse, "Everything created during the six days of Creation requires rectification" (*Pesikta Rabbati* 23). For God only began the work that He created *laasot* – in order that it should be perfected by man.

This first Shabbat, which heralded the suspension of creation, was not, then, the absolute conclusion of creation. Rather, it was merely the demarcation of one stage in creation. Shabbat serves both as a separation and as a bond between the divine work of the Creation and the human work of creation. This would explain the command to keep Shabbat just as God rested from His work, as our creation is truly part of the process of His Creation.

As we have stated, the prohibition on performing *melakha* on Shabbat means ceasing from all creative work. All the detailed laws and prohibitions merely elaborate and clarify this general command.

Even the prohibition of carrying on Shabbat, in its various forms – a prohibition that is considered an anomaly in halakha, since it seemingly does not entail any suspension of creative work – begins to make sense once we understand that Shabbat is a day of stillness, in which we suspend the practical-physical aspect of creation. The prohibition of carrying conveys the idea of a standstill, of upholding the status quo – standing at attention quietly and attentively.

THE ROLE OF REST

The essence of Shabbat, God's rest from the work of Creation, is not just suspension of work. There is an additional element as well: the command to rest. Here, too, we must stress the fundamental distinction between rest and inactivity. The same distinction we made between exertion and work – between a random action and a deliberate effort – exists between inactivity and rest as well. Inactivity is random inaction, complete desistance from any exertion, whereas rest entails the practice of deliberate, purposeful inaction in preparation for further action in the future. That is to say, although rest does not involve exertion, it, too, is a creative act, because it creates the possibility and prepares for all further creation.

In addition, rest has another, more spiritual aspect. In the course of continuous, routine work, it is generally impossible to appreciate the totality of the work that has been done, to attain perspective and plan for the future. Rest, on the other hand, enables one to take stock in this way, which is necessary for perceiving the spiritual significance of one's work. Thus, even though, with respect to exertion, rest is a state of stillness and passivity, with respect to the purposeful-essential aspect of work and creation, it is an incredibly dynamic activity.

The first Shabbat, too, was not just the sheer suspension of the Creation. Its significance was the summation, looking back on the Creation, finding its spiritual and meaningful content, and making it possible to raise the entire enterprise to a higher level. Only after a period of rest could work and creation be renewed in the second week, which was the week of man.

"And God blessed the seventh day and made it holy, because on it He ceased from all His work" (Gen. 2:3). Shabbat assumed an enhanced level of blessing and holiness precisely because of this cessation of active creation, because God took the time, as it were, to look at His creation and see all that He had made, and find that it was very good. Even loftier than this, Shabbat enabled finding the pure purpose that lay in this creation.

THE STILLNESS OF SHABBAT

Although the act of divine creation was a one-time event, it is also the paradigm and prototype for everything that happens afterward in the world through man and his actions. Just as the divine creation paused for summation, thought, and exaltation, so too, man – who continues the work of creation, who is the divine instrument for deliberate, purposeful creation – must cease his actions for one day of suspended creation, rest, and stillness: Shabbat.

Shabbat, the holy day of cessation and rest, is the culmination of everything that was done during the week. The stillness of Shabbat is a state of contemplation, a state of preparation for a deeper understanding of the essence of things, in a greater effort to attain their purpose.

Certainly, as long as Shabbat is perceived as a time of forced idleness, it becomes an incomprehensible, unwelcome burden. But this is not the true nature of Shabbat; its true nature is elevation from the mundane activities of the week to the attainment of a higher and holier level of creation.

Pekudei

WHY IS A TABERNACLE NECESSARY?

Parashat Pekudei concludes the book of Exodus and also concludes a series of *parashot* dealing with the Tabernacle. The particulars of the Tabernacle have given rise to many questions, which are discussed extensively in the Talmud and other sources. But before all these specifics, two fundamental questions must be addressed.

The first question relates to the time of the Tabernacle's construction. Why was the Tabernacle erected in the wilderness, a seemingly inopportune time and setting for such an endeavor?

The Song of the Sea includes the following passage: "Until Your people cross, O God, until the people You gained cross over. You will bring them and plant them on Your own mountain, the place You made to dwell in, the sanctuary of God, which Your hands established" (Ex. 15:16–17). From these verses, there would appear to be a planned order to things: First they cross the sea, then the wilderness; then they enter the Land of Israel, and only at the very end of this process do they build the Sanctuary. But in reality, the Tabernacle was built almost immediately after the parting of the sea. As early as the first year after the Exodus, the people received the command to build it, and at the beginning of the second year it was already dedicated.

To be sure, a distinction can ostensibly be made between the Tabernacle and the "sanctuary" mentioned in the verse. Nevertheless, it would seem that the Tabernacle should have been built at least fifty years later, after the entry into the Land, the conclusion of the wars of conquest, and the apportionment of the Land.

The second question, which is more general, pertains to the very need for a tabernacle or a sanctuary in the first place. When a person is moved to do something for God's glory, the best and most straightforward way for him to do this would seem to be on his own, in the manner that befits him. Indeed, that is precisely what was done before the Temple was built, even when the Tabernacle was already in existence, when the use of *bamot* (ritual platforms or altars) was permitted.

The truth is that a *bama* is less complicated than the Tabernacle in every respect, and is also much more accessible and personal; anyone can use it. In a reality where *bamot* are permitted, one who wants to bring a *korban* to God – and not just to worship Him through prayer and the observance of His commandments – does not need to rely on the Priests, nor does he need to travel a great distance. He himself can build an earthen altar or a stone altar anywhere, even in his own yard, and then he can bring *korbanot* and draw himself closer to God. Such service of God is direct and simple.

It appears that the essence of divine worship in general, and *korbanot* in particular, does not require a tabernacle and could have remained a private matter, for each individual to pursue personally. Consider the view of Nahmanides (Lev. 1:9), for example, who points out that *korbanot* existed from ancient times and are not necessarily dependent on a tabernacle or sanctuary. Even if we do not take into account our sages' interpretation that Adam brought a *korban* (Avoda Zara 8a), the Torah says explicitly that Cain and Abel brought *korbanot* at the dawn of man's existence. Apparently, the drive to bring *korbanot* is intrinsic to the human race. Every human being – not just the Jew – is entitled, according to halakha, to bring a *korban* to God, anywhere and anytime. We, the Jewish people, are the only ones who have been limited in this regard, in that we can only bring *korbanot* in the Tabernacle or in the Temple.

Instead of each person building his own *bama*, we were commanded to build the Tabernacle, which, in many respects, is a formidable and complex task. Here, again, the question is: Why is this necessary? What is it that can be found in the Tabernacle but not at a *bama*?

TWO WAYS OF SERVING GOD

Apparently, there is indeed a difference between *korbanot* brought at a *bama* and *korbanot* brought in the Sanctuary, a phenomenon unique to Israel. These are two different ways of serving God. Non-Jews who wish to serve God may bring *korbanot* anywhere, whereas the Jewish people were assigned a different way of serving God, in which they require a Temple.

The first way in which one can serve God – the way that is open to anyone – is on the level of the individual. One can lead his own life and try from within himself to achieve as much as possible in the service of God. If his "heart moves him" (Ex. 25:2), as we have seen, he can also make a private offering. If one gets up one morning, sees the sunrise, and feels that he must do something special for God, he can follow his instinct and bring a *korban*. Likewise, one who feels that he has committed a sin and needs atonement can visit the nearest *bama* and bring a *korban* as well. Whether it is a thanksgiving offering or an atonement offering, this offering is part of the person's divine service as an individual.

This service, which is available to Jews and non-Jews alike, can certainly bring a person close to God, but it has an inherent limit – the person remains within his limitations as a human being. This service derives from the individual's personal life, and therefore, even though it is has no restrictions, neither in the time nor in the place of the *korban*, the limitations inherent in this kind of divine service prevent one from breaking through to a higher level of intimacy with God.

The other way of serving God – the way that is unique to the Jewish people – is based on the principle that the individual does not remain where he is but, rather, is encouraged to transcend the limits and dimensions of his personality. In the case of the Jewish people, *korbanot* and divine service in general are connected with the need for the Tabernacle or the Temple. The Temple is not merely an instrument to enable man to approach God; it is also a two-way portal, a passage between the world and God. To be sure, there is the aspect of man turning upward to God from below in the Temple as well; but there is also the aspect of God turning downward from above. God dwells in the Temple, revealing Himself through it, as it says, "I will speak to you from above the Ark-cover" (Ex. 25:22).

These two ways of serving God are interconnected. In order for God to reveal Himself in the Temple, there must be an awakening of Israel from below. The place where God reveals Himself is the place where all eyes are raised to Him, a kind of beacon for religious devotion. God's revelation in the Temple does not happen automatically; it requires an awakening of the will, a certain element of longing. When such collective will does not exist – whether this is intentional or the result of some constraint – the portal remains closed.

The act of building a house for God may seem illogical at first. After all, "the whole world is full of His glory"! What is the point of establishing a physical place and instructing God to remain there? The truth is that while God is present everywhere, not every place contains a portal of revelation the likes of which we described above. In order for an earthly Temple to fulfill its purpose, our hearts must be open to it. When our hearts are not open to it, even the Temple cannot help us interact with God.

FORMING A CENTER

The aspirations of a large community of people are channeled through the Temple – not the personal longing of one individual, but the longing of the entire community of Israel. When the aspirations are concentrated together, this forms something that transcends the limits of the individual's personal will, and the Temple then becomes a place where God can come from above to dwell down below. From the combined aspirations of the community springs something that is not always visible to the eye. When the right connection is formed among Jews, there is a twofold, threefold, or ten thousand-fold magnification of what lies within each one of them. Batteries can be joined in such a way that each one remains separate, but they can also be joined in such a way that each battery adds its energy to the whole, strengthening it. This whole is necessary so that we not remain in a situation where each individual stands separately, so that the spiritual entity called "Israel" can continue to exist.

The standards of holiness required of the Jewish people as a whole are higher and stricter than those required of the individual, even if his heart has moved him. In the Temple, as in the Tabernacle, we attempt to raise the individual's standard to an entirely different level. Instead of the *bama*, which does not become invested with sanctity of place, a Sanctuary is built, around which the complete structure of the Holy and the Holy of Holies is formed. The Temple, which includes communal *korbanot* and other *korbanot* that cannot be brought as individual *korbanot*, was created in order to induce individuals to aspire to far more than they would when alone, to enable them to accomplish what they cannot on their own. When someone says, "What I have is sufficient for me," this is a sign that he is still stuck on the level of his private *bama*, whereas in the Temple he must transcend his own aspirations. The further he wants to go in the realm of the holy, the more is required of him in terms of purity, atonement, and ascent, level after level.

The Tabernacle and the Temple radiate inward, to the sacred, but at the same time exert an influence even on what is most profane. From the moment the Tabernacle is erected, it is meaningful not only when one is inside it, but even when one is just wandering in the wilderness. From the moment the Tabernacle is erected, the whole area around it receives a center, a focal point around which various camps are formed. The Levite camp and even the Israelite camp assumed sacred significance, and as a result, it became forbidden for certain people to be inside them. Once a Tabernacle exists, even one's own private tent is no longer what it used to be.

THE URGENCY OF ERECTING THE TABERNACLE

As we have seen, the proper order of things should dictate that only when everything is already in place – they have conquered the Land, appointed a king, and wiped out the Amalekites – is it possible to build the Temple. Such an order can only be actualized once the people arrive in the land of Canaan. In truth, after the People of Israel crossed the Red Sea, if they had acted properly, the construction of the Tabernacle/Temple would likely have been a thing of the distant future.

However, the construction of the Temple was not just a matter of convenience. If that were the case, the People of Israel would have postponed its construction four hundred years in anticipation of a period of quiet and calm – the optimal time to build the Temple. Instead, the construction of the Tabernacle began almost immediately.

The reason this happened is that after the sin of the Golden Calf, the reality faced by the People of Israel posed a great danger to them. If they had entered the Land immediately and begun to become involved in all that entry into the Land entails, it might have been possible to postpone the construction of the Temple. But the people faced forty years of wandering in the wilderness (at least according to those who maintain that the sin of the spies occurred before the construction of the Tabernacle), and during that time they could not be left in a scattered state, wandering about in an entirely individualistic manner. Sometimes, if one is not firmly raised higher than he aspired to climb, he is liable to descend much lower than he could have anticipated. The condition of the People of Israel at the time dictated the need for something that lay beyond their own spiritual dimensions. They needed an element that would raise them higher; for otherwise, they may not have reached the stage of entering the Land at all.

When it became necessary to warn the People of Israel not to sacrifice to demons, this was a sure sign that it was necessary to build the Tabernacle. In light of this, the construction of the Tabernacle became more than just an optional convenience; it became a necessity.

There is an adage that appears, in various forms, in many languages: "If you can't get through from above, try from below." But what should be done in the opposite situation, if you can't get through from below? Following the same pattern, it would seem that if you can't get through from below, you must get through from above. If the usual route is blocked, you must find another route; you must leap much higher than you had originally intended. In such a situation, one must ascend in holiness, in a way that is not at all commensurate with one's present level.

THE SILENT MAJORITY

The process that ultimately necessitates the "early" construction of the Tabernacle begins with the sin of the Golden Calf. When Moses descended Mount Sinai and said, "Whoever is for God, join me!" (Ex. 32:26), all the Levites rallied to him, and they killed many people – three thousand altogether. But this number is a small fraction of the total population of the People of Israel at the time. Assuming that these three thousand people represented those who created the Golden Calf and its hardcore followers, where was the remainder of the People of Israel?

It is clear that the majority of the people was not involved in creating the calf. If that is so, what happened? Apparently, once the calf was created, a large percentage of the people began to follow the calf along with everyone else. Moses was absent, and someone suggested that a calf should take his place. To be sure, the calf was not exactly like Moses, but this was an emergency; the calf would have to suffice. In this situation, even the seemingly levelheaded masses were drawn in to the allure of the calf.

The same question arises when Jeroboam sets up calves in Dan and in Bethel. What happened to all the good Jews who for so many years had gone to bring *korbanot* in the Temple? What happened to all those who learned Torah from Samuel, from David and Solomon? Until Jeroboam's time, there was a long period in which idolatry became taboo. King Saul took the first major steps, clearing the country of all sorts of idolatry, and David and Solomon continued on this path after him. This period of devoutness lasted for a relatively long time; yet when the calves are made, there is no popular rebellion. Everyone is simply swept along.

The reality, then, is that whenever there is a calf, there is a crowd – including many average individuals – that is ready to follow it. If that is the case, the Temple can no longer be delayed; it must be constructed immediately. In order to avoid a spiritual vacuum, in order to allow God to "dwell in their midst," the people must fulfill the command to "make Me a sanctuary" (Ex. 25:8) – precisely in the wilderness, and precisely during the forty years of wandering.

Leviticus

Vayikra
In loving memory of Yosef ben Rachamim, z"l
Family Vaturi

Tzav
In loving memory of Shoshanah bat Yosef, z"l
Family Vaturi

Shabbat HaGadol
Jacob Balass Trust/Frank Benjamin
In memory of Jacob Ballas, z"l, of Singapore

Shemini
In loving memory of Ze'ev Gedaliah ben Yitzchak Michael, z"l, Nissan 25, 5772,
a man who valued closeness to God and His Torah and eagerly awaited the final
redemption as foretold by our holy prophets.
Michael Schweitzer

Tazria and Metzora
In honor of Edward Lee's Bar Mitzva in London, May 1972

Aḥarei Mot
Dedicated to the memory of our late parents, Hans and Lala Diestel,
Hetty and Bernard Lever... with love, affection, respect and honor.
Gus and Judy Diestel

Kedoshim
With our warmest personal wishes to and great respect for
Rav Adin and Sarah Steinsaltz, may they be blessed with good health
and long life together, to continue their wonderful work.
It is our honor to be able to dedicate this parasha for our children and grandchildren.
Families: Goldschlager, Slonim, Gerschman & Sable

Emor
In memory of Michael Fox
My husband, my lifelong friend and a role model for so many,
both young and old, as an upright and faithful Jew.
Sheila Fox

Behar
In loving memory of Harriet, my dear wife, our mother and grandmother
Meyer Weitz and Family

Beḥukkotai
In honor of Yishai Yoseph ben Shlomo Zalman Moshe Halevi's Bar Mitzva
Ruth & Conrad, z"l Morris

Vayikra

THE BOOK OF HOLINESS

It is commonly said that the book of Leviticus deals with the laws of the *korbanot,* and indeed it does contain many of these laws. But the truth is that these laws also appear in Exodus, Numbers, and Deuteronomy, and even in Genesis, to some extent. What is more, while Leviticus itself does deal extensively with these laws, it is not devoted exclusively to them. If we had to connect Leviticus with the orders of the Talmud, we would say that, generally, it deals with material found in tractates Kodashim and Teharot. Most of the contents of these two orders appear in Leviticus, while a small part appears in Numbers. Additionally, Leviticus deals with a number of topics that are scattered throughout other books of the Torah as well, albeit in different contexts.

If, nevertheless, we must provide a general description of the book's theme, it is accurate to say that Leviticus deals with the various aspects of holiness. Holiness is found in all of the book's subjects, in the major principles as well as in the small particulars. This emphasis on holiness manifests itself linguistically as well: In no other book in all of Tanakh does the root K-D-SH (holy) appear so frequently.

Holiness is the context for all the subjects discussed throughout Leviticus. Even subjects that, at first glance, do not seem to pertain to the laws of holiness are included in Leviticus as part of the larger scheme of holiness and consecration in religious life. This holds true whether the subject is *korbanot* or matters of *tuma* and *tahara*; it holds true for the laws of forbidden sexual relationships in *Parashot Aḥarei Mot* and *Kedoshim*, and even for the interpersonal mitzvot. Thus, for example, the section on idolatry begins with: "Anyone of the People of Israel...who gives of his offspring to Molech shall be put to death," and ends with: "Sanctify yourselves and be holy, for I am God your Lord" (Lev. 20:1–8). Similarly, regarding forbidden foods, it says, "I am God your Lord who has set you apart from the nations. So you shall set apart the pure animals and birds from the impure...You shall be holy unto Me, for I, God, am holy, and I have set you apart from the nations to be Mine" (20:24–26).

Similarly, laws whose rationale appears, at first glance, to be related to law and order or to morality appear in Leviticus as deriving from the sphere of holiness. An example of this can be seen in the section on dishonesty: "God said to Moses, saying: If a person sins and commits a trespass against God by dealing deceitfully with his neighbor in the matter of an article left for safekeeping, or a business deal, or by robbery, or by defrauding his fellow" (Lev. 5:20–21). The case is that of one who robs his neighbor in one way or another, either openly or secretly. However, the Torah, in mentioning the obligation to return the stolen article, the withheld funds, or the deposit, focuses on another aspect of the act: "He shall bring his sin offering to God...And the Priest shall effect atonement for him before God, and he will be forgiven" (5:25–26). Beyond what he did to his fellow man, he committed "a trespass against God." This is a new factor, not a social factor but a kind of desecration. The sinner has desecrated something that was set aside as holy. Even interpersonal relationships are not discussed here from the standpoint of law and order or morality but from the standpoint of "a trespass against God."

Even the Ten Commandments, all of which are alluded to in *Parashat Kedoshim* (Leviticus Rabba 24:5), are viewed from a different angle, the special angle of the book of Leviticus.

DEFINITION OF HOLINESS

It is important to stress that if the general common denominator in Leviticus is the theme of holiness, then the definition of holiness here is not exactly the definition we would expect. Holiness is not only what one does or does not do in the Temple, but something that applies even in places that have nothing at all to do with the ritual holiness of the Sanctuary or the Temple. It is a spiritual quality in its own right, beyond the kind of holiness described by the Maharal, for example, who speaks of holiness as the aspect of standing apart from everything or as a type of detachment (*Tiferet Yisrael* 11). Here, holiness diverges from the ritual sphere and takes on a different meaning: something special or unique.

From the book of Leviticus it follows that if an ordinary person steals, he, too, impinges, somehow, on holiness. To defraud someone is "to commit a trespass against God." This may seem strange; what does stealing from one's neighbor have to do with God? However, the Torah insists that such a person has committed sacrilege, and therefore must make amends before God.

What all this adds up to is that holiness is a type of general refinement, perfection, and exaltation, not necessarily limited to one particular point or area. Holiness here means that there are certain acts that are so foul that one embarrasses not only himself, but God as well upon committing them.

When one refrains from committing a transgression, it may be because one simply has no desire to commit such an act. In contrast, it may be that one is able to refrain from committing the transgression despite his desires. The Midrash articulates this line of thinking: "I do have a desire for such and such, but what can I do, since my Father in heaven has ordered me to abstain?" (*Sifra, Kedoshim* 9). The general conception of holiness is, in a certain sense, "I have no desire" – I cannot do it; I have an aversion to such a thing; it is simply out of the question for me to stoop to such a base, low level and commit such a sin. A story is told of a *rebbe* who claimed regarding one of his Hasidim that the reason he does not sin is simply pride. For this Hasid, it seemed degrading that an exalted personality such as he should demean himself through sin.

There is a clever (though certainly not straightforward) explanation of the verse, "The wicked crows (*hillel*) about his unbridled lust" (Ps. 10:3): Does a wicked man resemble the great sage Hillel? The answer is that even a man as distinguished as Hillel the Elder is capable – when obsessed with "unbridled lust" – of bringing himself to a state that is so indecent that he reduces himself to the level of the basest of individuals. This can be seen in the case of all sorts of desires. A person can be distinguished, admirable, respected, and highly regarded; but when he is overcome with passion – suddenly, all the eminence peels off him, he debases himself and becomes a kind of four-legged creature, or even something lower.

When it says, "You shall be holy unto Me, for I, God, am holy" (Lev. 20:26), the Torah is talking about the glory of Israel: You are holy, you are uplifted; therefore, you must not degrade yourselves and sink so low. The requirement of holiness in Leviticus is thus a type of *musar*. There are children on whom this type of *musar* works very well. One need not hit his child or punish him, but merely say to him, "This kind of behavior is beneath you." Much of what is written in Leviticus about transgressions is based on this approach: "Is it possible that you would do such shameful things?"

The Midrash says that the meaning of "ascending and descending on it (*bo*)" (Gen. 28:12) is that Jacob's image was engraved on the Throne of Glory, and the angels were comparing the ideal image of the heavenly Jacob with his image as it actually appeared below (Genesis Rabba 68:12).[1] This is a very demanding comparison: Does Jacob's actual appearance correspond to his ideal image, to what he is capable of being? Likewise, the requirement of "You shall be holy, for I am holy" derives from the comparison of one's heavenly image with one's earthly image, as though to say: This is your source, this is your root, you originate from this ideal image; in light of this – how can you possibly sin?

That is why we say each morning: "My God, the soul that You gave me is pure." We start from above and continue below. It could be that during the day a person is occupied with all sorts of mundane things; nevertheless, he remembers that "the soul that You gave me is pure." The Talmud states that just as the beams of a person's house testify against him, so do his own limbs and his own soul (Taanit 11a). The Baal Shem Tov writes, "A person's own soul will teach him," meaning that one feels embarrassment when facing his own soul, his own heavenly image. In the same way, one is embarrassed in the face of the injunction, "You shall be holy unto Me."

---

1. According to this interpretation in the Midrash, *bo* refers not to the ladder but to Jacob.

The requirement of holiness is at the essence of a Jew's very existence. Hence, there are transgressions regarding which the Torah says, "I will cut him off," or "that soul shall be cut off." After a person does such things, there is no longer justification for his soul to continue its existence. Such a person removes himself from the circle of holiness and ceases to be part of the community of Israel, not just socially, but spiritually as well; he is lost in the sense that he is cut off from the source of life, from all that justifies his existence – precisely because it is holy.

EXCEPTIONAL RESPONSIBILITY

Our sages often refer to the book of Leviticus as *Torat Kohanim* (the Law of the Priests). Though it does contain many such laws, it is certainly not devoted exclusively to the Priests and their service. Nonetheless, the message that "You shall be My special treasure among all the peoples … You shall be to Me a kingdom of Priests and a holy nation" (Ex. 19:5–6), which is the essence of Israel's chosenness, appears in Leviticus with special emphasis. The Jewish people is "a kingdom of Priests" both literally and figuratively. We are, in a sense, the Priests of all mankind, with all the obligations that derive from this calling.

The prophets, too, speak of the exceptional responsibility that goes with being chosen as "a kingdom of Priests." Regarding other nations, for example, God does not always make a strict accounting, whereas regarding the People of Israel it says, "You alone have I known of all the families of the earth – that is why I will call you to account for all your iniquities" (Amos 3:2). This is not only because the greater the person, the greater his fall, and the higher his level, the lower his descent. Rather, there is improper behavior that an ordinary person can get away with, whereas a Jew is held up to much more intense scrutiny; if he does these things, it is considered a major blemish.

This distinction can be seen in connection with prophecy. The Talmud says that "The Holy One, Blessed Be He, causes His Divine Presence to rest only on one who is strong, wealthy, wise, and humble" (Nedarim 38a). These qualities are required only of the prophets of Israel, and they are connected with the holiness that is unique to Israel. In the case of all the other nations, a person who possesses none of these positive traits can still become a great prophet.

Bilam not only is not an admirable individual, he is a truly base creature. Nevertheless, the Midrash relates that Bilam's level of prophecy paralleled that of Moses himself: "Never again has there arisen in Israel a prophet like Moses – in Israel there has not arisen, but among the nations there has arisen. And who is that? Bilam son of Beor" (*Sifrei*, Deuteronomy 357). Bilam is the only prophet from among the nations of the world whose prophecy is included in the Torah. The daily morning prayer service begins with a verse spoken by him – "How fair are your tents, O Jacob, your dwellings, O Israel" (Num. 24:5) – and his prophecy reached to the end of days, to the end of all generations. Why is this so?

Apparently, in the case of nations of the world, prophecy is simply a matter of talent. The prophet can be a philosophical genius but totally incompetent in everything else, just as a peerless mathematician can be clueless in other fields of study. Among the nations, prophecy is a gift, a special quality that remains isolated from the rest of the prophet's essence. In the case of Israel's holiness and spiritual essence, however, such a thing could not be; there cannot be an exalted personality whose exaltedness is sullied.

This same point is echoed in the saying, "If someone tells you, 'There is wisdom among the nations,' believe it; 'There is Torah among the nations,' do not believe it" (Lamentations Rabba 2:13). Wisdom can be found anywhere. One can learn even from an animal – as it says, "Who teaches us by the beasts of the earth" (Job 35:11) – and certainly one can learn wisdom from someone who is not a member of the covenant. A person can be both a great mathematician and an adulterer, but it cannot be that someone who transgressed the laws that are found in *Parashot Aḥarei Mot* or *Kedoshim* is also a true Torah scholar. Torah, which belongs to the kabbalistic category of "wisdom of holiness," can be found only where there is holiness – and holiness does not go together with baseness. The requirements of holiness are much stricter.

Tzav

PIGGUL

Although the book of Leviticus is not the longest book in the Torah in terms of the number of its verses, it is the focus of the largest number of halakhic interpretations. There are halakhic interpretations on almost every verse in the book, despite all the repetition it contains. From the verse, "The sin offering and the guilt offering have exactly the same laws" (Lev. 7:7), for example, a multitude of halakhot is derived.

One of the more important passages in *Parashat Tzav* is the following:

> Whatever is left of the flesh of the offering must be burned in fire on the third day. If the person bringing the offering eats it on the third day, [the offering] will not be accepted. It is considered *piggul*, and it will not be counted in his favor. Any person who eats it will bear his guilt. (7:17–18).

From a halakhic standpoint, this verse is very important. Major portions of tractates Zevaḥim and Menaḥot deal with laws that derive from this passage, and there are several tractates in the Talmud that one cannot study without quickly encountering one of these laws, namely, *piggul*.

Piggul is created when, during one of the *korban* procedures, a person intends to eat or burn any part of the *korban* after the prescribed time limit for doing so. However, even though the law of *piggul* is derived from this verse, the verse itself technically does not speak of such a case at all; it deals only with *notar*, that is, what was left over from the *korban* and not eaten within the prescribed time limit. The actual law of *piggul* is derived from the words "it will not be counted (*yeḥashev*) in his favor." The use of the root Ḥ-SH-B implies that the disqualification of *piggul* relates to thought and is entirely a matter of intention. To turn a *korban* into *piggul*, one need not perform any action; the thought alone suffices.

At first glance, this law seems very strange. What kind of transgression is this? People have many illicit desires, but why would a Priest want to disqualify a *korban* by improper intention? Doing so brings neither physical nor spiritual enjoyment, so why would anyone ever want to do this?

The truth is that we have no record of a Priest ever rendering a *korban piggul*. In order to accomplish this, the Priest would not only have to be exceedingly wicked, but a Torah scholar as well, an unlikely combination of traits.

In the book of Amos, however, the prophet rebukes Israel: "Come to Bethel and transgress, to Gilgal and multiply transgression. Bring your offerings in the morning, your tithes on the third day. Burn thanksgiving offerings of leavened bread and proclaim freewill offerings loudly" (4:4–5). This is surely not a serious invitation but a sarcastic rebuke for sins committed there. He rebukes them: At the thanksgiving offering, you burn the leavened loaf instead of giving it to the Priest; instead of bringing the *korbanot* within their prescribed time limits, you bring them "on the third day." Why would a person want to burn the thanksgiving offering's loaf of leavened bread, or to bring *korbanot* precisely "on the third day"? Is it only out of contempt? As a rule, today as in the past, when people rebel against traditional religious practices, there is usually some kind of benefit or convenience to be gained by doing so. But what can be gained from bringing *korbanot* "on the third day"?

BURNING THE *KORBAN*

The answer to this question can be found in a different verse in this *parasha*: "Every meal offering brought by a Priest shall be a whole offering: it shall not be eaten" (Lev. 6:23).

There is a great deal of discussion surrounding this verse, but what clearly emerges from it is that the Priest does not partake of his own meal offering; the Priest's meal offering – including its remnant – is burned entirely.

The simple reason for this is that one cannot bring a *korban* and partake of it as well. When one brings a meal offering, while a Priest may eat most of it, nevertheless, the person who brought it did so without receiving personal gain. If a Priest were to partake of his own meal offering, it would be as though he gave something to God and then sat down to enjoy it, which is the very antithesis of the essence of a *korban*.

The act of giving is fundamental to a *korban*, and it even appears that the more sacred the *korban*, the less anyone may derive benefit from it. The inner *korbanot* are consigned to be burned entirely, and the less sacred the *korban*, the more the one who brings it may benefit from it. These include the firstborn, the tithe, and the Pesaḥ offering, which are the least sacred offerings, and of which the one who brings the *korban* eats most of the meat.

The burnt offering is, for the most part, consigned entirely to the fire. One brings a burnt offering in one of two circumstances: one violated a positive commandment (one is not obligated to bring the *korban* in such a case, however), or one's heart moved him to bring God a gift.

In addition, a proselyte, besides undergoing circumcision and immersion, brings a burnt offering of fowl. The reason he must bring fowl specifically is that a burnt offering of fowl is the only *korban* that is truly burned entirely, of which absolutely nothing remains. In the case of a burnt offering of cattle, the Priest is entitled to some benefit – he receives the hide. A burnt offering of fowl, however, though it is not a large offering – one turtledove or a young common dove – it is burned in its entirety.

By contrast, a peace offering is very easy to bring. The parts that are burned on the Altar are generally of no interest to the one bringing the *korban*, simply because they are forbidden in any case: The fat and the blood belong to God. When one brings a peace offering to the Temple, he basically enjoys a good meal. One sits in Jerusalem, eating fine meat, and what is more, one can take pleasure in the fact that the meat he is eating is sacred as well. What more could he desire? He has everything that he needs: sanctity, purity – and food. Such a *korban* resembles a festive Shabbat meal, whose consumption fulfills the mitzva of enjoying Shabbat. One can take pleasure not only from the delicious meal, but from the knowledge that he is performing a great mitzva as well – what more does one need?

CURTAILING THE CONVENIENCE

For this reason, the laws of *korbanot* contain an additional element – the laws of *piggul* and *notar*, which set time limits for partaking of the *korban*. The purpose of these laws is to ensure that the *korban* does not turn into a game, and that the consumption of the *korban* does not turn into a picnic. The time limits serve to curtail the element of convenience inherent in certain *korbanot*. Hence, the thanksgiving offering, which a person brings when he is in a good mood, is allocated an especially short time frame: only one day and one night. If a person experiences a miracle and wants to give thanks to God, he goes to the Temple and brings a *korban*. But once he does this, he must finish it as quickly as he can, for otherwise the meat will assume the status of *notar* and become unfit for consumption. Not only must he prevent this from happening, but he may not even think of consuming it after the time limit.

Amos said, "Come to Bethel and transgress, to Gilgal and multiply transgression" (Amos 4:4). What did they do there? In the Temple, there were limits that hampered people. But in Bethel and Gilgal, a person could plan a trip for the festival to Bethel, Gilgal, or Dan – all beautiful places to visit. He might plan to bring a large animal as a thanksgiving offering or a peace offering; the Priest will take his share, and he and his family can then stay a full week without having to worry about what to eat.

A *korban* is limited not only in that it cannot be eaten on the third or fourth day, but by the very fact that one may not entertain the thought of combining this religious ritual with some degree of pleasure. This is the essence of *piggul*, which, unlike *notar*, depends not on one's actions but on his thoughts. That is what happened in Bethel, Gilgal, and Dan: The people turned their holiday pilgrimages into extended vacations, furthering tourism and helping the local hotels. Instead of staying for only two days, they would stay for a week, enjoying the meat of the *korbanot*. They reasoned: Why should we hurry? Why create tension? Instead of this race to finish consuming the *korbanot*, let's change the regulation, so that a person will be able to bring a *korban* in a relaxed manner.

At the root of the matter, the obligation to bring a *korban* requires acknowledgement and understanding of the element of sacrifice that it entails. When one brings a *korban*, it is acceptable to relax to some extent, on the condition that this relaxation derives from a basic love of God and an awareness of His presence. But if this goes beyond relaxation, entering the realm of nonchalance and irreverence – that is where the problem begins.

A sacrificial act is fundamental to the process of bringing a *korban*, and this kind of act necessarily involves tension. The moment an attempt is made to relieve this tension, it is no longer a proper *korban*. This same reasoning can explain the concept of *piggul* as well. *Piggul* is not just a problem of bad intentions; it is about the attempt to make the process of bringing a *korban* more convenient. This *korban* is fundamentally flawed because the attempt to deprive it of the element of tension also deprives it of its essence – the burning, the dimension of the fire that burns within it continually.

We read in Tanakh of a "family feast offering" (1 Sam. 20:29); this is also the *korban* referred to in the verse, "The people, however, brought offerings upon the *bamot*" (1 Kings 3:2). These were not *bamot* dedicated to idolatry, but rather, *bamot* dedicated to God. Why, then, does Tanakh oppose the practice? The concern here is with this very same issue. Next to everyone's home there is a designated area for *korbanot*. A person would step outside his home, wash his hands, and announce: "Children, let us bring a *korban* today! We'll call our friends and bring a peace offering." This *korban* is dedicated to God in every respect: The animal is slaughtered, a blessing is recited, the blood is sprinkled, and everything that must be done is performed in sanctity and purity. Nevertheless, when a person brings these *korbanot* beside his home, partaking of them for as long as he desires, so that no piece of meat should, Heaven forbid, go to waste – the *korban* then loses its essence.

BURNING CONTINUOUSLY

These limits imposed on *korbanot* are not meant to needlessly make life difficult for people. They are simply an essential aspect of *korbanot*.

A *korban* is not just a matter of giving; it has an additional aspect: "A fire shall be kept continuously burning upon the Altar; it shall not be extinguished" (Lev. 6:6); "This is the law of the burnt offering. The burnt offering shall remain on the Altar's hearth all night until morning, while the fire on the Altar is kept going on it" (6:2).

This fire slowly consumes the parts of the *korban* throughout the night, until they are entirely consumed. This is not a public ceremony; on the contrary, it is a process that takes place precisely when the Temple is closed. Although some of the *korbanot* were burned during the day, most of them – especially on busy days – were burned at night, from the time of the daily afternoon *korban*, "all night until morning" – hours upon hours of Temple service done entirely in private. All the doors are closed, and several Priests regularly transfer the *korbanot* from the ramp to the Altar; and above, upon the Altar, they feed them into the Altar's main fire. The point of this service is that the Altar burns continuously. Whether a great ceremony is taking place, as in the *korban Pesaḥ*, or whether no one is present and no one sees, the Altar must always be aflame.

This theme of "a fire shall be kept continuously burning upon the Altar" pertains to the essence of the *korbanot*; and just as it pertains to physical offerings, so, too, does it apply to spiritual offerings.

A human being is in a constant state of burning. There is no extinguishing this burning; it has no end, and it continues day after day and night after night. In halakha, this concept is called *kayitz hamizbe'aḥ* – the requirement to provide burnt offerings for the Altar from public funds when the Altar is idle. The nature of the Altar is such that fire must burn continuously upon it, a *korban* must always be upon it; and even if no private individual brings a *korban*, the Jewish people as a community brings a *korban*, so that the Altar should never be without a burnt offering.

TWO PROBLEMS

These two concepts – (a) *notar* and *piggul* and (b) the continuous fire – are problems that are inherent to the life of a Jew who keeps the mitzvot.

The first problem is that of *piggul* and *notar*. The *korban* is disqualified not only when it is actually left over beyond the prescribed time limit, but even when one merely thinks about how much easier it would be if he were not so pressured. Even for a completely devout individual, it is natural to sometimes prefer that religious life be a little easier. Why is it difficult for many of us to get up in the morning and pray? Is it so painful? What bothers people is that it is a daily requirement, even when there is no time to pray, or when one is not in the mood – and this makes all the difference. The moment that one decides to change the rules and eat the *korban* on the third day, the Torah cuts in, "It is considered *piggul*, and it will not be counted in his favor. Any person who eats it will bear his guilt" (Lev. 7:18). One is taking something that was a *korban* and making a picnic out of it. If the intention is to make it easier, more convenient, more pleasant – "it is considered *piggul*"; it will not be accepted, it will not be counted.

The second problem is the continuous fire. To be sure, a person cannot live constantly in an elevated state of burning enthusiasm, and cannot tolerate a constant stream of momentous life events. Nevertheless, there is one aspect of our lives that must retain that constant spiritual high – the continuous fire. When one brings a *korban*, it must remain and burn upon the Altar. Although this may seem undramatic, we should remember that the continuous fire, which can burn quietly and in secret, must continue burning all day and all night. "A fire shall be kept continuously burning upon the Altar; it shall not be extinguished" (Lev. 6:6).

Shabbat HaGadol

The Shabbat immediately preceding Pesaḥ is known as *Shabbat HaGadol* – the Great Shabbat. The name is very old; it was certainly in use in the Middle Ages, although even then its meaning was not clear.

Some explain that *Shabbat HaGadol* was named for the greatness of the festival that follows it, which invests this Shabbat with special significance. Others interpret that the word *gadol* here should not be understood as an adjective but as a noun. In other words, it is the Shabbat of the *gadol* – the Shabbat on which the synagogue's greatest Torah scholar delivers a *derasha*. Some of the early commentators suggested a somewhat humorous explanation – that *gadol* refers to the length of the rabbi's *derasha*, which makes people feel as though this Shabbat were much longer than any ordinary Shabbat.

Since there is a certain calendric mobility in the Torah portions that are read throughout the year, *Shabbat HaGadol* does not have a fixed *parasha* that is read each year on this Shabbat. However, it does have a special *haftara* – Malachi 3:4–24 – which in many places is read each year on *Shabbat HaGadol*, and in some places is read only when *Shabbat HaGadol* falls on the day before Pesaḥ.

There are also several unique customs on *Shabbat HaGadol*, one of which is to read part of the Haggada in the afternoon, both as a reminder and as preparation for reading the Haggada at the Seder. In addition, as we noted earlier, the tradition in almost all Jewish communities is that the rabbi delivers a special *derasha* in the synagogue, generally on matters relating to the festival.

Only very few of the tens of thousands of *derashot* on *Shabbat HaGadol* deal with the central question of the *haftara*: What is its connection to Pesaḥ?

The third chapter of Malachi, like the entirety of this small book, contains prophecies on various subjects that do not fit together in a logical way, nor do they relate explicitly to the festivals. At first glance, it would seem that this *haftara* is associated with Pesaḥ because it contains general words of inspiration, which are connected with Pesaḥ in only a very general sense.

One possible answer is that the *haftara* is not connected specifically with Pesaḥ at all. Rather, the command, "Bring all the tithes into the storehouse, that there may be food in My house" (Mal. 3:10), is connected with the requirement of *biur hamaaserot*, which must be fulfilled by the day before Pesaḥ. This is the requirement to finish paying all agricultural dues in the fourth and seventh years of the seven-year agricultural cycle, and to recite the declaration of tithes in the Temple.

Thus, according to this explanation, the *haftara* is not connected with Pesaḥ itself but with a halakha that happens to relate to this time of the year. Indeed, the first day of Nisan was the beginning of the Temple's fiscal year, when people would bring to the Temple the new *shekalim*, and arrangements would be made for the whole system of *korbanot*, meal offerings, and Temple repairs for the coming year.

For this reason, there are communities whose custom is to read this *haftara* only in years when *Shabbat HaGadol* falls on the day before Pesaḥ, so as to recall the prophet's reproof precisely at the time when the mitzva was instituted.

This explanation fits especially well in light of the *haftara*'s first verse: "Then the offering of Judah and Jerusalem will be pleasing to God, as in the days of old and as in previous years" (Mal. 3:4). The prophet's statement served as a call to all those who did not give the tithes, and as an assurance of blessing to those who did fulfill the mitzva.

However, there is a certain difficulty with this interpretation. As a rule, *haftarot* relate much more clearly either to a subject or several subjects mentioned in the *parasha*, or to a certain period of the year (as in the three *haftarot* of admonition that are recited before Tisha B'Av and the seven *haftarot* of consolation recited after Tisha B'Av). In most cases, the *haftara* refers directly to a particular section of the *parasha*, or to an incident or law that is mentioned therein, whereas here the reference seems much more opaque. Moreover, there are many other places in the prophetic writings where the prophets refer explicitly to the Pesaḥ offering, and it would seem much more logical for those prophetic chapters to be read on *Shabbat HaGadol* rather than this chapter.

There is, however, another alternative. Although Pesaḥ is not mentioned throughout the bulk of the *haftara*, it does relate to Israel's redemption in general and to redemption that comes after dejection and distress in particular. Indeed, although most of the Haggada is devoted to remembering the Exodus, as the Torah instructs us to do, nevertheless, various sections of the Haggada allude to the redemption of the future as well. In addition to the role of Pesaḥ as a remembrance of past redemption, it also embodies a broader conception of the world order on a larger plane. The Haggada deals extensively with the suffering of the Egyptian exile, but it relates to redemption on a far grander scale as well.

This combination presents a view of history on the larger plane, that is, as a cycle that begins with oppression and suffering and ends with great redemption. According to the prophets, the sages, and the kabbalists, the redemption from Egypt is considered the prototype of the historical process. This amounts to a fundamental innovation compared with other conceptions, both ancient and modern, of human history. Some historians regard the course of human history as a path of decline, from the Garden of Eden to this world, which is becoming increasingly difficult and harsh. Others regard history as a directionless and purposeless cycle of growth and withering. To be sure, the Jewish worldview maintains that mankind began in the Garden of Eden, from which it was thrown into this world, with all of its distress and suffering. But this worldview also maintains that there is great hope for mankind, that ultimately the redemption will come, and with it the solution to the world's questions and suffering. This is a vision of a world that will ultimately reach not only the Garden of Eden but even higher.

The words of Malachi in this *haftara* likewise portray this grand design. Granted, Malachi begins with the complaints of the people of faith, who feel that precisely because of their faith, they lead difficult, restricted lives, and they ask questions that have no answers. As the prophet puts it, "You have said, 'It is useless to serve God. What have we gained by keeping His charge? We have walked about mournfully because of the Lord of Hosts'" (Mal. 3:14). This is a complaint not specifically about exile but about something much broader: divine concealment. Why is the world beset with the reality of, "Now we consider the arrogant happy. They have done evil and yet are built up; they have tested God and escaped" (3:15)? This question does not stem from one particular tragedy but, rather, relates to the course of life in its totality, a miserable life in which God does not seem to be involved at all. However, at the end of the prophecy, Malachi insists that days will come in which all the answers and solutions will be revealed, and the truth will be recognized. In those days, "you will come to see the difference between the righteous and the wicked, between him who serves God and him who does not serve Him" (3:18). And together with the answers and solutions, the time of reward will also come: "For you who revere My name, a sun of righteousness will rise, with healing in its wings" (3:20). This will be the time of clarification and response, when the righteous will ascend higher and higher and the wicked will descend lower and lower.

None of this pertains specifically to Pesah, although the account of the Exodus basically follows the same narrative arc, in which the wicked, brutal slave drivers are stricken and become wretched, while the downtrodden slaves emerge triumphant.

Thus, the end of the *haftara* reaches far back into the People of Israel's history: "Remember the teaching of My servant Moses, whom I charged at Horeb with laws and statutes for all of Israel" (Mal. 3:22), which takes us back almost to the starting point of our existence. The prophecy concludes with the end of days: "Behold, I will send you the prophet Elijah before the coming of the great and awesome day of the Lord" (3:23). With that, the great circle is closed: No longer shall there be exile followed by salvation, followed by exile, followed by yet another salvation but, rather, a final great redemption, "the great and awesome day of the Lord."

Indeed, at the conclusion of the Haggada as well, we recall with great enthusiasm the prophet Elijah, who symbolizes the great deliverance, the final redemption.

This prophecy is the final prophecy in Tanakh, and as such it contains the complete vision of Israel, from the first redemption to the final redemption. Although this chapter mentions the Exodus only indirectly, it expands that redemption into a vision for future generations, until the end of days. For all of these reasons, it is the perfect introduction to Pesaḥ.

Shemini

NO EXPLANATION

In *Parashat Shemini*, following the account of Nadav and Avihu, the section dealing with dietary laws begins – "to distinguish between the pure and the impure, between the living creatures that may be eaten and the living creatures that may not be eaten" (Lev. 11:47).

The distinction between the permitted animals and the forbidden animals raises a question that has occupied many commentators: What distinguishes the permitted animals from all the prohibited ones? Why is a hyrax worse than some other animal? What is wrong with camels and pigs? Why is sturgeon caviar worse than salmon roe caviar?

This question is not a new one, and similar questions can be asked regarding many other Torah laws. On this subject, however, the question is glaringly conspicuous. One of the reasons for this is the prominence of these laws in our daily lives and in halakha. Ever since we were exiled from our land and thus unable to fulfill most of the Torah's commandments, the dietary laws form a central part of Jewish life. Separating milk and meat, avoiding non-kosher foods, and using the appropriate silverware for each meal take up much of our time and attention.

There have been various attempts to resolve this question. Some have claimed that eating non-kosher animals is physically harmful, and from time to time claims arise regarding the danger of eating pork. It is true that pigs' meat is sometimes infected with worms, which can cause one who consumes the meat without sufficiently cooking it to contract a parasitic disease called trichinosis. But if that were the reason for the prohibition, instead of prohibiting pork the Torah could have given much better advice – that one must cook the meat thoroughly before eating it. Others have claimed that pigs are prohibited because they were used for idolatry, while still others have claimed the reverse, that pigs were not considered fit even for idolatry, so they are certainly unfit for our consumption as well.

There have been similar attempts to explain *tzaraat*, the leprosy-like condition described in the Torah. Maimonides, for example, explained that *tzaraat* is a type of disease. Ultimately, however, even he reached the conclusion that the *tzaraat* described in the Torah cannot be identified with any of the diseases known to him. On the contrary, especially in light of the fact that it can appear on houses as well as on flesh, *tzaraat* more closely resembles a miracle than a disease. In fact, Rabbi Shneur Zalman of Liadi writes that only supremely exalted individuals can be stricken with *tzaraat*, for only a spiritually exceptional person is worthy of experiencing such a miracle on his flesh (*Likkutei Torah, Tazria* 22b).

The same is true regarding *tuma* and *tahara*: no clear explanations exist. We do not know why hedgehogs, chameleons, lizards, and snails are *tamei*, while frogs are pure. There seems to be no reason why a frog, which is pure whether alive or dead, should be considered more exalted than a weasel or a mouse. However, the Torah distinguished between them, and we have no logical explanation for it.

Generally, attempting to justify mitzvot by portraying them as intended for physical or even spiritual benefit ultimately proves futile. This does not mean that such a justification is necessarily unfounded, nor does it mean that one should argue the reverse, namely, that pig meat is actually better than cow meat, only that God, knowing how good it is, nevertheless prohibited it to us. What it means is that this type of justification can never be the central consideration. It is better simply to rely on God and not attempt to give explanations.

TAMEI AND TAHOR

In the *parasha*, the words *tamei* and *tahor* appear in two completely different senses: in the list of animals that may or may not be eaten

(Lev. 11:2–23), and in the list of creatures that impart *tuma* when they are dead (11:24–46). These two lists are juxtaposed, even though there is no practical connection between them. Clearly, the statement, "it is impure for you" (11:4), regarding the camel and the hyrax has no relation – neither conceptually nor halakhically – to the statement "it shall remain impure until evening; then it shall be pure" (11:32) regarding the creeping things. The first statement denotes that the animal may not be eaten, while the second denotes that these creatures convey *tuma*.

Animals that may not be eaten are not, as a result, *tamei*. When they are alive, they certainly are not more liable to convey *tuma*; when they are dead, some are more liable to convey *tuma*, and some are less liable. For example, even though a snake may not be eaten, it is one of the creatures that do not convey *tuma*, neither when they are alive nor when they are dead.

Sometimes the two different senses of the terms *tamei* and *tahor* intermingle in the text, as in: "To distinguish between the impure and the pure, between the living creature that may be eaten and the living creature that may not be eaten" (Lev. 11:46); "Do not eat them, for they are things that must be avoided … and do not make yourselves impure through them, lest you become defiled through them" (11:42:43). Throughout the section, the laws of *tuma* and *tahara* and the dietary laws are intertwined.

This mixture demonstrates, first of all, that any attempt to explain these laws in a practical or rational way will prove extremely challenging.

But it is important to stress that this mixture is intentional, and signifies that although halakhically and functionally the two concepts have nothing in common, they nevertheless belong to one common idea. The terms *tamei* and *tahor* refer neither to the cause of things nor to the way they work but to the distance that must be kept from them. There are things that we avoid, and there are things that we do not avoid, and the distancing of the *tamei* – in all of the various senses of the term – is the subject of this section.

WHY WAS THE TORAH GIVEN?

In every generation and in every age, there are matters that a person simply accepts, without expressing any objections or casting any doubts. In

Maimonides' generation, for example, what was written in philosophy books was sacrosanct. In our generation, by contrast, philosophical literature causes no one to tremble, even philosophers themselves. To be considered a cultured individual, it is sufficient to pepper some of these ideas into one's conversation, without needing to acknowledge them as the basis of the world's existence.

Our generation is a generation of psychology rather than philosophy. Today, the study of the mind is what determines the essence of the human experience in the world. No one claims today that one should avoid pork because it causes intestinal worms, since all the mitzvot of the Torah can be explained as spiritual dimensions, relating to the human personality. According to this approach, the sole purpose of all mitzvot is to develop one's personality, each mitzva in its own way.

In this context it is worth quoting Yeshayahu Leibowitz, who said that the Torah was not given to mend the personality's torn pants. There is an element of truth in this. Whoever thinks that the exalted Torah was given so that man could attain peace of mind, lead a happy family life, love his fellow man, find favor in the eyes of society, or succeed in his affairs diminishes the Torah greatly.

It is true that one who is steeped in the world of Torah generally does not suffer corruption of character, but that is not the primary purpose of the mitzvot. On the other hand, the Torah would never command us to do something that clearly damages or destroys the body. The Midrash states, "Nothing that is evil descends from above" (Genesis Rabba 51:3). In other words, no mitzva would be given that causes damage, whether physically or spiritually. That said, it is still quite a stretch to then pin everything on this point and search for each mitzva's physical and personal benefit. God did not descend on Mount Sinai to provide information that can be found in a cheap psychology textbook – to explain how to improve one's life and how to behave better.

The psychological explanations for mitzvot are even worse than the medical explanations, which the Maharal criticized sharply, asking if it is conceivable that the Torah amounts to an article in a medical journal (*Tiferet Yisrael* 8). In his time, at least, medical and psychological texts were expensive and difficult to access. Nowadays, most of this information can be found easily, for free, on the Internet. If this is the case, could it be that for that purpose alone God Himself descended from the heavens?

A KERNEL OF TRUTH

To try to interpret the laws of *tuma* and *tahara* as expedients for personal development diminishes the Torah's glory. Moreover, one must also remember something that is true of the Torah in its entirety, from "In the beginning" to "before the eyes of all Israel." Although no individual can always uphold the truth, one must always remember that "the seal of The Holy One, Blessed Be He, is truth" (Shabbat 55a), and it can never be forged. One explanation for this, in the name of the Kotzker Rebbe, is that God's seal is truth because a seal must be something that cannot be forged, and truth is the only thing that cannot be forged: The moment it is forged, it ceases to be truth. It is possible to make forged peace, forged wisdom, or forged beauty, but there cannot be forged truth.

To be sure, there are times and situations in which it is impossible to appeal to truth. There are people who are not satisfied even when they are given a true explanation, because they are stubborn and short-sighted. Torah educators, from both earlier and later generations, have had to take this into consideration. Often the bald truth is not as exciting as a brilliant innovation, even if the latter idea may be faulty and questionable. Brilliant theories may appear to be the absolute truth, even when they are actually false. A person can live for twenty years on these falsehoods, satisfied with the lure of their cleverness, and never bothering to seek the actual truth.

When someone sinks to psychological or medical explanations, he need only peruse the section discussing the eight creeping things – for once, human psychology has little to say. What is the benefit of avoiding hedgehogs, chameleons, lizards, and snails? Why are the weasel and the mouse worse than the cat and dog? Why is it that earlier in the month of Nisan, this food is not harmful to one's body or soul, whereas a few days later, when the 14th of Nisan arrives, if one eats it, one's soul is cut off? Any attempt to impose artificial explanations on these laws – explanations relating to physical health or mental health – not only is problematic in itself but is a perversion of the truth, and that is truly unforgivable.

FOUR ENTERED THE *PARDES*

The Talmud relates that "four entered the orchard (*pardes*). They were Ben Azzai, Ben Zoma, Aḥer [Elisha b. Avuya], and Rabbi Akiva...Ben Azzai gazed and died...Ben Zoma gazed and was stricken...Aḥer gazed and became a heretic...Rabbi Akiva left in peace" (Ḥagiga 14b).

Maimonides explains that this "orchard" refers to the study of other wisdoms and other disciplines (*Laws of the Foundations of the Torah* 4:13; also see Rema, *Yoreh De'ah* 246:4), but the Vilna Gaon sharply criticizes this explanation. He argues that besides the fact that the explanation is fundamentally incorrect and constitutes an affront to the God of truth, it reduces the Torah to a mere antechamber leading to a great hall, a preparatory stage leading to the study of the other branches of knowledge. This interpretation sets as the highest level, as the goal, something that is not worth pursuing.

Rav Hai Gaon says that "it is not our way to cover up [the true meaning of] a matter and interpret it in a way that is not in accordance with the intention of the one who said it, as others do" (*Teshuvot HaGeonim* 99). When we set out to interpret words of Torah, we try to explain them strictly in keeping with the true intention of the one who spoke them.

This principle applies not only to methods of interpretation but also as a way of life. Sometimes, for various reasons, people build questionable, contrived explanations for the ideas in the Torah, reducing it to an antechamber that leads to a wretched hall. When, after several generations, a person finally understands that the glorious castle of his dreams is no more than a hovel, he asks himself: Was it all worth it?

Maimonides indicates that the lofty *Pardes* refers to Aristotle's metaphysics. However, several problems arise. First, this idea does not appear in the Torah at all. Second, it fails to explain the mysteries of the Torah. Finally, and most importantly, is it worth living and dying for this purpose? Is it for Aristotle's metaphysics that we sacrifice our entire lives?

And even if we argue that, in truth, whoever keeps the Torah and the mitzvot will succeed in his business dealings, in his marital life, and in his interpersonal relationships – still, is even this success worth living and dying for?

This idea can be seen, in the extreme, in the narrative sequence of the *parasha*. The *parasha* begins with the dedication of the Tabernacle, the fire that descends upon the Altar and the terrible tragedy of the sons of Aaron. On the day of the great revelation of the *Shekhina*, Aaron's two sons died "when they drew near before God" (Lev. 16:1), as it says, "I will be sanctified through those near to Me; thus I will be honored before the entire people" (10:3). And what follows the revelation of God's presence and the great tragedy that befell Aaron? What does the Torah offer as a reward? "These are the creatures that you may eat from among all the animals that are upon the earth" (see Rashi, Lev. 11:2). If the Torah commands all this simply for the sake of a diet – whether for the body or for the soul – then the dietary laws and their reward are truly not worth the cost.

When approaching the Torah, there is no point in considering the personal benefit to be gained, nor does one always find meaningful ideas. It is therefore good to recall the words of the Kotzker Rebbe to a man who came to him with questions about God: "A God who can be understood by anyone is not worth serving."

Tazria

A SIGN AND A WONDER

As it sometimes happens, this *parasha* is called *Parashat Tazria* even though practically all of it deals with matters relating to the *metzora*, while *Parashat Metzora* itself deals with those matters to a much lesser extent.

Maimonides writes that we do not actually know what *tzaraat*, as it is described in the Torah, is (*Laws of the Impurity of Tzaraat* 16:10; *Guide for the Perplexed* III:47). In modern Hebrew, the word *tzaraat* refers to leprosy, which may be what the Talmud calls "*baalei raatan*" (Ketubbot 77b). To this end, Maimonides writes that, according to his medical understanding, *tzaraat* does not resemble any known disease (*Commentary on the Mishna*, Nega'im 12:5).

Since this is not a medical matter, it becomes easier to understand the strangest part of this phenomenon – *tzaraat* on houses and garments. When it appears on human flesh, it is at least possible to think of *tzaraat* as a disease, but this is certainly not the case when it appears on inanimate objects. Moreover, houses and garments stricken with *tzaraat* are burned, a much harsher treatment than people who are similarly afflicted receive.

Another puzzle regarding *tzaraat* is the nature of its *tuma*, especially in comparison with other types of *tuma*. Generally, only living things that stopped living, either entirely or partially, can produce *tuma*. Indeed, among plants and inanimate objects, nothing is intrinsically *tamei.* Garments or other objects are generally only rendered *tamei*, but are not intrinsically so. In the laws of *tzaraat*, however, there exists an anomaly: A garment or house is itself an *av hatuma* (primary source of impurity), a phenomenon that is unique to *tzaraat*.

Maimonides' conclusion is that *tzaraat* is really not a disease. He says that *tzaraat* should be regarded not as an illness that is designated as *tamei*, but as "a sign and a wonder" that God uses to mark someone.

A DISCRIMINATING AFFLICTION

As we mentioned in the previous chapter, Rabbi Shneur Zalman of Liadi writes that *tzaraat* is an affliction that strikes only the most exalted individuals (*Likkutei Torah, Tazria* 22b). He cites the Zohar's statement that there are four spiritual levels that a person can reach, in ascending order: *enosh, gever, ish,* and – highest of all – *adam* (*Tazria* 48a). Similarly, the talmudic statement that "only you are called '*adam*'" (Bava Metzia 114b) is based on the assumption that *adam* is the noblest possible term for a human being. In light of this, it is curious that the term *adam* is used in connection with the mark of *tzaraat*: "If a man (*adam*) has on the skin" (Lev. 13:2); "If a *tzaraat* mark appears on a man (*adam*)" (13:9). The answer is that an ordinary person is not worthy of *tzaraat*. God does not bother to put a special mark on a person of no importance to show that he has acted improperly; that would be obvious even without the *tzaraat*. If a person is known to have serious faults and shortcomings, God does not need to let people know that he has sinned, nor does the person himself need a warning from heaven; he knows this on his own.

Only someone who is on a high spiritual level is eligible for and in need of such a sign. The Talmud says that the *tzaraat* marks are an "altar of atonement" (Berakhot 5b). Hence, to receive such a mark is truly indicative of a high level, of which the receiver must be worthy. In this connection, our sages note that in principle, the nations of the world should never be afflicted with boils. In practice, though, non-Jews nevertheless do experience this malady, so that they should not be able to claim that the Jews are "a nation of people afflicted with boils" (Genesis Rabba 88:1).

Clearly, not everyone who speaks slander gets *tzaraat*; for if that were the case, it would be very hard to find people who are *tahor*. The list of people in Tanakh who experienced *tzaraat* is quite impressive, rang-ing from Moses and Miriam to Naaman, Geḥazi, and Uzziyahu. When Miriam speaks slander, she gets *tzaraat,* and when Moses slanders Israel, he, too, perhaps deserves *tzaraat.* Naaman "was important to his mas-ter and held in high esteem, for through him God had granted victory to Aram. He was a mighty man of valor, but a *metzora*" (II Kings 5:1). Uzziyahu was a great king "who did what was right in God's sight," and "God made him prosper" (II Chr. 26:4–5). Geḥazi not only attended Elisha but was a great man in his own right (Y. Sanhedrin 10:2).

SPREAD OF THE MARK

Since *tzaraat* is not a disease but a mark and a sign, clearly there is something to learn from it. So let us focus on a few of the detailed laws connected with *tzaraat.*

The first point to consider is this: At what moment does an ordi-nary blemish become a *tzaraat* mark, which renders a person *tamei*? The surest sign that a blemish is considered *tzaraat* is that the mark continues to spread. If it stops immediately after it appears, it remains pure. This is true of all types of *tzaraat* described in the Torah. When a mark appears, this signals that perhaps there is something in the person's life that must be rectified. But it becomes *tzaraat* only when it begins to grow.

In the *Tokheḥa* section in Leviticus, in which God reproves the nation, we read: "If you remain indifferent with Me, I will be indifferent to you with a vengeance" (Lev. 26:27–28). Analogously, the preceding sec-tion states, "If your brother becomes impoverished and sells some of his hereditary land" (25:25), followed by, "If your brother becomes impover-ished and loses the ability to support himself beside you" (25:35), until finally, "If your brother becomes impoverished and is sold to you" (25:39).

The Talmud says that these verses in chapter 25 recount one story that unfolds progressively: A person can act improperly without real-izing this, in which case God then causes him to suffer a minor blow. If he still does not realize that he is in the wrong, God brings upon him another blow. And if he still does not realize this, God brings upon him yet another blow (Kiddushin 20a).

The same is true of *tzaraat* and its causes: So long as a person does not stop acting improperly, the *tzaraat* continues to spread. This applies to many different areas. Every person sins at some point in his life, for "there is no one so perfectly righteous on earth who does [only] good and never sins" (Eccl. 7:20). But when this happens, the sinner must recognize his error and stop himself from sinning further. If, however, he allows the stain to grow, it will become malignant *tzaraat*, which must be burned, destroyed, and eradicated.

"LET HER NOT BE LIKE ONE DEAD"

Another central element in the laws of *tzaraat* is that the mark contains dead flesh. The blood – the life – drains out, and therefore the flesh and the hair upon it turn white. When we say that "the wicked in their lifetime are called dead" (Berakhot 18b), this refers to *tuma*. A wicked person's *tuma* derives from the fact that he is essentially a dead creature. The element of death in the *tuma* of *tzaraat* shows that a person can die before coming to the end of his physical life; he can continue walking among us and nevertheless be a corpse. Like a corpse, a *metzora* conveys *tuma* by being together with someone or something under the same roof. The implication is that the *metzora* has already begun to die, and therefore even now renders everything that is under the same roof with him *tamei*. He may appear to be alive and kicking, but in truth he is a walking, breathing corpse.

It happens to people – both young and old – that they take upon themselves the fear of God, whether in a dramatic change or in a gradual process of spiritual growth. Such a person experiences a spiritual awakening and becomes like a new being. But this same person who was so inspired can sometimes begin to feel that he is partially dead. There is a respiratory disease called pulmonary fibrosis in which the lungs stiffen, becoming hard like wood. Even people who do not suffer from physical ailments can sometimes feel like a block of wood. A person who used to smile stops smiling; a person who used to be sensitive in so many ways suddenly turns cold.

Why does this happen? Justifications can always be found. A person may choose to be wary, thinking that to act otherwise would lead to sin or frivolity. One who continues along this path finds that each day another part within him dies. A person who was creative, or who was always joyful, bringing joy to others, now has become a sort of crushed creature, sulking in a corner. He dwells in isolation, outside the camp; it is a sign that something has gone wrong. In the past, he had experienced beauty, and it filled him with feeling; now, he feels nothing.

Such a person, who is dying little by little, continually reinforces this downward spiral by telling himself that the more dead he becomes, the more he deserves such a fate. He thinks that his dark, morose attitude to life is a form of devoutness, as we read in Malachi, "We have walked mournfully because of God" (3:14).

There is a concept in the Talmud that can often be difficult to comprehend: the notion of "movable realty" (Bava Kamma 12b). Slaves, for instance, are considered "movable realty" – they are human beings who possess the same legal status as one's land or one's house. In *Parashat Tazria*, we see something very similar – a dead man who continues to move around as if he is alive. The *metzora* is dead, and therefore conveys the same *tuma* that a corpse conveys. The only difference is that the *metzora* has not been buried yet. He is "movable realty." Holiness and all that stems from it are characterized by energy and vitality, while *tzaraat* is a form of death mark, sapping the very life force from the *metzora* who bears it.

"THE HEALTHY SKIN IS A SIGN OF IMPURITY"

Another law of *tzaraat* is very strange even in the context of other forms of *tuma*: "On the day that healthy skin appears on it, he becomes impure. When the Priest sees the healthy skin, he shall declare him impure. The healthy skin is a sign of impurity; it is *tzaraat*" (Lev. 13:14–15) – and the same law applies in all other types of *tzaraat* (see Rashi on 13:10). Normally, healthy flesh would seem to be a sign of recovery. But the Torah says the precise opposite: Healthy flesh is a sign of *tuma*, and he is sent back outside the camp.

The meaning of this law is that if vitality begins to emerge from the *tzaraat* itself, if the life that a person experiences flows from the mark, this, too, is a sign of *tuma*. Before, the *tzaraat* was merely a blemish; now, he is vitalized by it. This resembles a common sequence of events in a person's spiritual journey. At first, one simply cannot tolerate people who are unscrupulous regarding certain laws. He may react scornfully to people who neglect to perform the ritual washing of the hands, or who are careless when they trim their fingernails. As a result, he doesn't want to be around them, so he removes himself from society. After a while, this scorn for others becomes a source of vitality and pleasure for him. Before, he may have slandered others simply because he was haughty, whereas now all of his vitality comes from this vice. When one's fault becomes a flag and a banner, this is a much more serious problem. At first he viewed this character trait as a vice; now that he indulges in it enthusiastically, it is like putting a stamp of spiritual approval on an evil attribute. While beforehand he engaged in slander occasionally, now it is his whole life.

"The healthy skin is a sign of impurity." When healthy flesh begins to grow within the mark, when the affliction itself starts to become his life, this is not the vitality of recovery; it is vitality in which the affliction becomes a remedy, in which death becomes life.

SEEING ONE'S OWN FAULTS

An examination of the vices that, according to our sages, cause *tzaraat* yields a long list: haughtiness, arrogance, miserliness, *lashon hara* (spreading an evil report), and many others (see Tanḥuma, *Metzora* 10). Their common denominator is that they are all subtle evils. Regarding such subtleties it is appropriate that some kind of sign should be given from above, marking the sinner and indicating that the sin requires rectification.

Why is it so difficult to perceive these faults on one's own? Why does God have to mark them? It seems that these are all faults for which it is very easy to find some kind of justification, and that is why it is so difficult to identify them and rid oneself of them. When someone commits a blatant sin with full knowledge that what he is doing is wrong, he may experience pangs of guilt that prevent him from repeating such a sin. But what happens to someone who commits a sin and feels that it is a mitzva?

This is precisely the case of Miriam. Miriam wanted to give a reproof, feeling that her words should and must be said. Hence, if she had not been stricken with *tzaraat*, she would not have understood that she was out of line. The same is true of the other vices on the list. Haughtiness is often confused with pride, but they are actually quite different. Haughtiness pertains only to people of great stature, whereas pride can apply to anyone. A person can be covered in filth and be despised by all who meet him, and still think of himself as the greatest person in the world – this is the sin of pride. In the case of haughtiness, however, we are talking about someone who has ample reason to believe that he is on a high level, that he is a true *tzaddik*, but this perspective makes it impossible for him to see his own faults. Uzziyahu was a great king who was victorious in wars, built up the country, and was surrounded with honor and glory; he certainly had reason to believe that he was growing ever greater. The same was true of Naaman, "a mighty man of valor, but a *metzora*" (II Kings 5:1), who was the most important man in the kingdom.

The Mishna says, "A person may examine all *tzaraat* marks except his own" (Nega'im 2:5). What is the reason for this? After all, one may examine his own slaughtering knife; to be sure, a rabbi usually performs this examination, but this is only out of respect, or because a rabbi is generally more familiar with the relevant halakhot. One can also render halakhic decisions for oneself regarding the laws of *kashrut* if one has the requisite knowledge. In the case of *tzaraat*, however – where one would think that a certain measure of expertise would suffice – one may not examine the marks for oneself.

An additional oddity in the laws of *tzaraat* is the following: The Torah decrees that one must show the marks to a Priest, who must be the one to declare if the mark is *tamei*. But how does the Priest know? After all, not all Priests are Torah scholars! If, indeed, the Priest is unfamiliar with the laws of *tzaraat*, a Torah scholar stands at the Priest's side and instructs him to say "*tamei*" or "*tahor*" when appropriate (Nega'im 3:1). Thus, in a situation where the *metzora* is himself a Torah scholar, the following interaction is plausible: The *metzora* shows his *tzaraat* to the Priest; the Priest looks at the mark and asks the *metzora*, "Rabbi, what is the law in such a case?"; the *metzora* responds, "In my opinion, the mark is *tamei*"; and on that basis the Priest declares, "The mark is *tamei*," or, "The mark is *tahor*," rendering the person *tamei* or *tahor* respectively. According to halakha, this is a perfectly legitimate arrangement. Why, then, can't a person examine his own *tzaraat*?

The rule that "a person may examine all *tzaraat* marks except his own" applies not only to marks that appear on the skin; it applies even more to the marks that appear on the soul. This is because marks or faults, by their very nature, prevent one from seeing that he is afflicted. No matter how egregious the fault, one will still be certain that everything is all right. For him to become aware of his own fault, someone from the outside must tell him that he is *tamei*. For the same reason, one also cannot purify oneself. It is very difficult to determine when one's fault is gone, just as it is difficult to determine when it sets in. The nature of "marks" of this type is that they apply to the entire person, and it is very difficult to correctly assess them, especially when their meaning is unclear. Even after one knows what the signs are, the most one can say is: "There appears to be something like a mark on my house."

In all these matters, from slander and miserliness to haughtiness and the rest of the list, the question of ethical subtleties is so serious and complicated that there is almost no way of determining where the truth lies.

Speaking slander is a serious prohibition; on the other hand, it is a mitzva to expose hypocrites (Midrash Psalms 52). And if, by warning people that a certain person is a sinner, one performs a mitzva, it then becomes possible to constantly engage in the "mitzva" of slander. A circular pattern begins: If a person seems wicked, one may slander him; the more slander that is spoken about him, the more wicked he seems, and the more one may continue to slander him. Even in the Ḥafetz Ḥayim's book *Shemirat HaLashon*, there are a few sub-paragraphs discussing the various loopholes by which one may slander a person in a permissible manner. An ordinary person will likely never come to this, but a great man sometimes does.

Pride, too, can be a very important trait, and can serve a lofty purpose. The Talmud says that a Torah scholar should possess "an eighth of an eighth" of pride (Sota 5a), and of King Jehoshaphat it is written that "his heart was elevated in the ways of God" (II Chr. 17:6). Some people possess a small measure of pride – "an eighth of an eighth" – while others possess a larger, "elevated" measure.

"HE SHALL DWELL IN ISOLATION; HIS DWELLING SHALL BE OUTSIDE THE CAMP"

The remedy for *tzaraat* is that the *metzora* must remove himself from all categories. The *metzora* does not go to a doctor in order to be cured.

Rather, he is thrown out of the camp, out of human society – at most, he may interact with one other *metzora* – so that he should be entirely alone and engage in introspection.

Some of the ways in which people erroneously categorize themselves are based on social structures. If one constantly contrasts himself with others, then it will always be possible to find someone who is smaller and more contemptible than he is, someone who deserves to be vilified and slandered. It may then seem praiseworthy to oppress this other person physically, financially, and in any way possible.

When one is isolated with his *tzaraat*, one remains alone, and only then can one truly ponder one's own faults. Only after one is told that he is beset with faults and he is isolated with them can he begin to grapple with them until they disappear. If one remains isolated in this way for many years, it is because he has not dealt with his faults sufficiently. King Uzziyahu, for example, remained isolated until the day of his death, because he continued to feel that he was not at fault.

On the other hand, when a person is isolated, he is also liable to lose his sense of proportion. Hence, the Talmud says that one should not study alone, because one who studies alone is liable to err and then repeat the error over a long period of time (Berakhot 63b). Faults, however, relate to subtleties in one's personal conduct that cannot always be measured against someone else. What is more, another person's counsel is helpful only up to a certain point and cannot reach the root of the matter.

Once, a group of Hasidim approached the *Maggid* of Mezeritch and told him that they lived far away and needed someone to be their guide and teacher. They suggested Rabbi Menaḥem Mendel of Vitebsk (who in fact became a kind of successor to the *Maggid* after his death) and asked how they could determine whether he was the right man. What are the criteria by which to measure whether he is truly a great man? The *Maggid* responded, "Ask him whether there exists any method of avoiding pride. If he gives you such a method, you will know that there is no substance to him." When they posed the *Maggid*'s question to Rabbi Menaḥem Mendel, he answered, "What can I tell you? One person might wear sackcloth and filthy clothing, and his heart might still be full of pride, whereas someone else may walk erect and dress elegantly, yet his heart may be broken inside him. There is no method for this."

There are some ailments for which a remedy exists, and there are some for which this is impossible. One who has become *tamei* by contact with a corpse must go to the Priest in order to be purified; one who has a different problem must go to the elders and sages for a solution. In the case of *tzaraat*, however, if one is already great enough to receive such an affliction, this type of treatment does not help him. Indeed, the *metzora* does not go to the Priest to be cured; he goes to the Priest only after he is cured, so that he should look at the mark and issue a ruling. In all the stages of the process that precedes this ruling, even the Priest cannot offer him any help.

The only recourse for the *metzora* is to sit alone. He must keep sitting for as long as it takes to discover what is wrong and to set things right. The *metzora* is sent out to think, to relieve him of his preoccupation with business, to stop him from giving public sermons. Until he rectifies his problems on his own, he remains a *metzora*, and if the mark intensifies, his *tzaraat* spreads.

To remain alone is one of the best ways to attain self-rectification. One begins to reflect more and more on oneself and on one's path, the outer shells of one's personality begin to fall off, and sometimes parts of a person that were hidden behind these shells are revealed.

In the course of Jewish history, mainly in the time of the First Temple, there were many prophets, all of whom were extraordinary personalities who performed wonders in heaven and on earth, and yet none of this helped avert the destruction of the Temple and the exile. People sat and listened to the prophets and exclaimed, "What a wonderful *derasha*! What language! What Hebrew! What a pleasure to hear!" (see Ezekiel 33:30–32) – and then they went to sleep. Only during the transition between the First Temple period and the Second Temple period can one see a change in Israel's attitude toward the prophets. During the Second Temple period, there was a fundamental change for the better – Judaism began to deal with other matters. Why did this happen?

Apparently, the period of destruction and exile, the period characterized by the verse, "How does the city sit solitary" (Lam. 1:1), gave better moral instruction than all of the prophets combined. Apparently, solitude is incredibly effective. Then as now, people feel complacent, as long as they are in their own place, with an army to protect them and diplomatic relations with their neighbors – whether these neighbors are the Assyrians and the Egyptians or the Americans and the Russians – and with a great deal of money to build palaces across the country, all in accordance with national protocol. When the prophet comes and cries out in protest – it is easy to ignore him. But seventy years of "How does the city sit solitary" accomplished what all the prophets were unable to do.

Parashat Tazria does not conclude with the *metzora*'s complete rectification; only in the next *parasha* do we reach this stage. In this *parasha* we are still dealing primarily with the "isolated *metzora*," a *metzora* who has been given a warning. In the next *parasha* we learn how one who has gone through this entire period, who has experienced all that he needs to experience, can eventually make a full recovery.

Metzora

"KNOWLEDGE" REFERS TO THE ORDER OF TEHAROT

This *parasha* deals primarily with laws of *tuma* and *tahara*: *tzaraat* on people and on houses and the *tuma* of a *zav* and a *zava*[1] and of a menstruant woman. Whoever studies these subjects in detail discovers – as Maimonides writes in his introduction to the Order of Teharot – that even if he were to learn the laws of *tahara* a thousand times, he still would not know them, since they are so complex, complicated, and interconnected. The principles of the laws are not so complicated, but the details are so intricate that they are almost impossible to absorb.

Commenting on the verse, "There shall be faith in your times, strength, salvation, wisdom, and knowledge" (Is. 33:6), the Talmud states, "'Faith' refers to the Order of Zera'im; 'your times' refers to the Order of Moed; 'strength' refers to the Order of Nashim; 'salvation' refers to the Order of Nezikin; 'wisdom' refers to the Order of Kodashim; 'knowledge' refers to the Order of Teharot" (Shabbat 31a).

According to this interpretation of the verse, there appears to be a progression in the level of difficulty of the respective orders. The first orders, including the Order of Nezikin, are considered relatively easy to learn and understand, while the last two orders are

---

1. A *zav* or a *zava* is a person who experienced an abnormal discharge or flow, and is thus rendered *tamei*; see Leviticus 15.

notoriously difficult. This can be seen in the Talmud, where R. Aḥa asks a question relating to damages, and he is told, "When we get to [Tractate Zevaḥim] – ask your question there" (Bava Metzia 109b). In other words, the difficult questions are reserved for Zevaḥim, the first tractate in the Order of Kodashim, while the easy questions are asked in Nezikin. Now, in comparison to Teharot, even Kodashim seems simple and uncomplicated. It is virtually impossible to explain all the detailed laws of *tuma* and *tahara*, and it is even difficult to map out even a general framework for them.

Why are the orders of Kodashim and Teharot so difficult? The reason is that in the other orders, it is possible to follow the logic that guides the discussion, even without a strong knowledge base. Since the main line of thought is usually straightforward, it is possible to predict what will happen next and what the subject of the next discussion will be. When studying Kodashim, it is impossible to find the path within the maze. Even if one knows what the law is in the case of a guilt offering, for example, one cannot infer from this what the law will be in the case of the sin offering. It is very difficult to point to an inner logic within the various topics. In Teharot, the situation is similar. There exist review books that contain tables and charts explaining the laws of *tuma* and *tahara*, and it is plain to see that there is not even one guiding principle within these books, not only for the general categories of *tuma*, but even for the various details within each unique type of *tuma*. Thus, for example, there are aspects in which the *tuma* of a *zav* is stricter than the *tuma* of a corpse, whereas in other aspects the *tuma* of a corpse is stricter than even the *tuma* of a *metzora*.

One thing is clear: *Tuma* has nothing to do with uncleanness, a common misconception. It is not without reason that the concept of *tuma* does not exist in other languages, and that includes even related languages such as Aramaic. In the Aramaic Targumim, the usual translation for *tamei* is *mesaav*, a word that serves as the translation of *melukhlakh* (unclean) as well. Apparently, in Aramaic there is no word that corresponds precisely to the term *tamei*, and the same is true in English and other languages. In other languages it is always necessary to explain the term *tuma* with several other words, as it has its own distinctive character that does not exist in those languages.

Throughout history, and especially in recent generations, people have tried to explain that the laws of *tuma* and *tahara* are related to hygiene and physical health. These explanations are wrong, both in their general thrust and in their details. Even a superficial analysis of the laws of *tuma* is enough to demonstrate clearly that these explanations are off the mark.

For example, one might have thought that the *metzora* is sent outside the camp so that he should not infect others. But a study of the detailed laws reveals that, as Maimonides stated (*Commentary on the Mishna*, Nega'im 12:5), there exists no disease that fits the description of *tzaraat* in the Talmud and in halakha. Indeed, such a disease would be a scientific impossibility, and thus it is certainly not contagious.

Maimonides' conclusion is that *tzaraat* is actually a miraculous event. We probably have no idea at all what *tzaraat* on houses is or what *tzaraat* on garments is, and even the *tzaraat* that appears on people cannot be classified as a disease. In fact, our sages explain that, in principle, the nations of the world should never be afflicted with *tzaraat*, because essentially the whole matter of *tzaraat* pertains to Jews alone. However, in practice, they, too, get *tzaraat*, so that they should not say to the Jews: "You are a nation of *metzora'im*" (Genesis Rabba 88:1).

There are also various esoteric explanations regarding *tzaraat*, and their common denominator is that *tzaraat* has nothing at all to do with hygiene.

TUMA AND TAHARA – LIFE AND DEATH

It is possible perhaps to nevertheless attempt to give a very general explanation for the entire framework of *tuma* and *tahara*.

Throughout the Torah, from Genesis onward, the world is divided into two poles: life and death, and correspondingly, good and evil: "life and good," "death and evil" (Deut. 30:15). These matters are presented to us as the two extremes of existence, and every other element of existence falls on the spectrum between these two poles.

Death is presented in our literature not as a normal, natural phenomenon, but as a result of sin. Jewish thinkers throughout history have written that sin and death therefore are forever intertwined. The connection between them appears, for example, in the following interpretation:

On the words "engraved (*ḥarut*) on the Tablets" (Ex. 32:16), our sages expound, "Do not read '*ḥarut*' (engraved) but '*ḥerut*' (freedom), for no man is truly free unless the Angel of Death has no power over him… and as a result of their idolatry [at the sin of the Golden Calf] the Angel of Death came upon them" (Eiruvin 54a).

Likewise, the relation between *tuma* and *tahara* can be explained on the basis of this division. By way of analogy, it can be said that the creation of *tuma* resembles the production of a magnetic field. A magnetic field is produced when a drastic change occurs in an electric field. One of the ways this can happen is when an electric current that is moving through metal suddenly stops, in which case magnetization occurs. The new phenomenon is produced at the point of change, whether it is change from one extreme to the other or a more limited change. Similarly, *tuma* is produced when the complete current of life within an entity is stopped, whether in its entirety or in only one respect. Take, for example, the *tuma* of a corpse. This *tuma* occurs not because the corpse is not alive, nor because it used to be alive, but because it used to be alive and then this condition suddenly stopped.

What also emerges from the notion of the connection to life and death is a principle that applies throughout the laws of *tuma*. The stronger the current of life, the more intense the *tuma* will be if and when that life is stopped and cut off. The more life force that exists in an entity, the more intense the *tuma* generated by the negation of that life force will be. Conversely, the less life force that is in an entity, or the lower the level of its life, the less the *tuma* generated by the negation of its life force will be. We may not be able to explain all the minor questions of the laws of *tuma* and *tahara*, but this theory at least helps explain the overarching structure of these laws, in a general sense.

According to Teharot, the most severe form of *tuma* is that of a corpse. This is because when a person dies, the cessation of the current of life is the most drastic cessation of *tahara* possible. And when the deceased is a Jew, the *tuma* reaches its maximum height. When the deceased is not a Jew, the essence of his life was not quite so high, so the *tuma* generated by the cessation of that life is similarly less. This explains the seemingly paradoxical fact that a deceased Jew conveys *tuma* more than a deceased non-Jew does, and that a deceased human being conveys *tuma* more than a dead animal does. A deceased Jew conveys *tuma* more than a non-Jew because the life current that was stopped was on a higher level, and for the same reason, a deceased non-Jew conveys *tuma* much more than a cow does.

On a related note, not everything that dies conveys *tuma*. Creatures that we consider to lack a life force even when alive do not become *tamei* upon their death. According to the Talmud (Eiruvin 13b), a dead snake does not convey *tuma*. This is strange, as we usually think of a snake as the lowest animal in the world. Yet a snake does not convey *tuma*, neither when alive nor when dead. In truth, this should not be so surprising; a dead snake does not convey *tuma* because its life force is not sufficient enough to generate *tuma*. *Tuma* is produced by a fracture, by the tension of the sudden contrast between complete vitality and death. But when a creature is inherently insignificant, its death, too, is insignificant and does not generate *tuma*.

The basic concept is that *tuma* accompanies death or crisis, whether it is big or small; but while the entity is complete and healthy, it does not become *tamei*.

A simple example of this is the *tuma* of the menstruant woman. This *tuma* is connected to the natural destruction of life that is part of the woman's menstrual cycle. This is destruction not of actual life but of the lost potential for fertilization. As a result, the actual unfertilized egg cells that could have developed into new life are destroyed and flushed out of the body, and *tuma* results. It is still a normal occurrence and not considered an illness, yet it is connected with this same element of destruction – a partial form of death – and this, too, results in *tuma*.

A similar example is the *tuma* that results from a seminal emission. Even in the context of marital relations, and even if the relations result in procreation, an inevitable result of seminal emission is loss, a type of death. Each drop of semen contains a huge number of living cells, each cell carrying the potential for life, and the great majority of the cells – even in the best-case scenario of fertilization – are lost.

According to our literature, the white spot of a *tzaraat* mark indicates that something has died in that part of the body. If one looks at the symptoms of *tzaraat* that are described in the Torah, it seems that they serve to distinguish between *tzaraat* and ordinary illness. There are cases where the Torah says, "it is scar tissue from the infection" (Lev. 13:23), or, "it is merely scar tissue from the burn" (13:28), and therefore the mark is *tahor*. When the symptom is a result of an infection or other medical ailment, it may not be pleasant, but it is not *tzaraat*. When, however, the condition deprives the person of his life force, it is no longer defined as an illness, but is considered an impure affliction.

A *zava* experiences an impairment of her body's vitality as well. It is a result of a severe hormonal imbalance that prevents the woman from conceiving a new life, which explains the basis for its *tuma*.

RECEPTACLES

The intrinsic connection between the concepts of *tuma* and *tahara* and the life force of the entity apparently also applies to the distinction between things that are susceptible to *tuma* and those that are not. In the thirty chapters of Tractate Kelim, there are countless details that can drive a person crazy, but there are also several major principles, one of which is that the more perfect the vessel and the higher its quality, the more susceptible it is to *tuma*. This progression extends from high-quality metal vessels to low-quality earthenware vessels. If we were to understand *tuma* per se as a type of defect, this progression would be surprising. It would seem counterintuitive that a perfect and beautiful vessel would be susceptible to *tuma*, while an inferior or defective vessel would not be. In reality, however, the logic is just the opposite: Sensitivity to *tuma* requires some level of perfection.

A similar concept can be observed in the *tuma* of vessels. A metal vessel becomes *tamei* even if it has no receptacle. A wooden vessel requires a receptacle in order to be considered a utensil; but once it is labeled a utensil, it can become *tamei* through its outer surface as well; whereas an earthenware vessel cannot become *tamei* through its outer surface (Ḥullin 24b).

At first glance, this is quite puzzling. Why should an earthenware vessel not become *tamei* through its outer surface? According to an explanation attributed to the Kotzker Rebbe, an earthenware vessel is a utensil not by virtue of the material from which it is made but only in that it is a receptacle. Therefore, when something *tamei* touches the vessel's outer surface, the vessel does not itself become *tamei*, because its material is insignificant. Only when something enters the earthenware vessel's inner space, the part of the vessel that determines its status as a utensil, can the vessel become *tamei*, because only then does the vessel reach a level where it is even relevant to speak of *tuma*.

THE KEY OF CHILDBIRTH

The section of the *parasha* that deals with the *metzora* is preceded by the section on the *tuma* of a woman who has just given birth, and this in itself is truly striking. Why should the laws of *tuma* begin precisely with this form of *tuma*? After all, other forms of *tuma* are much more common and no less severe. Why, then, did the Torah choose to begin with the *tuma* that follows childbirth? Furthermore, in light of our explanation of *tuma* as a decline in life force, this *tuma* seems doubly anomalous.

Regarding *tuma* following childbirth, the Kotzker Rebbe said as follows: According to the Talmud, three keys remain in God's hand alone and were not entrusted to any emissaries: the key of rain, the key of childbirth, and the key of the revival of the dead (Taanit 2a). Since the key of childbirth is in God's hand, then apparently His spirit is present during the birth, after which it immediately departs – and this is the source of the tension that generates *tuma*. The *tuma* is generated not because the birth is something inherently *tamei* – on the contrary, it is a time when new life comes into the world – but because the birth involves a gulf between a high and a subsequent low, evoking the gulf between life and death.

The highly charged experience of childbirth and the fall from this high shortly thereafter derive from various aspects of the experience. First of all, the birth itself is an incredible miracle: One life is growing and developing inside another. We often take this for granted; we know how it happens and assume that it is natural. But in truth, the whole phenomenon of pregnancy, in which a woman bears two lives that suddenly separate from each other, is nothing short of miraculous. We hear a sense of wonder in Eve's exclamation of amazement and excitement upon giving birth to the world's first child: "I have acquired a man together with God!" (Gen. 4:1). Eve reflects on the birth and exclaims, "Look what happened! I did something together with God; I made a human being!"

From the physical, physiological standpoint, too, the process of childbirth is very similar to every other circumstance that creates *tuma*. Pregnancy demands tremendous changes in the way the body functions. Throughout the pregnancy, there is a continuous miracle transpiring in the mother's body, a miracle of creation, to which every other bodily function must adjust. When the process of childbirth begins, all of the body's systems speed up dramatically; massive releases of adrenaline and other hormones advance the labor vigorously, eventually enabling the birth of a child. Then, immediately after the birth, this unique and exceptional process, the miracle of creation, everything stops, not gradually but all at once. The chasm is huge. One moment the world is full of wonder, and the next moment it is already gone. The great disparity is what creates the *tuma*.

The intensity of this abrupt change is reflected, in a sense, in the phenomenon of post-partum depression. Most women experience a slight, fleeting feeling of sadness after giving birth, but sometimes this feeling turns into severe depression, which can be traumatic for both the mother and her family.

Even after all of this, we must remember and acknowledge that although we may have illuminated one general aspect of the laws of *tuma* and *tahara*, we will never truly be able to understand all of the complexities of these laws; questions will always remain. As King Solomon said regarding the laws of the red cow, "I left no wisdom in the world that I did not understand, but when I got to the section on the red cow 'I said, "I will get wisdom," but it was far from me' (Eccl. 7:23)" (*Midrash Zuta*, Eccl. 7).

Aḥarei Mot

The Midrash provides a long list of explanations as to why Aaron's sons died, ranging from the mundane to more lofty aspects: They entered the Holy of Holies, they brought unauthorized fire, they were intoxicated by wine, they were unmarried, they were haughty, and so on (Tanḥuma, Aḥarei Mot).

Some of the explanations, along with the plain meaning of the verse, "when they drew near before God" (Lev. 16:1), have a common denominator: The cause of the sin was overfamiliarity with God and His service.

The problem of overfamiliarity is a constant problem for those who stand before God and especially for the Priests in their role as God's servants. The focal point of the Temple is the daily worship known as the "Order of the Service." The courtyard, where the Outer Altar stands and where the Order of Service is performed, is essentially a platform that is elevated above the general public; the courtyard of Israel and the women's courtyard are situated below, and the large congregation assembled there merely stands and looks on, whereas it is the Priest who performs the bulk of the service. The Priests operate not only within the Temple courtyard but also behind the scenes; they are part of the whole process. They know all the routines and are familiar with everything that goes on.

Generally, a Jew would visit the Temple infrequently, on a festival or at some other time, and he would approach his encounter with great awe and reverence. By contrast, the Priest is constantly in the Temple, where he is personally involved in the process more than anyone else. He is like a member of the household, and that is precisely where his problem begins. He is so involved and such an insider that he inevitably starts to become overfamiliar with the proceedings. The Priests even have their own entrance to the Temple, and they come and go as they please; they even sleep in the Temple. Thus they are exposed to the danger of overfamiliarity, of insensitivity resulting from being so closely involved. When you are the expert, and others constantly rely on you, this situation breeds presumptuousness.

One can see how such a state can develop and deteriorate in the conduct of the sons of Eli. Eli's sons did not make light of the Service of the Tabernacle. They had faith, when it was necessary they went off to war, and they fulfilled their duty in protecting the Ark of the Covenant. But in the Tabernacle routine they acted haughtily. For example, a woman who had just given birth to a son would come to Shiloh, where the Tabernacle was then located. She has good reason to come, and good reason to be excited as well; this is a momentous experience. The Priests, however, are tired; they have already witnessed scenes like this thousands of times, scenes with which they are thoroughly familiar. And so the Priest goes up to the woman and immediately asks: "What about the meat?" He acts like a butcher in a butcher shop. Why does he act so insensitively? The Priests have spent their whole lives in the Tabernacle, and as a result, they feel like members of the King's household, and after a while, their fear and awe disappear. This does not mean that household members are never faithful or that they always have contempt for the proceedings, but they do run the risk of becoming habituated and overly familiar insiders.

JADED BECAUSE OF NEARNESS

The sin of Aaron's sons stems from their living within this familiarity, this habitual sense of comfort in their surroundings. When they enter the Holy of Holies without authorization, or when they bring unauthorized fire, or when they enter while intoxicated by wine, they do so because they feel that they are part and parcel of the system. Those who enter the Sanctuary are encouraged to first make preparations and immerse 310 times, and even after all that a sense of fear should still remain. The Torah states that "the firstborn was Nadav" (Num. 3:2); presumably, Nadav felt that he was already the High Priest. So he opens the door, moves the curtain and enters. The fact that this is a place where entry is strictly forbidden simply does not register with him, precisely because he is constantly so near.

In the Tabernacle, this problem is even more pronounced than in the Temple, because in the Tabernacle there is no sense of mystery. In the Temple, there is one chamber that is off limits, the Holy of Holies. In the Tabernacle that was built in the desert, the place of the Holy of Holies was previously a patch of desert like any other. Over one patch of desert the cloud suddenly stops, and the order is given to assemble the Tabernacle. If this spot is too grassy or stony, the structure is moved a bit. Here shall stand the Holy of Holies, here shall stand the Holy and here shall stand the Altar (see Ex. 26:33). While the Priests may understand, intellectually, that from now on it is forbidden to pass through the curtain, that it is forbidden to enter the holy place, and that one who enters the Holy of Holies is liable to receive the death penalty, it was likely difficult for them to feel this abrupt change in status.

Still, why is the sin of drunkenness treated so severely? They simply wanted to celebrate, to conduct a housewarming for the Tabernacle. If they then drank a little too much and entered the Sanctuary, is this really so problematic?

The problem of jadedness due to habituation is universal. When a person encounters death for the first time, it is a shocking experience; the first time one has to deal with a human corpse, one is usually frightened and shaken. But after being involved in this kind of work for a certain amount of time, jadedness begins to set in: The scribe begins to step on his holy parchments and the gravedigger begins to drag corpses from place to place. When a person holds a Torah scroll for the first time, it is a profound experience, but if you are the one who sits and makes the scrolls, and you are constantly surrounded with parchment, it becomes difficult to maintain the same feeling of awe and reverence as at the beginning.

A non-Jewish scholar writes in a work on Tanakh that Psalm 145 is one of the most beautiful verses that he has ever seen. Now, one who recites this psalm three times a day or more will find it very difficult to appreciate its beauty in this way, at most noticing that it is an acrostic. What is the source of this limited appreciation? It is not because he does not know it by heart, but precisely because he knows it by heart. The Kotzker Rebbe reportedly explained the words of the *piyut*, "Beauty and eternity pertain to the One who lives forever," that when a person looks at something beautiful a hundred times, it stops being special in his eyes. Beauty that lasts eternally pertains only to the One who lives forever.

This problem applies in more mundane matters as well. In our society, there exists a subdivision among religious Jews: a group of people who call themselves *benei Torah* (followers of the Torah). In ostensible contrast to their merely "religious" counterparts, these people consider themselves truly devoted to the Torah in all seriousness. The problem that this group experiences is the same problem that underlies the sin of Aaron's sons – overfamiliarity.

These *benei Torah* do not pray only once a year when the spirit moves them. They do not go to the synagogue only when there is a family tragedy; they go daily, three times a day. They are occupied with the Torah constantly. But because they are wrapped up in all this and live in the midst of all this, the danger arises that, little by little, they will become jaded by overfamiliarity. After a while, these people do not and cannot feel the emotions that spiritual novices feel. Why do our emotions run so high on the festivals and the Days of Awe? Because they come once a year, and we do not become desensitized to them. It is hard for a person to feel, three times a day, that he is standing before God. When someone who has never before been in a synagogue comes to visit, it sometimes happens that he is very moved by the experience. But when one regularly comes and goes, it becomes part of one's reality, part of one's daily routine.

Someone once complained to me that despite his great interest in mysticism over the years, he always remained "on the outside" and never actually underwent any kind of mystical experience. He added, "The only thing that I have from all that I did is that every time that I say '*Shema Yisrael*,' I feel a quiver."

Now, this person is no rabbi, and is certainly not considered pious. Yet how many truly pious Jews can say that every time they recite

"*Shema Yisrael*," they feel a quiver? The reason this happens is that we are too near, too habituated; even the holiness of the recitation of *Shema* has become banal and mundane.

A similar phenomenon exists also in Israeli society, regarding the hateful things that Jews often say about other Jews. If non-Jews were to attack and criticize Jews as harshly as Jews do to one another, this would no doubt provoke a great uproar. This phenomenon is not simply a result of baseless hatred; it is partially the result of the feeling that "I am among my own people." Precisely because we are so close to one another, we tend to disregard the constraints and limits of civility.

"I WILL BE SANCTIFIED THROUGH THOSE NEAR TO ME"

"Moses said to Aaron: This is what God meant when He said, I will be sanctified through those near to Me; thus I will be honored before the entire people" (Lev. 10:3). God is essentially saying that Nadav and Avihu are members of His household; they are children who grew up in His yard. Even if it would seem that they do not deserve such a punishment, "He puts no trust even in His holy ones" (Job 15:15). The Talmud states that God calls those who are close to Him to a strict accounting even for matters as slight as a hairbreadth (Bava Kamma 50a). Because of their closeness, they in particular must be held to a strict accounting, because even a hairbreadth can lead them off the straight path.

A similar story can be found in the *haftara* of *Parashat Shemini*, in the account of the death of Uzza (II Sam. 6). And it is again the same story in the account of the death of the people of Beth-shemesh, who "looked into the Ark of God" (I Sam. 6:19). There, we see that the Philistines perceived the Ark as a source of awesome fear and fright, whereas for the Jews, the Ark could be treated lightly and irreverently.

A similar incident occurs at the revelation at Sinai, immediately after which the Torah says, "And upon the nobles of the People of Israel He laid not His hand; they beheld God, and they ate and drank" (Ex. 24:11). The Midrash interprets that "they" refers to Nadav and Avihu, who ate and drank out of this feeling of overfamiliarity, and that God delayed their punishment so as not to spoil the joy of the giving of the Torah (Leviticus Rabba 20:10). Many have asked: Why, then, did God choose to postpone the punishment until the joy of the eighth day, the day of the dedication of the Tabernacle? Could He not have waited a few more days? As God was certainly not afraid that they would escape from Him, so what was the hurry?

The difference is that the revelation at Sinai was a one-time event, anomalous and unconnected in its background and context. By contrast, the Tabernacle is where all of Israel will subsequently come to bring *korbanot*. All the more so in the wilderness, when the Tabernacle's role was even more central, as all *shehita* took place in the Tabernacle, even when it was for the sole purpose of eating meat. Precisely there it was important to stress that "I will be sanctified through those near to Me" – that overfamiliarity can have grave consequences.

Overfamiliarity is ruinous to the person himself, and it leads to even greater ruin for others. Those who live in the midst of it can no longer discern what they are doing, but to others it appears to be unpardonable coarseness. While the Priest may experience the deterioration of his inner life, the layman looking on from afar experiences the fracture of his whole spiritual essence, because for him the Priest is the ultimate spiritual role model. Those who sit in the beit midrash are not so outraged, because they are already aware that not everyone who sits there is supremely holy. But for those for whom the Priest represents a kind of spiritual perfection, to see such a person acting disrespectfully is a desecration not only of his personal essence but of the whole cause that he represents.

The Talmud states that "a careless error in [Torah] study is considered deliberate" (Avot 4:13), and "credit is not extended in the desecration of God's name" (Kiddushin 40a). In the case of the desecration of God's name, God grants man no extensions, and he is punished whether he acted deliberately or inadvertently, and perhaps even whether he acted willfully or under duress: "For God will bring to judgment every deed concerning every hidden thing" (Eccl. 12:14).

In light of this, "I will be sanctified through those near to Me" is a warning directed precisely at those who are close and have been drawn near, who are constantly in the inner sanctum. They must always be aware that they stand before the holy. In their case, the penalties must be far more severe, so that "I will be honored before the entire people." They must remember why the Holy of Holies bears that name, and that the partition that separates the earthly realm and the holy realm must remain in place, even if they cross that boundary several times a day. To be sure, this presents a great challenge; it is much more difficult for a physician to feel the pain of others, and it is much more difficult for a gravedigger to maintain a high level of respect for the dead.

Unlike in other cases, in the case of the sons of Aaron, God, as it were, goes to the trouble of burning them Himself – "Fire came forth from before God" (Lev. 10:2). This is because Nadav and Avihu did something that is so understandable in itself but is so awful in its consequences for all involved. It is understandable because it is ingrained in man's nature, and its consequences are awful because they damage one's inner core. It is for this reason that the Torah views the sin of overfamiliarity with such seriousness.

THE TEST OF THE PRIESTHOOD

Every person, in one respect or another, draws close to God, and one must always remember that even though he may know what goes on behind the scenes, he must not lose the feeling of respect and awesome reverence; he must not feel that he is exempt from the duty of keeping his distance. This is certainly one of the most difficult requirements to fulfill. After one has already grown accustomed to being inside the Sanctuary, the true test is if one can still retain the attitude of an outsider, for whom the Sanctuary is still on a different plane. Is one capable of being on both sides simultaneously – to be inside, and nevertheless to feel like an outsider who has entered for the first time, knowing nothing of the experience?

There is a perpetual partition between the sacred and the profane, between the awesome and the ordinary. For the Priest, this partition is not smaller, but it is more difficult for him to abide by.

This tension exists in numerous diverse areas, all of which present the test of the priesthood: To what degree can one stand very close and yet remain in a state of awe and reverence, dread and trembling?

To straddle both sides simultaneously is nearly impossible; it is certainly one of the most difficult things that a person can do – yet that is what is required of a Jew. Rabbi Nachman of Breslov comments that in order to achieve this, one must be simultaneously extremely old and yet, in a sense, completely infantile. This requirement is against human nature, but nevertheless, as Jews we are called upon to do just this.

BURNING OF THE SOUL

The simple explanation of "when they drew near before God and died" (Lev. 16:1) is that God strikes these people and, as a result, those who are near recoil, and He is thus sanctified.

Sometimes, however, those who draw near suffer an even worse type of death: an internal death. The Talmud says of Aaron's sons: "Only their souls were burned, but their bodies remained intact" (Sanhedrin 52a). This kind of death can befall any of us today as well – one continues to fulfill mitzvot, to sway during prayer, but his soul has burned up and left him. "When they drew near before God," their souls were burned, "and they died."

There is a tradition that it is a mitzva to weep when speaking of the deaths of Aaron's sons. Indeed, one should keep this in mind, for it is truly worth crying over a spark of holiness that was lost.

Kedoshim

It is not for naught that the *parasha* is called *Parashat Kedoshim*. Holiness is undoubtedly a central motif in the *parasha*, throughout which expressions connected with holiness repeatedly recur.

This holiness, however, has a surprising aspect. In books that deal with holiness, the deeper they delve into the concept, the more profound it becomes, to the point that it is designated as the loftiest value that exists. As the Maharal explains, holiness is that which is transcendent in its essence (*Tiferet Yisrael* 37). By contrast, the concept of holiness that arises from *Parashat Kedoshim* seems completely different.

The *parasha* begins, "Speak to the entire community of Israel and say to them: You shall be holy, for I, God your Lord, am holy" (Lev. 19:2). The commandment to be holy appears in the context of God's holiness: You shall be holy as I am holy. But on the other hand, the commandments connected with this injunction do not appear to relate at all to the sort of transcendent holiness that the Maharal describes. *Parashat Kedoshim* is full of commandments, which include the prohibitions on stealing, lying, cheating, and so forth. At first glance, they do not appear to be special requirements or standards that an ordinary responsible person could not meet. On the whole, these are practices that are, more or less, commonly observed by the average person throughout the world, irrespective of religion or cultural background.

This puzzling question arises at the end of the section discussing forbidden sexual relationships as well. These laws begin with: "You shall keep My decrees and observe them, for I am God, who makes you holy" (Lev. 20:8), and they end with: "You shall be holy to Me, for I, God, am holy" (20:26). That is to say, one who keeps these laws is called holy. Thus, the same difficulty arises: How is a person who simply refrains from committing a few sins considered holy? Even if one complies with everything that is written here – a certain number of positive commandments and a certain number of negative commandments – is that all that is needed to be considered holy? One would think that attaining holiness would require special safeguards and practices; but from here it seems that as long as one refrains from a few contemptible acts, that is all that is required to be holy. How can this be?

This question recurs throughout the entire *parasha*. As a matter of fact, this *parasha* – which begins "You shall be holy" – contains nothing of a particularly holy character, and the definition of holiness that emerges from it is rather modest. It would seem to be devoid of any spiritual demand or attempt to elevate people to a higher sphere.

EARTHLY VIEW

The list of forbidden sexual relationships in this *parasha* corresponds to the list in *Parashat Aharei Mot*, where it says, "Do not follow the practices of the land of Egypt…and do not follow the practices of the land of Canaan" (Lev. 18:3). The passage concludes:

> Do not become defiled through any of these acts; for through all of these the nations became defiled…The Land became defiled; and when I directed My providence at the sin committed there, the Land vomited out its inhabitants…For all those abominations were done by the people who lived in the Land before you, and the Land became defiled. Let not the Land vomit you out for defiling it, as it vomited out the nation that was before you… You shall keep My charge not to engage in any of the abominable practices that were carried out before you, so that you not become defiled through them. (18:24–30)

In *Parashat Aḥarei Mot* these practices are presented as utterly abhorrent. Abominations and abominable practices, impure and disgusting – these are acts that the Land cannot tolerate, and it vomits out anyone who commits them. By contrast, when we come to *Parashat Kedoshim*, there is a significant change in tone. Previously, it said that the Land cannot tolerate one who does such a thing, whether he is a Jew or not; he is crooked, twisted, and perverted. In *Parashat Kedoshim*, however, although it does say that these are sins and that they bear penalties such as stoning and strangulation, it also says that one who refrains from doing these things is considered holy.

The repetition of the section on forbidden sexual relationships in *Parashot Aḥarei Mot* and *Kedoshim* represents two ways of looking at things. There is the heavenly view, which asks how it is possible to sink so low. But there is also the earthly view, which says that although corporal punishment and other severe penalties still apply here, still, one who guards himself against all these abominations is included in the category of "Keep yourselves holy, and you will be holy" (Lev. 20:7).

These are two different views of the very same thing. When a person is on a truly high level, there are things that he does not even consider doing; they are simply unthinkable. *Parashat Aḥarei Mot* addresses these people. But if a person is on a low level, suddenly everything looks different; suddenly, one who complies with all these laws is called holy. There are many actions that one would generally consider abhorrent and would never consider pursuing. But a person can change, as can his environment, and as a result, what was once easy to avoid can now be an extraordinary challenge. At this point, refraining from such improper behavior is no longer a simple task, but has become a matter of stubborn loyalty to one's views and principles.

There was a time when the typical pious Eastern European Jew had a beard and wore a long garment; this was a sign of his Judaism. When some of these Jews began to adopt the German style of dress – a short jacket and a trimmed beard – they were called *Deutsch* (German) by their peers in derision, an expression that indicated that such dress and demeanor were considered contemptible by other Jews. It was clear to the traditional members of the community that these Jews did not observe the mitzvot, and they were often even suspected of being apostates. This attitude was part of the way of life of Jews in Eastern Europe at the time.

In those times, there lived a great hasidic master known as the Ruzhiner Rebbe, who lived in a palatial home. One day, a visitor arrived at his home – one such *Deutscher*, with a short jacket and a trimmed beard – and he was received by the Rebbe immediately, without all the usual delays. He was granted a private audience with the Rebbe that lasted for hours. Afterward, to everyone's surprise, the Rebbe came out and personally escorted his visitor to the door. Everyone was shocked; what was the meaning of this? Finally, someone dared to ask the Rebbe: Who was this man who was so honored by the Rebbe? The Rebbe answered: "I asked God to grant me the privilege of seeing the *gadol hador* (greatest *tzaddik* of the generation) in which the Messiah will come."

This story expresses my point precisely. It may very well be that the *gadol hador* is someone of the type that one would least expect. The appearance of the visitor drew derision from the Hasidim, but they did not realize that in his own place and time he was not only a *tzaddik* but the *gadol hador* himself.

The personal secretary of the Kotzker Rebbe once related that when it was brought to the Rebbe's attention that his spoons were being stolen, he cried out, "Stolen? Is it not written in the Torah, 'You shall not steal'?!" The secretary then added that when the Rebbe said this, it made a tremendous impression on him – he truly could not understand how it was possible that someone would steal; in the Rebbe's mind, such a thing was impossible.

But there is another perspective on "You shall not steal" and "You shall not deal deceitfully or falsely with one another" (Lev. 19:11) – the earthly view. These matters are relevant; they exist in the world. While the heavenly view cannot fathom how people could act in such a way, the earthly view is grounded in reality, acknowledging the way of the world.

The earthly view can descend lower and lower in each generation. Sometimes one reads the descriptions of the most derelict characters from several generations ago, and one asks himself: These are the generation's most despicable people? Rabbi Shneur Zalman of Liadi writes that even the most sinful person in our communities nevertheless prays three times a day, wears tzitzit, and puts on *tefillin*. Nowadays, there are places where such a person would be considered the *gadol hador*, or if not that, then at least an important person. This is the essence of the earthly view: If a person truly does not steal, he is holy; and if by chance he does not swear falsely as well, then he is truly a righteous and holy Jew.

When the section on forbidden sexual relationships is read on Yom Kippur in the synagogue, it sounds completely different from when it is read in the comfort of one's home, whether one is poor or wealthy; because when one sits among the people, the words of the Torah become an actual possibility. The more respectable or cloistered one's place of residence, the less one's spiritual sensitivity is to the concept of "You shall be holy." Sometimes, when a person hears, sees, and discovers all these things from below, he finds that being holy is truly not a simple matter.

In the not too distant past, if someone would have said that Jews would leave their homes in the Land of Israel and commit idolatry in a far-off land, this would have sounded preposterous, simply implausible. Why would a normal person go somewhere and bow down before an idol and make an offering to it? Such a thing could not happen.

Now, when one reads through the list of mitzvot in the *parasha* from beginning to end, it is clear that there are places where this practice is common, widespread in fact, and there are places where such things are done in broad daylight. Suddenly, everything becomes a matter of "You shall be holy."

After three thousand years, *Parashat Kedoshim* has become relevant again. The earthly view is no longer far from us. I do not know how our fathers or our grandfathers explained to themselves the spiritual difficulty of being holy, that one who does not commit these acts is called holy. Now, as time has passed and the world has changed, the answer is unfortunately clear.

RESISTING JADEDNESS

There is an additional aspect of this same idea that we must address. We read in Micah: "What does God require of you: Only to do justice and to love goodness and to walk modestly with your God" (6:8). Overall, many of the requirements in *Parashat Kedoshim* fall under this same overarching message: "Behave like a responsible person." No more is required.

When we talk about the struggle of life from the perspective of an ordinary person, we speak of two types of enemies. On the one hand, there are overt embodiments of forces of evil. On the other hand, there is a subtler enemy that is no less potent and dangerous: erosion, where nothing out of the ordinary seems to happen.

The Talmud relates an incident in which R. Amram Ḥasida almost impulsively succumbed to the incredible temptation of sexual impropriety (Kiddushin 81a), demonstrating that sometimes even a decent and righteous man can suddenly find himself in a situation for which he is unprepared, and he engages in an exceptional struggle with base instinct. There are also other situations where there is no instinctual temptation, but only the slow and continual erosion of life.

The positive and negative commandments that appear here, and which characterize holiness, are things that generally do not suddenly erupt but, rather, are situations that a person gets dragged into gradually, where each time it becomes increasingly easier to be drawn in. Some people gradually become pressured by money. A livelihood is no longer an abstract concept but something very real and very painful. When a person suddenly falls into financial crisis, often this can be dealt with. But this does not always happen all at once. More often it happens gradually, where every day something else goes by the wayside, and it becomes more and more difficult to avoid rationalizing immoral behavior for the sake of supporting oneself and one's family.

Thus, are "You shall not steal" and "You shall not deal deceitfully or falsely with one another" truly sins that no ordinary responsible person would commit? When faced with a harsh reality, even such a person can become worn down and succumb.

The law of *shifḥa ḥarufa* (a half-betrothed maidservant) that appears here (Lev. 19:20–22) likewise fits into this pattern. This is a woman whose status is not exactly clear; she is half slave and half free. Her master succumbs to the temptation to sin with this woman precisely because of this muddled status. She is a half-married slave woman, and it all seems easier and less complicated.

For this same reason, the Torah says regarding the stranger, "Do not wrong him" (Lev. 19:33). After all, it is simple to cheat the stranger, just as it is also easy to oppress him and take advantage of him. One might rationalize that what he is doing is not a great sin; he is only cheating the stranger a bit, since he doesn't know the prices. It is actually beneficial, one may reason, to insult him a little, until he becomes more experienced and ceases to be a stranger. When he becomes a resident of the land, one of us, he himself will do the same to others.

One can see how "you shall not sow your field with a mixture of seeds" (Lev. 19:19) – the law of *kilayim* – may irk some people, and if there is a grocer who can truly comply with the law of "Do not falsify measurements, whether in length, weight or volume" (19:35), then to a certain extent he is indeed a holy person. The Tosefta says of Abba Shaul b. Butnit and R. Elazar b. Tzadok, who were grocers in Jerusalem, that they would take special steps to ensure that their customers received the full measure that was due them (Beitza 3:8). If this was the practice of ordinary grocers, these actions would not have been singled out in the Tosefta and credited solely to two of the most pious men in Jerusalem at a time when the Temple still stood. This does not mean that all the other people were thieves, only that one is constantly under social pressure not to be naïve. Everyone is tempted to take advantage of his fellow man, and many succumb to this temptation. In such a society, it is easy to rationalize: Everyone steals, everyone lies, and everyone cheats – why shouldn't I?

Constant erosion, along with the general atmosphere that immoral practices are accepted in society, create a situation in which when one does these things, on a large or small scale, they no longer feel like bad behavior, like sinful acts. Likewise, regarding forbidden sexual relationships, many commentators note that part of the problem stems from the daily reality and proximity. People who fall prey to these kinds of sins do not usually do so because they are suddenly seized with an uncontrollable urge. Rather, relationships develop gradually, until suddenly a person finds himself in a situation that he never would have believed was possible.

This process does not happen all at once, or because the burden of piety and morality is suddenly impossible to bear. It is just that bearing this burden on a daily basis is incredibly taxing. No individual demand in the Torah creates the sense of facing an abyss. Each of these is a minor battle over minor things, but the battles add up, and may seem to some like a war with no end in sight.

Bringing a *korban* every once in a while is simple. But to fulfill all the various major and minor requirements listed in *Parashat Kedoshim* every day is quite another story. Not for naught does the Torah say, "Everyone shall revere his mother and his father" (Lev. 19:3). Anyone who has any experience in this knows how difficult it is. It is something that we are faced with every day, and it can be especially challenging when one's father and mother are themselves not exceptionally holy people.

This struggle is the fundamental struggle for holiness. *Parashat Kedoshim* presents a long list of minor requirements, none of which is extraordinary on its own, but each one recurs day after day. The very requirement to maintain this routine without succumbing to jadedness and despair – that itself creates the highest levels of holiness.

"WITH ALL YOUR MIGHT"

We recite every day: "You shall love God your Lord with all your heart, with all your soul, and with all your might" (Deut. 6:5). Our sages interpret as follows: "'With all your heart' means with both your inclinations, with the good inclination and with the evil inclination; 'with all your soul' means even if He takes your life; and 'with all your might' means with all your money" (Berakhot 54a). But the order in this series of required sacrifices to God is strange: If one is ready to give to God with both of his inclinations, and he is even prepared to give up his life in service of God, it seems anticlimactic to end the series with the injunction to give up one's money in service of God as well.

The meaning of "with all your money" is not simply that the person is told to hand over his money. Rather, every person faces a life of wearying, unending toil. "With all your money" is not about the act of giving but about committing oneself to a type of life where he is aware of the sacrifices expected of him from the outset. One must face these sacrifices not once in his lifetime but every day – often three or ten times a day. In light of the erosion that we have discussed, it stands to reason that "with all your money" is actually the most difficult demand of the three. First comes "with all your heart," then "with all your soul," and if someone is truly courageous and holy, he can also serve God "with all your might." A lion or a bear can be struck down, but a million termites is a different kind of challenge altogether.

The secret to achieving this courage is "Sanctify yourselves and be holy, for I am holy" (Lev. 20:7). We agree to take upon ourselves the million termites of life, which appear every day and at every hour, from the time we rise in the morning until we go to sleep at night. The solution is to emulate God; when we bring God into the picture, we begin to understand the meaning of the verse, "I am God – I have not changed" (Mal. 3:6). God does not change; He remains holy no matter what the circumstances. "Who dwells with them in the midst of their impurity" (Lev. 16:16) – God has the ability to maintain life in the midst of impurity. *Parashat Kedoshim* states that we, too, can walk in His ways. Then and only then will we succeed in being holy like Him.

Emor

In the third section of *Parashat Emor*, we read about physical defects. From a halakhic standpoint, the laws of defects apply both to the *korbanot* and the people who bring them; both the *korban* and the Priest must be free of physical defect, according to the principle that "any defect that disqualifies a man disqualifies an animal as well" (Bekhorot 43a).

But there is another law of this kind that adds substance to our topic, and that is that judges, at least in the Sanhedrin, must be free of physical defects: "Just as the court must be clean in respect of righteousness, so must they be clear of all physical defects" (Yevamot 101a). A person with a physical defect can be one of the greatest sages of Israel, but to be a judge he cannot have a defect.

This law applies not only to a defect that would interfere with one's ability to function as a judge, but also to a defect that would not necessarily interfere with his work. A hunchback, even if he is one of the greatest sages of Israel, and however erudite he may be, cannot be a judge.

The term *mufla* appears in several talmudic sources in the context of the court system (e.g., Horayot 4b), but the meaning of the term is unclear. *Margaliyot HaYam* (Sanhedrin 3b) proposes that it refers to a great sage who, for a technical reason, cannot be a member of the court. For example, upon reaching a certain age, one is disqualified from being a member of the Sanhedrin that rules in capital cases. Also excluded is someone who is childless. Such a person could be the generation's leading Torah scholar, but he cannot be a member of the Sanhedrin. According to this interpretation, all sorts of people acted as adjuncts to the Sanhedrin, people who for technical reasons could not be members.

In the case of the Temple, at least, there is logic in the law that a *korban* must be without defect, and the same logic would explain why the Priest, too, must be without defect. This is the idea of "Try presenting [a defective animal as an offering] to your governor. Will he be pleased with you or show you favor?" (Mal. 1:8). Many other factors can disqualify a *korban*, beyond those featured on the list of actual defects. For example, an old or foul-smelling animal is disqualified from being a *korban*, even though it may have no physical defect. Clearly, the reason for this is that it is not proper to present such a thing to God. Since bringing a *korban* has an aspect of ceremony – "For I am a great King, says the God of Hosts, and My Name is feared among the nations" (1:14) – clearly it is an affront to the King if He is brought a defective *korban*. So, too, the King's servants must be pleasant in appearance, because if they are not, it is a defect in the King's honor.

In the Temple as well, there is an aspect of splendor. It is not a *shtiebel* where anyone can go in and act however he wants. It is a place that one enters with awe and reverence, which also includes external appearance. Hence, when a *korban* is brought, it must be free of any defect. The same goes for other features of the Temple; they must be the very best, because we are dealing here with the honor of God Himself. Because of this, the Temple vessels were made of gold. Can't God use iron vessels? Rather, gold vessels are used because this is the place of God's kingship, and kingship goes together with splendor.

All the vessels used in the dwelling of the Divine Presence must be perfect. Hence, if the Altar has a defect – even as slight as a notch that disqualifies a slaughtering knife, a notch that only a fingernail can detect – the Altar is unfit for use (Ḥullin 18a). The Priest's garments must be perfect as well, for the same reason.

To be sure, there is also the aspect of humility and lowliness in approaching God, as we read, "A heart broken and crushed, O Lord, You will not scorn" (Ps. 51:19), but the Temple of the King is not the place for it. It could be that a wretched person is precious in the eyes of God, but since externally he is full of defects, he may not enter the Temple and face the Divine Presence.

This explanation makes sense regarding the Temple, which is, in essence, the Sanctuary of the King, but why does the same rule apply to judges? Judges are generally esteemed for their wisdom, justness, and integrity – must they be pleasant in appearance as well?

A new mother once approached a certain *rebbe* in tears, holding her infant son who was born with crooked legs. The *rebbe* instructed her to relax, saying, "Don't worry, he will have a straight head." Indeed, the boy grew up to be a great rabbi, crooked legs and all.

THE *SHEKHINA* DOES NOT DWELL
IN A DEFECTIVE PLACE

We never know whether something that appears good is truly good. As it says, "Man sees what is visible, but God sees into the heart" (1 Sam. 16:7). The ability to see inwardly, into a person's heart, belongs to God alone.

Here, apparently, God requires of those who do His will a level of completeness, and not only from a spiritual standpoint. We might think that spiritual perfection is all that is important in the service of God, but it turns out that God expects perfection in all areas from His servants. This does not mean that someone who is not perfect in every way is worthless in God's eyes. Rather, there are concentric circles of closeness to the Divine Presence, and in the innermost circle God requires vessels that are whole, as it says in the Zohar, "The *Shekhina* does not dwell in a defective place" (*Vayeḥi* 216b).

On a related note, what are the qualities required of a prophet? He must be "strong, wealthy, wise, and humble" (Nedarim 38a). That he is wise and humble is not sufficient; he must also be strong and wealthy. Why should the two latter qualities make a difference? Let us say that a person is not strong; he is a small, withered creature. Does that interfere with his heart and soul, or with his ability to serve as a prophet?! Troubled with its implication, Maimonides reinterprets this talmudic statement, explaining that "wealthy" refers to one who rejoices in his portion and "strong" refers to one who overcomes his evil inclination (*Shemoneh Perakim*, ch. 7). But this is obviously not the simple meaning of the talmudic text; it seems clear that the Talmud is actually talking about someone who is physically strong and wealthy in the monetary sense. Thus, the Talmud requires of a prophet – a vessel for receiving the

Divine Presence – things that seem to be external qualities. He cannot receive the Divine Presence without these qualities because the "vessel" would then be incomplete.

The Talmud cites an interpretation that bears an incredible resemblance to a hasidic tale:

> The court declared: "Today is Rosh HaShana." The Holy One, Blessed Be He, then told the ministering angels: "Set up a platform and let the advocates and accusers step up, for my children have announced that today is Rosh HaShana." The court then decided instead to put off [Rosh HaShana] till the next day. The Holy One, Blessed Be He, then told the ministering angels: "Remove the platform and let the advocates and accusers go away, for my children have put off [the holiday] till tomorrow." What is the source for this? "For it is a law for Israel, Judgment [Day] of the God of Jacob" (Ps. 81:5): If it is not law for Israel, then, as it were, it is not Judgment [Day] of the God of Jacob. (Y. Rosh HaShana 1:3)

The point of this midrash is that the court's power derives not only from the fact that the judges are Torah scholars but due to the fact that they become a kind of instrument for the Divine Presence. What they decide is an expression of God's will; it has an effect both above and below.

Because they have this power, judges are required to be worthy instruments. This clearly does not mean that the scholar who sits in court is a kind of prophet, but he must have some form of divine power in order to voice God's will in deciding Jewish law. A session of the court involves an aspect of the dwelling of God's presence, and therefore the court is also called *elohim* (Sanhedrin 56b). For this reason, the ordination of Torah sages must be done specifically in the Land of Israel (14a), and their full authority can be exercised only in the Stone Hall inside the Temple, and not when they leave it.

INCLINATION WITH CREATION

If we take all of these laws not just in their halakhic context but also as the expression of God's true will, we may infer that He requires that those who approach Him be crowned in all forms of perfection.

In detailing the laws of blemished animals, the Torah says, "That which is crushed or mangled, torn or cut, you shall not offer to God, neither shall you do thus in your land" (Lev. 22:24). There are people whose whole approach to religious life is to be crushed and mangled, torn and cut. These people feel that the more they are downtrodden and oppressed, the more exalted and holy they become, and the greater their ability becomes to draw close to God. In the above verse, God says that the opposite is true; not only should such an animal not be offered to God, but "neither shall you do thus in your land." God does not want the crushed and mangled – neither inside nor outside.

We read in Psalms that "a heart broken and crushed, O Lord, You will not scorn" (51:19). What is the relation between the "crushed and mangled" – of which it says "you shall not do thus in your land" – and "a heart broken and crushed"?

A broken heart is a person's self-evaluation, in relation to others and in relation to God, and the result is the feeling that there is still much to accomplish. The opposite of a broken heart is what is called "obtuseness of the heart," as in the verse, "You grew fat, thick, and gross" (Deut. 32:15); it is the feeling of self-satisfaction, that everything is okay in one's life.

"Crushed and mangled" is someone who suppresses his drives – and along with them his ambition and creativity – which sometimes happens because of misplaced piety. Early Christian monks would often castrate themselves for this same reason – the desire to achieve holiness. Instead of struggling with one's evil inclination – a protracted struggle that can continue for years, in which one can never be certain that he is truly rid of the inclination – one simply removes the inclination entirely. One would think that this should be considered an exemplary act; it is certainly good-intentioned behavior. To be sure, there are inclinations that cannot be so easily cut off. Jealousy and honor, for example, are traits that cannot be eliminated from a person's consciousness. But if a safe, minor operation can solve the problem of sexual temptation forever, it would seem like the perfect solution to this problem.

Here, however, the verse teaches us not only that if a *korban* is bruised or crushed, it is then unfit to be brought before the King inside the Temple, but also that this approach should be taken in all areas of spiritual life.

Many *baalei teshuva* face this very problem. They observe that since they have become observant, they have lost all of their creativity. When they were sinners, whether big or small, they were full of vitality and creativity. Afterward, when they accepted upon themselves the yoke of God's kingship, they became truly "crushed and mangled, torn and cut," with all the accompanying ramifications. They may have a much less powerful evil inclination, but they have rendered themselves impotent in terms of creating good in the world.

When a brilliant mathematician, artist, or writer decides to apply his mind to Torah study, we hope that he maintains his ability to produce wonderful things, as he did in the past. But if he adopts the religious attitude of being "crushed and mangled," his brilliance amounts to nothing. He becomes a kind of insignificant, lowly creature who wanders through the alleyways. This is true not only of *baalei teshuva*, but also of those who merely decide to fill their hearts with pure religious devotion. They often begin to act crushed and stooped, small and broken.

What happened to willpower, volition, and desire? These traits can serve as tools for the evil inclination, but they can also be tools for creativity.

In this verse, God answers, as it were, the question of whether it is advisable for a person to remove his evil inclination if it means simultaneously removing his creativity. "That which is crushed or mangled, torn or cut, you shall not offer to God, neither shall you do thus in your land." This verse is also the source for the Torah's prohibition on castration, another indication that it is better to live with one's inclination rather than sacrifice one's creativity, whether in the Temple or elsewhere.

If a non-Jew wants to remove his evil inclination, we do not discourage him from doing so; neither is castration prohibited for non-Jews (Sanhedrin 56b). But for Jews, this is completely unacceptable. Similarly, a non-Jew's personal *korban* is only disqualified if it bears a significant defect, but for a Jew, any defect renders the *korban* unfit.

The Talmud states, "'Neither shall you do thus in your land' – even to castrate a dog is forbidden" (Ḥagiga 14b). Not only is it forbidden to castrate an exalted personality of Israel, but even a dog – an insignificant, lowly creature that wanders around eating carcasses in the street – may not be castrated, because the yoke of God's kingship does not mean being submissive, "crushed and mangled," even for one's animals.

One must constantly scrutinize where one is acting, where one is creating, and where one is living. In this *parasha*, God pronounces that He wants only sound, healthy people to join Him in His house – the more whole and upright the better. Judges, too, must be free of both moral and physical defects. God instructed Noah to take only healthy animals into the ark, and the same is true elsewhere as well. "Fortunate is the one You choose and bring near" (Ps. 65:5); God wants those He chooses and brings near to be healthy and physically sound.

On the verse, "You are children of God your Lord. Do not mutilate yourselves and do not make a bald patch in the middle of your head because of the dead" (Deut. 14:1), Rashi explains: "For you are children of the Omnipresent, and you should therefore be comely and not mutilated with hair torn out." God says that He wants His children to be beautiful, not full of cuts and marks. But isn't inner beauty more important to God than external beauty?

The truth is that we do not know the true reckoning of what is dearest to God. What we do know is that He wants people who are crowned in perfection, inside and out; and the finer this perfection is, the better.

THE REQUIREMENT OF PERFECTION

The requirement that the members of the Sanhedrin be well versed in all fields and disciplines is not connected to their professional work. The Talmud describes R. Yoḥanan b. Zakkai as the consummate man; there was nothing that he did not study: "Great matters and small matters – 'great matters' refers to *Maase Merkava*[1]; 'small matters' refers to the discussions of Abaye and Rava, washermen's tales and fox fables" (Sukka 28a). That he studied *Maase Merkava* and the discussions of Abaye and Rava is understandable, but why was it praiseworthy that he studied washermen's tales – the jokes and stories that washermen tell while they work – and fox fables? Because the definition of perfection is "You shall be holy, for I am holy" (Lev. 19:2). Just as God is crowned in all forms

---

1. The workings of the divine chariot.

of perfection, He also wants those who do His will to be crowned in all forms of perfection.

The same requirements cannot be demanded of everyone; not everyone can be wise like Solomon, a prophet like Moses, or strong like Samson. But it is not too much to ask that everyone avoid being "crushed and mangled ... blind, scabbed, or with scurvy" (Lev. 22:24).

An ox that has two broken legs and limps is a lot less dangerous than a big, healthy ox. As a result, it may seem that this limping ox is more of a *tzaddik*; he is physically unable to commit the same acts of violence of which his healthier counterpart is capable. It stands to reason, then, that we should go further: Let us remove both of his eyes and perform a few other operations on him, so that he cannot cause any damage whatsoever. Why should such a *tzaddik* of an ox not be brought as a *korban*? But this is twisted thinking: Is this ox really an appropriate gift for God?

Here we see what God wants and what He does not want. He wants things that are physically sound, with all the risks that this entails. An ox that has not been castrated is incomparably more dangerous and much more difficult to harness. But God does not want the castrated *tzaddik*; He wants the ox that is closest to perfection in all ways. If such an ox is dangerous – even murderous, at times – God is willing to take this risk.

Incidentally, this does not mean that halakha condones bringing as a *korban* an animal that has acted violently or otherwise inappropriately. An animal that had relations with a person, or that was worshiped, or that was condemned to be stoned, is unfit to be offered. If an ox actually used its power to commit some kind of offense, it is disqualified. But only an ox that is healthy enough to do such things in the first place can be brought as a *korban*, unlike the limping ox with the broken legs.

We read in Psalms: "Ascribe to God, O children of the mighty, ascribe to God glory and strength" (29:1). It is precisely the children of the mighty, the great and powerful people, the children of princes, who must ascribe glory to God, because "the voice of God comes in power, the voice of God comes in majesty" (29:4). Majesty and power demand a vessel that is capable of receiving them; broken vessels cannot bear them. That is the meaning of the verse, "the mighty in strength who do His bidding, hearkening unto the sound of His words" (103:20).

To be a *korban* and to be a Priest, one must be physically sound, along with the danger that this entails. For an animal to gore, to damage, or to have relations with a person is forbidden, but these despicable acts must be part of the whole range of possibilities. Only with the possibility of reaching what is truly evil can one fully achieve what is truly good.

The ramification, therefore, for the service of God – how one should see himself – is this: When we walk "mournfully before God" (Mal. 3:14), when we live with excessive fear of heaven, we are essentially heaping defects upon ourselves. The Torah does not vilify such a person. If it is necessary to transport burdens upon him, he will hold up; if he is needed for slaughtering, he is still fit to be eaten. Here, however, whether the meat is kosher is not the issue; here the issue is holiness. For ordinary consumption, we are not required to procure only the choicest meat; neither is it necessary to find the perfect ox for work in the field. But when it comes to holiness, there is a different standard.

We do not have a Temple, we do not have the service of the Sanctuary, and we do not have a Sanhedrin. But we still have God, and He remains the same: "I am God – I have not changed" (Mal. 3:6). He has not changed, and He still wants the same things.

Behar

At the beginning of the *parasha*, Rashi deals with the famous question, "What does *Shemitta* have to do with Mount Sinai? Were not all the mitzvot given at Sinai?" (Rashi, Lev. 25:1).

The answer that he gives is very surprising and not entirely sufficient: "Just as the laws of *Shemitta* were revealed at Sinai with all their general principles and details, so all of the mitzvot were revealed at Sinai with all of their general principles and details."

This answer explains what Mount Sinai has to do with *Shemitta*, but not at all what *Shemitta* has to do with Mount Sinai. According to Rashi, Mount Sinai had to be mentioned here in order to teach us that even though *Shemitta* is already mentioned elsewhere in the Torah, all of its principles and details were revealed at Sinai, and the same applies to all the other mitzvot as well. Yet even if this mitzva is the paradigm for the other mitzvot, the question still remains: Why was *Shemitta* the mitzva that was specifically chosen to be mentioned in connection with Mount Sinai?

The whole subject of "Shabbat of the Land" – *Shemitta* and the Jubilee year – is known to be a very important matter in the Torah, of far more importance than is ascribed to it nowadays, and one of the proofs for this is in the next *parasha*.

Toward the end of the *Tokheḥa* (the section of reproof in Leviticus 26), it says, "Then the Land will enjoy its *Shabbatot*...As long as it is desolate, it will enjoy the Sabbatical rest that you would not give it while you were living on it" (Lev. 26:34–35). The implication is that the great *Tokheḥa* refers specifically to the laws of *Shemitta* and the Jubilee year.

When Jeremiah discusses why the Land was destroyed, what emerges is that God overlooks forbidden sexual relationships, idolatry, and bloodshed, but He does not overlook neglect of the Torah (Jer. 9). In our *parashot* as well, a similar idea emerges. The implication here is that God overlooked forbidden sexual relationships and bloodshed, but not the laws of *Shemitta*. He is willing to forgive us for everything, but what ultimately creates the great destruction foretold in the *Tokheḥa* is the disregard of the laws of *Shemitta*. In the Mishna's list of sins deemed responsible for punishment coming into the world as well, it can be observed that neglecting the laws of *Shemitta* occupies a central place (Avot 5:8–9).

A WORLD THAT HAS CHANGED

We hear and read much about the difficulty that the *Shemitta* year entails, the great sacrifice that God requires of us. And the truth is that for a farmer who works the land, *Shemitta* obviously means a fundamental change in his whole way of life. This is doubly true when the majority of Jewish people in the world live in the Land of Israel, and when most of these people are farmers and agricultural workers.

In Josephus's *The Antiquities of the Jews*, he relates that over the course of Jewish history, many military defeats occurred during the *Shemitta* year or in the year immediately following it. The reason for this is that at the end of the *Shemitta* year or in the year that follows it, a country that is based on an agricultural economy has expended all its resources and is economically depleted. Hence, its ability to absorb suffering is at a low, and an enemy army can conquer it much more easily.

Today, however, we live in a different world. When a country subsists on agriculture, and its surplus – if it exists at all – is very small, this means that even an ordinary Shabbat is an economic burden, and certainly a whole *Shemitta* year is an unbearable burden. Therefore, in the times of our sages, it was indeed necessary to fight for the observance of the seventh year. As it says in the Midrash, keeping the laws of *Shemitta* truly required heroic strength and great fortitude (Leviticus Rabba 1:1). But the more that time goes by, and certainly in recent years, keeping the laws of *Shemitta* has become less and less of a hardship, the underlying reason being that most Israelis today are not farmers. For many years now, the only agriculture that most Israelis encounter – if they encounter it at all – is their little home garden.

While a farmer's perception of *Shemitta* is obviously different from that of the average Israeli, the difficulty of observing the laws of *Shemitta* is much lower than in the past. At the very most, it becomes one of the many nuisances that an observant Jew must deal with, another "annoying" halakha. Just as one must eat kosher food, and just as living in the Land includes observing the laws of *teruma* and *maaser*, *Shemitta* is now added to the list. However, these halakhot have long ago ceased to make much of a practical difference, even for farmers.

The concept of sabbatical – not just as a weekly day of rest but also as a legal regulation that entitles people to a year's vacation from their jobs – is becoming increasingly established all over the world. How can the economy survive this phenomenon? The answer is that the industrialized world lives on a tremendous surplus, and with it, a tremendous amount of waste. Modern society is based on the production of services, and most people in modern society engage in providing services, not in production of goods. This changes people's relationship to the land and their dependence on it, and this change has lessened the perceived existential significance of keeping the laws of *Shemitta*.

"FOR THE LAND IS MINE"

It appears that the whole idea of *Shemitta* has another meaning, one that is more relevant in our generation's reality. It is this meaning that is emphasized in this *parasha* as well. This emphasis is not connected with God demanding of us a great sacrifice; rather, the emphasis is on the question of who owns the land.

In the *Shemitta* year, and even more so in the Jubilee year, there is an aspect of suspension of property ownership by a kind of royal decree from heaven. Our sages call it an *afkaata demalka* – a royal suspension

(Bava Metzia 106a). God proclaims that He is suspending ownership of land and property, canceling all debts.

Such a suspension is not an anomalous idea. Ever since Greek and Roman times, and in other countries and other times as well, instances of this kind of decree have occurred. In the past, some countries instituted such a decree when they sensed that the economic situation was volatile. When they sensed that the pressures, the inequality, or the exploitation of a certain class had reached the point of being unbearable, the country would simply announce that it would stop paying its debts, and creditors would now have to write everything off as a loss.

In a certain respect, however, it appears from the Torah's account that the idea of *Shemitta* and the Jubilee year is not exactly suspension of ownership but something a little different; it can be called reinforcement of ownership.

An example of this notion can be seen in present-day reality: In the heart of New York City there is a large building complex called Rockefeller Center, home to landmark structures such as the GE Building and Radio City Music Hall. This whole area is actually private property, except that the owner implicitly allows the public access to it. For part of one day each year, the area is closed in order to make it known that it is not actually public space but private property. By closing it for one day, the owner reinforces his ownership. He declares that the public uses his property by right of use, not by right of ownership.

In the *Shemitta* and Jubilee years, the Owner reinforces his right to all possessions by suspending our usage rights. This can be seen from the fact that the "royal suspension" of *Shemitta* and the Jubilee year is not an absolute suspension and does not eliminate ownership of property completely. After the *Shemitta* year, the land does not become ownerless and does not go to whoever wants it. Changes do occur, but when the *Shemitta* year is over, the owner can begin to eat from his land's produce again. Everything is his, as before: The land is his, the trees are his, and the fruit is his. The *Shemitta* year was only an intermission.

When the Torah says, "Your cattle and the wild animals that are in your land may eat all its produce" (Lev. 25:7), this is because the suspension is not a true monetary divestment, where property is confiscated from its owner. It is simply that the owner of the land is taken down a notch and reminded that in reality, he is only a tenant. After all, the owner may eat from the produce of his field during the *Shemitta* year; the difference is that the neighbor's donkey is permitted to do so as well, as are all other animals.

An analysis of the laws of *Shemitta* shows that this matter of "and the wild animals that are in your land" is a very important detail. All the dates by which *Shemitta*-year produce must be removed from the house depend on whether the produce is still available to the animals in the field.

This point grounds the essence of *Shemitta* upon the fundamental restoration of ownership to God; He is the owner, and we are mere strangers and sojourners in His land. Once every several years, the ownership is removed from our hands, so that we should understand that although we are hereditary tenants who lease or hire the land, and we have a certain right of possession, the ownership itself is not ours.

The Torah describes another law that is related to this same point. When a "residential house in a walled city" (Lev. 25:29) is sold and is not redeemed during the first year after the sale, the house becomes the permanent property of the buyer and does not revert at the Jubilee year. By contrast, when a Levite sells his house, "the Levites shall forever have the right of redemption" (25:32). The reason for this law is rooted in the very idea we have been discussing. The Levites are the only ones who are expressly and openly designated as strangers and sojourners. An ordinary person who buys a portion of land says to himself that this portion belongs to him. The Levite, however, knows that his livelihood is provided by God, that he eats and resides as a tenant, since he is a servant of God. Therefore, the Levite cities are held under stronger possession, because in essence the Levites' possession of them is weaker. The Levites have more rights because they know that in truth nothing is their own. They know that they received these places as a gift, and they subsist on them only because God allows them to do so.

God is Master of the world and Lord of the earth (*Sifrei*, Deuteronomy 313), and therefore everything that is here belongs to Him. To ensure that we remember this, He takes away from us the exclusive right to use things, returning everything to its original residents – the animals, the beasts, and the dogs.

"IF YOUR BROTHER BECOMES IMPOVERISHED"

This is one aspect of *Shemitta*, which emphasizes the service, the owner-ship, and the fact that God is the Master of the world. The other aspect begins from the verse, "If your brother becomes impoverished" (Lev. 25:25).

As our sages understood it, this section concerns a schlimazel, a ne'er-do-well, who fails at all his endeavors. He has inherited land, but unfortunately, he does not succeed in managing it and is forced to sell it. Soon enough, he is forced to sell his home as well; he finally takes out a loan, with or without interest, and that, too, he is unable to repay. As a result, he has no other recourse – he must sell himself as a slave. But why is this section situated here?

I think that the point presented here is the other aspect of *Shem-itta*, the message of "All is from You, and from Your hand have we given to You" (1 Chr. 29:14). On the one hand, the emphasis of the *parasha* is that God is Master of the whole world and all who live within it; He gives and He takes away. This is the aspect that expresses the power of lordship. But there is also the other aspect of lordship. Lordship entails not only control but also commitment. The concept of "Whoever buys a Hebrew servant is like one who buys himself a master" (Kiddushin 22a) reaches all the way to God. If this is your servant, then you have a responsibility toward him. Just as the servant has obligations, so does the master. Just as a person can address his servant as "my servant," a servant can now address his master as "my master"; the master has a duty and an obligation toward him as well. Authority and dominion are not one-sided but, rather, demand involvement and concern from the master regarding his servants, and a responsibility to support them and provide for all their needs.

In light of this, what happens in the end to the poor schlimazel we spoke of earlier? God acknowledges that no matter how unfortunate this person is, he is His, so He must look after him. Likewise, when the poor fellow sinks even lower, "and he is sold to a stranger sojourning in your midst or even to the root of a heathen's family" (Tanḥuma, *Behar* 2) – he is sold to idolatry itself – he, too, remains under God's responsibility.

Such things have indeed happened. An acquaintance who was the Israeli ambassador to a Muslim African nation told me that one day the imam of the capital city came to him with quite a story. It turns out that this imam was a Yemenite Jew who, in search of a livelihood, wound up in Africa and did not do so well in business. But he had an advantage over the locals: He knew Arabic. He was therefore hired to read them the Quran until they would learn to read, study, and understand the text like he could. Eventually, he rose in the ranks to the point that he became the chief imam. Now that he had reached old age and had accumulated money, he asked the ambassador to somehow convince the authorities to let him make *aliya* and settle in Israel. Sure enough, the imam came to Israel and lived in Haifa for several years. This was a Jew who sold himself as an imam. He recited the Muslim prayers five times a day and read and taught from their holy text. This, too, could be a Jew's livelihood.

Even in such a case, God insists that this schlimazel is His. He is responsible for him. So He will make sure to pull him out, uproot him from these places, and bring him home.

The central motif in this *parasha* is that besides the message of "But the land shall not be sold permanently, for the land is Mine; you are merely strangers and sojourners with Me" (Lev. 25:23), there is also the message of "I am God your Lord, who brought you out of the land of Egypt" (25:38); "For they are My servants, whom I brought out of the land of Egypt; they shall not be sold as slaves" (25:42). And again: "For the People of Israel are servants to Me; they are My servants whom I brought out of the land of Egypt" (25:55). That is to say, they are My servants, My people; and since they are My servants and are Mine, they belong to Me, with all that that entails.

The picture that arises from both sides of the matter is that the entire *parasha* speaks of the same subject: God's servants and their service of God. How do they serve God? What is it like to be "called 'Priests of God' and termed 'servants of our God'" (Is. 61:6)? The answer given here is that just as they belong to Him in that He can confiscate and apportion their land, so, too, do they belong to Him in the sense that He is responsible for looking after their wellbeing and welfare for all time.

A KINGDOM OF PRIESTS

What, then, does all this have to do with Mount Sinai? *Shemitta* has to do with Mount Sinai in that this *parasha* is the essence of what happened at Mount Sinai. The revelation at Sinai represented the acceptance of the service of God in both senses: divine lordship and our service. In *Parashat Behar* this is expressed precisely, in detailed form; here, the Torah explains what it means that He is our Master and we are His servants, how this comes to expression, and what it relates to.

This is exactly what God told us at Mount Sinai even before the giving of the Torah. Those last moments before the Torah was given were moments in which God had not yet "forcibly imposed" the Torah upon us (see Shabbat 88a). And at that time God said, "And now, if you will obey Me and keep My covenant, you shall be My special treasure among all the peoples, for all the earth is Mine. You shall be to Me a kingdom of Priests and a holy nation" (Ex. 19:5–6).

The concept of "a kingdom of Priests" is the essence of our service. As the Ibn Ezra and others explain, "Priests" in this context means servants: You are God's servants. As the Torah relates, "Moses…set before them all these words…And all the people answered as one and said, 'All that God has spoken we will do'" (Ex. 19:7–8). God asks the people if they want to be His servants. The people answer that although they don't yet know the details, they do want to be the servants of God.

Here, too, in *Parashat Behar*, God says to us: "You are Mine." We cannot have true ownership of anything, but God will always provide for us, even when we act like schlimazels. If we think that we are successful on our own merits and that everything is our own, then God will simply take it back. But if we are unsuccessful and lose everything, He will provide for us.

All this we took upon ourselves already at Mount Sinai. Even then we agreed to be God's servants, His tenant-farmers – on condition that we would also receive usage rights.

Beḥukkotai

"IF YOU WALK CONTRARY WITH ME"

The *Tokheḥa* section in Leviticus 26 contains several repeated expressions, including, "If you walk contrary (*bekeri*) with Me." According to an interpretation cited by Rashi, this refers to the sin of interpreting every event in life as an accident (*mikreh*). When something bad happens, it is often easy to write it off as an accident. This can minimize the impact of such an event, disregarding its greater implications for one's life.

When one thinks of the last fifty or one hundred years, it is clear that this problem still exists in modern times. During this period, highly significant events occurred and various processes unfolded that greatly influenced the world and its inhabitants. Regarding each one of these events and processes, it is important to determine the lesson to take away from it. What can we learn from this? What is the conclusion to be drawn from it, and what should be changed as a result? These questions are relevant whether we are speaking about the Holocaust, about the establishment of the State of Israel, or about assimilation, which, although it may not seem as dramatic as the other events, is no less significant for the Jewish people in the long run.

Today, assimilation has reached proportions the likes of which we have not seen in over two thousand years. The majority of the Jewish people has no interest in Judaism. Not since the Hellenistic period, perhaps, have we lived in a time when to be a Jew is a matter of nationality, race, family, and other factors, but not a matter of religion. Statistics today show that for every second that goes by, there is approximately one less Jew in the world; not because he is killed, but because he assimilates among the non-Jews.

This situation, which pertains not just to anomalous individuals but to the entire community, is a tremendous change for us, and we have already forgotten how to deal with such a problem. We know how to deal with one apostate or what to do in the case of a minor misfortune; but how do we cope with the kind of traumatic phenomenon that affects an entire people? Assimilation today is an entirely different kind of problem from what we have dealt with in the past; it is a crisis like no other.

This situation is an example of what *Parashat Beḥukkotai* calls "If you walk contrary with Me"; it is clear that we have learned nothing from our history. To be sure, there are certainly individuals who have learned from past events. Those who abandoned their faith after the Holocaust had suffered through an incredible horror, and essentially said, "Master of the Universe, we cannot carry on anymore; we cannot say that our suffering was simply bad luck. If You exist, You are not watching; and if You are watching, then such a thing would not have happened." These people did not "walk contrary"; they did not attribute world events to chance. The events in our lives have significance, and if they indeed have significance, one cannot remain complacent in response to them; one must draw conclusions from them. But the people as a whole did not respond like these individuals did; instead, they learned nothing at all.

There are those who see a bird flying and chirping and are able to understand what the bird is saying. Rabbi Nachman of Breslov said that after reaching the Land of Israel, he learned why a heap of straw lies in the street lengthwise and not widthwise. Granted, these are arcane matters. But in our case, we are not speaking here about a heap of straw in the street or about hearing a bird chirping. We are talking about catastrophes, events that have shocked the whole world. Yet no response, no conclusion, and no upshot has been drawn from all of this – nothing at all. Everyone carries on as before.

BLAMING OTHERS

When, occasionally, someone does attempt to infer some lesson, the conclusion drawn is generally that someone else is to blame. It is in our nature to look around and search for a guilty party, to determine on whom to pin the blame. Blaming others is often a way of saying that everything that happened proves that one's approach was correct, and it was this other person who caused all the world's problems. Thus, nowadays there are Jews whose main principle of faith is that Zionism brought about the Holocaust. On all the other principles they are willing to compromise, but not on this one.

Conversely, when something good happens, it is the common practice of many people to take credit for it. Others were useful by not getting in the way, or at best they may have helped a bit, but I was the one who saved the day, whether by reciting psalms or by the force of my gun.

One way or another, everything that happens, whether good or bad, makes no impact and effects no change. This is the precise definition of "If you walk contrary with Me."

The *parasha* describes the horrifying consequences of this kind of attitude toward God:

> If you walk contrary with Me and will not obey Me, I will go on smiting you ... And I will send the beast of the field among you, which will rob you of your children, and destroy your cattle, and make you few in number, and your ways will become desolate. And if in spite of these things you will not be corrected unto Me, but walk contrary with Me ... I in turn will smite you sevenfold for your sins. And I will bring upon you an avenging sword ... When I break your staff of bread, ten women will bake your bread in one oven ... and you will eat and not be satisfied ... And you will eat the flesh of your sons. (Lev. 26:21–29).

All this because "you walk contrary with Me" (26:27).

There is a kind of mechanism in man whereby even when he is hit with one affliction after another, he remains unmoved. When retribution comes, everyone immediately looks at his neighbor instead of deep within himself and, as a result, nothing changes. So long as one knows who caused all these afflictions, it is easy to live with all the troubles. In spite of all the admonishment, everything remains as it was before.

One who does not walk contrary is one who attaches meaning, importance, and significance to everything that happens around him. But learning a moral lesson regarding oneself and not automatically looking to someone else is very uncommon.

During the Sinai Campaign, the previous Belzer Rebbe, who was well known for his holiness and piety, stood for two full days in prayer. He was not suspected of being a Zionist, nor did he suddenly become one. But this was a time of great crisis in the world, and there are times when a person changes his mind in response to a crisis, even if not by dramatic declarations.

The hope is that, beyond a certain point, a person can no longer truly claim that a momentous event was a chance occurrence, and he will then understand that he requires rectification and that he must examine his deeds.

"WE AND OUR FATHERS HAVE SINNED"

Toward the end of the *Tokheḥa*, there is another matter that is surprising in several respects: "They will then confess their sins and the sins of their fathers, in that they were unfaithful to me and walked contrary with me" (Lev. 26:40). The confession is not only for sins but also for "walking contrary with God" – that is, for the imperviousness that does not allow one to see things correctly. But what is the meaning of "they will then confess their sins and the sins of their fathers"? Every time we recite the *Viduy* and confess our sins, we use this very formula: "But we and our fathers have sinned," and perhaps for this very reason we no longer notice how odd it is. It makes perfect sense to confess one's own sins, with which one is well acquainted. I have sinned, gone astray, transgressed. But what right do I have to drag my father and grandfather into a confession of these sins?

It is only natural for a person to automatically justify the practices to which he has grown accustomed. People often defend their dubious practices by claiming, "This is how I was brought up, this is my style, this is my custom." Hence, when one wants to make a real confession, this confession cannot suffice with one's own problems. One cannot merely atone for one's own sins within one's own sphere, claiming that these are the only things that fall within one's sphere of responsibility and within the sphere of one's *teshuva*. Rather, one should consider that perhaps "we and our fathers have sinned." He should be willing to examine not only his own personal sins but also the sins of his fathers. Perhaps an error was made that encompasses more than what one did yesterday afternoon. One may have to go back five years, ten years, twenty years – perhaps there is an error that has persisted for generations.

Hence, the Torah says, "Those of you who survive will deteriorate because of their iniquity in the lands of your enemies, and they will deteriorate also because of the iniquities of their fathers. They will then confess their sins and the sins of their fathers" (Lev. 26:39–40) – because that is part of the reckoning. True soul searching must include not only the personal picture but the broader picture.

Whenever any major event happens, one must always ask: What does this mean? What does it imply? What are its implications? Such a comprehensive examination is always challenging for everyone involved, but it must be done; for if it is not comprehensive, the whole examination loses its significance.

ABHORRENCE

Not every sin is specified in the *parasha*, but there is one expression that appears twice, in two different but parallel contexts. At the beginning of the *parasha*, the Torah says, "I will set My presence among you, and I will not abhor you" (Lev. 26:11), and a few verses later, at the beginning of the *Tokheḥa*, it says, "If you reject My statutes and abhor My laws, so that you do not observe all My commandments and you break My covenant" (26:15); and the expression recurs repeatedly.

Generally, when discussing the performance of the mitzvot, one speaks of the practical side: what one must do and what one must not do, and how one must act in regard to laws, statutes, commandments, or covenants. Here, however, the expression concerns a different aspect of the mitzvot. Were they abhorrent or loathsome to you? This is an expression that does not relate to one's actions. Abhorrence pertains to a sphere that is outside and beyond the performance itself. It asks: In what manner did you perform the mitzvot? What did you feel toward them? With what emotion did you perform them?

Again, the issue here is not the actions one has taken that led to a transgression. The question of abhorrence relates to a different aspect. The process that leads to "you abhor My laws" begins with indifference. Indifference is soon followed by loathing, a feeling that the mitzvot are repulsive. Thus, a person can continue doing all that is required of him in practice, and yet loathe and abhor it. He carries out all the orders, but does not care at all about them; in fact, they disgust him.

On the verse, "because you did not serve God your Lord with joy and with gladness over the abundance of all things" (Deut. 28:47), it is said in the name of the Ari[1] that this is the root of, and reason for, all the punishments of the *Tokheḥa*. It is not because "you did not serve God your Lord" but because "you did not serve with joy." Because you do not serve God with joy, you suffer the whole, long *Tokheḥa*, ninety-eight curses in all. The reason for this is that what lies beneath deeds that are not performed with joy is "you reject My statutes and abhor My laws." It may seem unnecessary to perform a mitzva joyfully. Is it not enough to perform the laws in comprehensive detail? Must we be happy about it as well? The Torah's answer is yes – we must serve with joy.

In previous generations, when people would hear the recitation of the *Tokheḥa* in the synagogue – "If you walk contrary with Me"; "If you reject and abhor" – they would tremble in fear. In order to deflect self-scrutiny, many people would rationalize that the *Tokheḥa* applies only to the Torah reader, and not to them. This kind of thinking is vulgar and improper, not to mention ignorant. Nevertheless, it reflects an attitude of hearing the words of the Torah and experiencing a legitimate reaction – quivering with fear, feeling that the punishment described in the *Tokheḥa* may fall on him at any moment.

Nowadays, when the *Tokheḥa* is read in the synagogue, if the reader misses a cantillation mark or a vowel point, the congregants will stop him and tell him to repeat the verse with the proper pronunciation. The truth is that, in doing this, the congregants are following halakha. Why should this *parasha* be any different from all the other *parashot* in the Torah? Nevertheless, it should alarm us that the *Tokheḥa*, which used to inspire such terror, has been reduced to a *zakef katan* or a *mappik heh*.

---

1. Rabbi Isaac Luria.

Similarly, many people use the recitation of *Shema* simply as an opportunity to emphatically draw out the pronunciation of the letter *zayin* in the words "*lemaan tizkeru*"[2] (Num. 15:40); everything else stated in the *Shema* is irrelevant. "You shall love God your Lord" (Deut. 6:5) is unimportant; but to draw out the *zayin* – that is of real substance.

These examples show that many seemingly pious people do not actually care about the mitzvot; there is only contempt and abhorrence toward them.

"WHY IS THE LAND DESTROYED?"

In his introduction to *Tiferet Yisrael*, the Maharal writes at great length on the verse, "Why is the land destroyed … Because they have forsaken My Torah" (Jer. 9:11–12). The Talmud explains that "they have forsaken My Torah" means "they did not first recite the blessing for the Torah" (Bava Metzia 85b).

At first glance, the Talmud's explanation seems difficult to understand. For sins like bloodshed, forbidden sexual relationships, and idolatry, God does not react so harshly. They are certainly considered serious sins, but they are not the sins for which the land was destroyed and the Temple razed. God surely does not react this harshly to other offenses of similar insignificance. So why is the sin of neglecting the blessing for the Torah treated with such severity?

The Maharal answers that the people who "did not first recite the blessing for the Torah" were connected to the Torah without God's involvement. They followed all the mitzvot, but did not appreciate the very root of the matter. God was irrelevant to them, and it was because of this attitude that the land was destroyed.

The Midrash states that "God overlooked idolatry, forbidden sexual relationships, and bloodshed, but did not overlook contempt for the Torah" (Lamentations Rabba, introduction, 2). It is not that God forgave these major sins, only that these sins can always be rectified in this world or the next through *teshuva*, whether it is on one's deathbed

---

2. The purpose of this custom is to ensure that the word does not sound like "*tiskeru*," which would distort the meaning of the verse.

or even after his death. But regarding the sin of contempt for the Torah there apparently is no atonement.

The Talmud describes the *Shekhina*'s departure from the Sanctuary, detailing its movement from station to station, corresponding to its exile: From the Ark-cover to the cherub, from the first cherub to the second cherub, from the second cherub to the threshold of the Holy of Holies, and from there to the courtyard and then to the Altar, and so forth, until "it ascended and abode in its place" (Rosh HaShana 31a). But why should we care that the *Shekhina* has departed? Why does it matter precisely where God dwells? If He wants to live on the second floor, let Him live on the second floor; what does that have to do with me? This is the root of the problem: Man does not care about God, and so he is left only with the external aspect of everything.

The *Tokheḥa* comes in response to this attitude of contempt and abhorrence – and not necessarily because of the performance. God promises that if we follow His laws, He will look at us, "and I will not abhor you" (Lev. 26:11).

It could have been that when a person behaved in a certain way, he would simply make God feel nauseous; God would look at him and feel like vomiting. God therefore promises: "I will not abhor you." Despite all the sins, "I will not reject them or abhor them" (Lev. 26:44).

Numbers

Bemidbar
In honor of Rabbi Josy Eisenberg
Family Vaturi

Naso
Friends from Ra'anana

Behaalotekha
Anonymous

Shelaḥ
From Hanna, Gad, Simonetta, and Massimo Torrefranca
on the occasion of the 25th anniversary of the foundation of our family.
Torrefranca family

Koraḥ
Anonymous

Ḥukkat
In honor and remembrance of Rosetta Ester bat Avraham Avinu Avni Segre,
supporter of persecuted Jews in the valley of Lanzo, Italy, a lover of Israel.
The Segre Family

Balak
In honor of Yonah Pinchas Gedaliah ben David's Bar Mitzva
In honor of Nadav Yisrael Ben Michael Calev's Bar Mitzva
Ruth & Conrad, z"l Morris

Pinḥas
In loving memory of Izzy Herzog
לעילוי נשמת ישראל בן מנחם
From his wife and children

Matot and Masei
In honor of David Daniel ben Shmuel Moshe's Bar Mitzva
Ruth & Conrad, z"l Morris

Bemidbar

Parashat Bemidbar deals with, among other things, the service of the Kehatites. An important part of the Torah's description of their service is the warning to Aaron and his sons to take care to cover the vessels of the Tabernacle before the Kehatites draw near to carry them. The Kehatites, despite their important role as bearers of the sacred vessels, are not allowed to cover them:

> Do not let the tribe of the Kehati families be cut off from among the Levites. This is what you must do, so that they survive and not die when they come into the Holy of Holies. Aaron and his sons shall go in and assign each of them to his service and to his burden. They will then not come and see the sacred [objects] being covered, and they will not die. (Num. 4:18–20)

Regardless of whether "cut off" here means death by the hand of God or by the laws of man, regardless of whether this is an obligation, a prohibition, or a warning, it is clear that, for the Kehatites, witnessing the "covering of the sacred" involves mortal danger.

To bring the matter into sharper focus, let us first note something that may seem obvious at first: The Levites generally, and the Kehatites, from whom the Priests emerged, in particular, are not ordinary people who get out of bed each morning and go to work. They are people who are dedicated to the service of God – "They are wholly given unto Me from among the People of Israel" (Num. 8:16). Yet despite the fact that the Levites are an eminent family in Israel, a family dedicated to God's service and solely responsible for carrying the sacred vessels, they are forbidden to witness the "covering of the sacred." Only a small group of Priests is permitted to cover the sacred objects; anyone else who does so puts himself in mortal danger.

SHATTERING THE SACRED

Every feature of the Temple was also included in the Tabernacle. In the Temple, there was an Outer Altar and an Inner Altar, and in the Tabernacle there were two altars as well. In the Temple there was a Sanctuary and a Holy of Holies, and only those who were on a certain level of sanctity and purity were allowed to enter, and so it was in the Tabernacle. Nevertheless, there is an essential difference between the Tabernacle and the Temple.

In the Tabernacle, despite the sanctity of the Holy of Holies, when the trumpets were sounded everything was moved. And when everything was moved, the place that previously had been the Holy of Holies ceased to be the Holy of Holies, and everyone could then walk on that place with impunity. Men and women, *zavim* and *zavot*, menstruant women and women who recently gave birth – they all are permitted to tread on this place.

What is more, in the Temple nothing would move from its place. The Ark of the Covenant was kept in a secluded place, closed off by a curtain, and not everyone could even look upon it. In the Tabernacle, by contrast, when the trumpets were sounded and it was time to move on, the Levites would take the Ark of the Covenant upon their shoulders and go. The Incense Altar, whose corners were sprinkled only once a year, was carried by four strong Levites, and the same goes for the Menora and all the other vessels of the Sanctuary. Ten minutes earlier, the Ark of the Covenant was something that no one was allowed to hold; to touch its poles was forbidden, and even to look at it was impossible. Now, suddenly, these Levites must take it upon their shoulders and go. Before, the Ark was a place where the *Shekhina* dwelled, and now it is loaded onto a wagon and taken away. The Talmud relates that the boards of the

Tabernacle were often thrown from wagon to wagon (Shabbat 96a). The Levites removed the boards as one would dismantle any other building.

The transition from relating to the Tabernacle as God's holy Sanctuary, to dismantling it and transferring it elsewhere is not simple, and it even involves danger. The very heart of the difficulty, the most dangerous stage, is of course at the point of transition, and that is why the sacred vessels must be covered when the Levites come to take them: "They will then not come and see the sacred objects being covered, and they will not die." Only the Priests, who are God's actual servants, and not servants of servants, may enter within, and they alone have the authority and permission to go in and cover the sacred. Others lack the authority and permission to do so; for them, such an act is fraught with danger. A Levite may not watch the Priest draw near and wrap the vessels in cloth. The concern is that he will not be able to bear the difficulty of the scene, and therefore he may not be present at this stage. Only after the covers have been placed upon the sacred vessels may the Levites draw near and carry them.

DISMANTLING THE SACRED

As long as one stands at a distance from the sacred, as long as one does not touch it and does not deal with it, and it remains in its place in its existing condition, one can see the sacred and stand in awe of it. But what happens when one has to dismantle the sacred? How does one switch from the stage where everything is sanctified to the stage where the sacred must be carried on one's shoulder?

In 1 Samuel, we read that when the people of Beth-shemesh gazed upon the Ark, a great plague broke out among the people. Our sages explain that the plague broke out because the people showed disrespect to the Ark (Sota 35a–b). But why did they do this? Where did this disrespect come from?

As long as the Ark of the Covenant sat in the Tabernacle in Shiloh, no one dared touch it, and even the Philistines showed it reverence, until they could no longer maintain this reverence and eventually returned the Ark to the People of Israel. But the people of Beth-shemesh looked at the Ark and said to it disdainfully, "Who angered you, so that you became angry and [therefore] did not save yourself from captivity? And now who appeased you, so that you became reconciled and came of your own accord?" (Rashi, Sota 35b). The people accused the Ark of ruining their perfect world, where everything was simple and clear. Until now, they knew where everything stood, but the Ark came and spoiled the order of things. For the people of Beth-shemesh, it was no longer possible to relate to the Ark as before; it was no longer the same sacred vessel.

The difficulty was coming to grips with the fact that the sacred vessel that was captured by the Philistines and moved from place to place was still the same sacred vessel that it was originally. It was hard to believe that just as it was sacred in the Holy of Holies, it is still sacred even now, and will continue to be so tomorrow as well, when it will be established in a new place. How could they absorb this truth? How could they witness the sacred vessels being taken in this fashion again and again?

In this *parasha* we have, in effect, a general acknowledgment that not every mind can bear. Not everyone can deal with the fact that what was once sacred is now voided of its sanctity; that something that could not be seen or touched or related to is now freely handled by the Levites.

THE ESSENCE OF STUDY

The truth is that this fundamental problem is not limited to the Tabernacle; it applies to the world of learning as well – to study in general and to the study of Talmud in particular.

There is an essential difference between one who studies *Kitzur Shulḥan Arukh* and one who is considered a true Torah scholar. If someone knows an entire tractate by heart, it can certainly be said that he is well versed in that tractate. But one who asks a novel question, pointing out an objection or a refutation that no one had ever thought of before, even though everyone has seen the page of Talmud in question, so that now neither Rashi nor *Tosafot* can be understood – he is considered a tremendous scholar.

Why is this so? Instead of praising him for his actions, we should take him to task for them – this scholar took something whole, something complete, and ruined it! He took a subject that was previously easily understood, and he shattered it. Why, then, is he called a scholar? What is the virtue in this? When one studies a page of Talmud with the commentaries of Rashi, *Tosafot*, and other early commentators, one begins to wonder: What are they doing with my page? Before Rashi and *Tosafot*, there was a simple, smooth page of Talmud; the commentators then enter the equation and tear it to pieces! What is more, the attitude is that the stronger and sharper one's questions, the more praise one deserves.

Almost everyone has some kind of desire to destroy or ridicule something; there are people who have a special talent for destruction. One always has qualms about whether or not to destroy something, but when one knows that in destroying he is performing a mitzva, and that he may enjoy it – he does it wholeheartedly. Just as this evil inclination exists regarding the physical, it exists regarding the spiritual as well. When a person is told to critique someone, he will usually waste no time in tearing him to pieces.

This is essentially how traditional Torah study works. We demonstrate that the first *Tanna* did not understand the last *Tanna*, and that the latter does not know what the former is talking about. There was a period when the "*ḥillukim*" method was prevalent, where the objective was to show that the questioner and answerer did not understand each other, and neither of them understood the Mishna. This is how talmudic discussions were reconstructed. Thus, a person's level of scholarship was judged not by how much he studies and how much he knows but by his ability to dismantle the Talmud into its smallest elements, so as to reconstruct it.

The study of Talmud and Torah study in general is essentially a matter of breaking things down into their composite parts. The greater one's ability to break things down, the greater the depth of one's learning. If one studies only *Kitzur Shulḥan Arukh*, he will know all the information that is written in the book, but not more than that. For such a person, nothing exists outside the *Kitzur*. But what happens when he begins to study Talmud or *Arba'a Turim*? What happens when he studies the full *Shulḥan Arukh* with all the commentaries? It becomes clear that everything that is presented so clearly and simply in the *Kitzur* is not at all simple: There are suddenly countless conflicting opinions, and it becomes difficult even to keep track of all of them. This is not limited to minor differences of opinion. Some differences range from one end of the spectrum to the other. For example, there is a difference between *minhag Sepharad*, *minhag Ashkenaz*, and *minhag Sepharadim* on the question of whether one counts the weeks or the days first in *Sefirat*

HaOmer. In *Kitzur Shulḥan Arukh*, these matters are treated very simply: This is what one must do, this is what happens in every case of error, and that is all. In this simplified world, one knows what is forbidden and what is permitted, what is ideal and what is not ideal. However, the more one studies in depth, the more one begins to break things down and take them apart.

The story is told of a new student at a certain yeshiva who attended the lectures of the *rosh yeshiva*. The *rosh yeshiva* would address Rashi's commentary, saying, "I don't understand Rashi!" and explain why his commentary was puzzling. Then he would turn to *Tosafot* and say that he doesn't understand *Tosafot*. Then he would turn to the Talmud and say that he doesn't understand the Talmud, and so forth. After a while, the new student wrote home: "Thank God, I already don't understand ten pages of Talmud!"

When one begins to study a page of Talmud, he believes that he knows everything, or almost everything, and that all he needs to do is to fill in a gap or two here or there. When he gets further into the sub-ject, if he really delves into it, he discovers that he understands neither Rashi, nor *Tosafot*, nor the Talmud, nor the *Rishonim*, nor the *Aḥaronim*; and the more he delves into it, the less he understands. As he discov-ers more and more questions and peculiarities, the effect is cumulative: Things become increasingly complex.

Torah study is, in a sense, a kind of battlefield. One takes a page of Talmud, cuts it into pieces, and reduces it to dust and ashes. One takes a halakha, which he knows exactly how to implement in practice, and begins to demonstrate that it is built on compromises – between the Shakh and the Taz or between Rava and Rabba. It is not a matter of merely sharpening the mind, where one looks for problems for no rea-son; these problems can actually be found everywhere, in every subject of Torah study. And for one who deals with matters of faith, the matter becomes even more complex than this.

When people explain to children that a man with a long white beard sits in heaven, holding a stick in one hand and a candy in the other, this may be an unsophisticated conception of the world, but it is simple and clear. After one begins to study, and the more one learns, the world does not become simpler and smoother. On the contrary, in a certain sense it becomes more and more complicated, more and more complex. What this means is that study entails a kind of traumatic process, a process of breaking things apart.

VARIOUS LEVELS

As we see in the *parasha*, not everyone can bear the process of dismantling the sacred. There are various levels in this notion: Anyone who is *tahor* may touch the boards of the Tabernacle, but not everyone can perform the dismantling and the assembling, the carrying and the dragging. Most people are not allowed to participate in this process of changing from sacred to profane and back again. They do not touch the dismantled Sanctuary; for them, there is only a complete Tabernacle. Anyone of Israel may visit the Sanctuary, and when a person wanted to eat meat, he would bring his animal to the Tabernacle forecourt to offer it as a peace offering. But when it came to dismantling, carrying, or assembling the Tabernacle, he is told that he has no part in this work; for him, the Tabernacle may only be seen in its complete form.

This point can also be observed in the formation in which the camps would travel in the wilderness. Whether they would travel in square formation or in a straight line (see Y. Eiruvin 5:1), the Tabernacle was always in the center, surrounded by the Levite camp. The various Levite families were likewise on different levels: Some would handle the outer boards; some would enter the interior; some would handle the hangings of the forecourt; some would handle the boards and the sockets; and some would handle even the sacred vessels. But even those who handled the sacred vessels could not draw near and cover them. Although the Levite knows what he is carrying, he does not actually see it.

Similarly, in Torah study, some people can only tackle the simplest types of questions, while others can ask deeper, more incisive questions. Sometimes, when a student begins to cross the boundary of his spiritual limitations, we advise him not to push further: There are questions that even an outstanding scholar should not ask, for he would not be able to bear the dismantling of the sacred and its subsequent reassembly. For this reason, every student must assess himself and determine his personal spiritual level.

Someone once remarked that in order to attain the proper fear of heaven, one must study Maimonides' *Guide for the Perplexed* from the end to the beginning, so as to begin with the answers and end with the questions. The meaning of this strange statement is that sometimes people begin with the questions and do not have the strength to continue to the answers, so they remain with the questions and never emerge from them.

Everyone must ask questions in order to learn. Even a small child must be encouraged to ask questions, for this is the only way he will understand. However, the distinction is in the type of questions one may ask. Some people can ask only very simple questions, and one must accordingly supply them with simple explanations. Other people can take apart deeper matters. The ordinary person's problem is not that he is unable to take the Tabernacle apart and break it down, but that he cannot always reassemble it.

DEMOLISHING IN ORDER TO BUILD

What happens later, when one wants to relocate the holy? How does the new location suddenly become holy? How does this place become the Holy of Holies? How can one be exposed to all the questions and contradictions, and after all that, still relate to the subject with the proper awe and fear? This level of spirituality is not easy to attain. It is a problem that is inherent in Torah study, in faith, and in Judaism: How can one question, take apart, demolish, and rebuild, and at the same time preserve the sense that one is in the realm of holiness?

Only those who can bear it – the sons of Aaron, the Priests – may enter the inner Sanctuary and dismantle it. Only they can they see "the sacred [objects] being covered" each time, because only Aaron was on such a level that he remained whole after the shattering of the sacred.

We read in Psalms: "With the wholehearted, You act wholeheartedly... and with the perverse You are wily" (18:26–27). This notion can be applied to such a person: On the one hand, he can be wholehearted and guileless, but on the other hand, he can be wily as well. The Midrash describes how Aaron would make peace between people: He would go to two people who had quarreled, whether it was a husband and his wife or a man and his friend, and shamelessly lie to both of them. He would approach one, saying, "Your friend so-and-so is now weeping bitterly"; then he would approach the other and tell him the same thing. When the two would next meet, it would be in a spirit of love and brotherhood (*Kalla Rabbati*). Aaron could be wily "with the perverse" and, in spite of this, remain wholehearted – as the Priest is described in Malachi, "a messenger of the Lord of Hosts" (2:7).

The hallmark of the Priest is that while he has the ability to cover the sacred, he is still afraid to approach the Altar after doing so. Aaron is afraid, "for who is he that would risk his life to approach Me?" (Jer. 30:21). Hence, he is the one who may cover the sacred, handle the vessels, and move them from place to place. Some people may only see the vessels, others may disassemble them, but only a select few may see the removal of the essence of the sacred. Only one who serves God wholeheartedly may do this, one who has nothing else but the worship of God. Outsiders "who attach themselves to God, to serve him" (Is. 56:6) are shielded from this experience. Only one who does inner, hidden service, totally committed to serving God, may enter the Sanctuary and cover the sacred.

It could be that one who disassembles the Tabernacle might be able to reassemble it in a different form, such that it is no longer the Tabernacle. For this reason, there are questions that not everyone may ask – not because they have no answers, but because after one has struggled with them, it will be impossible to build the Sanctuary properly on its site, and then one risks remaining in a void. Not to mention the two matters in the same breath, but an example of something similar is found in the laws of idolatry. For an idolater to nullify an idol, it suffices to spit at it, throw something at it, or chip one of its fingers. The assumption is that after treating it this way, he will never again regard it as an object of worship. A Jew, however, cannot nullify an idol. No matter what he does, it will always remain an idol.

When the Tabernacle is dismantled, it does not wander randomly; it must follow a certain course. It is dismantled and reassembled in order to ultimately reach the Temple – "the place You made to dwell in" (Ex. 15:17). To get there takes centuries. The path is not straight – it is long and winding, but it is the only way to make progress.

In the Tabernacle, as it is so often in our lives, we dismantle in order to build. Something is uprooted from its place in order to be rebuilt more fruitfully in a new place.

The prohibition on destroying holy vessels – "You shall break down their altars…You shall not do so to God your Lord" (Deut. 12:3–4) – does not apply to this process. We are commanded to dismantle the Tabernacle time and again, so that we can rebuild it elsewhere. This demolition is an extension of God's will – "at God's command they encamped, and at God's command they journeyed" (Num. 9:20) – and it is always a constructive act, as the Talmud says, "The destruction of the old is building" (Nedarim 40a).

Thus, the Tabernacle constantly moves forward, toward the chosen place, ever advancing to the eternal house of God.

Naso

THE LEVITE FAMILIES

Parashat Naso consists of several subjects, each one of which is basically self-contained: the section on the *sota* (suspected adulteress), the section on the *nazir*, the priestly blessing, and the offerings of the princes. I would like to discuss the matter that appears at the beginning of the *parasha* – the service of the Gershonites.

In terms of content, the beginning of the *parasha* is connected to the previous *parasha*. After the division of the flags and the division of the camps comes the division of the Levite families, each family in its assigned place and standing. *Parashat Bemidbar* ends with the service of the Kehatites, and *Parashat Naso* begins with a description of the service of the Gershonites and Merarites.

The description of the service of the Gershonites follows the pattern of the description of the service of the other Levite families, the Kehatites and the Merarites. The verse, "Take a census of Gershon's sons also, by their fathers' houses, by their families" (Num. 4:22), is an almost verbatim repetition of the verse from the preceding *parasha*, "Take a census of Kehat's sons among the Levites, by their families, by their fathers' houses" (4:2). The Merarites, too, are described as being counted "by their families, by their fathers' houses" (4:29).

Clearly, then, we are dealing with one section. It is also clear that even though it seems that the same thing is repeated, each Levite house appears independently and is described uniquely. The Kehatites are characterized one way, the Gershonites another way, and the Merarites yet another way. But the question remains: Why does a new *parasha* begin with the Gershonites? What stands out in the case of the Gershonites is the statement "of Gershon's sons also." What is the meaning of the word "also" here?

The Kehatites have a clear designation: "This is the service of the Kehatites in the Tent of Meeting: the Holy of Holies" (Num. 4:4). The Kehatites dealt with the Holy of Holies. Except in a few cases, the Ark of the Covenant was not carried by the Priests but by the Levites – specifically the Kehatites. It was their responsibility to carry the contents of the Sanctuary, the sacred vessels: the Menora, the Table, and the Incense Altar.

The service of the Kehatites did not consist of backbreaking labor. Rather, it was work in the sense of conveying the essence of things. One's ability to bear the Ark of the Covenant was not a matter of physical strength. It is difficult to imagine how they carried the Ark of the Covenant, particularly in light of the talmudic statement that the Ark-cover's thickness was one handbreadth (Sukka 5a). To create a cover with a thickness of one handbreadth, even without including the cherubim in the equation, required a huge amount of gold, and the weight of such a cover would be well over a ton. Our sages acknowledge this, explaining that this was not an issue, as "the Ark would carry its bearers" (Sota 35a). This is an essential point. The Levite who would lift the Ark was not actually lifting a heavy load; he was lifting a supernatural object. Our sages say that "the place of the Ark is not included in the measurement" (Yoma 21a), because the Ark of the Covenant exists half in this world and half in another world. It exists between the material and the spiritual. Hence, the whole matter of carrying the Ark, the Table, and the Menora transcended the physical carrying.

Thus, the service of the Kehatites was service of people who are on a lofty level. Indeed, the Kehatites did not remain within the limits of this service. Many eminent people came forth from their ranks. One of them was a descendant of Korah, the prophet Samuel, whose level of prophecy was equal to that of Moses and Aaron: "Moses and Aaron among His Priests, and Samuel among those who call on His name"

(Ps. 99:6). And it is not only Samuel. Anyone who opens the book of Psalms can see that this family accomplished many other profound things: "For the leader, a psalm of the songs of Koraḥ" (44:1). Once, they carried the Ark of the Covenant; and even when they stopped carrying it, they continued to produce great people from their midst. These people continued to bear the Ark of the Covenant, if not physically then spiritually.

Unlike the Kehatites, the Merarites were simple porters. They carried the boards, the basic structure of the Tabernacle. They took the whole structure, the entire house – but not the sacred vessels. All over the world, there are people who must do the simple work, the menial labor. They could be exalted people or humble people, but in a certain respect, everything depends on them.

In this respect, the Gershonite families occupied a middle position. "This is the service of the Gershonite families: to minister and to carry" (Num. 4:24). The Kehatites dealt with spiritual matters. Though the service of the Merarites was not intellectual work, when they were finished a house stood. They took a hammer and nails and built something. If the Merarites performed the heavy lifting, and the Kehatites dealt with the important, exalted matters, what was left for the Gershonites? The answer is that the Gershonites carried everything in between. They collected and folded all sorts of things, including various materials and ropes.

Sometimes, it is much easier to be one of the simple porters than to be a member of the Gershonites. To be sure, a Merarite could not be an angel, nor could he perform the work of the angels, but his responsibility was clear and defined, and at the end of each day he knew that he accomplished something. But a Gershonite was neither an angel nor a porter – he was in between. The Gershonites certainly engaged in holy work, but not of the highest sort, like the Kehatites. For the Gershonites, it was easy to feel that they were not accomplishing anything.

Because of this, the Torah emphasizes, "Take a census (*naso et rosh* – literally, raise the heads) of Gershon's sons also," because these people must be remembered, they must be uplifted and told, in essence, that the Kehatites did not take all the plum jobs – "Raise the heads of Gershon's sons also."

This is also the reason the *parasha* begins with the census of the Gershonites and is not connected with the preceding *parasha*: It is a way to give honor to the Gershonites. Instead of again sandwiching them in the middle, between the Kehatites and the Merarites, they are given the honor of beginning a new *parasha*.

THE GERSHONITE FAMILIES – MIDDLE PEOPLE

Needless to say, this distinction between people is not limited to Kehatites, Gershonites, and Merarites; it can be applied to almost anyone. Some people are like the Kehatites who carried the holy Ark, and tend to gravitate to roles of this type in all their undertakings. Whether they pursue these roles because of some inner stimulus, or a feeling that society, or their external reality, is pushing them in that direction, they know that they are going to be something special. When a person has a passion to become a Jewish leader – if not tomorrow then sometime in the future – this is because something burns within him and gives him strength to work hard to achieve his aspirations.

Others are like the Merarites; all they want is to be a decent person, a good worker, to do an honest day's work and earn a living. They will never do anything out of the ordinary, because no one ever discusses matters of great importance with them. Such people could perhaps achieve more, but they remain within their limits. Many people prefer not to be appointed to high positions, but to just remain an ordinary worker, because in many respects this greatly simplifies one's life. They exemplify the Talmud's statement, "'You will eat the fruit of your labor; you will be happy, and it will be well with you' (Ps. 128:2). 'You will happy' in this world, 'and it will be well with you' in the World to Come" (Ḥullin 44b). There is "fruit of your labor" whose great virtue is "you will be happy in this world." One knows where the work begins and where it ends, and there is no need to deal with one's conscience. It is easy to be a decent person, to fulfill one's responsibilities in life.

When a person does not aspire to great things, he can make for himself a peaceful, simple life. Indeed, many people live this way. One's life remains simple even when difficulties arise, God forbid. This does not cause inner dilemmas, and he does not struggle with God in matters of faith. If he needs money, for example, he looks for work to increase his income.

Someone once said: The rabbi is so unfortunate! Even when he recites the *asher yatzar* blessing (after using the bathroom) he must make a whole production out of it, with special contemplations and mystical thoughts. Many people have no such problem; they recite automatically not only *asher yatzar* but also the blessings of the *tefillin*, winding them, kissing them, and winding them once more without paying the slightest attention to the meaning behind the process. When he comes home from work, he watches television for a while, then goes to the synagogue, attending a Torah lesson between Minḥa and Maariv. Afterward, he'll watch some more television, recite the *Shema,* and go to sleep. In this way, his life will be a good life. Such a person could have been one of the Merarites.

The problem is in the case of the Gershonites. A Gershonite is not on such a level that he can put on *tefillin* in a state of ecstatic reverie. On the other hand, he is not one of the simple people whose lives are without delusions and without pretensions. The Gershonites cannot do the lofty work of the Kehatites, nor do they want to do it; on the other hand, they are not assigned the simple, menial work either. They are in the middle, torn between the two extremes. What happens to the middle person? He cannot live like the Merarites, because if he does so, it will eat him up inside. However, he is not really on the level of the Kehatites either.

This is often the tragedy of career-long assistants and subordinates. They have enough authority and intelligence to cause a headache, but on the other hand, they do not have enough power to make major decisions. *Pirkei Avot* speaks of such people: "In our hands is neither the tranquility of the wicked nor the suffering of the righteous" (4:15). Suffering of the righteous – because a *tzaddik* undergoes a certain kind of suffering simply by virtue of being a *tzaddik*, accepting his suffering with love. One who decides to be wicked has a certain kind of tranquility as well. What happens to someone who is neither one nor the other? He has neither suffering nor tranquility, or alternatively, he has both suffering and tranquility. Here stands a man who is not sure why he receives these blows, and when he rests he knows that it will not last long; shortly he will be jolted awake again.

"Raise the heads of Gershon's sons also"; give these people, who have neither the tranquility of the wicked nor the suffering of the righteous, a role in the Tabernacle. The Torah tells the Gershonite that he may never reach the level of the Kehatites, who bear the Ark of the Covenant, for he is not cut out for that. The ease and tranquility of placing the boards on the wagon and accompanying them will likewise not be the lot of the Gershonite. Instead, the Gershonite must realize that his service will always include both service of love and service of carrying. That is his lifetime vocation.

The Gershonites receive their very own *parasha*, an honor that was not bestowed upon the Kehatites and the Merarites. They were given this honor because they suffer on both accounts. They suffer because they want to grow and they have insights into profound matters, but they are unable to realize this or put their lofty aspirations into practice.

"ENTHRONED UPON THE PRAISES OF ISRAEL"

In the description of the *ofanim* and the *hayot* who raise themselves toward the seraphim, we find this same distinction. Some angels fly above, and some remain in the middle. The seraphim "were standing above, at His service" (Is. 6:2) – they are holy angels, and they burn with His light. The *ofan*, who is both an angel and a wheel, must watch this seraph fly above, whereas he, the *ofan*, is tied down below. Had this *ofan* been simply a wagon wheel, this would not have bothered him. His problem is that he is both an angel trying to ascend and a wheel that cannot ascend. On the other hand, this tension is precisely what makes him holy.

The *ofanim* and the *hayot* raise themselves toward the seraphim – they, too, want to be above; they constantly try to ascend higher. Even though they are essentially porters who perform simple labor, they must somehow rise up. Hence, it is said that, in the uppermost realms, the *ofanim* and *hayot* ascend higher than the seraphim. This is not because they are on a higher level, but precisely because they live amidst this contradiction and distress.

The seraphim ask, "Where is the place of His glory?"[1] because when they speak of God, they know that however holy they may be, He nevertheless is inaccessible to them. No matter how high they ascend, God is above and beyond. "Holy, holy, holy" (Is. 6:3) means that God is above, beyond, from the other side, from another reality, in a different world.

---

1. From the *Kedusha* of the *Musaf* service on Shabbat and Yom Tov.

By contrast, the *ofanim* say, "Blessed is the glory of God from His place" (Ezek. 3:12). Their spirituality consists of revealing God's presence in the physical world. The seraphim can fly around the divine chariot, and they are very holy, but they elevate neither the divine chariot nor God. Those who elevate Him are the *ofanim*, the wheels that are tied down below, which will never be seraphim. From where does an *ofan* get such power to elevate? It is precisely because he is miserable, and precisely because he admits that he cannot be a seraph. He is tied down, relegated to a life of labor. However, the *ofan* still knows that he is not a simple wheel; he knows that seraphim exist and that a divine chariot exists, and thus he will always aspire to higher things.

The problem of the Gershonites is the problem of the *ofanim* and of all those who are in the middle. On the one hand, the Gershonite knows that he is not an angel. On the other hand, he is not a simple wheel either who is happy with his lot. The *ofan* of the divine chariot is an angel, and the source of his power is the fact that he endures suffering, through which he elevates and bears God's glory.

The essence of the Gershonites applies to mankind in general. A person has enough self-awareness to know that he is not satisfied with his lot in life. He is too corporeal to be an angel and too divine to be an animal. The significance of man as a unique creation lies in his imperfection, and it is on this account that God does not suffice Himself with angels alone.

Before man's creation, the angels came to God, saying, "Does His Majesty want someone holy? Take Michael. Someone to decide halakhot? Take Gabriel. Do You want someone who can generate new insights? Assign two or three angels to work on novel Torah ideas. Do You want simple creatures that eat grass and moo? You already have such creatures."

The angels did not complain about the cows, goats, sheep, and swallows. Only when man was created did the angels have something to say. If God had created man strictly as a holy soul, the angels might have extolled him (Genesis Rabba 8:10). If man had been created as a kind of advanced ape that wanders around the world, this too would not have troubled the angels. But God created man, and that is the problem. On the one hand, man was given a soul, which constantly urges him to ascend, yet on the other hand he was given a body, which constantly pulls him down. Thus, God formed a creation that, from its very inception, has existed in a state of contradiction.

We read that God is "enthroned upon the praises of Israel" (Ps. 22:4). He sits on a throne of sighs, of those who say, "Master of the Universe, I am not on a very high level, but I still want to uplift myself." These are the "praises of Israel" on which God is enthroned. The complaints of the angels echo those of many people. These people are constantly distressed by their station in life. They are not simple farmers, because internally they would always be restless. They are not built to be angels either – so what remains? The poor fellow sits there, torn from above and from below. It would have been much better if God had omitted the creation of man entirely, leaving a pleasant, simple world.

God ignored the angels and created man, because He knew what they did not know. What man accomplishes with his torn inner self the angels cannot accomplish with all of their perfection. The Gershonites are neither here nor there, but God appreciates them. Hence, the *parasha* begins, "Raise the heads of Gershon's sons." We conclude the previous *parasha* by stopping in the middle of the subject, to give the Gershonites the honor they deserve. This is precisely the meaning of "enthroned upon the praises of Israel."

The Talmud relates that God has an exalted angel upon whom we cannot gaze, who is taller than all the *ḥayot*, and who stands behind the Throne of Glory, wreathing crowns for his Maker from the prayers of Israel (Ḥagiga 13b). Down below, there is a Jew who is neither an angel nor a seraph, but from time to time he becomes bitterly sad and says: "Master of the Universe! I would like to do something for You." Then this exalted angel lowers his whole stature so as to bend down and take these words, with all the mud that is stuck to them. And he is told to clean them, polish them, and make of them a crown for God, as the Midrash says, "'Israel, in whom I will be glorified' (Is. 49:3) – as The Holy One, Blessed Be He, is crowned by the prayers of Israel" (Exodus Rabba 21:4). What is written in God's *tefillin*? "Who is like Your people Israel, a unique nation on earth" (II Sam. 7:23) (Berakhot 6a).

The concept of "Israel, in whom I will be glorified" is in one respect awful and sad. But in another respect, it is our glory as human beings, and God glories in it.

Behaalotekha

LET THEM BE YOURS ALONE

In this *parasha*, we read of the fascinating incident of Eldad and Medad. God commands Moses to appoint seventy men who will share the burden of the people with him. Everything proceeds according to plan, until Eldad and Medad begin to prophesy in the camp. The seventy prophets all received a kind of "*hekhsher*" from Moses, certifying the legitimacy of their prophecy. By contrast, Eldad and Medad were prophets without a license.

When Joshua sees them prophesying, he says that a prophet without a *hekhsher* should be imprisoned. At this point, Moses gives a memorable response: "Are you jealous for my sake?" (Num. 11:29). It is unclear if this is a rhetorical question.

Moses then makes a trenchant comment: "Would that all of God's people were prophets, that God would put His spirit upon them." This is a point that can be applied to Torah study, to general piety, and to many other matters. Is it necessary, or even possible, to confine these matters to a limited number of people who are most qualified for them? Should one restrict the matter or spread it around? When one possesses Torah, piety, wisdom, or knowledge – should one disseminate it? Is it better to keep it whithin oneself – "Let them be yours alone" – or should "others share with you" (Prov. 5:17)?

This is actually a general question about the nature of the Jewish people. Should only the worthy enter the inner sanctum, while the unworthy remain outside, or may anyone who desires presume to enter?

I posit that this was the argument between Moses and Joshua, an argument that continued over the course of the generations. In a certain sense, this was also the dispute between Beit Hillel and Beit Shammai (*Avot DeRabbi Natan* 3) whether to teach Torah only to the wealthy or to the poor as well. Before Hillel's time the custom was that one could not enter the beit midrash without paying an entrance fee. Admission was not open to all comers; one had to demonstrate one's seriousness by being willing to pay. Beit Hillel's position was to open the beit midrash so that whoever wanted to study could come and study.

In describing Yehoshua b. Gamla, the Talmud says, "That man shall be remembered for good, for were it not for him, Israel would have forgotten the Torah" (Bava Batra 21a). Yehoshua b. Gamla founded a chain of popular schools that allowed all Jewish children to learn Torah, an innovation at the time. It is not that this innovation never occurred to anyone before. Rather, beforehand people took a different approach, saying that if someone is not completely cut out for such study, he should not study at all. If someone truly wanted to study, they claimed, he will ultimately find his way on his own.

The last time this dispute broke out between the two approaches was in Yavne. A large part of the dispute with Rabban Gamliel in Yavne and his dismissal had to do with this argument. As long as Rabban Gamliel was president, there was a doorkeeper at the entrance to the beit midrash. This doorkeeper enforced Rabban Gamliel's proclamation that anyone "whose inside is not the same as his outside" may not enter the beit midrash. The Talmud relates that after the doorkeeper was removed, four hundred benches were added to the beit midrash, implying a vast increase in the number of students learning there. Rabban Gamliel was then greatly disheartened, saying, "Perhaps I withheld Torah from Israel!" He was then shown in a dream four hundred casks full of ashes, as though to tell him not to be overly upset, as these new students were not worth very much. The Talmud concludes: "This, however, really meant nothing; he was only shown this to appease him" – in truth, Rabban Gamliel had made the wrong decision (Berakhot 28a).

But who was this doorkeeper? Who could possibly recognize whether a person's inside is the same as his outside? The answer is that the doorkeeper just stood there and announced, "If anyone's inside is not the same as his outside, he should not enter the beit midrash." That was all that was necessary to deter most people from entering. But what Rabban Gamliel did not know was that there were people whose hearts were broken inside them, people who were thirsty for Torah, people whose insides were indeed the same as their outsides – and yet when such a person would heard the announcement that whoever's inside is not the same as his outside should not enter, he would begin to doubt his own integrity nonetheless. He would remember the dubious things he did in the past, and question if perhaps he was not worthy of entering the beit midrash and studying. So he would not enter. The only people who would enter without any hesitation were those to whom it was obvious that their insides were the same as their outsides. According to this explanation, the casks full of ashes symbolize the students who entered before the doorkeeper was removed, and not the new students.

THE WHOLE JEWISH PEOPLE

This dispute, and Moses' question to Joshua, is a real problem. It cannot be said that Joshua was a petty person, envious and narrow minded, and he therefore understood nothing. Joshua was a supremely exalted individual; he just had a different perspective and a different approach.

This same issue appears in several places in the Torah. For example, after the sin of the Golden Calf, God says to Moses, "Leave Me alone, and I will destroy them … and I will make you a nation greater and more numerous then they are" (Deut. 9:14), and yet Moses resists: "Blot me out from the book You have written" (Ex. 32:32); under no circumstances! Why does he resist? If God had said to Moses, "I shall abandon the People of Israel and place My spirit on Yitro's people," Moses' outcry would have been understandable. Why are Yitro's people considered better than my people? But Moses' essential complaint relates to the question of ownership of the Torah. Who are the elect? Is the Torah only for special individuals, or is it a Torah for everyone, even for ordinary people, even for people who sinned because of ignorance or obtuseness? Who are the chosen? Only unique individuals, the elite, those who exemplify the legacy of Moses? Or do the chosen include others as well, like Koraḥ and other rebellious, transgressive individuals among us?

Moses fights precisely over this point. He fights for the Jewish people as a national community. Does the Jewish people have to be composed entirely of select individuals, where one by one everyone has been checked, or does the people include all types? Moses is neither overly forbearing nor overly forgiving, but on this principle he refuses to compromise. He does not condone the actions of sinners, but he is adamant that they are included in the Jewish people. Moses struggles, as it were, with God over this point, and avers to God that if He wants to build a nation out of exceptional people only, "blot me out from the book You have written."

"WOULD THAT ALL OF GOD'S PEOPLE WERE PROPHETS"

The resolution of this question is not simple and unequivocal, since there are different aspects to it, but ultimately we are all disciples of Moses, and the answer that he gives to this question is unequivocal: "Would that all of God's people were prophets, that God would put His spirit upon them" (Num. 11:29). If it were up to Moses, he would want not seventy prophets but 600,000 prophets – as many prophets as possible. According to this principle, all God wants is that whoever is capable of receiving should receive, whoever is capable of absorbing should absorb, and whoever is capable of doing should do.

For Moses, this is not a minor detail but a major principle. He says that he is sorry that not all the people are prophets. They all should have become prophets, and if only they all would have wanted to be prophets. All his life, Moses regrets this, and in the description of the giving of the Torah in Deuteronomy, he complains that the people sent him to speak with God and did not want to hear Him themselves. Essentially, he accuses them, telling them that they had an opportunity to be prophets – notwithstanding the pain that experiencing one's soul taking flight entails – and yet they renounced the opportunity and decided to be commoners.

To be sure, it is difficult to be a prophet, and most of the prophets in Tanakh did not enjoy being prophets. Being a prophet means paying an extraordinary personal price, and it appears that none of the prophets ended up being happy with the job. Only one prophet seemed to have wanted to be a prophet: Isaiah, who embraced the role. Isaiah proclaimed, "Here I am; send me" (Is. 6:8) – and even of him we read that "My servant Isaiah has gone naked and barefoot" (20:3) and "I did not hide my face from insults and spitting" (50:6). Prophecy is not a simple matter, neither in this world nor in the inner world of the prophet. This is the lot of Isaiah, and this is the lot of every prophet.

Yet Moses nevertheless says, "I would like you to be prophets; I would like you to want to be prophets." From Moses' standpoint, ideally the process of creating a prophet would be simple. One would find a person in the street, grab him by the collar and say to him, "God wants you to be a prophet!" Instead, what actually happens is that we tell the person that as long as he has a *kippa* on his head and attends synagogue, we are satisfied with his spiritual standing and we will leave him alone.

The question that Moses raises here is this: What does God want from each and every member of the Jewish people? What does He require of him? What are His expectations for such a person?

We find a similar approach in Jeremiah: "No longer will they need to teach one another, saying: 'Know God'; for all of them – from the least of them to the greatest – will know Me" (31:33). Likewise, we see this perspective in the ideal portrayal of the end of days: "For the land will be filled with knowledge of God as water covers the sea" (Is. 11:9).

MOSES THE MAN

According to our mystical literature, one of the reasons that Moses needs the seventy prophets is that he is such a great man that he simply does not understand what people want. It is not that he is not wise enough. Rather, it is like sitting next to two small children who are quarreling over a candy wrapper. Would an adult intervene in such an inane dispute?

When Moses says despairingly, "I am not able to bear this entire people myself alone, for it is too much for me" (Num. 11:14), it is because he looks upon the people who say "give us meat" in this same way. He cannot understand how people can cry over onions and garlic; it seems impossible to him. So he says, "I cannot deal with them." When he meets with all the leaders of thousands and leaders of hundreds, and they are all crying over the onions and garlic, he feels exactly like a beleaguered adult among bickering children; he does not understand them.

Moses, the man who speaks with God face to face, the man who towers over all the people, has trouble dealing with the people in daily life. In spite of this, he refuses to compromise on the principle that everyone should have access to the Torah. Although he cannot deal with them, he does not want to give up on them either. He does not simply abandon the people or send them back to Egypt, as they implied they would prefer, keeping only the sensible, intelligent ones in his company. Nor does he refuse to interact with the general populace, insisting on communicating only with those to whom he can better relate. Instead, he puts himself on the line for each and every one of them, because the two issues are unconnected. Although they are foolish and he cannot relate to them, they deserve the Torah just as the wise do.

THIS GREAT NATION

The Torah makes two seemingly contradictory statements. On the one hand, it says, "Not because you are more numerous than all the other nations did God embrace you and choose you; for you are the smallest of all the nations" (Deut. 7:7). On the other hand, it says, "This great (*hagadol*) nation is certainly a wise and understanding people" (4:6). Is this nation a large nation or a small one?

In truth, however, *hagadol* does not refer to the nation's size – we are a rather small nation – but to Israel's chosenness. We are great in that we are a wise and understanding people.

In certain generations the people are more wise and understanding, and in other generations they are not, but the dispute between Moses and Joshua does not concern the reality but the ideal. Should one accept the status quo that there is a certain percentage of people who are ignorant, or should I combat this phenomenon? Moses says that he is absolutely unwilling to accept the given situation. He wants at least 600,000 prophets; for Moses, less than that is insufficient.

Since we all are Moses' disciples – we therefore call him "our master" – it is our responsibility to recognize that Moses' words and actions here convey a profound teaching. In this *parasha*, the teaching goes beyond the details of practical halakha – how to make a *tallit katan* and a *tallit gadol* and when to bow during *Aleinu*. It has real ramifications for the question of how to view the Jewish people.

Moses issues a declaration: He says that he does not want to abandon the small people, leaving them small forever. Moses knows that such people exist; he himself suffers from their smallness, lowness, and inferiority – but that is a separate matter. Despite the suffering, he wants all of them to receive the Torah from the Almighty: "Would that all of God's people were prophets, that God would put His spirit upon them."

Shelaḥ

WHAT HAPPENED TO THE SPIES?

At the center of *Parashat Shelaḥ*, we come to the section on the spies and the subsequent punishment received by the wilderness generation.

The Torah describes how the spies were chosen: "One man each for every patriarchal tribe. Each one shall be a person of high rank ... They were all worthy men, leaders of the People of Israel" (Num. 13:2–3).

The central question that arises is how people who, as the Torah attests, were sent "at God's bidding" (Num. 13:3) and "were leaders of the People of Israel" can stand up and say that they do not want to enter the Land of Israel. To be sure, they speak on the basis of a military assessment of the reality, and each one of them may have been a general, but the question in essence still remains.

Moreover, our sages point out that the spies did not lie: "Three spoke the truth and were uprooted from the world: the spies, Doeg, and the sons of Rimon the Beerothite" (*Avot DeRabbi Natan* 45). So, too, Caleb's argument against them is not that they are lying; he merely disagrees with their conclusion that "we cannot go forward" (Num. 13:31), saying, "Let us go ahead, and we shall gain possession of it" (13:30). So it was not for speaking falsely that the spies were punished. Hence the question: If the spies spoke the truth, why were they uprooted from the world?

"A LAND THAT CONSUMES ITS INHABITANTS"

One approach is that the dispute here is actually much more basic than a question of fear of the Canaanites or a question of military strategy. In what many consider one of the narrative's key sentences, the spies say that the land "consumes its inhabitants" (Num. 13:32). With this sentence, they raise a fundamental issue – whether to go to the Land of Israel or not.

Life in the wilderness is almost like being part of a Kollel, whose members receive a monthly stipend to support their full-time Torah study. The Jews in the wilderness received manna morning and evening, and were provided with all their basic worldly needs. Moses and Aaron, the Sanhedrin, the leaders, the princes, and the chiefs had all that they required, and they were thus able to sit all day long and study Torah.

In this respect, entering the Land is really a downward step, because it "is a land that consumes its inhabitants." When one lives in the wilderness, one can live a complete spiritual life. But when one enters the Land of Israel, one's spirituality is placed in extreme danger.

This danger begins from the outset of the people's entry into the Land. As soon as each person receives his plot of land, he must immediately begin to work it. In commenting on the verse, "He who works his land will have plenty of bread" (Prov. 12:11), the Talmud explains that only one who enslaves himself to his land can have plenty of food; otherwise, it does not work (Sanhedrin 58b). A farmer must constantly be subservient to the soil. He cannot put his work off until the next day or the next week, because he is bound by agricultural seasons and times. One must sow at a certain time, plow at a certain time, and reap at a certain time – this cannot be manipulated.

In this respect, farming is more difficult than almost any other type of work. Most kinds of work can bend, to a certain extent, to a person's own priorities and can be put off. A farmer cannot take a vacation whenever he wishes, and he cannot rest whenever he wishes. This holds true to this very day. One who is responsible for milking the cows must get up early in the morning every day. The cows do not ask him how late he would like to sleep each day.

The problem of entering the Land is the problem of assuming responsibility for the physical, financial, and practical sides of life. All of this responsibility means that one no longer lives in a calm world, where he can sit in peace and study Torah. One is going to a place where one's life will be occupied by constant work, the work of life with all that it entails. It is an entirely different world. As opposed to all the spirituality that existed before, when one could bask in the beauty of the Clouds of Glory above him, here the Clouds of Glory are nowhere to be seen; all that remains are clouds of rain and clouds of dust. This is what those who enter the Land must contend with.

If a person lives on manna in the wilderness and wants to keep Shabbat, there is nothing easier than that. But if he lives in the Land, or any land, to keep Shabbat means sacrificing work days, and often he cannot afford to lose these days. This is true of Shabbat and Yom Tov, and of all the mitzvot in general as well.

"A land that consumes its inhabitants" means that a person who previously spent his time sitting and learning, without the pressure of worldly cares, now must shoulder the burden of real life. When such a person enters the Land and has to integrate into it, it literally consumes him.

When the spies say that the land consumes its inhabitants, they are basically saying that this is a normal country, a land like all others. Don't think that every morning there will be a miracle, that sustenance will fall from the sky. It might be a wonderful land, but still, people are born there and people die there. There are wars, there are difficult times, there is agriculture, and people have to work. In the midst of all this, the spies claim, we will lose our whole individuality. So it is better for us to remain in the wilderness. Why go to the Land of Israel and lose our identity, our distinctive character?

This argument, in various forms, can be heard frequently even today, often from worthy men, leaders of Israel. Why, they ask, should we lose our abstract spiritual essence, our Torah, and our manna, solely in order to go to the Land of Israel? It is better to remain in the wilderness. Entering the good and spacious land means entering a world that has a lot more obligations, difficulties, and challenges. In a certain respect, this can be considered an advantage, but not every person will feel this way. This is precisely the dispute between the spies and Caleb.

To be sure, the Torah seems to have answered this question unequivocally, but apparently it continues to reverberate among the Jewish people: Is it better to live in the wilderness or in the Land of Israel?

For Jews living today in Israel, this is a daily question. One who lives in a different country can say that there are certain professions that are morally uncomfortable for him. Being a soldier might be considered reprehensible, because it involves killing people. A policeman must patrol the streets and see all the filth that is out there. Cleaning sewers is disgusting; it is beneath one's dignity. No matter where one lives, one can allow oneself to desist from these activities in the hopes of avoiding dirtying oneself physical and spiritually. When one lives outside of Israel, there is no true responsibility; one lives up in the air, detached from reality.

But when one lives in one's own land, all these constant responsibilities – concerns of war and diplomacy, current events, and other matters – become an integral part of one's life. American Jews are great patriots, but how many of them serve in the US Army? The United States is a country where one can choose for oneself the pleasant elements and ignore the others. But when one comes to one's own country, one must deal with everything; there is no way of evading it. Every normal country requires a certain amount of Shabbat desecration. Even on Yom Kippur, there are all sorts of vital services that must operate around the clock. Electric company workers cannot just take the day off to pray in the synagogue. The operation of these services on Shabbat and on Yom Kippur is not a result of the country being full of heretics; it is because the country requires these services, and people cannot just choose the pleasant elements.

To be sure, the wilderness is not an ideal place to live, but it is much more convenient. Nowadays in Israel, we are raised and educated to appreciate the Land of Israel and its preeminence, but many Jews throughout history have demonstrated indifference in this regard. Some maintained that if one sits and studies about sacrifices, it is as though one has offered sacrifices, and if one sits and studies about tithes, it is as though one has separated tithes (Menaḥot 110a). R. Yehuda maintained that it is forbidden to go to the Land of Israel from Babylonia because of a Torah decree (Ketubbot 110b–111a). The Talmud also says that R. Yehuda loved the Land of Israel very much and would therefore recite a special blessing over balsam oil: "Who creates the oil of our land" (Berakhot 43a). Thus, R. Yehuda demonstrated his love of the Land of Israel by sitting in Babylonia and reciting a special blessing over a fruit of the Land of Israel – what could be better than that?

The spies reached the conclusion that there is no inherent problem with the Land; the problem is the transition from the wilderness to the Land. Their argument is constantly part of our life. Why is this whole headache necessary? What does the Land of Israel possess that makes all this worth it?

THE MATERIAL WORLD

Moses clashes with the spies not because he wants to turn the Jewish people into peasants who work the soil, but for a much more profound reason. Moses regards life in the material world as a challenge and treats it as a goal to strive for, in spite of the problems that are involved.

This is also the difference in character between Moses and Elijah. Elijah ascended on high, whereas Moses – even though he was on a higher level than Elijah – did not ascend. Moses had a sense for the physical; he had a true love for the Land. As the Midrash relates, Moses asked to become a small bird so as to reach the Land of Israel and at least touch it in some way (Deuteronomy Rabba 11:10). His request was rejected, meaning that even in his death he did not ascend on high.

The problem of the spies is akin to the question the angels asked God regarding the giving of the Torah. According to the Midrash, the angels asked, "Why do You need this creature? If it is because you want them to say 'Amen. May His great Name be blessed,' then we will say it; why do You need man? Are we not pure enough, not fine enough?" Moses, as the representative of human beings, represents the advantage that the material has over the spiritual; he speaks of man's superiority and preeminence within the world.

The question, "What is man that You should be mindful of him" (Ps. 8:5) is surely relevant, for man is "dust of the earth" (Gen. 2:7) and is indeed pulled downward. However, Moses' argument begins from this same point. In his opinion, man's greatness springs precisely from the fact that he is a material creation. The *piyut* "*Ve'avita tehila*," which is recited in the *Musaf* service during the Days of Awe, speaks of the fact that God has angels and seraphim, and yet man is His glory. Man's distinction is that he exists in the world, with all the troubles and difficulties, and nevertheless succeeds. It is precisely his dual nature that gives him the ability to ascend higher.

Maimonides, who thoroughly appreciated the spiritual world, said that in the World to Come, the soul leaves the body and exists in an entirely spiritual world. According to Nahmanides and many others, who said that in the World to Come the body will still exist, the culmination of Creation will indeed feature the resurrection of the dead, but the world will still be based on the principles of nature.

The spies are the ones who introduced the view that the physical is dirty and undesirable, and that one must adhere strictly to the spiritual. Opposing them was Moses, who replied that even though the land has its difficulties, and even though the manna is wonderful and convenient, it is better to live on simple wheat, which is fertilized with cow manure.

God tells Moses that He wants to start over again with better people, people who are more spiritual, and He suggests that He will blot out the Jewish people – "and I will make of you a mightier nation" (Deut. 9:14).

But Moses answers that if He had wanted spiritual beings, He would have sufficed with the angels. But He wanted people, so He must deal with the problems of people. Moses wanted to include all the rebellious individuals in the Jewish people, including rabble-rousers like Koraḥ, Datan, and Aviram. He wants them all, because otherwise everything could have been accomplished with angels.

Essential parts of the Torah are connected with the material world. Whether the subject is *tefillin* or the case of an ox that gored a cow, the Torah almost always deals with the material. Occasionally, we read of matters that relate more to the spiritual, but almost the entire Torah relates to this world, because there is great significance in the material. One cannot recite a blessing over a spiritual etrog; a physical etrog is required.

Until recently, the accepted scientific view was that there are two separate systems in the world: matter and energy. Today, scientists say that matter and energy are different aspects of the same thing. There is a law of conservation of matter and energy, along with Einstein's famous formula describing the precise nature of the relationship between matter and energy: $E = Mc^2$. According to this formula, even a small object contains enough energy to burn the entire world. So, although energy has various advantages, in matter everything is much more concentrated. To be sure, matter is less controllable than energy, since matter contains elements that interact with other elements according to electromagnetic patterns, but the potential for the release of energy from matter is in fact much greater. So we see that the material world has greater potential for powerful spirituality than the world of the spirit itself.

THE DANGER AND THE ULTIMATE PURPOSE

In this dispute, Moses does not claim that his approach entails no dangers and descents; he says only that this is the path and the objective. The Land can be "a good and spacious land"; nonetheless, it might ultimately prove to be "a land that consumes its inhabitants."

Moses intentionally leads the Jewish people on a path that goes into the world of matter, knowing full well that the path entails entering a war, and in war people are wounded and die. When one enters the world, the danger is that I will come to see the material world in which I live as the most important thing. We learn that Jacob finally decided to leave Ḥaran when he dreamed that the bucks were mounting the sheep. Then Jacob said, "When I left the Land, I dreamed of angels ascending and descending from heaven. If I have begun dreaming of goats and sheep, it is a sign that I must return to the Land."

The danger of the world is that a person can be consumed by it. Hence, when one enters the Land, one must take care that this does not happen. Joshua, as it turned out, did not succeed in this, or if he did, it was only for a short period. During the period of the Judges, the Land of Israel really was "a land that consumes its inhabitants." For four hundred years it swallowed up the People of Israel, as can be seen from quite a few examples. Consider, for instance, the private temple of Micah, with his idolatry and his Levite attendant (Judges 17–18). So, too, when the Danites visit his temple, they do not go in order to stop him, but to take over his objects of idolatry for themselves.

When people are swallowed up by the land, it becomes apparent that all the spirituality that was possessed by the previous generations, or that these people themselves possessed when they were young, has disappeared, for there are vegetables to harvest and goats to milk.

Nevertheless, it is worthwhile to lead the People of Israel into the Land, because that is the ultimate purpose.

In a certain sense, the entry into the Land of Israel is like Creation and the dangers that it entailed. When God created the world, He chose to dwell down below in the material, physical world. Even though "against your will you were formed...and against your will you die" (Avot 4:22), some believe that if they have already come down to this world, it is best to be free of worries, like the embryo that studies with an angel in the womb. But God does not want this. He wants us to live as a human beings in the midst of the world.

Koraḥ

WHY DID WRATH GO FORTH?

Parashat Koraḥ deals with strife. Several works that enumerate the mitzvot even list a special negative commandment derived from the *parasha* prohibiting strife: "One should not be like Koraḥ and his party" (Num. 17:5). There are several questions relating to the quarrel of Koraḥ and his followers, and I would like to focus on one of them.

This is not the first time that people quarrel with Moses; he had dealt with similar conflicts several times already. They complained about him, argued with him, even tried to throw stones at him. But this case is different. The rebellion here is led by respected people: Koraḥ, Datan and Aviram, and another group of *tzaddikim* – leaders of Israel, 250 princes of the community. All the leaders of this quarrel are intelligent people, and there is almost no violence. The most extreme thing that happens is that Moses summons them and they do not come. And yet, strangely, Moses' reaction is much sharper than in other cases.

In the other quarrels, Moses sometimes falls on his face, sometimes pleads for Israel, and once he even utters a curse. But here his response is extraordinarily severe: "Moses became very angry... If these men die the common death of all men... then God has not sent me. But if God creates something entirely new, so that the ground opens its mouth... you shall know that these men have spurned God" (Num. 16:16–30). Moses wants the earth to swallow them up, which is no ordinary punishment. He wants God to implement a supernatural event for this purpose alone. The spies, too, it would seem, deserved to be swallowed up by the earth, but they died in an ordinary plague. There are other people throughout Tanakh, great and small, who were condemned to death by the sword or by strangulation, but this is something else entirely.

This question appears in the literature and is even alluded to in *Pirkei Avot*, where it says that one of the ten things that were created on the eve of the first Shabbat at twilight is the mouth of the earth that swallowed Koraḥ and his followers. Moses calls for something that is beyond the natural order to intervene in the dispute and decide it. What exactly is Moses so angry about? What made this dispute different from all the others?

EVEN MY ALLY

Quite a few answers have been suggested for these questions, the most basic of which is that this is a dispute with a close associate.

It is one thing to be in a dispute or a quarrel and to feel the antagonism of someone who hates you for one reason or another. But when the antagonist is a person who should be one's ally – that is much worse. King David, who likewise was confronted with such a reality, expresses this feeling: "Even my ally in whom I trusted, who shared my bread, has been exceedingly false to me" (Ps. 41:10).

So, too, in the case of Moses: The disputes until now have always been with outsiders, and Moses can basically relate to them with equanimity. Koraḥ, however, is not an outsider; he is Moses' cousin, a relative. When such a dispute comes from within, it is much more painful.

When David faces antagonism from Goliath, it is completely different from his later conflicts with Avshalom and Aḥitofel. It is a feeling of desperation and realization that one cannot rely on anyone.

After the sin of the Golden Calf, when Moses calls out, "Whoever is for God, join me" (Ex. 32:26), all the Levites – including Koraḥ – gathered around him; they all rallied to his side. The Levites are not just Moses' tribe; they are also his loyalists. Just as the emperor has a personal guard whose members have special rights, the Levites act as Moses' royal guard, whose duties include guarding the Sanctuary. Disloyalty within this guard is much more painful and harmful than disloyalty in any other group, and it is also much harder to pardon.

"THAT GOD SENT ME"

Another unique aspect of this dispute is the nature of the claims put forward by Koraḥ and his followers against Moses, claims that are much more far-reaching than any other claim advanced against him thus far. In the dispute of Koraḥ and his followers, the complaints, for the first time, do not relate to a practical problem but to a fundamental religious question. Koraḥ says, in essence, that Moses is certainly a great man – he does not deny this – but that Moses also adds his own content to God's will.

This claim can be interpreted as a personal attack against Moses, but the truth is that it extends much further than that. Moses' argument with these people relates to the way in which God chooses to reveal Himself and communicate with the people. Moses says that he appointed Aaron because God told him to do so. If God had instructed him to appoint the son of Shelomit, daughter of Divri, the blasphemer, he would have done so as well. He is merely God's instrument and nothing more than that; and since he is an instrument of God, Koraḥ has no right to blame him.

Until now, when people would rebel, they were opposing God and thus also His anointed. People always had complaints – they complained of hunger, of thirst, and of the long and arduous journey – but Moses never appeared as an independent element. God and Moses always went together, already from the outset, after the parting of the Red Sea: "They believed in God and in His servant Moses" (Ex. 14:31). Even when, nevertheless, there were complaints against Moses, they were not about him as an individual but about God and His anointed.

Here, however, something new and strange happens. Koraḥ and his party are basically like the original Reform Jews who say that they are for God, for the Torah, and for the Sanctuary, but not for any of the "later additions." Moses' supposed "later additions" are what the rebels complain about.

This is a very serious matter, because it relates not only to the people's perception of Moses' role as the instrument of God, but also to a time and to a place that are more essential and important. Before the revelation at Mount Sinai, God says to Moses, "I will come to you in a thick cloud, so that the people will hear when I speak with you. And then they will believe in you forever" (Ex. 19:9). We rely on Moses not as a secondary source, not as an additional element on account of his being a great and wise man. Faith in Moses as God's prophet is fundamental to our faith, and it is not for naught that Maimonides establishes this as one of the fundamentals of Jewish faith.

Moses is not only God's servant; he is God's emissary in all matters, and the *Shekhina* speaks from his throat. This is a fundamental truth in our faith. In light of this, Moses responds sharply:

> By this you shall know that God sent me to do all these deeds, and that I have not done them of my own mind. If these men die the common death of all men and share the common fate of man, then God has not sent me. But if God creates something entirely new, so that the ground opens its mouth and swallows them up with all that is theirs, and they go down alive into Sheol, then you will know that these men have provoked God. (Num. 16:28–30)

He sends them to Sheol because they are impinging upon a deep and basic point; they are undermining the foundation of the Torah's message.

Even the spies – though they claimed that God could not conquer the Land for them and overcome all the difficulties that this would entail – did not undermine the foundation of the Torah's message. To be sure, they lacked faith in God, but they did not show a lack of faith in Moses as His emissary. If Moses is merely a microphone, there is no reason to quarrel with a microphone, even if it shouts at me. Here, in the case of Korah and his followers, there is an attempt to separate between God and Moses. This alarms Moses, because such a separation undermines the people's ability to continue receiving the Torah – both regarding the Written Law and the Oral Law. This rebellion must be completely eradicated; these people must be wiped out, without leaving even a remnant. What is left for posterity is only the "reminder to the People of Israel … that [they] not be like Korah and his party" (Num. 17:5).

The dispute of Korah and his followers seems like a minor incident, much less serious than other parallel cases. In contrast to what the spies demand – "Let us assign a leader and return to Egypt" (Num. 14:4) – all Korah and his followers want is permission to offer incense. Moses could have simply allowed them to do this and then gone back to sleep. But the truth is that this is not just a dispute about appointments. The dispute here touches upon a very deep point. Hence, even though it does not present an immediate threat, it requires more thorough eradication.

In the other quarrels, we see the entire community – "The whole community began to complain" (Num. 14:1) – they all begin to yell. When the people cry out for a hot breakfast, there is an immediate solution; Moses can deal with the people who, "like the beasts" (Ps. 49:13), cry and yell for meat. This is simply an instance of infantile behavior, not reflective of any deeper problem. In our case, however, those who create the turmoil are making logical arguments regarding basic tenets of our faith. The fact that the ideas were put forth by the elites of the nation makes their actions even more dangerous. The real, difficult dispute is not with people who are not looking to satisfy lusts but, rather, with those who are looking to change and replace the basic principles of our belief system.

ALL THE PEOPLE IN THE COMMUNITY ARE HOLY

A third related point is that Koraḥ and his followers use Moses' own words against him.

What do Koraḥ's followers say? "You take too much upon yourselves, for all the people in the community are holy, and God is in their midst. Why do you raise yourselves above God's congregation?" (Num. 16:3).

In the incident of Eldad and Medad, Moses said almost the same thing to Joshua: "Would that all of God's people were prophets, that God would put His spirit upon them" (Num. 11:29).

In essence, Koraḥ and his followers reminded Moses that he wanted people who would be more involved – he wanted prophets. Here were 250 people, all of whom were volunteering to fill these roles. There had been only one High Priest; here were 250 potential High Priests. Their objective was to open to all what until now had been restricted.

In the Jewish people, there is an aristocratic class composed of Torah scholars. This is basically the ruling class: all the appointments and honors go to them. But this class is not an exclusive club. If you want to belong to this class, you are not asked who your father was or whether you have respectable in-laws; anyone can belong to it. In this respect, the crown of Torah is truly accessible to all; whoever wishes to study is invited to do so.

Korah and his followers continue, noting that while they appreciate that the aristocracy of Torah is open to all, there is another class – the class of the priesthood – and that class is closed. The rebels demand that the priesthood be opened to everyone as well, so that anyone who is inspired to become a Priest – or even a High Priest – can do so.

Many generations later, this is indeed what happened. Throughout the book of Kings, we read that "the people still brought sacrifices and burned offerings upon the *bamot*" (1 Kings 22:44). According to almost all the commentators, these *bamot* were dedicated to God, in sanctity and in purity, and not to idolatry. A Jew who was seized with a spirit of holiness would summon his entire family, immerse in a *mikve*, don white clothing, and make a whole offering to God. When *bamot* were permitted, this was certainly considered a mitzva.

In the time of the Tabernacle and the Temple, however, the *bamot* were prohibited. In the Temple, an ordinary person is a minor adjunct; he merely buys a ticket. He can bring his offering, and he can even perform the ritual of laying one's hand upon it, but from that point onward it already is not his affair.

There is much to be said, then, for Korah's demand to open the priesthood class. Underlying a person's desire to be a Priest, then, is not just a desire for honor but a true desire to express oneself in the realm of holiness. The argument raised by Korah and his followers reflects not simply a desire to break down barriers but a desire for personal involvement. They argue that instead of forming a structure where the Priest does everything and there is no room for individual expression, it is possible to bring in other people as well – Levites and Israelites.

We do not have a complete list of Korah's followers – according to the Midrash, they even included members of the Sanhedrin (Numbers Rabba 16:21) – but whatever the case may be, we are dealing here with the leaders of Israel, "princes of the community" (16:2). These distinguished people simply want to serve God as Priests; they, too, want to serve in the inner Sanctuary. This is a legitimate request, a holy and serious matter.

In light of all this, the question is compounded: What fault did Moses find in them? What is more, the dispute of Koraḥ and his followers became the archetype for unworthy disputes throughout our history: "What dispute was not for the sake of Heaven? The dispute of Koraḥ and his whole party" (Avot 5:17). This is difficult to understand. After all, they say that their objective is that all the people in the community should be holy. The question of whether to reach out to the whole community or to remain concentrated in a small, limited circle is a dispute that continues for many generations and is a real, important question. Why, then, is this considered a dispute that is not for sake of Heaven?

BEHIND THE SLOGANS

The dialogue between Moses and Koraḥ's party is odd. On the surface, it appears as though Moses' responses do not relate to their claims. They claim that they want to participate in the Order of Service, and Moses replies, "Is it but a small thing to you that the God of Israel has set you apart?" (Num. 16:9). They accuse him of deceiving them, not fulfilling his promise to bring them to a land flowing with milk and honey, and Moses replies, "I did not take a single donkey" (16:15). What does Moses mean by this?

The implication is that Moses simply does not believe that these people are acting for the sake of Heaven. Here he expresses his view of the dispute – that it is dishonest; behind its stated claims lurk other motives.

Koraḥ and his followers use slogans implying that their motives are for the sake of Heaven, but there is reason to believe that this is not the case. The Midrash says that behind Koraḥ's claims lies his desire to be the head of the Kehatite family (Numbers Rabba 18:2). When the appointments were made, he was passed over, a snub that made him angry, envious, and frustrated. Koraḥ was smart, wealthy, and probably a great man as well; he was able to convince everyone that his motives were pure and holy. In truth, however, according to the Midrash, behind the façade of this great man lurked a personal grudge.

Datan and Aviram, of whom we know nothing other than what we read here, also seemingly wanted to receive something but did not get it. They cried out as though an injustice had been done to them, while nothing actually happened other than that they could not tolerate

Moses, simply because he was greater and wiser than they were. This is a case of envy and resentment, hidden behind the rhetoric.

One can learn a lot from this about disputes that are seemingly for the sake of Heaven. People often use slogans of holiness, but what lies behind these slogans is often nothing but personal pettiness. Even when all slogans are for the good of the party, or for the good of the world, one should still search for what lies beneath them, below the surface. Sometimes one finds there a small, frustrated person who wanted to receive something and did not get it. He is envious of someone else and cannot do anything about it, and so he tries to attack him in some other way.

Recently, it has been said that there is a remedy for every form of hatred except for hatred that results from envy. For hatred caused by envy, gracious gestures by the other side will never help, because the source of the hatred is not an act of injustice, but a deep-seated feeling of jealousy.

In saying, "I have not taken a single donkey, nor have I harmed a single one of them" (Num. 16:15), Moses is emphasizing that the dispute did not start on the basis of an injustice. In general, if one causes someone to suffer, even justifiably, it is understandable that this could lead to the development of a grudge. But in the dispute with Korah and his followers, no such suffering was caused, no offense was given; the whole incident was a direct result of envy.

There is no remedy for such hatred, and because of this, Moses needed to eradicate them completely.

Ḥukkat

In this *parasha*, the matter of the death of the righteous appears twice: once in connection with Miriam and a second time in conection with Aaron. At first glance, this subject appears here simply because of the historical succession of events in the wilderness. Our sages, however, offer an additional explanation: "Why is the account of Miriam's death juxtaposed to the section on the red cow? To inform you that just as the red cow effects atonement, so does the death of the righteous effect atonement" (Moed Katan 28a).

The first question we should ask here is this: What is the significance of the death of a *tzaddik*?

Second, how is the death of the righteous analogous to the laws of the red cow? After all, the simple understanding is that the red cow is not a *korban*, and it does not effect atonement but, rather, *tahara*, whereas in the case of the death of the righteous, the issue is atonement.

ABSENCE OF A SPIRITUAL ESSENCE

Upon every death, and certainly upon the death of a *tzaddik*, there are mourners and there is loss. When a person who lived with us in this world suddenly leaves it – especially in the case of a great individual whom we needed and depended on – we feel a void, in the simplest sense of the word. In this respect, the death of the righteous is truly the world's loss.

Still, the Torah often specifically recounts the deaths of many *tzaddikim*, sometimes briefly and sometimes at great length, so it appears that the death of a *tzaddik* has special significance, beyond that of a regular person's death.

Why is the death of the righteous so significant? After all, Miriam is hardly mentioned in the Torah. Why, then, is her death so resonant with meaning for us? Let us also recall that at the time of Miriam's death, many prominent members of Israel died as well – tribal heads, tribal princes, members of distinguished families – and yet the Torah does not specifically announce the death of any of these other esteemed individuals.

In this context, the Talmud makes a distinction between two types of loss. The first type is the death of someone whose absence, at least in a certain sense, can be measured. It is possible to define certain things that are missing and how much they are missed, and all of them are deficiencies that can basically be filled. The concept of filling that void is called "one who fills the place of his forefathers" (Shabbat 51a), which implies that although someone departed from the world, his son can ably replace him. In this regard, there is a famous witticism often ascribed to Charles de Gaulle: "The graveyards are full of indispensable men." This is a type of absence that can be filled naturally.

Granted, there are differences between people and their modes of behavior. It is impossible to fill a person's absence exactly, even if he is a private individual, and this is true of everyone. Every human being was created in the image and likeness of God, and "man was created single" (Tosefta, Sanhedrin 8:4). Hence, even the lowliest person is irreplaceable. Every person has individual significance, an individual and unique personality, of which there is no exact copy; for if there were such a copy, the person need not have been created.

Yet in spite of all this, in a practical sense, the work that most people accomplish in their lifetimes can usually be replicated by their successors.

The second type of loss is the death of a truly irreplaceable person, which creates a deficiency that cannot be filled. The issue of the death of the righteous is partly connected with the fact that a *tzaddik* cannot be completely replaced by anyone else. One can perhaps do the same things that he did, but for the unique combination of attributes possessed by this personality – there is no substitute. In such a case, even a son who is a worthy successor of his forefathers, both in wisdom and in fear of sin, cannot be an exact replica of them; he is never exactly the same thing.

This is not intended as disrespect toward the younger generation. There are roles in which sons or successors are certainly capable of replacing their predecessors. The fathers carried out a certain function in the world, and the sons continue to fulfill it – and sometimes even exceed it. Therefore, even in the wake of the fathers' inimitable personal greatness, the feeling of emptiness in the world upon their deaths is not absolute.

However, when a *tzaddik* leaves the world, the concern is not about a function whose performance is now lacking, but about the absence of a spiritual essence. Not everyone has such a personality, one that is irreplaceable, for which there is no substitute.

Most eulogies, especially one for important people or Torah luminaries, contain the following basic message: We know where to find gold and silver, "but where can wisdom be found? And where is the source of understanding?" (Job 28:12). Our loved one has gone; who will replace him? Who will succeed him?

In truth, however, there are only a few people who are on this level and of this nature. From the distance of generations it can be seen, amidst the full array of people and personalities throughout history, that most great figures were great only for their own time. Often, the loss of an outstanding personality seems inconsolable and irreparable; yet after a while, it becomes apparent that a successor exists. There have been only a few people for whom we indeed have had no replacement. When a person cannot be replaced by another, this is an essential deficiency, and the death of such a person can be treated like the death of the righteous.

When someone is not just a key figure or an important person but a unique phenomenon, the likes of which we will not see again, the date of his death truly carries significance. When someone on such a level dies, this date has significance not only in the lives of individuals but also in the life of a whole community and sometimes even for a whole nation. When the Torah mentions that a certain person died, this can only mean that he was truly a unique personality, incomparable and irreplaceable.

Regarding Miriam and Moses, this clearly seems to be the case, since they did not have children who could replace them in a significant way. Aaron, however, has a son who succeeds him as the High Priest. Indeed, the Torah mentions this in the context of his death. Nevertheless, Elazar can never become another Aaron. It is easy – sometimes too easy, as history has demonstrated – to appoint a High Priest, but it is impossible to make another Aaron; not necessarily because he was the first, but because he was a unique personality.

THE *TZADDIK* IS NOT DEAD

Because of the objective vacuum that is left in the world upon the deaths of such *tzaddikim*, it is impossible to say with certainty that they are dead.

This notion is stated explicitly regarding Jacob. The Talmud, in Taanit 5b, relates a strange anecdote. R. Yitzḥak, upon arriving in Babylonia from the Land of Israel, tells R. Nachman that Jacob our patriarch is not dead. R. Nachman, who was a forceful personality, says to R. Yitzḥak, "Was it for naught that he was bewailed and embalmed and buried?!" The Torah not only mentions his death but also describes in detail how he was embalmed and buried, and you say that he is not dead?! Elsewhere, the Talmud describes how R. Bana'a visited Abraham and found him conversing with Sarah, very much alive (Bava Batra 58a). Other such examples exist as well.

The same applies to all of the "seven shepherds" – the spiritual fathers of the Jewish people. Although it is not said of all of them that they did not die, there is a traditional understanding that all of them have an ongoing existence within the Jewish national community.

Maimonides, in his introduction to his *Commentary on the Mishna*, for example, does not want to say that Moses died; he refuses to utter this idea. He therefore says that "this was his death for us, since he was lost to us, but life for him, in that he was elevated to Him. As [our sages], peace be upon them, said: 'Moses our Master did not die' (Sota 13b); rather, he ascended and is serving on high."

All of this signifies that such a person, as it were, cannot die. To say that such a person died is equivalent to affirming that the world lacks a vital component that is integral to its existence. When an ordinary person dies, the world can exist without him. But for a supremely unique individual, to say that he ceases to exist seems almost blasphemous. Hence, we say that this person is dead and not dead; he is dead, but he remains alive in some form.

LIFE AND DEATH – PURITY AND IMPURITY

The death of the righteous has an additional aspect. In various sources (e.g., Zohar, *Haazinu* 296b), the death of the righteous is called a *hillula* (literally, "celebration").

Indeed, nowadays the practice in several places – a practice that sometimes far exceeds proper proportions – is to hold a full-fledged celebration on the anniversary of a *tzaddik's* death, to the point that at times the celebration is larger than the funeral that was held upon his death itself. This practice relates to a different aspect of the *tzaddik's* death – the atonement that it brings.

The Midrash frequently addresses the notion that the death of a *tzaddik* atones for the generation (see Exodus Rabba 35:4). A simple reading of Isaiah 53 demonstrates this concept as well – that a *tzaddik* bears the suffering of the generation and atones for its sins in his death.

In order to understand this better, let us talk a little about the *tuma* that results from death. One of the major principles of the laws of *tuma* and *tahara* is that the more dead something is, the more *tamei* it becomes; and the more alive something is, the less *tamei* it becomes. This holds true in the great majority of the laws of *tuma*, and it can be seen in the *tuma* that results from a seminal emission and in the *tuma* of the menstruant woman: In both cases, there is a kind of partial death, which, in turn, generates an aspect of *tuma*.

However, within the whole array of impurities, one of them is exceptional – the *tuma* of a woman following childbirth. This *tuma* seemingly has nothing at all to do with the sphere of death; on the contrary, birth is the formative event of life – the opposite of death.

Hence, let us be a little more precise. It appears that *tuma* is created during the transition between life and death – either when life is cut off or when it emerges. To put it very simply, the moment of birth is the moment in which the soul enters the body completely, and the moment of death is the moment in which it leaves the body. If we view our life in this world as a closed unit, a circle, we could say that a line going through it intersects it at two points: at the point of entry and at the point of exit. The events are similar, in that body and soul are in transition, and the connection between them is changing. At these two points, life in this world is intersected.

In this sense, the idea of atonement resembles the idea of *tuma*. Just as death, whether full death or partial death, leaves *tuma* in its wake, death similarly generates a point of purity, of atonement, which likewise results from the fissure, the temporary connection, between the worlds. The more alive the person who dies is, the more complete the nature of this purity will be.

We say that the death of the righteous atones, but the truth is that death in general atones, not only for the righteous but for the wicked as well, as it says, "This sin shall not be atoned for you until you die" (Is. 22:14), and "his death is his atonement" (see Sanhedrin 6:2). The most serious sins are atoned for through death, and the more difficult the death, the greater is the apparent atonement. The atonement attained by someone who is given the death penalty is unlike the atonement attained by someone who dies peacefully in his bed.

Although the sources are not clear on the subject, we have a tradition that any Jew who is killed by non-Jews is called *kadosh*. Not only when a person dies for the sanctification of God's name, in which case it is certainly appropriate to speak of *kedusha*, but even when a Jew is killed by non-Jews because of his crimes and sins, and according to some, even when he is killed by non-Jews in a traffic accident, he is called *kadosh*. To a certain degree this is also atonement and, as a result, the person ascends to a higher level. In this sense, his death atones not only for his sins but also for his life, because it changes the characterization of his life.

The *tzaddik's* death atones for the sins of the whole generation and of the whole world, because the greater and more alive the person who is uprooted from the world, the more significant the changes in purity and atonement generated by the transition are. Hence, when the *tzaddik* leaves the world, the breach in the partition between the worlds makes an impression, in that it changes part of the nature of the world.

Just as in the case of *tuma*, partial death is also a type of death, so, too, in the case of purity, partial death is an opening to the realm of *kedusha*, as our sages say that not only do the deaths of *tzaddikim* atone for our sins, but even their suffering atones.

Why is it that in the Temple we effect atonement with blood and not in some other way? Why does atonement have to be effected by taking a living creature and killing it? Why do we make sacrifices by taking their lives? How can we understand the atonement through the scapegoat, the goat for "Azazel," which, according to halakha, atones for all sins, both deliberate and inadvertent, and whose atonement exceeds that of the sacrifices? After all, the only thing this act of atonement entails is killing the goat. Would it not be nicer and more sensible to simply set the goat free? Yet we do not do this; instead we kill it, thereby attaining atonement.

We effect atonement with blood because death creates a change in the world's nature; it creates a reality of atonement and purity. Thus there is a double paradox: On the one hand, childbirth imparts *tuma*; on the other hand, death effects atonement. Both childbirth and death constitute transitions beyond the bounds of reality, inward and outward. One is a transition into the world, while the other is a transition out of the world.

THE TWO SIDES OF DEATH

When our sages compare the *tahara* effected through the red cow and the atonement effected through the death of the righteous, this is because they indeed share a common aspect.

Regarding the red cow, King Solomon said, "I said, 'I will get wisdom,' but it was far from me" (Eccl. 7:23; *Midrash Zuta*, Eccl. 7). This section is full of unfathomable elements, full of paradoxes, like the law that the water renders everyone *tamei* except someone who is himself *tamei*, and other conundrums. But the basic conundrum regarding the *tahara* attained through the red cow is connected precisely with the subject we are dealing with.

One who comes in contact with the severe *tuma* of a corpse can only achieve *tahara* and atonement through the death and subsequent burning to ash of an animal. The atonement is produced through something that completely perishes from the world.

If *tahara* could be achieved through the usual process – immersing in the "living water" (Num. 19:17) of the *mikve*, the matter would have been understandable. *Tuma* and the living water can be regarded as opposites: One is death and the other is life. But the fact that the purification from death proceeds through death, through annihilation, is the basic problem in the matter of the red cow, beyond any other detailed halakhic questions.

This would explain, in a different way, the atonement that arises from the death of the righteous.

The death of the righteous is indeed a tragedy. When a *tzaddik* leaves the world, one would expect the world to become much darker. This man enlightened the world, and now darkness has come to the world in his absence. Such a picture of darkness appears in the Talmud's deptiction of the transition from Moses to Joshua: "Moses' countenance was like that of the sun; Joshua's countenance was like that of the moon" (Bava Batra 75a). Sometimes it also happens that the master's countenance resembles the sun, but the disciple's countenance resembles the moon during an eclipse. Sometimes a son is "the father's leg"[1] (Eiruvin 70b), and sometimes he is even less than his father's leg.

The death of a *tzaddik* is indeed a gloomy occurrence but, on the other hand, it is also a moment of release, of rebirth, an illumination of life. When a child is born in this world, he departs from one world and is born to another world. So, too, when a *tzaddik* dies, he undergoes a reverse process – he departs from this world and returns to the other world. This point creates the paradox in which *tuma* and atonement coincide.

The transition between worlds can be described by the following anecdote. A man was once very ill, and he dreamed of recovering. He dreamed that in the heavenly court, he was sentenced to return to life, and he was escorted back. On the way, his escorts found a corpse, and they forced him to enter it. He cried and wailed, as he did not want to enter the corpse. After he was forced to enter the corpse, he awoke and discovered that he had returned to life.

This anecdote can also describe the process of birth. Every morning upon arising, one's soul is taken and forced to enter the body. Thus we recite each morning, "My God, the soul that You gave me is pure." The soul is uprooted from its own world and thrown into another world.

---

1. That is, the son steps into his father's place.

Why do Moses and Aaron die on the top of mountains? Why does Aaron wear the priestly garments when he goes off to die? The answer is that these *tzaddikim* do not go down when they die; they go up. At his death, Aaron in effect does exactly what he does upon entering the Holy of Holies on Yom Kippur – he atones for the entire community. Aaron's death is essentially an act of sacrifice, an act of self-annihilation. Just as when he offers *korbanot* he wears the High Priest's garments, so, too, when he ascends to the final *korban*, he goes up to die in his priestly garments.

Why does Aaron do this, while most others do not? Why doesn't every High Priest ascend to the top of the mountain? Why don't all rabbis go up to Mount Nebo?

One of the reasons for this is that Aaron represented a unique personality. He was not merely a *tzaddik*; he was a perfect *tzaddik*. For such a person, even his death takes on a unique nature. Hence, every such death must be recounted in the Torah and commemorated. Such a death not only creates a void in the world, but also creates a change in reality.

For this reason, Miriam's death appears in the Torah as well. It does not matter what role she filled in her life; for all we know or care, she may have stayed at home and knitted. But Miriam represented an irreplaceable personality that departed from the world.

The death of the righteous is marked in reality, engraved in time. Sometimes the event is commemorated only for one generation or only in a certain place. At other times, as in *Parashat Ḥukkat*, the event is established forever because of its singular nature that will never recur.

Balak

The name of a *parasha* is generally based on its first words, and therefore this *parasha* is called "*Parashat Balak*," but the truth is that it should be called *Parashat Bilam*. Without a doubt, Bilam is the hero of the *parasha*, all of which revolves around his personality and actions.

When one examines the Torah's description of Bilam's character, taking the text according to its plain meaning, what emerges is that, on the whole, Bilam is a pretty decent person. But when one examines the words of our sages, one can see that they took a much more negative view of Bilam.

There is a well-known principle, commonly applied to midrashim, that we tend to attribute evil actions to evil characters, and we likewise tend to attribute good actions to good characters. This concept can certainly be applied to Bilam. The Talmud explicitly says that regarding those listed as having no share in the World to Come, you should not overly expound to their discredit the biblical passages dealing with them, "except in the case of Bilam: Whatever you find written about him, interpret it [to his discredit]" (Sanhedrin 106b).

BILAM'S VIRTUES

Bilam's prophecy is the only one cited in the Torah that is not spoken by Moses. As the Midrash comments on the verse, "No other prophet like Moses has arisen in Israel" (Deut. 34:10), "In Israel he has not arisen, but among the nations he did arise. And who was he? Bilam" (Numbers Rabba 14:34). We see here that this idea actually emerges from the plain meaning of the verse. As a rule, the Torah cites only the words of Moses, whereas here another prophet's words are included. Apparently, Bilam's prophecy is so profound and momentous in its scope that it is truly worthy of inclusion in the Torah.

Indeed, this is quite a statement. If our sages had said that Bilam is as great as Joshua, that would have been fine. But they say that he is comparable in greatness to Moses! Moses is not just an exalted personality, a wise man, and a great leader; he is in a different league altogether. "With him I speak mouth to mouth, in a vision and not in riddles" (Num. 12:8). He is a man who merited speaking with God face to face, with unconcealed vision, with unobscured perception. Hence, to say that among the nations of the world there arose a man like Moses is a major compliment.

Bilam's prophecy is important also in its content. In Bilam's prophecy, we not only see into the future, but we also see the grand vision of the Jewish people. Here, all at once, appears our whole distant future. This is not a vision of a day or of a hundred years; this is a vision that reaches to the end of days. The famous words, "A star shall go forth from Jacob" (Num. 24:17), were not spoken by Moses; they were spoken by Bilam. Bilam is the one who speaks of the end of days, the ultimate end, how the whole world collapses and the Jewish people remains.

What is more, Bilam not only possessed lofty spiritual powers, like the ability to see far into the future and perceive what is hidden – many others have been naturally endowed with such gifts, without any connection to prophecy. Bilam is a prophet of God, a human being with a live connection with The Holy One, Blessed Be He.

When there is a prophet of God among the nations of the world, that is something unique. When our sages identify Pharaoh's three advisors, it is no coincidence that they join together Job, Yitro, and Bilam. These three people had one thing in common that sets them apart: They were gentiles who drew near to God – each one in his own way, according to his individual character. They were people who were isolated within the world, people who reached an understanding of God from within themselves, through their own thought and inner contemplation.

In spite of all this, our sages list Bilam in the pantheon of the most evil characters in our history. They took Bilam, an exalted personality on a lofty level, and although they did not deny his prophecy, they portrayed him as the ultimate degenerate. Even Rashi, in explaining the verse, "Have I been in the habit of doing thus to you?" (Num. 22:30), refuses to explicitly cite the words of our sages, instead sufficing with, "as is found in Tractate Avoda Zara." How did such a great man come to this? What happened to him? Why did our sages blacken his name?

SELF-CENTEREDNESS

To get to the root of the matter, we must understand our sages' assessment of Bilam.

In *Pirkei Avot*, our sages compare the disciples of Abraham and the disciples of the wicked Bilam:

> Whoever exhibits these three traits is a disciple of Abraham our patriarch, and [whoever exhibits] three other traits is a disciple of the wicked Bilam. The disciples of Abraham our patriarch have a generous eye, a modest spirit, and a humble soul. The disciples of the wicked Bilam have an envious eye, an ambitious spirit, and an arrogant soul. What is the difference between the disciples of Abraham our patriarch and the disciples of the wicked Bilam? The disciples of Abraham our patriarch enjoy [life] in this world and inherit the World to Come... but the disciples of the wicked Bilam inherit Gehenna and descend into the nethermost pit. (Avot 5:19)

This passage gives expression to the conception that Bilam was not just a particular individual, a historical figure, who took part in certain historical events. Bilam transcends his own personal story; he produces disciples and represents a whole school that stands in contrast to Abraham's school and his very way of life.

Our sages' comparison of the disciples of Bilam and the disciples of Abraham is not connected with the incident of the donkey or with other matters but, rather, is connected primarily with one exclusive sphere. If we take all of our sages' comments regarding Bilam together, it is clear that the emphasis is on Bilam's self-centeredness: "an envious eye, an ambitious spirit, and an arrogant soul." By contrast, in the case of Abraham, the point is exactly the opposite: "a generous eye, a modest spirit, and a humble soul," as reflected in the verse, "I am but dust and ashes" (Gen. 18:27).

Bilam's self-centeredness can be observed not just in the small details pointed out by our sages, but even in the phraseology of his prophecy.

When a prophet prophesies, he expresses the prophecy through the faculties of his individual personality. Hence, even when he is in a prophetic state, it is still possible to speak of his spiritual nature as distinctive and unique to him as an individual.

Proof of this may be adduced from the talmudic statement that "whoever acts arrogantly... if he is a prophet, his prophecy departs from him" (Pesaḥim 66b). This notion is derived from Deborah the Prophetess, who boasted in her song that "the rulers ceased in Israel, they ceased, until that I arose, Deborah, I arose a mother in Israel" (Judges 5:7). As a result of this impropriety, the *ruaḥ hakodesh* departed from her, and she had to be urged, "Awake, awake, Deborah, awake, awake, utter a song" (5:12). Even though the words are spoken in the framework of a prophetic utterance, when a person makes such a statement, it shows something about his personality.

So, too, in Bilam's prophecy it is evident that he communicated his prophecy through his own faculties, through a self-centered outlook. To be sure, his declaration essentially expresses complete homage to God, and he speaks in the manner of the prophets: "Even if Balak were to give me his house full of silver and gold, I would not be able to do anything great or small that would violate the word of God my Lord" (Num. 22:18). Neither silver nor honor will buy him; he will not sell himself. However, his phraseology indicates an "ambitious spirit"; he has grandiose ideas – the example he gives is no less than a "house full of silver and gold." This reflects more than just an aberration of character. A critical, penetrating analysis of Bilam's language reveals that it goes far beyond that; it is a problem of essence.

GOD HAS SET THE ONE OPPOSITE THE OTHER

Bilam can be characterized as a great intellectual, theologian, and philosopher. His experience proves that it is possible to reach great achievements – even prophecy – by immersing oneself in the study of God. Therefore, the fact that our sages hold him to an elevated standard, instructing us to interpret all the passages about him to his discredit, should be viewed in light of this background.

Hence, our sages' real argument with Bilam, their essential attitude toward him, stems from their assessment of him as a personality that stands in contrast to that of Abraham. All the other minor matters that are brought up can be termed secondary interpretations.

What separates Abraham from Bilam is the distinction between the inner holiness and the outer husk. This is the root of the matter, the point that makes the difference, and it is on this point that our sages criticize Bilam.

Before every character analysis, there are prefaces and groundwork. Even if these factors do not dictate the complete results of the investigation, they will always determine the tone, the color, and most importantly, the meaning of the conclusion. Two people can work equally with the same data, reaching basically identical conclusions, and still produce major differences in other respects.

The difference between the disciples of Bilam and the disciples of Abraham relates to the starting point of this groundwork. The point of departure for one who serves God is that he serves God and is setting out to search for Him. In contrast, the philosopher is simply setting out to search. This results in a major difference between them. The kabbalist and the philosopher have the same fundamental question regarding the disparity between God and the world: How can they be joined together in one system? This question is rooted in the fundamental question of both the faithful and the philosophers. And it can be formulated in two ways. The philosopher's reasoning begins as follows: There is a world. If there is a world, how could there be a God? The kabbalist begins differently: There is a God. If there is a God, how could there be a world? Each one of these approaches leads to a different conception of the world.

When our sages chose to contrast Bilam and Abraham, they did so because there truly is a profound similarity between them. They both searched, and they both found the way to God by themselves. The difference between them is what happens when they encounter the unexplained and the unexplainable, where God tells them to do something that is against their essential nature. Both Bilam and Abraham face situations that are strongly paradoxical, and in their respective situations Bilam remains Bilam and Abraham remains Abraham.

Bilam has his own interests, which he continues to pursue. By contrast, when Abraham encounters a contradiction that, from the standpoint of the truth, is more painful to him than what Bilam goes through, he is willing to go ahead with it. For Bilam, the question is whether he will be able to receive money and honor. For Abraham, his whole physical and spiritual life is put into jeopardy because of this tension; he is confronted with a contradiction of everything that existed before. But despite the contradictions, Abraham is willing to continue walking with God.

It is difficult to imagine how many logical contradictions and extraordinary questions Abraham must confront when he must perform the *Akeda*. His whole world is being destroyed. Not only his emotional life, but everything that he has, everything that he knows, everything that he was promised, everything that he understands – everything is being destroyed all at once. All that will remain in his life is God.

Very likely, Abraham was tempted to tell God that he can go no further. He might have cried out to God, "If You want to kill the child, take the knife and kill the child. But how can You put me into this situation? After condemning such acts throughout my whole life, do You expect me to commit such an act?!" However, Abraham does not say this, and this is a fundamental reflection on Abraham's character.

A seminal verse in Job reads, "Though He slay me, yet I will trust in Him (*lo ayaḥel*)" (13:15). Traditionally, the word *lo* is read as if it was written as "*lamed-vav*," meaning "in Him." However, the Masoretic text actually spells the word *lo* "*lamed-aleph*," meaning "not," which turns the meaning of the entire verse on its head: "When He slays me, I will not hope." At first glance, the difference between the *ketiv* (written version) and the *kerei* (read version) seems trivial – it is the difference between a *vav* and an *aleph* – but it is actually a fundamental difference, because it determines the way in which a person approaches events and how he responds to them.

THE *TZADDIK* SHALL LIVE BY HIS FAITH

Another difference between Abraham and Bilam, which is emphasized by our sages even more than the previous one, is the difference between isolated, abstract thought and the aspiration to live one's faith. For Bilam, this difference stands out prominently. Bilam can have the most profound insights and the most subtle understanding; nevertheless, he can remain Bilam, without perceiving a contradiction in this.

In the course of Bilam's prophecy, he poses a rhetorical question: "Who has numbered the seed of Israel?" (Num. 23:10). The Talmud explains that Bilam was essentially saying, "'Would He who is pure and holy, and whose ministers are pure and holy, look upon such a thing?!' Thereupon his eye was blinded, as it says, 'the saying of the man whose eye is closed' (24:3)" (Nidda 31a).

There are people for whom there is always an abysmal chasm between the abstract, the exalted, the pure truth, and life itself, down to the simplest level. For such people, "He who is pure and holy and whose ministers are pure and holy" is truly not meant to look upon such things. According to this approach, there is a basic intellectual partition between two worlds. There is one world in which the mind functions brilliantly, reaching the highest levels of understanding of the divine. But there also exists another world, which consists of what one does in one's spare time. Adherents of this approach are not willing to admit that this latter part has anything to do with the former part. Study and pure thought belong to a world that is complete and pure in itself, unsullied by one's individual personality.

The Kotzker Rebbe would ask how it is possible that our sages call Bilam a prophet (Bava Batra 15b). Can an evil prophet truly exist? If there was any question as to the accuracy of this characterization of Bilam, the later events involving the daughters of Midian and the way that Bilam is eventually killed make it clear that he was evil.

The Kotzker Rebbe explains that although a Jewish person cannot be both, a non-Jew can be both a prophet and a vile person; the two have nothing to do with each other. This is because when the perception and insight of prophecy remain rooted in the realm of thought and abstraction, they do not have constant influence on the person. In such a case, the whole person does not participate in the process of struggle and relationship between man and God; he sends his brain to the battle, and the brain does excellent work. But this kind of service detaches man's emotional side, his human side, from his rational side. There is no connection to the human element; it deals solely with abstract elements.

By their very nature, the Jewish people insist on the mixture of heaven and earth. They insist on the constant fusion of the physical and the spiritual, and on the attempt to combine the abstract elements with the concrete elements; for the spiritual and the mental are not sufficient for us. We have expressions such as, "Whoever says that he has only [an interest in the study of the] Torah [but not its observance] does not even have [to his credit the mitzva of studying the] Torah" (Yevamot 109b), and, "Whoever studies the Torah but does not keep it, it would have been better for him had he died at birth" (Tanḥuma, *Ekev* 6). It would have been better for one who is interested only in abstract thought not to have been born at all. We fundamentally disagree with such an existence. A person's spiritual endeavors must reflect the notion of "all my bones cry out" (Ps. 35:10); they should include all of human experience.

For a non-Jew, the intellectual sphere can be open entirely. This does not mean that the divine image is not fully present in him, or that a non-Jew cannot be a genius in mathematics, physics, or chemistry; that would be patently false. Similarly, a non-Jew can be an outstanding philosopher who deals with theological matters, and he can channel all his talents and abilities into that realm and achieve great things.

The perceptual realm is essentially an alienated realm, in which only conceptions, perceptions, and insights exist. Israel's unique holiness does not glory in the perception of abstract divine matters, because in these matters the human intellect can apply itself without any connection whatsoever to holiness, thus avoiding any effect on one's personality.

Israel's holiness begins with this mixture of the spiritual and the physical, which is part of our abiding pain. We read in Ecclesiastes that "he who increases wisdom increases pain" (Eccl. 1:18). Wisdom here does not refer to intellect but to the connection and fusion that must exist at the nexus of two worlds. Pain is the Jew's heartache when he asks himself what he should do now that God has endowed him with this new wisdom.

Wisdom, then, is an awesome responsibility: Each and every word of Torah creates a clamor, crying out to the person who learned it: "What have you done with me?" In this respect, each new insight that a person attains becomes in itself a point of criticism against him.

On the verse, "Rejoice, O youth, while you are young! Let your heart cheer you in the days of your youth … But know that for all these things God will call you to account" (Eccl. 11:9), the Midrash explains:

> "Rejoice, O youth, while you are young" – in the Torah that you learned when you were young; "Let your heart cheer you in the days of your youth" refers to Mishna, "and walk in the ways of your heart and in the sight of your eyes" refers to Talmud, "But know that for all these things God will call you to account" refers to mitzvot and good deeds. (Ecclesiastes Rabba 11:8)

That is to say, a person will ultimately be asked: Which mitzvot and good deeds did you perform as a result of all these words of Torah that you learned?

THE INFLUENCE OF STUDY ON THE PERSONALITY

What do Bilam's disciples gain when they talk about transcendence, about the soul, about insight? When a disciple of Bilam wishes to gain insight into the divine, he studies a certain theological issue, like divine attributes or divine providence, spending several hours on it, and after attaining a certain insight into the issue, he relaxes on his couch, or in his barrel if he is like Diogenes, and says, "Ah! How beautiful!" And that is all.

For such a person, every theological conclusion that he reaches serves only to magnify his ego. The Baal Shem Tov spoke of a personality type called *re'uma*[1] (*Baal Shem Tov on the Torah, Vayera* 17). This type of person is always saying, "Look (*re'u*) what (*ma*) I am! I have something! It is exceedingly small, amounting to almost nothing (*ma*). But nevertheless, look (*reu*)!" Such an individual need not be a university professor in order to boost his own ego by spreading his ideas; he can also garner attention by sitting in a barrel in the marketplace – so everyone can see his "humility."

---

1. Possibly a reference to Nahor's concubine Re'uma (Gen. 22:24).

By contrast, for a disciple of Abraham – or, for that matter, of Moses, who said, "What (*ma*) are we?" (Ex. 16:7) – the more he beholds, the more he shrinks and contracts. And if nevertheless something overcomes him, it is the will to go and do something with these words and matters that does not let him sit in peace. The new insight that he received does not remain in the abstract but, rather, forces him to change something within himself. A person of this kind is not tested on the question of whether the insight that he perceived is a true insight, but on the question of whether he follows a true path. If it is indeed a true path, then it must somehow lead him to build, do, and act in a truly essential way – whether in relation to himself or in his relationship with his peers, with his parents, or with God.

Bilam's disciples, like Bilam himself, are extraordinary people who remain frozen in a spiritual wasteland, where they can analyze all the formulas for everything in the world, whether it is theology, Talmud, Hasidism, or Kabbala. Some live in a mathematical Gehenna where they refine formulas, and others live in the emptiness of an intellectual vacuum where everything is possible. Bilam lived in a world where everything that is connected with abstract thought ceases to be meaningful, and this is the path that he teaches his disciples.

Bilam is not just a simple non-Jew who wanders around on his donkey. He truly can forgo the silver and the gold, and he has backbone. Bilam avows that he is a scientist, a theologian; for him, this is the truth, from which it is impossible to swerve. All this seems to be a lofty dimension, yet it is the complete antithesis of holiness, because it is woven together with the character of the person who lives in it, the vile character of Bilam.

BILAM THE SOOTHSAYER

In conclusion, let us briefly address Bilam's end.

As we have seen, Bilam is a great prophet whose vision extends to the end of all generations; he is as great a prophet as Moses himself. But in truth, Bilam was destined from birth to fall into the abyss of aimless intellectualism, and that is essentially what characterizes his death. The Torah's description of this incident is strange: "The People of Israel slew Bilam son of Beor, the soothsayer, with the sword, along with their other slain" (Josh. 13:22). Suddenly, Bilam ceases to be a prophet, a man of God, and all that remains is "Bilam the soothsayer."

Bilam was not an ordinary soothsayer; he was a soothsayer on the intellectual plane, and it was there that he performed his incredible tricks. He did not use a crystal ball; he used his ideas. Ultimately, when the final judgment is rendered, he is no longer "Bilam the prophet" but "Bilam son of Beor, the soothsayer." Though Bilam's profession made him stand out in the crowd, in the end he was just another person who was ultimately slain along with the Midianites. The slain Midianites were not intellectuals, so they put him in an honorable place – "upon their slain" (Num. 31:8), so that he should be on top, so that everyone should recognize his uniqueness – but that is the pinnacle of his existence.

The story of Balak and Bilam does not end with the death of the latter. Actually, this only begins a new chapter in our history, where we must always take great care in deciding what to do with new knowledge and understanding. How should the words of the Torah be implemented? Which paths should be followed? Hence, the Torah continues with Pinhas and moves on to Joshua, marching forward into the distant future.

Pinḥas

THE CHARACTER OF THE PRIEST

> Pinḥas, the son of Elazar, the son of Aaron the Priest, has turned
> My wrath away from the People of Israel, in that he was very
> zealous for My sake among them, so that I did not consume the
> People of Israel in My jealousy. Therefore say: "I give to him My
> covenant of peace." (Num. 25:11–12)

The combination of "in that he was very zealous for My sake" and "I
give to him My covenant of peace" seems strange. Why should Pinḥas
receive a "covenant of peace" simply for killing two people?

In the Talmud and midrashim, there are many descriptions of the
Priests' character, and generally they fall into two groups. One view is
that if you see a Priest who displays impudence, it is a sign that he is not
really a Priest (Kiddushin 70b). Pashḥur, a Priest in Jeremiah's time, had
four thousand slaves, all of whom became mixed up in the priesthood.
In light of this, every bad-tempered Priest, who does not display proper
character, is apparently a descendant of those slaves and therefore does
not only lose his credibility as a Priest, but is not even considered a Jew.

The characterization of the Priest as a man of love and kindness
appears in the Mishna as well, where it says, "Be among the disciples
of Aaron, loving peace and pursuing peace, loving people and drawing

them near to the Torah" (Avot 1:12). This is not a new idea; it is expressed frequently in Tanakh. For example, we read, "He walked with Me in peace and uprightness and turned many away from iniquity. For the Priest's lips keep knowledge, and people seek the law at his mouth; for he is a messenger of the Lord of Hosts" (Mal. 2:6–7).

However, the Talmud also states that the reason for intricately "folding" a bill of divorce is that there were hot-tempered Priests who, in their anger, would impulsively divorce their wives (Bava Batra 160b). This irascibility is not a defect in their priesthood but is rather part of their nature, and therefore it is precisely a bad-tempered Priest who is authentic.

Zealousness of this type can be found in the Torah as well, in connection with Levi in the Shekhem incident, where we find an expression that evokes the events of *Parashat Pinḥas*, though the situations are different. In his fury, Levi asks, "Should our sister be treated like a prostitute?" (Gen. 34:31). Indeed, it can be said that Levi and Pinḥas displayed identical character traits.

The similarity between the two does not end there. This quality of hot-headedness is ascribed to the Levites following the sin of the Golden Calf. Moses needed help in implementing what amounted to a minor massacre, so he called out, "Whoever is for God, join me!" (Ex. 32:26). In response, all the Levites rallied to him. They obey Moses' order with great zealousness, for which the Torah praises them: "Your Urim and Thumim belong to Your pious one ... who said of his father and mother, 'I do not see them'; neither did he acknowledge his brothers nor know his own children. For they kept Your word and guarded Your covenant" (Deut. 33:8–9). Somewhat astoundingly, the plain meaning of this is that the tribe of Levi is praised for having killed people. To be sure, it was all done out of righteous zeal and for the sake of Heaven, but the fact remains that they are praised for a murderous rampage.

Indeed, in Jacob's blessings to his sons, Levi – together with his brother Simeon – is remembered for his hot temper, irascibility, and zealotry.

The Zohar distinguishes between two groups within the tribe of Levi: the Levite and the Priest (Zohar, *Bereshit* 266b). The Priest corresponds to the attribute of love and mercy (*ḥesed*), while the Levite corresponds to the attribute of strength and justice (*gevura*). However, if one looks into this, what emerges is not so simple. After all, the primary service of the Priests is butchery. The Priest's task is to slaughter the *korbanot*, receive the blood in a service vessel, convey it to the Altar and sprinkle it. He lives constantly in the midst of blood. The Levites, by contrast, sing songs, open the gates, and serve as the honor guard in the Temple. On the blessing given to the tribe of Levi, "Smash the loins of those who rise up against him, so that his enemies rise no more" (Deut. 33:11), Rashi explains that this is a prophecy about the Hasmoneans, who consisted of Priests of the tribe of Levi. The Hasmoneans would arise, take Israel's defense into their own hands, and lead a war. Thus, we see that the Priest's character clearly contains an aspect of making war and zealously championing God's cause.

The nature of the priesthood, then, is characterized by contradiction. On the one hand, there is zealous passion, bloodshed, and war; and on the other hand, there is something very different – a character that is entirely one of blessing. What, then, is the true character of the Priest?

We find a similar phenomenon in connection with Elijah. There are many stories about Elijah, and in all of them Elijah appears as a loving figure. When someone seeks assistance or is in trouble, Elijah always comes to his aid. There are hundreds of these stories, from the time of the Talmud until our own time, about Elijah's sudden appearance, always as a loving figure.

However, if we look at the depiction of Elijah in Tanakh, it is clear that he is not a figure of love and mercy. First of all, Elijah brings famine and death to the world by declaring that there will be no more dew or rain "except by my word" (I Kings 17:1). Elijah's conduct with the prophets of Baal also does not seem like that of a kind, loving person: All told, he personally slaughters four hundred of them. That is Elijah the man. When someone comes to arrest him (II Kings 1:9–12), Elijah consumes him and his fifty men in fire. When someone else arrives, Elijah burns him, too, along with another fifty men. When Obadiah, who according to the Talmud was himself a prophet, meets Elijah, he shakes with fear (Sanhedrin 39b), and many other accounts show that Elijah was surrounded with an aura of real fright.

When Elijah comes to Mount Sinai, and God asks him, "Why are you here, Elijah?" (1 Kings 19:9), he says, "I have been very zealous." This is the essence of Elijah, as the Zohar states, "Pinḥas is Elijah" (Zohar, *Ki Tissa* 190a).

On the other hand, when Elijah is referred to after his death, his character appears quite different: "Behold, I will send you the Prophet Elijah" (Mal. 3:23). Elijah, who personally smote the land by the sword in his lifetime, now shall "turn the heart of the parents to the children, and the heart of the children to their parents" (3:24). It is not the terrifying Elijah, but this Elijah whom we call upon when we are in the midst of trouble, praying that he will come and offer help to great and small alike.

THE NAME OF GOD IS ZEALOUS

This leads us to the question of the role of zealousness (*kin'a*) in religious experience. What does the Torah mean when it says that Pinḥas "was very zealous for My sake" (Num. 25:11)?

There are two types of *kin'a* that appear in the Torah, which are often connected and intertwined. The first is jealousy, when one wants to be like that person in some way. The second type of *kin'a* is zealousness. When one is zealous for someone's sake, it means that one bears some strong emotion toward that person. For example, in the case of the *sota*'s husband we read that "a spirit of jealousy (*kin'a*) came over him, and he expressed feelings of jealousy (*kinei*) about his wife" (Num. 5:14). This *kin'a* about one's wife can be interpreted not only as "jealousy" but as "zealousness." This zealousness is rooted not in hatred but in love; it comes from the attribute of *ḥesed*, not from the attribute of *gevura*.

Hatred can appear in various forms, some of which are aggressive, but its essence is indifference toward the one hated.

The Talmud defines a bearer of hatred not as someone who curses his fellow man and yells at him, but as "anyone who, out of enmity, has not spoken to his fellow man for three days" (Sanhedrin 3:5). Take, for example, Joseph's brothers, who "could not speak peaceably to him" (Gen. 37:4). When one cannot speak to someone, this is considered strong hatred toward him. In a certain sense – and this is true on the kabbalistic level as well – stern judgment, hatred, and fear are all one attribute, whose basis is breaking off contact with a person. If the attempt to break off contact fails, the next step is to use direct antagonism and violence. One who hates another person does not want to see him, but sometimes in order to reach this goal he must confront the very person he wants to avoid.

Zealousness for someone stems from the attribute of love. The attribute of love has several levels. There is the level of affection, where one is happy to have a certain thing, but he does not long for it or seek it out. When it goes beyond this – when there is an intense longing and desire when that thing is lacking – that is a sign of a higher degree of love. One who loves something, whether it is a beverage, money, or anything else, feels a void when it is not beside him.

This idea is true in spiritual matters as well. One type of person stands in the synagogue on Rosh HaShana or Yom Kippur and prays because everyone else is praying. But there is a higher level: "I remember You upon my bed, and think of You in the night-watches" (Ps. 63:7). The plain meaning of the verse describes one who wakes up at night, if only to turn over to the other side, and immediately longs for God's presence. To be sure, few people are on this level, but this is a level for which to strive.

There is an even higher spiritual level: the level of *kin'a*. One who is truly zealous not only loves something but cannot bear the fact that others can possess it as well. This desire for exclusiveness can sometimes reach a state where one cannot love two things at once.

The essence of *kin'a* is described in the verse, "Love is fierce as death, jealousy (*kin'a*) strong as Sheol" (Song. 8:6). The verse is not speaking disparagingly of zealousness, but in its praise. When love is fierce as death, when *kin'a* is strong as Sheol, it is like a great fire. What underlies *kin'a* is that one cannot accept a relationship that is not exclusive, and that the moment the relationship is no longer unique, it becomes extremely distressing. "I have loved you, says God" (Mal. 1:2); He loves us so much that if we give our love to another, He will not forgive us. Hence, God is zealous – "the name of God is Zealous (*Kana*)" (Ex. 34:14). "You alone have I known of all the families of the earth" (Amos 3:2) – this is a choice of love.

Interestingly, almost every halakhic opinion agrees that worshiping God in tandem with another deity is prohibited only for

Jews. "Except to God alone" (Ex. 22:19) is a formula that applies only to Jews. For non-Jews, if a person believes in God and in another deity as well, he is not considered an idolater, since he nevertheless believes in God. For the People of Israel, however, "I have loved you, says God" – you are beloved and unique to Me, inseparably and intimately connected with Me. God is jealous when there is someone else.

MY COVENANT WAS WITH HIM

When Pinḥas – "in that he was very zealous for My sake" – kills Zimri, his act stems from the aspect of "My covenant of peace": His zealousness stems from the attribute of love, not from the attribute of stern judgment, and this explains the dual identity of the Priests. When it comes to lost love, many people comfort themselves, saying that "there are plenty of fish in the sea." But one can only say this if one's love is not unique and irreplaceable. For Pinḥas, however, his zealous attitude toward his relationship with God dictated his actions.

Kin'a – the feeling of total commitment and exclusiveness – is rooted in love, not in hatred. In his prophecy to the Priests, Malachi describes the covenant that was given to the tribe of Levi: "My covenant was with him, of life and peace" (Mal. 2:5). It is no accident that Malachi's description is based on the verse from this *parasha*, "I give to him My covenant of peace" (Num. 25:12). The attribute of love, from which the Priest stems, assumes various aspects, forms, and modes, and there are times when it cannot restrain itself. Hence, the same Elijah who says, "I have been very zealous" also reconciles parents with their children and children with their parents.

This observation also explains why the "messenger of the covenant," who is present at every *brit mila*, is Elijah and not – as one might have expected – Abraham. Elijah is the messenger of the covenant because he is characterized by total commitment. *Brit mila*, which signifies our unique relationship with God, is based on this same element of commitment, on the complete communion of the two sides. Just like in the case of the Priests, there is simultaneously both blood and love. *Brit mila* is indeed a covenant by blood, but not the blood of hatred; like every covenant, it is an expression of total commitment and love.

Matot

CREATING SANCTITY

"When a man vows a vow to God or swears an oath imposing an obligation on himself... he must do whatever he expressed orally" (Num. 30:3). This idea is very puzzling: How can it be that if a person says that he will not do something, it becomes actually forbidden for him to do it? Why is it that "he must do whatever he expressed orally"?

It is logical that a person should incur the penalty of lashes for eating pig meat or for working on Yom Tov. Here, however, we discover that a person can receive lashes even if he merely declared that he is designating a certain book as a sacrifice, and then went ahead and studied that book. Why is it that simply by saying something, one can generate a new prohibition, and be punished by merely breaking his word? What is the source of a person's ability not only to establish a prohibition but also to create a situation where the attendants of the court must ensure that he does not break his word?

The Torah presents here a whole new array of prohibitions. There are prohibitions that the Torah imposes, to which God subjects us. But there are also prohibitions of another type, a world of obligations that one can create for oneself. By means of various kinds of vows, one can build a whole structure that has all the authority of Torah laws, which emanated from Sinai.

Our sages say that a vow takes effect only "by what is itself forbidden by a vow" (Nedarim 13a); that is to say, a vow takes effect only if one makes it in the same way that one consecrates a *korban*. In essence, a vow is similar to consecrated property. Just as a person can create consecrated property, he can also cause a vow to take effect.

Here, too, the same question arises: How can a lowly person, undistinguished in wisdom, fear of God, and holiness, cause something to become sacred? How is sanctity created?

The following anecdote may help to illustrate the problem. There was once an exalted personality who was an outstanding Torah scholar and a great man. After his *rebbe* died, he was crowned the *admor*, the chief hasidic rabbi of the town. One day, he met the town rabbi, who was a *mitnaged* with a tendency to insult people. The rabbi asked him, "Reb Avrum, I don't understand: Beforehand, you were just a person like everyone else. Now, you have become the holy *admor*. How did this happen?" The new *admor* answered him in his characteristic manner: "Look, it is like designating *teruma*. There is one kernel that is like all the other kernels; it looks exactly the same. But when a Jew takes this kernel and declares, 'This is *teruma*,' it actually becomes *teruma*; it has the sanctity of *teruma*, and all the laws of *teruma* apply to it. So, too, when Jews choose someone and elevate him above the community, he becomes holy." Not to be bested, the town rabbi responded, "This approach also has a drawback, for the Mishna states that if a deaf mute, an imbecile, or a minor separate *teruma*, it is not considered valid" (Terumot 1:1).

Essentially, this discussion raises exactly the same problem that we raised above. The question does not begin with the *admor*; it actually begins with the kernel. How is it possible to say that this kernel is now sacred? How can it be that one can take a kernel and declare that, from now on, it is a sacred kernel, and in fact it then is immediately rendered sacred?

This is not a halakhic question, but a more fundamental problem: What is the source of this power to consecrate? From where does one get the ability to invest something with sanctity and change its essential nature?

If one were to knock on the table and announce, "From now on, this table shall no longer be made of wood; it shall be made entirely of gold," the rest of the people in the room would laugh at him, and rightfully so. What does it matter that he said it is gold? By contrast, if that same person says, "From now on, this table is sacred," this statement has an immediate effect; the table objectively becomes a sacred object, and one must treat it differently. The same thing happens in the case of *teruma*. Previously, it was produce like any other produce. Now, one must treat it with great respect and follow all the laws that now apply to it.

Generally, an object derives sanctity from its relation to the sacred. There is the inherently sacred, the essentially sacred, and a sacred object is that which relates to the sacred in some way. This understanding would explain why a Torah scroll is sacred. To be sure, the scroll was written in ink by a human being, but its sanctity does not come from this. Rather, it received its sanctity from that fact that it contains holy matters. Nevertheless, this still does not explain the source of man's ability to bestow sanctity upon anything in the world simply by pronouncing that it is sacred.

ARRAY OF SANCTITY

In the case of vows and consecrated property, we see that besides the ordinary powers of sanctity and prohibition, a person has the power to cause an array of sanctity to take effect on additional things. We see, then, that holiness is not a defined, limited spiritual dimension – a holy time, a holy place, and a holy people – because we, too, have, in some way, the ability to expand holiness through our own power.

This ability expresses itself in all the various sanctities – in the sanctity of place, in the sanctity of time, and even in the sanctity of Israel.

Regarding the sanctity of place, the Talmud states that it is possible to expand the Temple and the courtyards (Sanhedrin 14b). There we see that, in principle, there is nothing impeding the expansion of this sanctity. In order for this expansion to take effect, a king, a prophet, and two thanksgiving offerings are required. In addition, there is no halakhic impediment to the expansion of the sanctity of Jerusalem – the city borders may reach all the way to Damascus, if that is our desire. All that is required is that the sanctification be implemented properly.

We routinely add to the sanctity of time by accepting Shabbat early, at the expense of the mundane weekday. The custom in Jerusalem is to add an additional segment of time to Shabbat, beyond what is added in most places. Moreover, one who wants to accept Shabbat as early as midday on Friday can do so.

What is possibly most surprising of all is that one may even add to the sanctity of Israel by accepting proselytes. We take a non-Jew who knows that he is a non-Jew, and we convert him. How can we do this? After all, many kabbalistic works discuss the concept of the Jewish soul, which is special and unique. Yet now, when a non-Jew decides that he wants to become a Jew, we allow him to do so. The act of circumcision itself, a requirement for acceptance into the Jewish people, does not make one a Jew; there are countless people who are circumcised for one reason or another, and none of them becomes a Jew as a result. Certainly, immersion in a *mikve* does not make one a Jew; otherwise, anyone who would bathe in the ocean would become a Jew as a result. What allows a non-Jew to become a Jew is our decision to extend the sanctity of Israel to him. Once we do this, he truly becomes sanctified with the full sanctity of Israel.

Just as it is possible to make a vow and to create consecrated property, it is also possible to dissolve and nullify vows, and to retroactively dissolve the sanctity of consecrated property (Arakhin 23a). This, too, is part of our ability to create sanctity. It is also possible to dissolve the sanctity of *teruma* and *maaser* (Nedarim 59a). One can approach a rabbi and say, "I declared that this should be *teruma* and I now regret having done so." As a result, the *teruma* ceases to be *teruma*, and this is essentially the case regarding consecrated property as well.

One of the common questions on this subject relates to slaughtering consecrated *korbanot* outside the Temple. When a person slaughters a consecrated offering outside the Temple, thereby incurring the punishment of *karet*, why couldn't he obtain the retroactive dissolution of the animal's consecration, thus retroactively absolving himself of sin?

On this basis it would be possible to save oneself from all sorts of punishments. For example, if a consecrated ox becomes mixed with a thousand other oxen, none of the thousand oxen can be used.[1] But

---

1. Since it is a "whole creature" and is important, it cannot be nullified through a majority of permitted animals.

in such a case, why not retroactively dissolve the ox's sanctity and thus solve the whole problem?

Many Torah scholars have investigated questions of this kind – whether there is a time limit beyond which it is impossible to dissolve the sanctity of an object, or whether there may even be a prohibition against doing so.

Vows can be released and nullified because the power to make a vow is what gives one the power to nullify it; if one consecrates something, one can seek the release of its sanctity as well.

Nowadays, thank God, we are generally more restrained in making vows, compared to former generations. To be sure, problems with vows still exist, but they are not as they once were. Nevertheless, before the Days of Awe, as well as in the *Kol Nidrei* prayer, people cleanse themselves of vows, demonstrating that it is possible to erase the very sanctity that we create.

THE POWER TO BUILD AND TO DESTROY

The section on vows says something about our power to create, and also about our ability to nullify our creations. It is within our power to create another dimension within an object, and it is also within our power to remove and nullify this dimension.

Some claim that the power to consecrate and to make vows is connected with Israel's essential holiness, which can be seen in the verse, "You shall be holy unto Me" (Lev. 20:26). But in truth, vows and consecrated property are not unique to the Jewish people. Rather, they stem from man's creation in the image of God. Indeed, non-Jews are obligated by such vows just as we are (Nazir 62a). Man can generate sanctity in things because he himself is connected to holiness. As a result, he can do things that at first glance seem relegated to the domain of God.

When the Torah says that "he must do whatever he expressed orally," it says something momentous about man's essential nature, similar to the Talmud's statement that if *tzaddikim* want to, they can create worlds (Sanhedrin 65b). Presumably, even one who is not a *tzaddik*, and who cannot create a world, can create a new reality with his pronouncements. We have within us the ability to connect elements from life and form from them a different reality. Putting aside the halakhic aspect of vows, the subject of vows comes down to a very basic question: What is man? *Parashat Matot* teaches that man is endowed with the power to build and to destroy. By the power of speech alone, man can build a world – a new reality – and with the same simple act, destroy it.

Parashat Matot begins uniquely: "Moses spoke to the heads of the tribes…This is the word that God has commanded" (Num. 30:2). Our sages say that this is the prophetic manner unique to Moses, as all other prophets prophesied with the introductory formula, "Thus says God," whereas Moses prophesied with the introductory formula, "This is the word" (*Sifrei*, Numbers 153). It is no coincidence that Moses' unique prophetic manner is featured here: "This is the word" – a momentous matter is stated here.

WHOEVER VOWS IS AS THOUGH HE BUILT A *BAMA*

On many occasions, our sages seem to frown upon the whole institution of vows: "Rabbi Meir says: 'It is better not to vow than to vow and not fulfill' (Eccl. 5:4) – better than both is not to vow at all" (Tosefta, Ḥullin 2:17). And if someone made a vow, he should go to a learned person and absolve the vow rather than fulfill it, for "whoever vows is as though he built a *bama*, and whoever fulfills [the vow] is as though he burned incense upon it" (Nedarim 59a). This analogy to a *bama* requires explanation.

Why do people make vows? Most vows are made either due to a quarrel, where each person forbids himself to interact with the other, or due to anger, where a person becomes angry at a person, animal, or even an inanimate object, and prohibits it for himself in his frustration. He tries to open a door, but it does not open – so he makes a vow. In any case, when a person makes a vow, this vow becomes endowed with life. "You have been snared by the words of your mouth" (Prov. 6:2). You said something and thereby created a new reality in the world that possesses objective force.

When one makes a vow never to eat a certain food, one constructs a framework that has a certain sanctity, like consecrated property. The difference, however, is that this vow is not dedicated to God, but to one's own pride. The vow is a *bama*, built in response to being denied one's desires. A *bama* can serve one of two purposes: the slaughter of a consecrated offering outside the Temple or idolatry. A vow is the same way; the purpose of the vow might be pure and holy, but more likely this is not the case – it is a form of idolatry.

Hence, our sages say that if one has already built a *bama*, the best thing to do is to destroy it immediately. Likewise, if one has already made a vow, it is best to run quickly and nullify it.

There is a common refrain throughout the book of Kings: "The people still brought sacrifices and burned offerings upon the high places (*babamot*)" (1 Kings 22:44). To this very day, people continue to bring sacrifices and burn offerings on all sorts of *bamot*. It is a mitzva to destroy such *bamot*, and it is certainly not a mitzva to offer *korbanot* upon them. If one fulfills a vow that one made, one is essentially offering a *korban* upon this *bama*. The *bama* was constructed – possibly for the sake of idolatry – by making a vow, and by fulfilling that vow one offers a *korban* upon it.

WHAT REMAINS FOR US?

Nowadays, when it is no longer possible to offer *korbanot* to God, nevertheless, we still have the ability to dedicate things to Him. When a person wants to dedicate something to God, the Torah provides a way to construct special sanctity for all sorts of things. One can take time and dedicate it, conferring true sanctity upon it. If one says, for example, that he will study Torah at a certain time, sanctity is conferred upon that time. If one says that he will dedicate a certain place for studying Torah, sanctity is conferred upon that place. This is very significant, for it shows that we still possess the power to create genuine sanctity.

If one wants to go further, he can also make himself holy. *Parashat Matot* lists the booty collected during the war against Midian, including sheep, cattle, donkeys, and even people, regarding all of which the Torah delineates how much must be set aside as tribute to God. One can understand this as a broader statement about our relationship with God: One can take oneself and devote part of oneself to God.

As weak as one may be in other areas, every person possesses the power to generate real, objective sanctity. When a person vows to study Torah, his study will not always necessarily be on the highest level. Nevertheless, he succeeds in creating sanctity, like the sanctity of the

Altar, sanctity that rests upon a designated time or upon the commitment to study itself. He promised, and now he sits down and fulfills his vow, thereby changing something within himself.

Even if we cannot build a real altar, a vow enables us to build a small altar, and to exercise our ability to generate holiness in the world.

Masei

"ITS COURSES WANDER; YOU CANNOT KNOW"

Parashat Masei begins with a detailed description of the People of Israel's long journey following the Exodus from Egypt: "They journeyed and they camped … They journeyed and they camped" (Num. 33:5–49) – on and on for forty-two journeys. What is the meaning of this lengthy review? Why does the Torah need to tell us all this?

One point that emerges from most of the commentators is that "these were their stops along the way" (Num. 33:1) is not a straight line that proceeds in a clear route. This is true of life as well: A person's path is never smooth and straight, just as on the People of Israel's path there were many complications along the way. Their path is full of twists and turns, the route is unclear, and the direction is unknown.

According to the map, it is not at all clear, for example, where the People of Israel were located after the conquest of the country of Sihon and Og. In order to conquer the Bashan, which was located in modern-day Syria, they went north, and afterward they apparently retraced their steps and came all the way back. This is surprising, since from the Bashan it is possible to avoid the Jordan entirely and enter the Land from the north. Yet instead they go all the way back south until Jericho. Why precisely Jericho? The answer to this, too, is not clear. Throughout this entire journey it appears that they do not follow a normal route.

All the journeys that appear in the *parasha*, like all of the Torah's narratives, tell the story of the inner life of both the People of Israel as a nation and of each individual Jew. What happens in the Torah is the basic pattern, the mold for everything that happens to the Jewish people throughout the ages. Everything is cast in this mold, and we pass through it again and again, although not in all the details of things but certainly in their general thrust, in the experiences that they represent.

Today, too, we are in a wilderness; not in the wilderness of Sinai but, as Ezekiel calls it, "the wilderness of the peoples" (Ezek. 20:35) – in exile. We have been wandering in the wilderness of the peoples not for forty years but for more than two thousand years, and the length of each one of these journeys has been multiplied several times over. Each station in our history corresponds to a station in the wilderness of Sinai. The Torah says that in the wilderness of Sinai, we "remained in Kadesh for many days" (Deut. 1:46), which may correspond to the many days that we resided in a certain place – three hundred years, four hundred years, or six hundred years. Jewish life stays and concentrates in one place for a certain time, and then it picks itself up and begins to move about from place to place.

All these journeys, like the other points of passage in the Torah, have one thing in common: Each one of them signifies a transition point, a point of stopping and change. But the distances and the travel time between them are not the same. During the forty years of travel in the wilderness, the People of Israel experienced forty-two journeys, but the time between each journey was not always a year. Sometimes a year would pass between two stops, while at other times only half a day. Thus, when we travel through the world on our journeys through history, we do not know our present station; what is more, we do not know how long it will take until we reach the next station.

We are in one of the books of the Torah, but we do not know which one. Are we in Deuteronomy or in Leviticus? We proceed from station to station, but we do not know which station is which. Are we in Abel-shittim or in Mithkah? Sometimes many years go by until we have an idea where we are in the narrative, and sometimes we will never know our location.

This is the meaning of the verse, "Its courses wander; you cannot know" (Prov. 5:6). There is a course or path that runs through the ages, and this is the course of the journey from exile to redemption. It is a course whose number of steps is unknown; neither the distance between the stations nor how much time is spent at each station is known. Sometimes it appears as though we are now approaching the Land of Israel, but then it becomes apparent that although we are truly very close, there are still many more stations to go.

The individual, too, experiences these journeys and travels on this path. "These were their stops along the way" – the stops of all people, only that we do not know what the stations are called. "And they journeyed from Mount Shepher and encamped in Haradah" (Num. 33:24) – when does a person move between these two stations? The names of these two stations are easy to understand. When is one in a beautiful mountain (*har shefer*), and when is one in a state of trembling (*ḥarada*)? When is one in a low station, and when is one in a lofty station? This is the meaning of "Its courses wander; you cannot know."

The holy name on which the *Ana BeKo'aḥ* prayer is based is the name of forty-two letters, corresponding to the forty-two journeys of the People of Israel in the wilderness. This name is connected with the transition from one reality to another. Hence, *Ana BeKo'aḥ* is recited at times that involve this kind of transition, such as during *Sefirat HaOmer*, which is a time when we undergo a process of change, of transition from exile to redemption and the giving of the Torah. We also recite it during *Kabbalat Shabbat*, at the time of transition between the weekday reality and Shabbat reality. This name is the name of "these were their stops along the way," the name that alludes to the inner processes of the worlds.

HE MADE THEM WANDER IN THE WILDERNESS

At the beginning of the *parasha* (Num. 33:1), Rashi tells a story: A father takes his ailing son to a distant place; because he is ill and dazed, he sees nothing and is not aware of what is happening. Afterward, when the father and son return home along the same route as before, the father points out all the places along the way where they stopped. He says to his son, "Although you do not remember, we stopped in all these places. Here it was difficult, here it was good, etc." This is the meaning of "these were their stops along the way."

Nowadays, we, too, feel that we are wandering and moving about, without understanding the meaning of it all. In the future, however, once God brings us to the redemption, He will also tell us about all the stations along the way. He will tell us where this station was and where that station was; which stations were difficult stations and which were easy; which were the important stations and which were unimportant.

Part of the difficulty of the wilderness, which is also a perennial trial for the Jewish community and for the individual, is that if one could understand where one's steps are leading, one would know his exact distance from the final destination, and one would know what the solution is: Everything would be simpler. The great difficulty is that just when it seems that we are going northward, we suddenly begin to move southward; just when we think that we are ascending the mountain, we suddenly begin our descent.

This problem is the source and essence of the whole conception of Jewish destiny. If we understood all the nuances of the process leading to redemption, and saw clearly that we are progressively drawing nearer to it, everything would seem different. But since we do not know this, we need only recall that "these were their stops along the way," for the community and for the individual. We constantly re-experience the same journeys; we stand and we fall. Some of us are swallowed up by the earth and some of us escape. Sometimes we sin and sometimes we act righteously. There is a station where one can receive Torah, and there is a station where one is liable to be burned by a divine fire. Sometimes the stations switch positions, and if one would know exactly what the stations were, one would be able to take precautions. Only when we reach the final station will we be able to say with confidence that we have reached the point we were destined to reach.

This is our story, which we will be able to read and understand only at the end of time, when we reach the final station. Then we will receive the meaning of the map by which we have traveled, and this will enable us to explain our history and the events that have befallen us.

The path from Egypt to the "good and spacious land" is long and arduous, a path that traversed "the wilderness of the peoples." Only at the end of the path will we come to the point at which it will be possible to understand both the "going forth" and the "journey." Only then will we comprehend the meaning and the content of all our experiences over the years.

Deuteronomy

Devarim
In honor of Shlomo Zalman Moshe ben Zvi Halevi's Bar Mitzva
Ruth & Conrad, z"l Morris

Va'ethanan
In honor of Yisrael and Golda Koschitzky
Koschitzky Family

Ekev
In honor of Betty Jean Mervis

Re'eh
In honor of our wedding anniversary
Scott and Sally Saunders, London

Shofetim
In honor of Sir Trevor Chinn's Bar Mitzva
Dedicated by Sir Trevor and Lady Susan Chinn

Ki Tetzeh
In honor of Alan Lee's Bar Mitzva in London September 1970

Ki Tavo
In honor of Ralph Goldman, z"l

Nitzavim
Anonymous

Vayelekh
In honor of the Ruth and Conrad, z"l Morris Family

Shabbat Shuva
In memory of Rolf O.J. Fritzsche
Reuven, z"l
Barbara Hines

Haazinu
In honor of our father Chaim Ben Menachem Mendel a"h
David Deitz Family

Vezot HaBerakha
In memory of our beloved mother and grandmother,
Gertrude Sichel, an Eshet Chayil.
Esther and Romie Tager
Joseph, Simon and their families

Devarim

EIKHA

During the week of *Parashat Devarim*, we encounter the word *eikha* three times: in the weekly Torah portion – "How (*eikha*) can I myself alone bear your trouble, your burden, and your strife" (Deut. 1:12); in the *haftara* – "How (*eikha*) has the faithful city become a harlot!" (Is. 1:21); and in the reading of *Megillat Eikha* on Tisha B'Av – "How (*eikha*) does the city sit solitary" (Lam. 1:1).

Although *eikha* itself is a neutral word, and can be used to mean "how" in any context, it has taken on a very specific connotation; it has become an expression of sorrow and pain. In connection with Tisha B'Av, for example, *eikha* is a central motif, and there are quite a few *kinot* that are entirely devoted to elaborating on the meaning of the word.

In this respect, there is a deeper connection between the *eikha* of Moses, Isaiah, and Jeremiah, and they all express the same sorrow and lamentation. The *eikha* of Moses is the beginning, the key to the entire matter: "How can I myself alone bear your trouble, your burden, and your strife?" From this original question, there is an inner development over the course of generations that continues for centuries, through the *eikha* of Isaiah until the *eikha* of Jeremiah.

"YOUR TROUBLE, YOUR BURDEN, AND YOUR STRIFE"

In light of the word *eikha*'s association with mourning and expressions of sorrow, we should try to understand what led Moses to use this key word precisely here.

At the sin of the Golden Calf, for example, Moses certainly had a lot to say. However, one thing he does not say is, "How (*eikha*) could you have made the calf?" The sin of the Golden Calf was very serious; indeed, our sages expound on the verse, "When I visit, I will visit their sin upon them" (Ex. 32:34), that some small portion of all punishment is due to the sin of the Golden Calf (Sanhedrin 102a). Nevertheless, although he takes harsh steps against the calf's worshipers, Moses does not treat that sin with the same gravity as we find here; he does not regard it as a major problem. So, too, in the case of the sin of the spies, despite its seriousness and its great influence on the Jewish people's future, Moses does not use the expression *eikha*.

What, then, bothers Moses here in *Parashat Devarim*? Our sages say that God had forewarned Moses and Aaron that leadership over the People of Israel would not be easy for them: "He said to them: You should know that they are stubborn and troublesome. Nevertheless, assume leadership over them, even though they may insult you and stone you" (*Sifrei*, Numbers 91).

The Talmud cites a dispute as to whether the verse, "They would gaze after Moses until he entered his tent" (Ex. 33:8) should be interpreted as praiseworthy or derogatory. According to one opinion, the people gazed at Moses because they considered it a privilege to behold him. According to another opinion, however, the people looked at Moses with ill will and said, "Do you see his neck? Do you see his legs, his backside? How does he get so fat? It is all from our money!" When Moses would be late, they would say, "He is busy thinking about us, devising some new plan, some new decree with which to afflict us." When he would be early, they would say, "He has some family problem – he apparently got into an argument with his wife" (Y. Bikkurim 3:3).

Moses was a man whose every act influenced our world and the realm of heaven; God spoke with him face to face, the skin of his face shone with a brilliant light – and yet the people would slander him to his face and behind his back; they would provoke him, falsely accuse him, and quarrel with him. "Your trouble, your burden, and your strife" was part of Moses' divine service, and he knew it. Though even from the beginning he was not eager to become the leader of the People of Israel, he understood his responsibility and accepted the assignment, knowing full well what he was getting into.

A *tzaddik* once complained to his Hasidim that he could no longer endure the constant flow of people coming to him and bothering him with all sorts of questions, problems, and stories. One of the Hasidim, a sharp young man, answered him in front of everyone: "*Rebbe*, return the money." In other words, if you are a *rebbe*, you take this upon yourself; if you are not a *rebbe*, return all the money that was given to you over the years. If you agree to accept responsibility, you receive "your trouble, your burden," and when there are quarrels, you receive "your strife" as well.

"MYSELF ALONE"

What, then, was Moses' problem here? Why did he sigh and cry out *eikha*?

The cantillation mark *etnaḥta* generally determines where the stress should be placed in a verse. In the verse, "How can I myself alone bear your trouble, your burden, and your strife," the *etnaḥta* falls on the words "myself alone (*levadi*)," and this was the root of Moses' problem. The problem began with the fact that Moses was alone. What truly ate at him was that all of "your trouble, your burden, and your strife" fell only on him.

Moses did not mean to say that he needed a certain number of attendants, soldiers, and bodyguards at his disposal. Rather, his complaint was that no one else besides him really cared. So, too, when he complained, "Did I conceive this people, did I give birth to them?" (Num. 11:12), it was not because he had a hard job. There, too, Moses' problem was that no one else cared – "I am not able to bear this entire people myself alone" (11:14).

In order to understand the wilderness generation, there is something important to remember: One who is privileged to experience God's voice – even if it is not His actual voice but a *bat kol* or an echo of a *bat kol* – he has merited something that will remain with him throughout his life. Here, an entire nation – men, women, and children – stood and heard God speaking. This is an indelible memory that will never leave these people. Our sages say that the wilderness generation was a generation of knowledge, and that it included many people who were worthy of being prophets (Leviticus Rabba 9:1). Nevertheless, no one except Moses was interested in the momentous challenges of leadership. That generation was not lacking in people of stature, leaders of Israel, but each one was only willing to fulfill his own role. Even those who were appointed leaders of hundreds or leaders of thousands would go to work from eight in the morning to three in the afternoon, punch the clock, and go home. Moses' dilemma is not that there are problems, but that others do not get involved. They go about their lives and do not feel responsible for what is happening to their own people.

Accordingly, when Joshua said to Moses regarding Eldad and Medad, "My lord, Moses – stop them!" (Num. 11:28), and Moses responded, "Are you jealous for my sake?" (11:29), this can be understood as an expression of wonder: Are you truly jealous for my sake? So many people stood there and did nothing, and now Joshua comes and says: "My lord, Moses – stop them!" Can it be that finally there is someone who cares?

This concern shown by Joshua is also what marks him as a candidate who is fit to lead the people after Moses' death. However, Joshua is also criticized. When he says to Moses, "There is a cry of war in the camp!" (Ex. 32:17), and Moses replies, "It is not the sound of the victorious; it is not the sound of the defeated; it is the sound of song that I hear" (32:18), we understand the reply as a kind of reprimand: Here is Joshua, who is destined to be the next leader of Israel, and he does not know what kind of sound this is! Israel's leader must be able to distinguish whether people are crying or shouting, whether they are celebrating or wailing. Nevertheless, Joshua is chosen as the successor to Moses, the one "who shall go out before them and come in before them"; he is the "man in whom there is spirit" (Num. 27:17–18). He is chosen because he cares, and that is the decisive factor. Everyone else wants to sit at home in peace; they are not willing to give of themselves for the sake of the Jewish people.

Yitro suggests to Moses that he should search for "men of truth, who hate improper gain" (Ex. 18:21), or as Moses himself puts it, "wise and discerning men" (Deut. 1:13). The Talmud notes here that Moses had found men who were wise but not discerning (Eiruvin 100b). But what is the difference between a wise person (*ḥakham*), who is easily found, and a discerning person (*navon*), who is rarer? A wise person can understand things, but a discerning person goes beyond this; he can infer one thing from another. A wise person can be given an order, and he will carry it out properly, whereas a discerning person creates things on his own. It is this latter type of individual that Moses could not find.

Moses laments the fact that he could not find people who would join him in bearing a greater share of responsibility. "Carrying the thickest part of the beam" – a Hebrew idiom meaning to delve into the heart of the matter – derives from a simple metaphor: A tree is generally wide at its base and increasingly narrow as it rises. Some people choose to get at the root of things, to be involved in the essence, at the point where the trunk is thick, whereas others prefer to approach the tree where the trunk is thin. Moses bewails the fact that, in the end, there is no one else who will accompany him as he enters the thick of the crisis; he is left by himself.

To a great extent, Moses' problem in the wilderness, and Israel's problem afterward as well, is that people are not proactive in involving themselves in things, but instead wait for things to be done for them.

Moses was a great leader, and as long as he was alive, things held together for the People of Israel. Maimonides explains that the difference between Moses and all the other prophets was that Moses could approach God with any question he might have had: "Stand by, and I will hear what instructions God gives about your case" (Num. 9:8). And yet, his lofty level notwithstanding, he could genuinely say to the people, "I still live in your midst" (Deut. 31:27) (*Laws of the Foundations of the Torah* 7:6).

But what happens after Moses dies, in Joshua's time and afterward? At first, monumental events were still occurring, and the emotional excitement was high, but soon enough everything fell apart. After the Elders, who outlived Joshua, also died, everyone began to practice idolatry. At first glance, this seems incredible, since there had already been several generations of education in Torah and Judaism in one form or another. The problem was that people were willing to be recipients but not creators, an unsustainable dynamic for maintaining a positive relationship with God.

CONFIRMED AND ACCEPTED

When one longs for and deeply identifies with something, there may be ups and downs, but he will continue to pursue it for as long as he is able. Here, however, there is an entire people that is continually in need of support, motivation, and prodding. The force of inertia can only move it forward for so long; eventually the force peters out.

The deterioration continues and even becomes more acute, from the time of Moses until Jeremiah's time. From a historical standpoint, throughout this period the Jewish community appears to be apathetic toward God. The question is not how many wicked people and how many righteous people there are – there will always be a significant number of people in each category. The question is whether there are people who are creative, who take the initiative, who can lead. Throughout this whole period, the impression is that the people are merely passive beings; only sporadically do we find more active, self-motivated individuals.

Each time the name of another king is listed in the book of Kings, it is accompanied by a short summary of the nature of the king's reign. This summary generally reads either, "And he did what was evil in the eyes of God," or, "And he did what was good in the eyes of God." The question that immediately arises is: What about the entire community? What did everyone else do? According to Tanakh, King Uzziyahu had an army of over 300,000 soldiers (II Chron. 26:11–13). What did these soldiers all think? The Jewish people was ruled by kings like the wicked Menashe, on the one hand, or Hezekiah, who was fit to be the Messiah, on the other – and the public seemed to be indifferent to this contrast. How can this be? The answer is that the people are passive and not active; they do not show drive but are driven. This reality only changed during the time of Jeremiah.

Only at the start of the Second Temple period, beginning with Ezra and Nehemiah, can one detect a change, a new beginning. Although there are prophets, political leaders, and others who are concerned and take action, now, for the first time, there is a Jewish community that is not dependent on any one of these individuals. In the covenant that appears in Nehemiah 10, what stands out is that it is written in the plural. Throughout the covenant, a recurring motif appears: "We have taken upon ourselves." The covenant is not built on one person who dictates it; the signatures of many people are affixed to it. Finally, the Jewish community decides its own fate and acts on its own initiative.

During this period, the structure of the Jewish people was essentially transformed. "The Jews confirmed and accepted upon themselves and their descendants" is a structure entirely different from the decision or undertaking of one individual. When Haman decreed that the Jews should be exterminated, the Jewish people decided as a community to die rather than submit, give up their Judaism, and assimilate among the non-Jews. Unlike the coercion and pressure on the Jewish people from above to fulfill the Torah in the wilderness period, and unlike the passivity that characterized the people from the time of Moses, here the people begin to be independent.

"HOW HAS THE FAITHFUL CITY BECOME A HARLOT?"

This explains the connection between "How can I myself alone bear your trouble, your burden, and your strife?" which would seem to be a relatively minor complaint, and Isaiah's harsh accusation, "How has the faithful city become a harlot!" (Is. 1:21). There is a real connection between the two, because it may very well be that the city "in which righteousness once lodged, but now murderers" (1:21) is this way precisely because of the situation in Moses' time.

A country cannot enforce a just social order from above; it is not enough to have a king and a police force. They can punish and coerce, but these tools alone will not be effective for long. When "everyone loves bribes and pursues payments" (Is. 1:23), no legal system will work. In a civilized society, if a murderer is on the loose, he will inevitably be caught, because the public will not tolerate him. When no one tolerates him, when such a person is totally unacceptable, he will be unable to survive. Conversely, when there is a platform for wickedness and injustice in the midst of a society, then no matter what the state institutions do or legislate, it will not help change the face of that society.

That is exactly the situation that Isaiah describes. Not everyone took bribes; presumably, there were a few corrupt Priests, a few officials who sought bribes, and a few false prophets. The question is how the people as a whole reacts to this. Apparently, no one was willing to get involved and confront the problem. To be sure, no one likes the corrupt regime – everyone knows that corruption is bad for the nation in the long run – but no one goes out of his way to do something about it. No one rocks the boat and no one protests. As a result, the reality of one form of corruption after another can be expected.

When there is no one whose heart – and not just his *kippa* – has been touched by the fear of God, and there is no activism from within, society sinks lower and lower. Sodom is an extreme example of this, and in fact, Isaiah turns to the People of Israel and tells them that they are "chiefs of Sodom" and "people of Gomorrah" (Is. 1:10). What fundamentally characterized society in Sodom? Their basic law was: "What is mine is mine, and what is yours is yours" (Avot 5:10). Everyone has his own house and his own possessions; "You don't interfere in my business, and I won't interfere in your business." Since these are the laws of the country, when one goes out of one's way to act righteously, to do justice – this is a serious crime, because it interferes with the natural order that the people of Sodom held to.

When "How can I myself alone bear" develops and branches out, it is only a matter of time until its extreme extension – "How has she become a harlot" – comes into fruition as well. This is also the explanation for the analogy to a harlot: A woman who goes about recklessly and is careless about her relationships has a good chance of degenerating and becoming a harlot.

"HOW DOES THE CITY SIT SOLITARY?"

"How does the city sit solitary" (Lam. 1:1) is the extreme extension of "How can I myself alone bear." Lack of involvement and lack of real interest in things progressively increase over time. At first, one does not love the good; then he does not hate the evil. Then he becomes apathetic to the evil; as time goes on, he is willing to accept it tacitly, and eventually he is even willing to agree to it outright. He begins to cooperate with it, then he commits a transgression in practice, then he initiates a transgression, and finally he becomes a leader of transgressors. As we have stated, from apathy to harlot takes a while, but ultimately that stage, too, is reached. After the moral degeneration come the social and political degeneration, the final stage of that same process. If no one cares, there can be no national community, no unity, no agreements; only "How does the city sit solitary."

The Midrash comments on the verse, "Her leaders were like harts" (Lam. 1:6), that just as when it is intensely hot, harts turn their faces one beneath the other, so the great men of Israel would see a transgression committed but turn their faces away from it" (Lamentations Rabba 1:33). The same notion is repeated in the Talmud: "Just as the hart, the head of one is at the side of the other's tail, so Israel of that generation hid their faces in the earth and did not rebuke each other" (Shabbat 119b). Even the righteous among the people do not want to get involved, instead insisting on keeping their heads down; what other people do is none of their concern.

Moses said wistfully, "Would that all of God's people were prophets, that God would put His spirit upon them" (Num. 11:29). This was not a wish for every person to truly receive the spark of prophecy, but a desire that the entire People of Israel should become involved in what is happening.

It stands to reason that the disaster of the destruction of the First Temple and the Babylonian exile was precisely what reversed and cured the decline, which began with the *eikha* of Moses and ended with that of Jeremiah; for only then did the understanding sink in that we have nothing to rely on but the personal involvement of each one of us.

After the sin of the Golden Calf, when Moses cried out, "Whoever is for God, join me!" (Ex. 32:26), only the Levites answered his call – a rather small group, all of whom were members of Moses' family. By contrast, when Cyrus said, "Whoever among you of all His people… let him go up" (II Chron. 36:23) – not as an order but merely as a statement granting permission for people to go up on their own initiative – a large congregation went up, without anyone pushing them to do so, and without a leader standing in front, urging them on.

THE POWER TO CHANGE

When one is self-motivated, one has the power to accomplish things and bring about change. When one gets into something with all one's heart, with all one's soul, and with all one's might, this has real power that constantly grows stronger. When one does something for trivial, selfish reasons, the result, too, will reflect this, even if it is a matter that relates to Torah. As a Jewish leader once remarked, "Why do the *maskilim* win? Because they do their falsehood truly, whereas we do our truth falsely."

The change that has come about since the period of "How does the city sit solitary" is an instructive lesson that we learned from exile. It is the awareness that when one person is left alone to deal with everything, this is a situation that leads to disaster. There is only one way out of this predicament: for every person to get involved. Only when we adopt this attitude will new opportunities begin to arise.

Va'ethanan

WHAT IS IDOLATRY?

Parashat Va'ethanan, part of Moses' long farewell speech to the People of Israel, deals extensively with the topic of idolatry. The command to keep far away from any trace of idolatry and paganism is presented together with all the central events of the *parasha*, from the historic spectacle of God's revelation at Sinai to the pronouncement of the Ten Commandments, to the warnings about the future – the entry into the Land and the process of acclimation that goes with it.

But what is idolatry? Why is the Torah so concerned about it, why does the Torah caution so much against it, and what is the source of its attraction?

Apparently, the Torah's preoccupation with idolatry is rooted in the fact that it is not defined as a collection of forbidden objects but, rather, depends on man's intention. Moreover, idolatry can manifest itself in many different ways, some of which do not necessarily resemble the traditional image of an idol. Anyone can take an object and cause it to become an idol; it does not have to be a pre-existing idol like Dagon or the Moabite Chemosh.

When one worships an object, he makes it an idol, whether it is the image of a man or the image of a donkey, the image of a louse or the image of a fish. When the Torah says, "You shall not make for yourself a graven image nor any manner of likeness of anything that is in heaven above, or that is on the earth beneath, or that is in the water under the earth" (Ex. 20:4), this means that we should not think that something has to be important or unique to be an idol; anything can be an idol.

What is the halakhic definition of idolatry? "If one slaughters [an animal] as a sacrifice to the sun, the moon, the stars, the planets, Michael the Archangel, or a tiny worm, it is regarded as an idolatrous sacrifice" (Tosefta, Ḥullin 2:18). The inclusion of Michael the Archangel in this list may seem strange: What could be the problem with sacrificing to Michael, "the Archangel who stands beside Israel" (Semaḥot, Ḥibbut HaKever 1:1)? Nevertheless, one who worships anything other than God, even an archangel, turns that object into an idol.

SEPARATING THE MASTER

The essence of the matter is that anything that is removed from the framework that the Torah established and set up independently becomes idolatry, even if this entity seems like something inherently holy or positive.

The *piyut* "*El Mistater*," a hymn that is often recited on Shabbat at *Seuda Shelishit*, states, "The strong one unites the ten *sefirot* as one; he who separates the Master will not see lights." The ten *sefirot* are one whole, and this whole must remain unified. When one removes one of its components, it becomes impossible to see the light.

An expression of this idea appears in the Midrash in connection with the sin of the Golden Calf. God says, "I go forth in My chariot so as to give them the Torah … and they unhitch one of the animals of My chariot" (Exodus Rabba 43:8). That is to say, at the revelation at Sinai, Israel beheld the divine chariot with its four *ḥayot*, and they took one of the *ḥayot* and began to worship it. The ox's face in the divine chariot is an angel, but when it was worshiped at Mount Sinai it became the exact opposite of an angel. If Israel had taken the divine chariot in its entirety, that would have been perfectly acceptable. But when they removed one of its parts, that constituted the sin of the Golden Calf, for which we are paying a price to this very day. As our sages say, every affliction that falls upon the Jewish people is part of the interest paid for the sin of the Golden Calf (Numbers Rabba 9:49).

This point becomes all the more pronounced when we consider Solomon's "sea" – the copper basin in the Temple that stood atop twelve oxen (1 Kings 7:23–25). When twelve oxen are placed in their designated positions in the Temple, not only is this unproblematic, but the oxen even add to the sanctity of the Temple. But to take one small calf and place it in the Temple by itself would be a grave sin. When one separates something from the whole, one holds on to a mere fragment of the pure form. The moment one removes it, no matter how holy it was, it turns into an idol.

On the verse, "gods of silver and gods of gold, you shall not make for yourselves" (Ex. 20:20), Rashi expounds:

> "Gods of silver" serves to lay down a prohibition regarding the cherubim … If you make any change in them by making them of silver and not of gold, they will be regarded by Me as idols; "and gods of gold" serves to lay down a prohibition against adding to the number of cherubim. For if instead of the prescribed two you make four, they will be regarded by Me as gods of gold.

If one adds a cherub, it becomes idolatry; if one removes a cherub, it becomes idolatry as well. Even though it comes from the Holy of Holies, it becomes idolatry. Once one breaks it off, it loses its holiness, as it has been severed from the whole.

This difficulty exists in many places and areas within the Jewish world. Just as half a Torah scroll is invalid and does not have the sanctity of a Torah scroll that is intact, so, too, when a piece is removed from the Torah, the piece has no sanctity but, rather, has the *tuma* of idolatry. It makes no difference whether that piece contains text concerning the mitzva of Torah study or love of the Land. Thus, the Talmud declares that "whoever says that he has only Torah [but not its observance] does not even have Torah" (Yevamot 109b). If a person takes the Torah itself and empties it of all its content, then he is left with nothing – not even Torah – because he neglects the connection to the living God.

Our sages say that if one wishes to convert to Judaism and accepts upon himself the entire Torah "except for one thing," he is not accepted (*Sifra, Kedoshim* 3:8). The reason for this is that acceptance of the Torah requires acceptance of the entire package, down to the last word. This is certainly true regarding the omission of verses like "*Shema Yisrael*," but it is also true regarding verses that are seemingly less critical for one's faith, like, "Timna was a concubine" (Gen. 36:12). As Maimonides puts it, "There is no distinction between 'The descendants of Ham: Cush and Mizraim' (10:6), 'and his wife's name was Mehetabel' (36:39), and 'I am God your Lord' (Ex. 20:2) and 'Hear, O Israel' (Deut. 6:4), for it all is from the mouth of the Almighty, and it all is God's perfect Torah, pure, holy, and true" (*Commentary on the Mishna*, Sanhedrin 10:1).

One can be totally committed to some matter; but when it is a commitment to one thing only, it is liable to become what psychologists call monomania: an obsession with one thing.

For example, a man once wrote an entire five hundred-page book about lice. The problem with lice is that they can live only on human beings; if put on mice or on monkeys, they die. So in order to research the lice, the author grew them on his own flesh. Here we see that, for the sake of research, one can sometimes go to incredible lengths. And if a person can have such commitment for louse eggs, it is no wonder that there can also be commitment to Torah study or to the Land of Israel. But so long as a person is crazy about one thing – he is crazy, regardless of what that thing is. This is not to say that raising lice is equal in value to the love of the Land or to Torah study, but it is essentially the same phenomenon. The test of the legitimacy of such devotion is whether the object of one's obsession is an element within a greater system, or whether it has assumed supreme importance in itself.

THE ALLURE OF OVERSIMPLIFICATION

The urge to worship idols contains within it a very religious aspect – the desire to wholly devote oneself to something. In truth, however, this desire has the potential to uproot the world of Judaism from its place. What draws people to do this?

A person is liable to be drawn to such complete devotion when he is faced with many elements within his spiritual life, each one of which points in a different direction, like the fingers of the hand. This is disturbing and confusing, and so as not to remain in a state of confusion, one is liable to choose one element and give it a separate status, thus clarifying and simplifying one's world. This element is not necessarily forbidden, contemptible, or vile; it can even be something profound, important, and even holy. But it has been uprooted from its context, and so it loses its connection to true holiness.

In 1977, the BBC produced a documentary television series called *The Long Search*, whose purpose was to cover all religions. To introduce the show, representatives from each religion were invited to speak for three or four minutes about their religion. I was asked to speak about Judaism, and through this experience I discovered how difficult that task is.

When one speaks about Christianity, one can effectively and accurately summarize the essence of the religion in two or three sentences. Even Islam and Buddhism can be summarized in a few sentences. But how can one summarize Judaism? To be sure, we believe in one God, but that does not set us apart from the other monotheistic religions. We of course believe that people must fulfill mitzvot, but that, too, does not truly set us apart. We believe in all sorts of things – the problem is that there seems to be no one element that fundamentally defines our belief system. One can say that Judaism is belief in God, belief that He chose the Jewish people and gave them the Torah and the obligation to fulfill it – but this, too, is merely a superficial definition.

It would be convenient if it were possible to find one simple slogan of three or four words, and to say that this is the entire Torah. But the truth is that there is no slogan that encapsulates the entire Torah. I once met a Jew who wanted to declare publicly that all the religions basically aspire to the same thing – love. It would not be correct to say that we are against love; we are clearly for it – both love of God and love of man. It is just that the Torah contains many other things as well.

Moreover, the Torah contains many things that appear contradictory. One can make a whole collection of seemingly oppositional verses: On the one hand, we have, "Love your neighbor as yourself" (Lev. 19:18), while on the other, "he shall be put to death" (Ex. 21:15–17); one verse says, "Love the stranger" (Deut. 10:19), and another says, "do not let a soul stay alive" (20:16), and there are many other examples of this.

For each of these pairs of contradictory verses, which is correct? The answer is that both are correct. The Talmud says, "Great is knowledge, since it is placed between two names, as it is written, 'For a Lord of knowledge is God' (1 Sam. 2:3)" (Berakhot 33a). That is to say, the verse's placement of the word "knowledge" between two holy names shows that it is a great thing. The Talmud continues, asking: But then this applies to vengeance as well, as it is written, "Lord of vengeance, O God" (Ps. 94:1)! The Talmud answers that this is correct: Vengeance, too, in its proper sphere, is a great thing. Thus, knowledge is important, love is important, and vengeance is important. Likewise, "Do not let a soul stay alive" is important, "Love the stranger" is important, "You shall love God your Lord," and "You shall fear God your Lord" – everything is important. This can be very confusing: How can one live one's life constantly jumping from one important thing to its equally important opposite?

Such a requirement creates a high level of stress that for a normal person is almost impossible to bear, and that is what makes people want to separate one element from this confusing tangle of ideas. For them, this element will be the most important one, the true essence. Whether they choose an important element or not, this choice is always based on the difficulty in coping with the complicated aggregate of elements that make up our belief system. People want one flag, one direction, and for that they try to uproot a single isolated element from the Torah, in order to simplify their world. They feel that they know what is important – and the rest is commentary.

Even one whose connection to Judaism began with one particular element, and who understandably fixates on this element as a result, must bear in mind that this is only a part of the whole. One cannot hold on to a mere tatter. If one is holding on to the corner of God's garment, it does not matter which tassel one is clutching: The moment one grasps part, one must also grasp the whole. If not, one assumes the aspect of Saul, who was left only with tatters – "God has torn the Kingdom of Israel away from you" (1 Sam. 15:28).

THE NECESSITY OF COMPLEXITY

The concern about idolatry is constant because it is a gradual process. It begins with small offerings like flowers and songs. These lead to animal sacrifices, and eventually to human sacrifice as well. The problem is not just the distorted proportions but the fact that ultimately everything drains into one place and all the rest is forgotten.

Because of this, religious experience requires great wariness. One must take great care to avoid removing parts from the holy chariot, as it were, setting them up as independent objects of devotion. Hence, whenever one enters into a spiritual attachment or connection, even when it is for an important purpose, one must take care not to become involved in idolatry. When engaged in these spiritual areas, one must remain in a constant state of awe and fear, always questioning whether one has exceeded the limits. One must not lose a sense of proportion, going out of bounds and – consciously or unconsciously – rejecting the essence of man's relationship with God.

Sometimes there are urgent matters that one must carry out with devotion. But whenever this happens, one must be wary and remain aware of where the limits are. For the moment that one exceeds these limits, one breaks the Tablets.

There is an old joke that after the Tablets were broken, some people came and snatched up individual fragments, each person with his own "Thou shalt not." Some snatched for themselves "adultery," some took "murder," and some took "stealing" – everyone took a fragment. The truth is that it does not matter what one took from there, because once the Tablets were broken, they were no longer the Tablets; they became mere stone fragments. The Tablets were holy objects only when they contained all Ten Commandments. To be sure, they were kept as a remembrance even after they were shattered, but they no longer possessed holiness, despite having been inscribed with the finger of God Himself.

On the whole, to be a Jew is difficult because it requires one to adapt to opposites. One can feel that Purim is an enjoyable holiday, or, on the contrary, he can feel that Purim is unpleasant, while Tisha B'Av is enjoyable. But the Torah that commands us to drink and rejoice on Purim is the same Torah that tells us to weep and fast six months later, and we are required to adhere to both, each one in its proper time. God wants us to love Him "with all your heart" – the whole range of what is in the heart, the entire spectrum: the joy and the sorrow, the uplift and the letdown, the descent and the ascent – where we give everything and receive everything at the same time.

There was once a large fire that broke out in a town. A Jew stood beside the fire, crying, dancing, clapping his hands, and declaring with great fervor, "Blessed are You, O God…who has not made me a heathen." The other townsfolk asked the man, "What does this blessing have to do with your dancing beside the fire?" He answers, "If I were a heathen, my god would be consumed in the fire as well. So I am thankful that my God remains alive and well." The man was right: When one reduces one's entire faith to one pillar, what happens when that pillar suddenly falls apart and collapses under him? What does one do when his whole world falls apart?

It is hard to be a Jew, because Judaism requires of me to be at once extreme and moderate, calm and wild, to dance and to crawl. This is the complex nature of life that we must accept, even though the evil urge constantly knocks on the door, tempting us to reduce it all to one thing.

The Talmud relates that R. Ashi asked King Menashe, "Since you were so wise, why did you worship idols?" Menashe answered him, "Had you been there [in those times], you would have lifted up the edge of your garment and run after me" (Sanhedrin 102b). There are times when one must guard oneself against such tendencies vigorously. This is rarely simple, because when one lives in such an environment and such an atmosphere, it is hard not to be infected by it. Everyone is saying the same thing, so it is easy to be swept along and shout it together with the crowd.

We must combat this tendency, proclaiming, "This is your God, O Israel, who brought you out of the land of Egypt" (Ex. 32:4) – this time addressing the true God and not any Golden Calf that may come along. We must repeat, a thousand times if necessary, "This is your God; there is none else!"

Ekev

Parashat *Ekev*, like the *parashot* that precede it, tells the story of the Jewish people in the wilderness. Although it contains a few mitzvot, it is primarily a review of the past and a look into the future of the Jewish people. However, whereas the center of *Parashat Va'ethanan* features the giving of the Torah and the events surrounding it, the center of *Parashat Ekev* features the sin of the Golden Calf and the other sins of Israel in the wilderness. In the following *parashot*, the Torah goes on to discuss mitzvot, some of which appear for the first time, and some of which reiterate and supplement previously given mitzvot.

The Torah needed to recount the major events because many of them occurred in the first and second years after Israel had left Egypt, and most of Moses' current audience could not clearly remember all these events. Some of the people were very young then, and many were not even born yet. These people who are about to enter the Land are members of a new generation; for them, Egypt is either an old memory or a place known only from stories told by their parents. In contrast, their present setting is very strange, almost timeless, a state in which they encamp, remain static, or journey on without a clear direction and without a specific purpose.

Moses proceeds to plot the course that henceforth leads swiftly and directly to the Land of Israel. But for now, these people are suspended between a blurred past and an unclear, albeit promising, future.

Both the encampment on the east side of the Jordan after its capture and the array of preparations for the entry into the Land and the war against its inhabitants are a continuation of the impermanent reality of the wilderness. In addition, during their stay on the east side of the Jordan, the People of Israel still primarily subsist on the manna, and they are protected and united as the Jewish people in one camp. Only upon their entry into the Land did the People of Israel's world become more normal. To be sure, the entry is at first accompanied by overt miracles, but this develops into a diplomatic and military campaign that essentially takes place in the real world.

But the whole course of events in the first three *parashot* of the book of Deuteronomy is not just a historical report of the events that occurred. On the one hand, Moses adds explanations and supplements regarding matters known only to him, such as his negotiations with God and his efforts to keep the People of Israel from annihilation. On the other hand, in addition to words of reproof relating to the past, he also includes general guidance for the future. His words contain great promises about victory and conquest, about expanded borders and prosperity, along with warnings not to become ensnared by arrogance and assimilation.

Moses' words in the book of Deuteronomy, and particularly in this *parasha*, are a mixture of very disparate elements. On the one hand, they are a detailed and precise reiteration of Israel's sins in the wilderness. But on the other hand, they are words of encouragement: Despite all the sins and transgressions, Israel is God's people, over which He watches with His providence. The wilderness and its terrors are described at length, but so is God's sheltering protection. Recollection of the sins is always accompanied by recollection of the forgiveness. For the future, too, momentous promises are accompanied by multiple warnings.

TOWARD NORMALIZATION

Unlike the previous *parasha*, which deals primarily with exalted matters – the giving of the Torah, the Ten Commandments, and the section of *Shema* – *Parashat Ekev* deals with the breaking of the Tablets and with sins, and includes the section of "It shall come to pass, if you obey" (Deut. 11:13), whose subject is not only intimacy and attachment but also the acknowledgement that people have to account for their actions.

This *parasha* is situated at the point of transition from the special, unworldly existence of the wilderness to normalization. The Land of Israel is depicted here as a different world, one that seems to resemble our own ordinary world. Life, which until now has been under the general protection of God's providence and marked by certainty, is about to be individuated into deeds, policies, and personal responsibility, and marked with the awareness that there are no longer steps that transcend the actions of human beings.

In this context, special significance is attached to Moses' remark to the People of Israel that they have left the land of Egypt, where water is always available, and are about to arrive in another land which "drinks water from the rains of heaven" (Deut. 11:11) – it relies on rainfall, which is uncertain by nature, to survive. The difference between the two lands boldly underscores the difference between life in the wilderness and the stark reality of life in the Land of Israel.

Although the *parasha* also contains general guidance and matters dealing with God and faith, they are only an introduction to themes that are repeated with greater clarity throughout the entire book. As long as the People of Israel are in the wilderness, they live under the Clouds of Glory and under the leadership of Moses, who is not entirely a man like any other man. Henceforth, they will be entering a world of personal responsibility and personal work, a world without a feeling of protection that shields them and saves them from their sins and errors and from all the troubles around them. In a certain sense, Moses' words are like a father's parting words to his maturing children, when he explains to them that from now on they are going to live in a different world, by no means a worse world but a world that is certainly different. From now on they will be entering a system of life in which people have to work for a living, conduct themselves properly so as not to be harmed, know their place, and not stray from the proper path.

A NEW GENERATION

The Torah provides no account of how the People of Israel reacted to Moses' long speech. The end of Deuteronomy features parting words, preceded by many chapters of guidance and instruction.

Upon Moses' death, do the people feel like abandoned orphans? From the Torah's final chapters, it appears that feelings are mixed. On the one hand, there is definitely pain and sorrow over the departure of their leader, the father of all Israel. On the other hand, one gets the sense that the listeners, like many young people at the beginning of their path, hear the words without truly internalizing them. Perhaps their inner sense tells them that all the reproof and moral instruction are true, but belong to the past. They find it difficult to relate to Moses' warnings about pitfalls they are likely to encounter in the future, or about the new life they are about to lead.

The truth is that Moses does not want to discourage or dishearten them. All that he wants to do is to explain to them that they are now mature and on their own.

He concludes by saying, as many parents tell their children in such a situation, that all he wants is for them to get through life's pitfalls in the best possible way. Although there may not always be good results, that is the way of the world.

A new generation has arrived, and after all the memories, instructions, and warnings, it will ultimately make its own way, its own mistakes, and its own improvements as well.

Re'eh

Throughout our history, our sages have tried to find ways to explain the order of the content of Deuteronomy. In Deuteronomy, particularly beginning with *Parashat Re'eh*, each *parasha* contains many mitzvot, more than in most *parashot* of the Torah, and these mitzvot are not arranged in any clear structure or pattern. Some of these mitzvot are merely a repetition of matters already recorded previously in the Torah, while others are new mitzvot that have not been mentioned previously. There are no guidelines explaining the sequence of the mitzvot in every *parasha*, or the more subtle order of the various verses and commandments.

It is interesting to note that this very lack of clear continuity between the topics, the fact that matters that would seem to be unrelated are juxtaposed, has itself become a source not only of aggadic interpretations but also of a number of halakhic rulings. Our sages note that even scholars who generally do not draw conclusions from the juxtaposition of different subjects admit that in the book of Deuteronomy, such juxtaposition exists for a reason. Indeed, the order (or lack thereof) in the book teaches us that halakhic inferences may be drawn from one subject to another within the Torah. This kind of interpretation is found in quite a few subjects in Deuteronomy, despite our lack of an established method of arranging the verses and the mitzvot in one overall system.

THE SITE THAT GOD WILL CHOOSE

Parashat Re'eh, too, contains many mitzvot and topics, some of which are found only in the book of Deuteronomy, and some of which reiterate, more or less, previously mentioned material. Here, too, it is difficult to find a logical sequence for the mitzvot that appear in the *parasha*.

Nevertheless, we can point to a common aspect that is mentioned, and sometimes even stressed, in many halakhot in the *parasha*: A considerable number of these mitzvot are connected to holy space – the Land of Israel in general and the site of the Temple and the holy city of Jerusalem in particular. While the name "Jerusalem" is not mentioned at all in the Torah, nor is its location noted – the Torah calls it "the site that God your Lord will choose from among all your tribes, to establish His name there" (Deut. 12:5) – nevertheless, this *parasha* specially emphasizes its significance to the People of Israel. Whereas other *parashot* do not deal with the holiness of the Land of Israel but with general mitzvot, many of which are not connected with the Land of Israel, *Parashat Re'eh* is unique in this regard.

The emphasis on the chosen place extends through the *parasha* by way of various major mitzvot. The beginning of the *parasha* deals with the laws of the *korbanot*, in which the connection to "the site that God will choose" (Deut. 12:5) is emphasized, a choice that invalidates all the other places in the Land – all the more so outside the Land – for bringing *korbanot*. Then we encounter the mitzva of *maaser*, which is not the same as the *maaser* mentioned earlier in the Torah (Num. 18). There, the reference is to the first tithe, the tithe given to the Levites, whereas here the reference is to the mitzva of the second tithe, a major part of which involves bringing the *maaser* to Jerusalem and consuming it there. The mitzva of *Shemitta* is another commandment connected strictly with the Land of Israel; it cannot be fulfilled anywhere else. Another law, which would appear to pertain to a different sphere but which is likewise connected to the Land of Israel, is the mitzva of the city of refuge, whose laws do not apply outside the Land. The connection to Jerusalem is found in the section on the festivals at the *parasha's* conclusion as well. Even though the section is essentially a reiteration of what has been stated previously, the mitzvot of making a pilgrimage and observing the three pilgrimage festivals specifically in Jerusalem are specially emphasized here.

Thus, the great majority of the subjects treated in the *parasha* – both the mitzvot that are described in detail as well as the matters that are only outlined here and are elaborated upon later (like the blessing and the curse given upon Mount Gerizim and Mount Ebal) are connected to Jerusalem or to other places within the Land of Israel.

The introduction to the many laws that appear in this *parasha* and in *Parashat Shofetim* states, "These are the statutes and the ordinances that you shall carefully observe in the land that God, the Lord of your fathers, is giving you to possess" (Deut. 12:1). Thus, even laws that are not expressly connected to the Land of Israel are communicated in the atmosphere of preparation for life in the Holy Land, which is endowed with special sanctity and which serves as the setting for these laws.

Hence, we can easily understand that the Land has a special sensitivity and intolerance of defects. This sensitivity pertains not only to major defects such as sins of sexual immorality, regarding which the Torah stated previously that the Land will vomit out its inhabitants (Lev. 18:25), but to other laws as well, many of which are not obviously connected to the Land. The laws of forbidden foods, for example – which were already detailed in Leviticus with an emphasis on the sanctity of God, the sanctity of Israel, and the connection between them: "Sanctify yourselves and be holy, for I am holy" (11:44) – are repeated here in the context of the preparations for entering the Land, as though to say that it is inappropriate for the Land's inhabitants to eat things that are not compatible with the uniqueness and special nature of the Land of Israel.

HEAVENLY PEOPLE

Another major subject in the *parasha* that is connected in a different way to life in the Land is the special warnings against idolatry. The People of Israel must reach the Land of Israel, conquer it, and rule over it by exercising total control, without leaving even a trace of its former cultures. Deuteronomy is full of warnings stressing apprehension over the ancient inhabitants of the Land, mainly because of their culture and religion.

It appears that more than concern over the direct influence of the nations on the Jewish people, there is concern over the character or feeling of the place, which create a sense of closeness to the gods of the nations, both near and far. Indeed, we know that these commandments were never completely fulfilled. Not only at the beginning of the Land's conquest but even hundreds of years thereafter, enclaves of other peoples still remained, and apparently not without reason. It seems that the Jews who came to settle in the Land had a misguided sense that connection to the land must be accompanied by some kind of inner attachment to the rules of the gods of the land. The descriptions in the book of Judges show that the people followed religious/superstitious patterns of behavior and symbols connected specifically with the land. This happened because the People of Israel came from a completely different way of life. The patriarchs were shepherds, and their descendents still defined themselves as "Your servants are shepherds, both we and our fathers" (Gen. 47:3). Even while they were in Egypt, performing forced labor for Pharaoh and his servants, the Jewish people never had a direct connection to the earth and to agriculture.

In this respect, even in the first generation that conquered the Land, Jewish society was detached from the earth and had found the sources of its livelihood in various other ways. Hence, the connection to the earth involves not only a professional change but also a change in consciousness. When the People of Israel entered the Land, they had to learn to adapt to a world of seasons, agriculture, and an almost sensual connection to the land and its labor. When they found in the Land a preexisting practical and cultural foundation of connection to the earth, it is very difficult to distinguish between the professional, technical, agricultural side and the idolatrous element that was connected with it.

These considerations do not inherently create a desire for outright idolatry, but instead lead to the development of a mixed life: The people worshiped God, since this was their way of life and their ancestral tradition, but they also frequently gave in to the temptation to worship Baal, which represented a connection to the earth and to the land. The people saw no contradiction whatsoever in this bifurcated spiritual loyalty. In Jeremiah 44, for example, Jeremiah criticizes women who still worship idols without realizing that Judaism absolutely rejects religious syncretism. Hence, precisely upon the people's arrival in the Land of Israel, it was necessary to strongly emphasize that under no circumstances may the popular cultic customs of the land be accepted.

For this reason, the *parasha* contains the laws of the idolatrous prophet, the laws of one who entices others to go astray, and the laws of the apostate city. In the last case, the inhabitants of the apostate city change the laws of the Torah, adding various embellishments in order to "complete the picture" of a belief system that they perceive to be lacking. All three of these cases are versions of the enticer, who seeks "to lead you away from God your Lord, who brought you out of the land of Egypt, out of the house of bondage" (Deut. 13:11).

The repeated emphasis on maintaining distance from idolatry derives from the need to recall Judaism's uniqueness, otherness, and apartness. Israel must remember that ultimately they are "a people that dwells apart" (Num. 23:9), that the customs and traditions of the nations cannot apply to them.

It is not without reason that the expression *am haaretz*,[1] whose meaning in Tanakh is rather neutral, over time became a derogatory term. For in spite of the Jewish people's attachment to the Land of Israel, they still are not "people of the land" but "people of heaven."

---

1. Literally, "people of the land."

Shofetim

The first letter of the word *tamim* – the letter *tav* – in the verse "Be wholehearted (*tamim*) with God your Lord" (Deut. 18:13) is traditionally written in Torah scrolls larger than the other letters of the word. Rabbi Naftali of Ropshitz, who was known to joke at his own expense, and even more so at the expense of others, once said that the reason for the large *tav* is so that there should be room inside it for everyone, so that no one should consider himself too big and great to fit into this wholeheartedness.

What does it mean to "Be wholehearted with God your Lord"? It is not so simple to determine what type of person qualifies as *tamim*.

The first person to whom this attribute is assigned is Jacob, who was a "wholehearted man (*ish tam*) who stayed with the tents," unlike Esau who was "a skilled hunter" (Gen. 25:27).

The designation *ish tam* is so closely identified with Jacob that the great Tosafist Rabbeinu Tam was given this name because his first name was Jacob. We generally envisage an *ish tam* as a type of lowly creature, a pale young man, an idler, who sits in the tent and does not know how to perform even the simplest of tasks. Yet from the Torah's account, Jacob does not seem to fit this description at all. He is not simple and naïve; on the contrary, the Talmud says that when Jacob met Rachel and told her that he was her father's brother, he said to her, "I am his brother in deception" (Bava Batra 123a). Sure enough, Jacob uses this craftiness to ultimately emerge unharmed by Laban.

In modern Hebrew, a *tamim* is a naïf, a person whose mental capacities may be lacking in some way. But this is not the plain meaning of "Be wholehearted with God your Lord" and of the word *tamim* as it generally appears in the Torah. Rather, the Torah speaks of *temimut* in the sense of wholeness and wholeheartedness.

This distinction can be seen by considering the context of our verse. Moses tells the People of Israel that if they want to know the future, they must not be like all the other nations who "listen to astrologers and diviners" (Deut. 18:14). Rather, they must "be wholehearted with God your Lord" – be completely with Him. When people want to see something that is hidden from them, some will attempt to see the concealed item by straying outside stealthily. King Saul, for example, reasoned that if he could not know the future – neither via the Urim and Thumim nor via the prophets – he will go outside the Torah's framework and visit the woman who consults ghosts. When something is interesting and intriguing enough, it is very tempting to go outside to get a glimpse.

"Be wholehearted with God your Lord" means that we must be wholly with Him, just as Ḥamor and Shekhem described Jacob's family to their fellow townsmen: "These people are completely with us" (Gen. 34:21).

To be wholehearted with God your Lord means to be completely in God's domain and not to go outside to get a glimpse of the future. As such, *temimut* is truly a simple matter. It is the simplicity of one who lives within a world of wholeheartedness.

THE ABILITY TO ACCEPT

Another difference between the *tamim* and the non-*tamim* is the ability to immediately accept new things, whether it is another person, idea, or subject, without constantly asking if perhaps the opposite is the case.

Temimut is measured by a person's initial reaction: Does he immediately block out everything that he encounters, or does he come with the willingness to listen and accept? After the initial acceptance, there is certainly room for investigation and examination, study and search, and sometimes one in fact discovers that the thing in question must be rejected. But one's initial reaction is what determines if one is a *tamim* or not.

Rashi comments that an *ish tam* is "one who is not sharp in deceiving." Some explain that the reference is not to one who does not know how to deceive or does not understand what deception is; rather, "sharp in deceiving" refers to one whose first thought is how to get the best of the other person: "You do not trust others because you yourselves are untrustworthy" (Is. 7:9).

The Midrash relates that when God offered the Torah to the Ishmaelites, they asked, "What is written in it?" whereas the People of Israel immediately said, "We will do and [then] hear" (*Mekhilta DeRashbi*, Ex. 20:2). The Talmud cites the words of a certain sectarian: "You are a rash people, who gave precedence to your mouths over your ears [when you said 'We will do and (then) hear']." Rava answered him: "We, who walk in integrity, of us it is written, 'The integrity of the upright will guide them.' But of you, who walk in perversity, it is written, 'but the perverseness of the faithless will destroy them' (Prov. 11:3)" (Shabbat 88a–b).

This is exactly the essence of *temimut*: A *tamim* is one who immediately says, "We will do and then hear," rather than always making sure to first ask what is written.

Does this mean that it is easier for Jews to fulfill the Torah than it would have been for the Ishmaelites or the Edomites? One could argue just the opposite: It is true that the Ishmaelites could not accept "Do not commit adultery" and the Edomites could not accept "Do not murder" (Ex. 20:13), but the Jewish people had difficulty accepting all Ten Commandments, from beginning to end. Nevertheless, the Jewish people's approach was that because the Torah came from God, it was their responsibility to accept it before delving too deeply into the details. If there are problems later on, they can be dealt with, with the necessary struggle, coping, and reckoning, internally and externally.

The difference between Israel and the nations is the difference between *temimut* and the sense that everything must be investigated. It is the willingness to accept a thing as it is, without feeling the need to first dismantle it, extract the inner mechanism, and see how it works, and only then consider whether to accept it.

A COMPLEX WORLD

When one loses the ability to see something new and simply go with it – whether because of one's own personality, the society in which he lives, or the education that he received – this is a poisonous way to live one's life. Such a person will never again be able to see things in a straight way. This actually happens to some people. They reach a state where they assume that behind every smile lurk dark thoughts. They lose the simple ability to recognize and accept the good in things.

It is difficult to be *tamim*. Perhaps it is easy for one who has never suffered disappointments in his life. For someone who has never been kicked from behind, it is easier to relate to people according to the expressions on their faces. He feels much more comfortable with people; if someone smiles at him, he smiles back. The problem exists primarily with those who have already encountered dishonesty in interpersonal relationships. Yet even these people are charged with maintaining their *temimut*, and this is not easy at all.

Part of what people learn in the course of their lives, for better or for worse, is that the world is complex, and not everyone is the same inside and out. Despite the need to live one's life with *temimut*, this, too, is an experience that one must learn: Although not everything that appears unpleasant on the outside is unpleasant on the inside, and although not everything that seems frightening should actually cause alarm, the reverse is also true; not every nice thing is actually as nice as it appears. However, sometimes people take this distrust too far, and are no longer able to accept anything at face value.

After Adam ate from the Tree of Knowledge, he may have wanted to spit it out, because he probably discovered immediately that the pleasure of knowledge is accompanied by much pain. What is difficult and tragic is that once man tastes the fruit, after the slightest lick from the Tree of Knowledge, it is very hard to spit it out.

A righteous Jew once came to see his *rebbe* and said to him, "When I pray, I see facing me letters of fire." The *rebbe* informed him that the letters represent the contemplations of the Ari on the prayers. The Jew replied, "*Rebbe*, I would prefer not to see those letters, and to pray with the intention that I used to pray with." The *rebbe* answered,

"In order to study the contemplations of the Ari and yet not see those letters, one must be on a much higher level than yours."

What, then, can be done? According to the *Responsa of the Rivash* (No. 157), Rabbi Shimshon from Kinon used to claim that he prayed with the mentality of a young child, that is to say, with the same *temimut* or simplicity that a young child has. Rabbi Shimshon of Kinon, author of *Sefer HaKeritot* on the rules of Talmud, was one of the greatest rabbis of his generation, and part of his greatness was that after all that he knew and heard, he was able to pray "with the mentality of a young child."

Nowadays, prayer requires spiritual effort that in earlier generations was not as necessary. One's spiritual work in prayer is not just to remove distractions or extraneous thoughts, but that people cannot relate to the matter of prayer itself; rather, they feel that they must conduct all sorts of analyses of prayer. Nowadays, when one wants to have proper intention in prayer, he must conduct linguistic, historical, and philosophical analyses, and even esoteric or exoteric analyses, and cannot accept the prayer as it is. He cannot contemplate the *Selaḥ Lanu* blessing without debating whether the phrase *meḥol lanu* follows the rules of grammar or not, and other such questions.

When one hears the blowing of the shofar, notwithstanding all the halakhic matters connected with it, one must remember the simple question, "Shall a shofar be blown in a city, and the people not be alarmed?" (Amos 3:6). The time of the blowing of the shofar is designed for this alarm, but instead of alarm, many people focus on how long the shofar blast lasted, whether the *shevarim* tones were satisfactory, and whether the shofar blower became confused and blew ten times instead of nine. It could be that when one heard the blowing of the shofar as a child, one experienced fear of judgment and fear of God. But now that one has grown up and studied the *Shulḥan Arukh*, one experiences neither of those fears. Instead of the simple aspect of alarm inherent in the shofar blowing, it has turned into a science of shofar blasts. I can imagine that, even facing Mount Sinai, there was some wise and learned man who stood up and said, "Nu, how long was this shofar blast?" I am sure that there were several God-fearing people there who, when they heard the sound of the shofar "growing louder and louder" (Ex. 19:19), made sure to count how many seconds it lasted.

In a certain sense, after having already encountered so many individual, disjointed parts, it becomes very difficult to see the whole, the *temimut*. The Talmud expounds on the verse, "Attend (*hasket*) and hear, O Israel" (Deut. 27:9), saying, "First be silent (*has*) and only then analyze (*kattet*)" (Berakhot 63b). First there is a stage of listening, of accepting. Only then is it time to discuss and analyze, to break down and reconstruct. If one engages only in analysis without retaining the ability to receive, the idea is no longer alive; it is only dissected parts.

A pathologist who performs autopsies often knows more about the human body than anyone else. However, in a certain sense he now knows less, in that he was never given the whole in its perfect form. All that he has to work with are dissected parts.

This is true of a vast array of things, ranging from faith to prayer. Integral to prayer is the appeal for the strength to serve God wholeheartedly. This is an ability that we generally have when we commit sins but less so when we perform mitzvot. When a person commits a sin, he does not consider how many prohibitions it entails, and how this sin is shameful and contemptible. While the sin is being committed, he has the ability to forget the sin itself and somehow to be wholly invested in the performance. One should pray for the ability to perform the mitzvot just as wholeheartedly, without all the surrounding considerations.

I began with Rabbi Naftali of Ropshitz's comment on the *tav* of the word *tamim* – that at times it may seem that one is already a great man. It is good that the blowing of the shofar causes the eyes of children to fill with tears. But if one believes that he is a great, learned man, who has studied so much about the halakhot of shofar blasts, it is hard to imagine reacting this way. Yet what Rabbi Naftali of Ropshitz says is that even for such a great man, there is room for him to enter into *temimut*. Indeed, he is obligated to do just this.

"I HAVE STILLED AND QUIETED"

Each year, *Parashat Shofetim* is read close to Rosh HaShana, and the nature of Rosh HaShana is that it always arrives, whether I want it to or not. On this great day, the Day of Judgment and the Day of Remembrance, there is an aspect of "I have stilled and quieted" (Ps. 131:2). Indeed, on Rosh HaShana the mitzva is not to blow the shofar but "to hear the sound of the shofar" – to listen and to accept. The new beginning on Rosh HaShana is significant because it sets the direction of one's progress, and if one begins at a wrong angle, there is a higher chance of continuing this way in the future.

Rosh HaShana is, without a doubt, a day of intense prayer. The custom on Rosh HaShana is to read chapters of Psalms; indeed, many people read through the entire book of Psalms twice. One of the reasons for this is that if one must finish reading the entire book twice, one cannot do it with the contemplations of the Ari, nor even with the commentaries on the bottom of the page; one must read it as one reads a book – simply read and react. Sometimes there is a positive reaction and sometimes there is a negative reaction, but there is always a reaction.

Many learned, God-fearing Jews will not have time for all this. When these people read Psalms, they will likely not reach chapter 131, a chapter that demonstrates how to be truly wholehearted with God:

> A Song of Ascents; of David. O God, my heart is not haughty, nor mine eyes lofty; neither do I exercise myself in things too great, or in things too wonderful for me. Surely I have stilled and quieted my soul like a weaned child with its mother; my soul is with me like a weaned child. O Israel, hope in God from this time forth and forever. (131:1–3)

Just as a young child sits with his mother even after he is weaned, a great and learned man can likewise sit this way in prayer, even after attaining vast amounts of knowledge and interpretations. When one faces God, "My soul is with me like a weaned child."

Ki Tetzeh

EXPOUNDING UPON JUXTAPOSITION

Parashat Ki Tetzeh is full of diverse topics. According to Maimonides' enumeration of the mitzvot, this *parasha* contains over seventy mitzvot, and several observations can be made regarding the connection between the various subjects in the *parasha*.

According to the Talmud, though it is disputed whether halakhic inferences can generally be derived from the juxtaposition of two topics, all agree that in the book of Deuteronomy such inferences may be drawn (Berakhot 21b). The reason for this is that Deuteronomy is full of repetition of material that is found earlier in the Torah. Because the reason for this repetition is not always clear, our sages provided us with this tool to help us identify distinctions between two otherwise identical passages or verses.

It is said that the Torah can be interpreted in seventy ways, and so many Torah fundamentals are derived by exegesis, often by expounding upon the juxtaposition of two sections. An examination of the various juxtaposition-based interpretations by our sages reveals that the laws derived by this kind of interpretation – particularly in the book of Deuteronomy – are very basic laws.

Juxtaposition can explain the reasons behind many laws. For example, why is the wayward and rebellious son punished with the death penalty, a punishment that seems overly severe? Our sages say, based on the juxtaposition of the section on the wayward and rebellious son to the section on those to be executed by the court, that "the wayward and rebellious son is condemned on account of his inevitable end" (Sanhedrin 72a): He is punished when still a boy so that he should not commit more serious crimes in the future.

Another type of juxtaposition-based interpretation teaches us not only the reason behind the law, as in the case of the wayward and rebellious son, but the actual law itself. For example, the fact that one is liable to receive the punishment of lashes for violating a negative command (that has no associated positive command) is inferred from the juxtaposition of the section on lashes to the section of "Do not muzzle an ox when it is treading grain" (Deut. 25:4).

A much more basic type of interpretation is when there is juxtaposition within a section. In *Parashat Ki Tetzeh*, a basic law is derived from the juxtaposition of words in the Torah, as in our sages' interpretation of the words, "she leaves...and becomes" (Deut. 24:2), linking the woman's marriage to another man with her divorce from her former husband (Kiddushin 5a).

Thus, very basic laws are derived from the juxtaposition of sections. Still, in this *parasha* the combination of subjects is so puzzling that, according to Ibn Ezra, although many have already tried to find connections and links within the *parasha*, they succeeded only on the homiletical level (Deut. 24:6). No one has been able to show how all the subjects in the *parasha* fit together.

CATEGORIES OF MITZVOT

Parashat Ki Tetzeh deals with both major categories of mitzvot: those between man and God and those between man and his fellow man. From here, as well as from other places in the Torah, it appears that our most common method of categorizing mitzvot into groups is not a division that the Torah seems to follow.

The lack of this division is evident in the Torah in various ways. Not only is there no differentiation between mitzvot concerning the man-God relationship and mitzvot concerning interpersonal relationships, but, most surprisingly, neither is there differentiation between major and minor matters, between major principles and mitzvot that seem supplementary or marginal. There are matters that we would categorize as basic principles, on which the world stands and, by contrast, there are matters that we would categorize as details. In the Torah, this type of distinction seems to have no place. Even within the Ten Commandments, major and minor precepts are, to a certain extent, equated. Prohibitions against idolatry, adultery, and murder, which are major doctrines, appear beside prohibitions such as "Do not covet" (Ex. 20:14) and "Do not take the Name of God … in vain" (20:7), which, as serious as they are, are not often thought of as equal in severity to the former prohibitions.

Why is there no differentiation between categories of mitzvot? It seems clear that it is not the Torah's purpose to present a system of laws to prevent people from eating each other alive. It is also clear that the Torah is not a book of remedies; that is not the basis on which the Torah stands. The fact that the diverse categories of mitzvot are mixed together in the Torah, and that we are unable to explain the sequence of the subjects, teaches us an essential lesson: If we are to receive the Torah, the only way is to accept it as it is. We can receive the Torah only if we accept it with all its various components, because the Torah itself does not differentiate between them or see any difference between them.

In this *parasha*, precisely because it is replete with various subjects and themes, it is possible to delve into the Torah's essence. There are very few other places where there is such a mixture of major and minor precepts, more important and less important, daily matters and matters that arise once in a lifetime, as in this *parasha*. It teaches us that in the Torah there is no such thing as more important and less important mitzvot. The totality of all the mitzvot, in all the different areas, forms a kind of definition of the Torah's essence. There is a bridge that stretches from here to God – for the Jewish people, there is no other bridge (according to Maimonides, this applies to all the nations as well) – and this bridge goes through the Torah. The Torah is what connects man to God. All other paths that man tries to find may seem acceptable, but they are flimsy. The wind carries them off; they are merely products of the imagination. A person can imagine that a path exists from here to there, but altogether only one path extends from our reality to God, and that is the path of the Torah.

THEY COME FROM ONE SHEPHERD

The Torah contains several instances where the juxtaposition of sections is extraordinary and calls for interpretation. Toward the end of *Parashat Shofetim*, the Torah details the mitzva of destroying the Canaanite cities: "Of the cities of these nations, which God your Lord is giving you for an inheritance, do not let a soul stay alive. You must wipe them out completely" (Deut. 20:16–17). This is followed by a second mitzva: "When you lay siege to a city and wage war against it a long time…You may eat of them but you must not cut them down. For the [existence of] man is the tree of the field" (20:19). The Canaanite city must be destroyed and all its inhabitants wiped out, but when one comes across a fruit tree, you must not harm it. This juxtaposition is very difficult to comprehend. The Torah seems to condone incredibly harsh actions when they are performed in the context of war. But cutting down a tree – that is where the Torah draws the line!

There is a whole list of mitzvot that present this difficulty. A siege is laid on a city "until it is subjugated" (Deut. 20:20), and many people are killed in the war, yet in the very next verses, when a slain person is found and "the identity of the slayer is not known" (21:1), the members of the Sanhedrin perform an intricate ritual of measuring the distance to the nearest city, because they must atone for its residents.

On the one hand, we "do not take the mother along with her young" (Deut. 22:6), and "do not muzzle an ox when it is treading grain" (25:4), where the Torah spares no detail in its concern for preventing the suffering of the ox; yet at the end of the *parasha*, after the command, "Fathers shall not be put to death because of sons, and sons shall not be put to death because of fathers" (24:16), we are commanded to obliterate the entire people of Amalek.

Thus, in order that donkeys should not be overworked, or so that birds should not see their young taken from them, the Torah institutes special laws in this *parasha*. There is concern for trees, donkeys, and sometimes even people, as in the case of taking a pledge upon giving a loan: "You shall not go to sleep holding his pledge" (Deut. 24:16). Yet the same *parasha* in the Torah that is so merciful to animals is full of mitzvot commanding us to administer blows and lashes, and sometimes even to kill.

The upshot is that, in truth, it is far from simple to always give the Torah a friendly face, because the Torah contains many different aspects, sometimes ranging even to the extreme. One can fill an entire book with quotations from Tanakh on how peace is a paramount value, but one can also write a book demonstrating just the opposite, filling it with quotations seemingly supporting the antithesis of peace. Instead of citing, "And they shall beat their swords into plowshares" (Is. 2:4), one can cite, "Beat your plowshares into swords" (Joel 4:10). The problem with both of these theoretical books is not that they would be inaccurate, but because they would be portraying the Torah as a product of only one aspect.

The *parasha* contains a small mitzva that one generally does not have the opportunity to fulfill – the mitzva of chasing away the mother bird before taking her eggs. The Talmud says of this mitzva, "If one says, 'Your mercies extend to a bird's nest'…he is silenced" (Berakhot 33b). One explanation for this prohibition is that "he makes the commands of The Holy One, Blessed Be He, simply acts of mercy, whereas they are merely decrees" (Megilla 25a). But what is wrong with saying that God's commands are rooted in mercy? Why must we insist that God's commands are "merely decrees," a seemingly arbitrary system?

From here and from other places as well, we see that the Torah's basic structure is not built on bringing people satisfaction. There are mitzvot in which one can experience spiritual exaltation, and there are mitzvot in which one cannot. It is hard to tell someone who is receiving forty lashes in court that he should be excited about fulfilling the mitzva. One who says, "Your mercies extend to a bird's nest" tries to show that the Torah is based on human logic, as though the Torah were a book of remedies or a guidebook for life, whose purpose is to teach people how to lead a proper life. But the truth is that God's commands are indeed merely decrees, and the only way for us to comprehend the Torah is as a bridge between us and God.

THE WORK OF GOD

When one tries to define and reduce the Torah to one aspect, one is left with only part of the Torah, one that is essentially deficient. Usually, the intention is to give the Torah a human face, a face that can be comprehended in its totality and entirety. However, the Torah is the work of God, and thus cannot truly be defined in such a way; it cannot be fashioned like a human face.

Sometimes, when one looks at the world, one's immediate reaction is, "Why does everything go awry? Why are there so many problems?" If one were to build a machine to fulfill a certain function, one would surely strive to create an efficient product. In the world, however, everything goes awry. It is not clear, then, what the world's purpose is and what function it fulfills.

The sequence of sections in the Torah teaches us that the world cannot be compared to a machine that a person might create. When a person builds a device, he does it in a way that he hopes will efficiently fulfill certain purposes. However, when God creates something, He does not operate on a level that we can comprehend; He creates a unique structure that is built according to His own plans. When a human being attempts to study this structure, he will never be able to entirely understand it, regardless of the number of attempts he might make, and no matter how much he tries to learn how it works. One can live in the world, but there is a limit to one's ability to change it. The Torah, too, is the work of God, and all one can do is stand before it and gaze upon it.

The Kotzker Rebbe was once asked how he understands God's frequent mercilessness, and he answered with one sentence, "A God who can be understood by anyone is not worth serving." That is the essence of it. If one thoroughly understands God and feels that he can make improvements on Him, then such a God is no longer worth serving.

Our attempt to understand everything and create a unified and complete picture is an attempt to take God, or at least the Torah, and make it a simplistic plaything, and that is precisely what the Torah forbids. The fact that some *parashot* seem to juxtapose disparate elements means that while each one of these elements can be understood on its own using a range of exegetical tools, one must always understand that the Torah is merely a bridge to God. One end is here on earth and the other end is in heaven, and it is on this bridge that God wants us to walk. If we do this, we will find that the other end of the bridge reaches to the highest heavens.

Ki Tavo

Unlike *Parashat Ki Tetzeh*, which has an abundance of laws, *Parashat Ki Tavo* contains few halakhot. Instead, *Parashat Ki Tavo* is replete with curses.

The Talmud states, following the implication of the passage, "These shall stand to bless the people…and these shall stand for the curse" (Deut. 27:12–13), that at Mount Gerizim and Mount Ebal there were two formulas. Those standing for the curse pronounced the curses as they appear in the Torah, and those standing for the blessing pronounced an opposite formula: "Blessed is he who does not make a graven or molten image," "Blessed is he who does not dishonor his father and mother," and so forth (Sota 32a).

If a "blessing formula" was in fact pronounced, why does the Torah cite only the curses and not use the positive language of the blessings? Why is the blessing formula only implied and not written in the Torah explicitly? While it is true that the Torah generally tends to be concise, positive language could still have been used, especially in light of the Talmud's assertion that the Torah goes to great lengths, often employing circumlocutions, in order to use clean, decent language (Pesaḥim 3a).

TOO MUCH GOOD

It is far simpler to create a curse than to create a blessing. This is not because people are generally wicked, but because the moment something diverges from its usual order, it is already a curse. Normally, there is more of a basis for curses than for blessings, because only the optimal state is considered a blessing. Whether it is too hot, too cold, or too rainy, if it is not perfect then it is a curse. Thus, the margin for the optimal is very narrow, and if conditions incline even slightly to one side, it is already no longer optimal. As the Talmud says, "Your people... can endure neither too much good nor too much punishment" (Taanit 23a). Even if one is given more and more of something, he will not necessarily be better off.

The pauper says, "Give me neither poverty nor riches, but provide me with my daily bread" (Prov. 30:8). That is to say, both a pauper and a wealthy person face unique problems and trials connected to their station. One should not strive for maximum prosperity, because this does not guarantee that the situation will truly be better. In fact, after a little too much prosperity, it stops being pleasant; after a little more, it becomes unpleasant; and finally, it becomes painful. In anything concerning the physical pleasures of this world, there is a stage at which the more one receives, the more unpleasant it becomes.

In light of this, there is more of a basis for curses than for blessings in our world. But despite this, we have one powerful claim to make before God when we pray for blessing: By now, all the curses described throughout Tanakh – those in Leviticus, those here in Deuteronomy, and those in Ezekiel – have all been fulfilled. I knew a woman who was the only girl to survive the Vilna Ghetto. She and her family were very far from Judaism, and she said that she was moved to return to observance when she encountered the *Tokheha* section in *Parashat Behukkotai*; she saw that everything that is written there came true. People did not think or believe that these things could come about, and the fact that all the curses came true caused her to experience a change of heart. While all the curses seem to have been realized, however, we are still waiting for the fulfillment of many of the blessings.

The Talmud relates that Rabbi Akiva and his colleagues once saw a fox emerging from the site of the Holy of Holies, and Rabbi Akiva laughed, saying, "So long as Uriah's prophecy ['Therefore shall Zion for your sake be plowed as a field, and Jerusalem shall become heaps, and the mountain of the House as the high places of the forest'

(Mic. 3:12)] had not been fulfilled, I was afraid that Zechariah's prophecy ['Old men and women shall yet sit in the broad places of Jerusalem' (Zech. 8:4)] might not be fulfilled. Now that Uriah's prophecy has been fulfilled, it is quite certain that Zechariah's prophecy will be fulfilled" (Makkot 24a).

In this sense, we, too, should laugh. God was faithful in bringing upon us the curses, so He will surely bring upon us the blessings as well. So long as all these things had not been fulfilled, one could say that it will happen in far-off times. But now that, in our times, curses that no one would have believed would occur have come about, the blessings, too, will surely be fulfilled.

Even the final curse, "There you will offer yourselves for sale to your enemies as slaves and maids, but there will be no buyer" (Deut. 28:68) – which no one would have believed could occur – we have witnessed in recent memory.

LEAVING THE SHELTERED ENVIRONMENT

In this *parasha*, as in other places in the Torah, many harsh things are described. Why are so many curses necessary? Why is it necessary to threaten the people with such dire consequences for disobedience? Why can't the Torah always speak pleasantly?

Seeing as the Torah nevertheless frequently insists on expressing itself in the form of curses, apparently this is necessary. Although the Torah certainly contains its share of blessings, it is truly difficult to be a Jew, and the curse section written here only emphasizes just how difficult it is. While we can understand the need for both the carrot and the stick, it is still a great challenge to accept this reality.

One of the main purposes of yeshivas, beyond allowing students to study Torah for its own sake, is to prepare students for the future. Despite this, a yeshiva is essentially a closed place, a sheltered environment, and a yeshiva student cannot truly feel how difficult it is to be a Jew. In such an environment, one struggles primarily with subtleties and nuances of faith and Torah. To be sure, there are occasionally major struggles, but the challenges and temptations faced by a yeshiva student are immeasurably fewer than the temptations that exist outside. As a result, it is sometimes hard to leave such a sheltered environment, and because of this, many students indeed avoid leaving this shelter at all. However, when these students are forced to leave, for one reason or another, this becomes a moment of dangerous crisis.

There was a time when psychologists discouraged parents from telling their children frightening stories. Now, however, the opposite is encouraged; the claim is that if children never hear about the dark side of life, they will grow up with a distorted view of life. If we shield them from evil, telling them that the world is entirely delightful and everyone is good, they will have difficulty coping with the real world when they grow older.

Death, for example, is frightening, and there were societies – such as the kibbutzim of the past – that distanced children from any exposure to it. I once attended the funeral of a teacher in a certain kibbutz, and I didn't see anyone under the age of twenty-three; they had all avoided coming. This attitude is an attempt to push aside the fact that such a thing exists.

A person like that who emerges from a sheltered environment and faces reality will have a harder time dealing with it. At one stage or another, everyone encounters lies and deceit, and when a child grows up under the illusion that there are no thieves and liars in the world, the result may be a major personal crisis.

THE CHALLENGE

Despite the Torah's message that, "It is not in heaven … It is not beyond the sea … It is something that is very close to you, in your mouth and in your heart, so that you can do it" (Deut. 30:12–14), in our world it is hard to be a Jew. The Torah merely says that it is possible, that the Torah contains nothing that a person cannot live up to. But this does not mean that it is easy, because we live among human beings and not in a sheltered environment where there is almost no exposure to the evil inclination.

To be sure, our sages advise us that "if this repulsive scoundrel [the evil inclination] confronts you, drag him to the beit midrash" (Sukka 52b), but sometimes we forget that the scoundrel is with us in the beit midrash as well. As the Kotzker Rebbe once remarked, "*this* scoundrel" implies that there is yet another scoundrel: the one in the beit midrash.

All of this is not meant to frighten us. The purpose of the curses is to make us aware that following the Torah presents a great challenge, and the more we are exposed to the world, the greater the challenge becomes. It is a challenge that comes along with both blessings and curses. We must remain undaunted by these curses, rising to meet the challenge.

Nitzavim

LET HIM DO *TESHUVA* AND BE ATONED FOR

At first glance, the content of *Parashat Nitzavim* seems identical to that of the preceding *parasha*. Although this *parasha* has fewer curses and perhaps fewer blessings than *Parashat Ki Tavo*, it repeats the same essential elements. Nevertheless, a difference in mood can be discerned, a difference that makes *Parashat Nitzavim* the more appropriate *parasha* to read before Rosh HaShana.

In *Parashat Ki Tavo*, the blessings and curses stand opposite one another and create a somber mood, a feeling that there is no way out. By contrast, in *Parashat Nitzavim* there is a certain optimism that does not exist in *Parashat Ki Tavo*. *Parashat Nitzavim* speaks of *teshuva*, conveying the message that all is not lost, and that there is a way to set things right. It has a tone of hope that says that there is a way out of the distress, and this hope changes the mood of the entire *parasha*.

The curses in *Parashat Ki Tavo* conclude with the following description: "God will bring you back to Egypt in ships, by the way that I said you would never see again. There you will offer yourselves for sale to your enemies as slaves and maids, but there will be no buyer" (Deut. 28:68). In *Parashat Nitzavim* the conclusion is quite different: "When all these things have befallen you – the blessing and the curse...and you will reflect on them...and you will return to God your Lord and obey Him" (30:1–2).

Parashat Ki Tavo can be summarized as follows: "If you do what is good, you will prosper; but if you do not, you will suffer." In this *parasha*, too, there is a similar connection between "life and good, death and evil" (Deut. 30:15). But here, there is also the way of *teshuva*: "And you will reflect… and you will return to God your Lord" (30:1–2). The difference between the *parashot* is the factor of *teshuva*.

What is the essence of *teshuva*? The fact is that people sometimes make poor decisions, and these decisions often lead to suffering. For example, one might find himself in a difficult situation, and he might decide to relieve himself and his family of their troubles by jumping off the roof. This kind of story does occur; it is unfortunately part of our reality. But what happens if, on his way down, when he reaches the fifth floor, he decides that it was not wise to take this step? The problem is that he has already fallen; he has committed an irreversible act. Correspondingly, one would think that when a person commits a sin, it should be like the person who has jumped off the roof. Remorse in such a case is useless. But because of the existence of *teshuva*, an act can become reversible; there is a way to stop in the middle of a fall and turn back the clock.

The Midrash relates the following:

> Wisdom was asked: What should be the sinner's punishment? Wisdom answered: "Evil pursues sinners" (Prov. 13:21). Prophecy was asked: What should be the sinner's punishment? Prophecy answered: "The soul who sins shall die" (Ezek. 18:4). The Torah was asked: What should be the sinner's punishment? The Torah answered: "Let him bring a guilt offering, and his sin will be atoned for." The Holy One, Blessed Be He, was asked: What should be the sinner's punishment? He answered: "Let him do *teshuva*, and his sin will be atoned for." (*Pesikta DeRabbi Kahana* 24:7)

The punishment of death for a sinner is not excessive. One who sins is, by the laws of nature, like one who swallows poison. However, the innovation of *teshuva* lies in the possibility of reversing this reality.

CHOOSE LIFE

Parashat Nitzavim contains, besides the element of *teshuva*, an additional element that likewise is not found in the preceding *parasha*: the element of persuasion. *Parashat Ki Tavo* establishes the facts, as a physician does: "If you follow my instructions, you will live another three months. If you do otherwise, the consequences will be different." In *Parashat Nitzavim*, however, we find, more than once, persuasion to choose one option over the other: "I call heaven and earth to witness against you this day: I have put before you life and death...Choose life" (Deut. 30:19).

When Moses tells the People of Israel that the options are life and death, he is merely stating the facts. But then he adds, as good counsel: "Choose life, so that you may live." Moses says that the people already know the consequences that each path will bring, and the choice between the two is theirs to make. Still, his advice is to choose life. Indeed, our sages themselves pointed out that after Moses shows them what the path to blessing is and what the path to curse is, and sets the two choices against each other, he asks them to choose the good path (*Sifrei*, Deuteronomy 53).

The same point is found in the case of Joshua as well. Joshua is Moses' servant, and in a certain respect he is also his complement. Moses and Joshua are often regarded as one unit, sharing a division of labor. There are many things that Moses starts and Joshua finishes, that Moses sets up and Joshua establishes. As a continuation of Moses' words, Joshua, at the end of his life, suggests to the People of Israel, "God took you out of Egypt, gave you the Torah, and brought you into the Land, and we have reached a state of rest and security. Now, the decision is in your hands: If you want, serve God; if you are loathe to serve God, 'I and my household will serve God'" (Josh. 24).

BLESSING OR CURSE

The Torah speaks of choosing the good, and advises us to choose life. However, when one must implement the choice in reality, it is not always clear which path to choose; distinguishing the blessing from the curse is not always simple. If the reality were clear to us, we would not commit so many errors.

Sometimes one makes a decision based on his perception of the reality, and afterward – even if it becomes clear that the decision was made on the basis of mistaken assumptions – he can no longer withdraw the decision that he made. One chooses what he thinks is a blessing, and he ends up being totally subservient to it, even though it has already become a curse for him.

In other instances, the question whether something is a blessing or a curse is completely subjective. For one person it could be a curse, but for someone else it could be a blessing. It could be that now it is a curse, but at another time it will be a blessing.

In all these matters, one's perspective is often the deciding factor. The Talmud relates of Naḥum Ish Gamzu that no matter what befell him, he would declare, "This, too (*gam zu*), is for the best." Even when he was without hands and legs, he continued to say, "This, too, is for the best" (Taanit 21a). One can lead a perfect life, and yet his whole life might feel like a curse, depending on his perspective. Thus, the choice between blessing and curse is partly subjective: How does one regard the events that transpire in one's life?

It is common to bless someone that he should have God-fearing children who will become great sages. However, the nature of such a blessing depends on the perspective of its recipient. Some would rejoice upon receiving such a blessing and would respond, "The same to you!" However, others – particularly those who are not themselves God-fearing individuals – might become distraught upon receiving such a blessing, regarding it as a terrible curse.

When one encounters something of this nature, one must look at it, scrutinize it, and consider what may result from it. It often happens that it is the individual who decides whether it is a blessing or a curse; it is not a matter of knowing the future. If one decides to accept something as a curse, it will only grow worse, while if one decides to accept it as a blessing, it will fulfill that initial perception.

There was once a captain who, on a voyage, saw various lumps floating near his ship. He drew them out of the water, but they stunk up the whole ship, so he threw them back into the water. What he did not know was that these lumps were actually ambergris, an incredibly rare and valuable substance secreted by sperm whales that is used in some perfumes. When one possesses such a lump knowing that it is a blessing, it means that one was fortunate enough to happen upon a great treasure. But if one does not know what this lump is, it seems worthless. One throws it back into the ocean and is happy to have gotten rid of it.

This is a very significant point regarding the Torah as well, since the entire Torah can be considered a blessing or a curse. We have 613 mitzvot; this might seem like a huge number – who can meet so many requirements? This perspective turns the whole Torah into a curse. However, an alternative perspective is found in the Mishna: "The Holy One, Blessed Be He, wanted to give Israel merit; He therefore gave them a large amount of Torah and mitzvot" (Makkot 3:16).

Is Jewish identity a source of joy and pride, or a source of shame and disgrace that one tries to get rid of? The brilliant poet and apostate Heinrich Heine said, "Judaism is not a religion; it is a curse." When one knows that he will never be rid of his Judaism, he sometimes experiences this as a terrible curse that dogs him his whole life. In his own eyes, he was born with a kind of genetic defect. By contrast, the Maggid of Kozhnitz would say, "If I were sure that I was definitely descended from Abraham, Isaac, and Jacob, I would put aside my hat and perform the Cossack dance in the street, for having this merit."

Blessing and curse do not necessarily exist in two separate worlds; sometimes they are in the same place. The Talmud states that the *tzaddikim* in Paradise sit and enjoy the splendor of the *Shekhina* (Berakhot 17a). In Paradise, there is no eating or drinking, only enjoyment of the Torah. There are people who deserve to be sent to Gehenna, but should really be sent to Paradise. For some people, an eternity of constant Torah study would be the greatest form of torture.

To choose life is to see things from the right perspective, to choose the good aspect in everything. It is not just the question of whether or not to be a Jew, whether or not to keep the mitzvot. One can decide to be a good Jew and yet perceive one's Judaism as a kind of curse: Against one's will one lives, against one's will one dies, and against one's will one is a Jew. There is nothing worse than perceiving the Torah as an inherited burden, because there is absolutely nothing that one can do about it.

This distinction is emphasized by the Ari in his interpretation of the passage, "All these curses will come upon you, pursue you, and overtake you…instead of (*taḥat*) serving God your Lord with joy and with gladness over the abundance of all things. You will therefore serve your enemies" (Deut. 28:47).

The simple explanation of the passage – as we find in *Targum Onkelos* – is: Instead of serving God with joy, you did not keep the mitzvot, and therefore all these curses will come upon you and overtake you.

The Ari, however, explained that the word *taḥat* should actually be translated as "because." That is to say, because you did not serve God with joy, "you will serve your enemies." Punishment comes not because you did not serve God, but because you did not serve Him with joy and with gladness; it comes because you accepted the Torah as a punishment and as a curse.

"Choose life," therefore, relates not only to the choice itself, but also to the manner in which one chooses.

"HOW GREAT IS YOUR GOODNESS"

There are good things in life whose excellence can be conveyed to others by explanation, and there are things that one can learn only directly, through personal experience. When one is able to see the goodness of God – "How great is Your goodness that You have hidden away for those who fear You" (Ps. 31:20) – it is a personal experience that cannot be taught or communicated to others.

Every Shabbat, we recite a similar verse: "Taste and see that God is good" (Ps. 34:9). Taste cannot be received from others. In order to perceive it, one must taste it himself. This is a fundamental point within the Jewish experience. Although one who has experienced the delight of the Torah can forget part of his learning, he can never forget the pleasure, the taste, and the feeling of that experience.

There are certain tastes that everyone can recognize; a child generally does not have to be persuaded to eat candy. But there are some things that require sophistication to appreciate. A child must grow in maturity to appreciate the taste of a salty dish. This is not because the dish is not tasty. Rather, tastes change, and in order to appreciate certain tastes, one must first grow up a little.

Similarly, few people can appreciate complex music. Everyone, except perhaps a deaf person, can listen to and enjoy a simple melody.

But to enjoy music that is complex, like a symphony, one must first learn to appreciate it. It could be that after one learns to enjoy such music, he will no longer be able to listen to simple music; it will be too vulgar for him. This is true not only of relatively abstract things like music; it is also true of good wine and many other things as well.

When the Torah says that we have before us "life and good," sometimes a shell must be cracked to reveal the good. Sometimes one must chew quite a lot before the good can be tasted. Sometimes one must educate himself, and many years might pass until one can discern what is truly good. Things that are obviously good are easily perceived, but to perceive the things that are truly good, one must develop this skill over time.

"Choose life": To get into the matter, to absorb it, to gain an inner understanding of it, one must make a great effort, an effort aimed at experiencing the spiritual flavor of life.

Vayelekh

A t the beginning of the *parasha*, Moses calls Joshua and transfers to him the leadership of the Jewish people, and from this moment
on, Joshua is the leader of Israel in practice.

Nevertheless, Moses is still the central figure in the coming *parashot* because they form a festive conclusion to his period of leadership,
a conclusion whose essence is the song in *Parashat Haazinu* and the
blessing in *Parashat Vezot HaBerakha*.

In addition to the two mitzvot outlined in *Parashat Vayelekh* – the
mitzva of *hak'hel*[1] and the mitzva of writing the Torah – this *parasha* is
composed of two central matters. The first, which begins the *parasha*,
is a description of the people's entry into the Land of Israel: "God your
Lord is the one who will go over before you; He will destroy these
nations before you, so that you will dispossess them... He will do to
them as He did to Sihon and to Og... And you shall deal with them in
full accordance with the commandment" (Deut. 31:3–5). The second is
Moses' conclusion: "For I know your rebellion and your stiff neck. Even
while I am yet alive with you this day, you have been rebellious against
God; and how much more after my death?" (31:27).

---

1. Assembling the entire people once every seven years to hear the reading of the Torah
   by the king of Israel.

This conclusion is puzzling. In the course of the book of Deuteronomy, Moses lays out before the People of Israel all that he has to say, all his words of encouragement, the blessings and the curses, and so on. Upon concluding, he summarizes by saying, "I told you all of this because you must be aware of it, but I know you well: Just as for forty years you did not listen to my words, all the more so after my death." We would not have expected that Moses would conclude his speech with such a harsh declaration. "For I know that after my death you will become corrupt and turn aside from the way that I have commanded you. Evil will befall you in the end of days, because you will do what is evil in God's sight, angering Him through the work of your hands" (Deut. 31:29).

Why does Moses have to phrase his message so pessimistically? Why end this way?

I WILL BEAR, I WILL SUFFER

There are several definitions for the term "optimist." There are people who, by their very nature, always hope for the best. There are people who go further; they look on the bright side of everything.

There is a positive side to this tendency: Such a person knows that things will always be good, an attitude that surely gives one great encouragement at certain points in his life. On the other hand, people usually cannot sustain this level of optimism. They inevitably reach a breaking point and cannot continue with such a rosy attitude toward life.

The optimistic approach – the assumption that everything will always be all right – is a way of building a kind of sheltered environment for oneself. Even if one sees someone who appears to be a bad person, surely inside he has a heart of gold. It may take a lifetime to discover, but ultimately everyone is good on the inside.

A child with such an attitude who arrives in school will very quickly become the target of bullies. In practice, those who grow up in a sheltered environment ultimately reach a breaking point. When they are exposed to life outside their sheltered environment, they are very vulnerable, and they sometimes cannot recover from their injury.

Someone who grows up in a place where he is protected and sheltered may grow and develop faster, since his environment is more sterilized and germs do not reach him, but if even one hole is made in this bubble, and he contracts the slightest illness, this will end his life. In far-flung regions of the world, it was often the case that the native people had little immunity to diseases that we consider commonplace. When expeditioners carrying the common cold would arrive, there were cases where this ailment proved fatal for the natives since they had not developed immunity to it. A secluded world can remain a good world as long as there is nothing to bring it down.

The Torah does not encourage us to live in such a world, and conceals from us neither the facts of life nor the facts of the world. The Torah begins with the determination that "the inclination of man's heart is evil from his youth" (Gen. 8:21), and concludes with "I know… that you will become corrupt" (Deut. 31:29). Throughout the Ḥumash, from Genesis to Deuteronomy, the world is described as inwardly and outwardly difficult, and in this regard the Torah does not spare even the *tzaddikim*.

"I know that you will become corrupt" is a tragedy: For forty years in the wilderness, Moses works constantly to bring the People of Israel closer to God, and yet at the end of his life he is forced to admit that in a few more years, all his work will have been for naught. At the time of Joshua's death as well, there still were people who had witnessed the guiding hand of God's providence at every step and turn, and yet after all that, he, too, admits, "I know that you will become corrupt."

This statement can be viewed as a result of either pessimism or despair, but actually Moses is providing the Jewish people with the ability to bear difficulties in the future. Had we not heard his words, it would seem to us that everything is on the verge of collapse. When a good state of affairs is followed by a fall, it often seems as if the period of goodness was a failed attempt, and that the true end is near. Often, something momentous and positive begins, but after a while there is a feeling that it has failed to live up to expectations.

Here Moses tries, difficult as it may be, to prepare the people in advance for the descent. When Moses says, "I know that you will become corrupt," he does not mean to frighten them but to prepare them for the reality that life is full of ascents and descents. While Moses is clearly not a person who sees the world through rose-colored glasses, this, too, is essentially a form of optimism. All in all, the Torah is optimistic, in that it shows the possibility of rectification, but at the same time, it makes clear how challenging this can be.

When Moses takes leave of the people, he tells them that until now everything has gone easily. The prevailing feeling is that they will enter the Land of Israel and life will be simple from then on. But the world is not made that way, Moses explains, and one must prepare for difficulties and falls as well.

Parashat Vayelekh states, "And it shall be there for you as a witness" (Deut. 31:26). Moses here testifies, "I have said that there will be descents and falls; I do not promise that from now on everything will be better. I do, however, promise you that the end will be good, but you must be aware that on the way it may be difficult." Knowing this does not lessen the difficulty for the people, nor is it a way for Moses to say, "I told you so." Yet Moses' statement makes it possible for the people to get through the difficult period when it comes.

The Holocaust was an awful experience for the whole Jewish people, but the severest blow was to those who did not believe that such a thing could happen. People in Western Europe were struck twice: They were struck physically, by death and degradation, and they were struck spiritually, because they could not imagine that the world of Beethoven and gentility could commit such atrocities. When one's assumption is that such a thing cannot happen, the blow is unexplainable. It is not less painful when one knows of it in advance, but if one is prepared for a blow, one is more capable of bearing it.

This can be seen in all areas. The army that is victorious in war is the army that is able to overcome difficulties. In the business world as well, the companies that are able to survive tough times are the companies that were prepared for them in advance, and so are able to absorb losses.

In life, there are descents, falls, and troubles. No one ever wants to be the one to suffer them, but they do happen, and one must be prepared for them. Moses' intention here is not to predict evil events or to rescind his previous statements, but rather to prepare the people for a fall and to warn them that if they are not prepared, their whole world will collapse.

BE STRONG AND TAKE COURAGE

In the Torah, there are many commands that, although they are not counted among the 613 mitzvot, we must fulfill them and take them seriously. One such command is the expression that is repeated three times in our *parasha* and several times in the same connection at the beginning of the book of Joshua – "Be strong and of good courage."

The same idea appears in Psalms 27, which we recite during the month of Elul and the Days of Awe: "Wait for God; be strong and take courage, and wait for God" (Ps. 27:14). Before the problems begin, "wait for God." After the problems are over, "wait for God." And in between, "be strong and take courage."

The command to take courage means not being shaken by problems and not being shattered by troubles, because breaking down in the face of problems is the most dangerous thing one can do. There can be war and other problems, but the greatest danger – in war and in life – is when one is unable to absorb a blow and persevere.

The repeated and emphatic use of the expression "be strong and of good courage" is a call not only for courage in the colloquial sense, but also for a tenacious effort to hold on tightly and steadfastly to one's faith. The secret to serving God is resilience: "Seven times the *tzaddik* falls and gets up" (Prov. 24:16). What characterizes the *tzaddik* is not that he does not fall, but that after the fall he gets up. The wicked fall once and they are finished; they stay down. They do not necessarily begin wicked, but they end up that way, since they do not get up. One who is "strong and takes courage" can withstand almost anything. He can accomplish a great deal and succeed in all that he does. But one who is not "strong and of good courage" has no resilience.

The Talmud states:

> In the time to come, The Holy One, Blessed Be He, will bring the evil inclination and slay it in the presence of the righteous and the wicked. To the righteous it will have the appearance of a high mountain, and to the wicked it will have the appearance of a thread of hair. Both the former and the latter will weep. The righteous will weep, saying, "How were we able to overcome such

a high mountain?" The wicked, too, will weep, saying, "How is it that we were unable to conquer this thread of hair?" (Sukka 52a)

One of the explanations of this passage is that every person experiences trials, and each trial is a thread of hair. The righteous person passes over one thread of hair and then another and another until, over the course of his life, an entire mountain of hair has piled up. By contrast, the wicked person gets stuck at the first thread of hair. When their lives are shown to them, the righteous are shown the mountain they were able to overcome, whereas the wicked are shown only the first thread of hair that stopped them at the start.

During this period, as we approach Rosh HaShana, many people make all sorts of commitments, whether on Rosh HaShana itself or during the *Aseret Yemei Teshuva*. Some people commit to rectifying a certain character flaw, while others add stringencies and additional observances. Everyone, at least for a minute or two, is serious in his intentions. But the year drags on, and indeed can drag a person down. The Talmud says that a year contains 364 days (besides Yom Kippur), corresponding to the numerical value of the word *hasatan* (Satan), who lies in wait and, dressed like everyone else, circulates among us.

Those who make resolutions and fail to fulfill them should take heart. After all, if people would fulfill all the resolutions that they made, then by the time *Shabbat Shuva* arrives each year, the world would look different. However, already between Rosh HaShana and *Shabbat Shuva*, people cannot maintain their commitments. Even between the *Ne'ila* service on Yom Kippur and the *Maariv* service that follows it, people manage to forget.

"Be strong and of good courage" should be understood in the sense of "Though he may fall, he is not utterly cast down" (Ps. 37:24). To fall is part of life, but to be cast down need not be. That is the message Moses conveys at the end of the *parasha*: Come what may, even if one falls, "he is not utterly cast down."

When a person commits a sin, he is liable to become broken, torn, and devoid of courage. If this happens and, as a result, the sinner collapses, he can no longer return. All sins can be rectified, positive commandments as well as negative commandments; but when a person falls and collapses, there is no rectification.

Parashat Vayelekh is not optimistic in the ordinary sense of the word; there is no show of might and power, singing and shouts of joy. On the contrary, it states that "you will become corrupt." We read this either before or after Rosh HaShana, and it means that we must be able to continue, even after "you will become corrupt."

There was once a *tzaddik* who worked as a merchant for many years, and in his business dealings he experienced ups and downs. He would say, "If you lost in business, you lost money; nothing happened. But if you lost your courage, you lost everything."

So, too, *Parashat Vayelekh* says that whether you fall or not, whether you become corrupt or not, no matter what happens – "be strong and take courage."

Shabbat Shuva

Shabbat Shuva – or as it also called, *Shabbat Teshuva* – is the Shabbat that falls out during the *Aseret Yemei Teshuva*, between Rosh HaShana and Yom Kippur. Since Rosh HaShana can fall out on various days of the week, the Torah reading on this Shabbat is not set: Sometimes it is *Parashat Vayelekh*, and sometimes it is *Parashat Haazinu*. What is set aside especially for *Shabbat Shuva*, however, is the *haftara* (Hosea 14:2–10), from which the name *Shabbat Shuva* is derived.[1]

Teshuva is a central theme on this Shabbat, since it is one of the *Aseret Yemei Teshuva*. However, there is an essential problem in the combination of Shabbat and *teshuva*.

Teshuva is commonly understood as inner change that entails a certain amount of retrospection focusing on the negative aspects of one's past conduct. This is because one who is satisfied with and happy about everything he has done regrets nothing, whereas the will and ability to do *teshuva* result to a great extent from the repudiation of the past and the need to distance oneself from it.

To be sure, *teshuva* also has an aspect of rejuvenation, of erasing the past and rewriting oneself, a refreshing aspect of hope for a new beginning. But this aspect, too, contains within it the rejection and destruction of what once was.

---

1. The *haftara* begins with the word *shuva*, meaning "return."

This negation, which can be dramatic and even painful, is found frequently in the words of the prophets. When the prophet says, "Rend your hearts, not just your clothes" (Joel 2:13), the emphasis is not on the act of rending the clothes but on rending the heart.

This aspect of *teshuva* has a time and a place – both in daily prayer, which includes petitions for *teshuva* and forgiveness, and also on certain days of the year that are dedicated to this spiritual work of *teshuva*, with the soul searching and pain that it can entail.

Shabbat stands in contrast to all of this. Shabbat is supposed to be a day of joy, reconciliation, and both spiritual and physical rest. As we recite in the Shabbat prayers, "In love and favor You have given us Your holy Shabbat as an inheritance." For besides the prohibition of work on Shabbat, there is also a general duty to call Shabbat "a delight" (Is. 58:13). Shabbat rest entails not only the cessation of physical work but also the attainment of inner calm and tranquility. For this reason, none of the Shabbat prayers and hymns focuses on *teshuva* or forgiveness. For this reason, too, *Viduy* is not recited on Shabbat, for confession is a part of *teshuva* that involves recollection of sin.

This raises a question about the very name "*Shabbat Shuva.*" Can such a combination of words actually exist in the same phrase? Is it possible to do *teshuva* on Shabbat in an appropriate manner?

The answer to this question is that *Shabbat Shuva* joins Shabbat and *teshuva* not on the simple, ordinary level but on a much deeper level. In fact, the very term *teshuva* hints at a different understanding of this concept than what we are accustomed to hearing. We do not call it *ḥarata* (remorse) or *shevirat lev* (broken-heartedness) but, rather, *teshuva* – return. This return can be accomplished very quickly: One who commits a sin can try to return to the time that preceded this sin. But the return can also be more difficult and complicated, as in the case of someone who, after years of following an improper path, seeks to return to a point before he set out on that path.

For one kind of person, *teshuva* means a return to his childhood days, to a time when his world was more in harmony – with himself, with his family, and with God. But there is another kind of person for whom not even his childhood offers him a secure point from which to return to God. In such cases, *teshuva* takes on a deeper meaning: return to the "original source," the source of a person's being even before his physical life in this world. *Teshuva* on this level, which takes a person farther, beyond his life and deeds in this world, involves much less conflict or confrontation with past defects or blemishes, for it is like a total rebirth, a beginning almost from the point of origin.

Conceptually, Shabbat, too, includes an element of return and restoration of things to their source. To be sure, *shevita* means cessation of action, leaving everything in a state of rest. But the word *shavat* is also connected to *shiva*, meaning "return." Shabbat is a return to a point prior to our coming into being. On the one hand, Shabbat is the completion of everything that exists, but on the other hand, it is a return to the state before Creation, to a state of non-existence, to the day before the first day.

This conception of Shabbat as a state of existence that preceded the world is found, for example, in the *piyut*, "*Lekha Dodi*," which describes Shabbat as "the source of blessing." In other words, Shabbat is not an epilogue to the six days of Creation but a kind of prologue.

The sense of return that is found both in *teshuva* and Shabbat is the heart of the connection between the two. We are encouraged to think little of the past and much more of what could yet be; we do not obsess over our sins, but instead focus on the exaltation of *teshuva*.

On this Shabbat, as on *Shabbat HaGadol*, the synagogue rabbi customarily delivers a *derasha* to the entire congregation. As a rule, the *derasha* deals with matters that are meant to rouse the heart to *teshuva*, but takes into consideration the fact that on Shabbat one should not recall or bring up the difficult matters and painful memories that are generally spoken of when we attain *teshuva*. On *Shabbat Shuva*, we emphasize the *teshuva* of love, not the *teshuva* of remorse and pain. This kind of *teshuva* is a return that is not only based on love, but can only be achieved by returning in the way of love.

The special *haftara* of this Shabbat begins with the words "Return, O Israel" (Hos. 14:2). These words contain the essential message of this Shabbat: the call to return to God.

To be sure, most of our prophets emphasize *teshuva*, for this was their main purpose – to inspire the Jewish people to leave its evil ways and choose the good path. However, most of their prophecies are full of harsh rebuke about sins and the punishments that the individual and the nation will suffer because of those sins if they do not attain *teshuva*. It is not for naught that the Talmud describes the words of the prophets as "words of complaint," referring to the prophets' complaints about Israel and about their sins.[2]

By contrast, Hosea's prophecy read in this *haftara* contains very few words of rebuke, petition, or supplication for the abrogation of punishment. The essence of the *haftara* is a call for complete *teshuva*, for leaving sin and for following a new direction. It also contains words of conciliation, acceptance, and reassurance for those who seek *teshuva*.

What is more, although there are prophecies of consolation in the words of other prophets as well – regarding the future redemption and the good times that will come – those prophecies generally do not deal with the causes of the exile and the suffering. In this *haftara*, however, there is a unique combination: Although it is not a prophecy of redemption but an explicit call for *teshuva*, nevertheless, it consists entirely of words of consolation and conciliation.

These words of comfort, stated with great tenderness, are meant to inspire people in a different way: Look how good it is for people who seek shelter under the wings of the *Shekhina*! Look how much love God bestows on His people and on all who love Him! The *haftara*'s general tone resembles the words of encouragement that one offers to a sick person: How good it will be when you recover! How well you will feel, and how many blessings you will enjoy! Indeed, this is how Ibn Ezra interprets the verse, "I will heal their backsliding, I will love them freely" (Hos. 14:5): "Backsliding in the soul is like illness in the body; thus the words 'I will heal.'"

Finally, the other prophets' words of rebuke deal primarily with *teshuva* out of fear – fear of sin and fear of punishment – whereas in the *haftara* chosen for *Shabbat Shuva* we are encouraged to seek *teshuva* out of love, a *teshuva* whose whole essence is drawing near to God. In this way, the *haftara* reflects the essence of this Shabbat: a conciliatory call to spiritual awakening and drawing near to God.

---

2. See *Shita Mekubetzet*, Bava Kamma 2b.

423

Between the majesty of the judgment on Rosh HaShana and the majesty of the forgiveness on Yom Kippur stands this Shabbat, *Shabbat Shuva*, whose whole essence is the relationship of two lovers between whom a misunderstanding has arisen. Now, as they resolve the misunderstanding, they hold each other in a loving embrace.

Haazinu

THE SONGS OF MOSES

The Song of Moses, which is the essence of *Parashat Haazinu*, corresponds in many respects to the first song of Moses – the Song of the Sea. These two songs are similar in that they are comprehensive poetic compositions written in lyrical language. Both songs exhibit many poetic images and distinctive language that, like the language of epic poetry, makes use of special terms and ancient forms.

The distinctiveness of these two songs also has a halakhic expression: Neither of them is written in the Torah scroll in ordinary sequential style but in a special way that graphically emphasizes the elements of the poetic line, whether through parallelism or in some other way. This written form is very ancient, and it is mentioned in the Mishna as a proper form (Masekhet Soferim 12:7–9).

The distinctiveness of these songs in comparison to other sections in the Torah, most of which are prose or poetic prose, is that from the outset they were meant to be poetry, whose basic characteristic in Tanakh is a fixed meter. Most of the pure poetry in Tanakh can be found in the latter books of the Prophets and some of the books of the Writings, and while the Torah occasionally contains short poems (like the Song of the Well in *Parashat Ḥukkat*), the poetic sections in the Torah are exceptional.

Although the sanctity of these words of song is no less than that of the other parts of the Torah, the songs differ in that they contain a personal element. Throughout the Torah, Moses acts as a scribe, taking dictation from the Almighty; he is completely transparent and introduces nothing of his individual personality. These words of song, however, like other words of prophecy written with divine inspiration, contain a personal nuance that stems from the prophet's personality as well. This is why when two prophets prophesy the same content, each expresses it in his own personal style, so that in a certain respect the uniqueness of the style is the proof of the prophecy's authenticity.

Indeed, the songs of Moses contain an element of his individual personality. Hence, they express not only specific content but also his emotion at the time he recited them. Thus, the difference between the Song of the Sea and the Song of Moses in *Parashat Haazinu* lies not only in their content but also in the general message and the overtones that they convey.

Be that as it may, the Song of the Sea and the Song of Moses stand apart from similar songs in Tanakh, such as the Song of Deborah and the Song of David. Although these songs feature God's mercy and power as their main subject, they both consist of the statements of the poet himself, whereas the songs of Moses are completely devoid of any explicitly personal element. Moses does not speak of himself, neither in the Song of the Sea nor in the Song of Moses. Here, too, he tries to function as merely the instrument, not the poet.

THE SONG OF THE SEA AND THE SONG OF MOSES

The Song of the Sea is primarily a song of victory and praise for God's salvation, whereas the Song of Moses summarizes the past and turns to the future. The song of praise for the victory at the sea primarily relates to the past, to the events that transpired, but it also contains wishes and words of prophecy for the future. By contrast, while the Song of Moses certainly contains references to the past, it is conspicuously concerned with the future.

The two songs can be distinguished from each other in that the Song of the Sea is Moses' song for, and in the name of, all of Israel, whereas the Song of Moses is his personal message to the People of Israel.

When Moses sings the Song of the Sea, he sings it together with all of Israel – "Then Moses and the People of Israel sang" (Ex. 15:1). They all, in one way or another (see Sota 27b), participate with him in the words of praise and thanksgiving.

In the Song of the Sea, there is also another aspect that gives a positive tone to the vision of the future. Now that Moses' leadership is completely accepted by all of Israel – as it says in the introduction, "They believed in God and in His servant Moses" (Ex. 14:31) – Moses is able to sing as Israel's representative.

Moreover, Moses was then in the company of his confidants Aaron and Miriam, not only his own flesh and blood but also his helpers and assistants, and they, too, participated in this song.

Above all, the Song of the Sea was the beginning of a road that was meant to be one of increasing ascent, from God's mountain to the Holy Land, a path that is full of hope, with no worry or fear.

The Song of Moses is a song of the end of the road. It is sung at the end of the forty years of wandering in the wilderness, at the point where Moses conveys to Israel his parting words. Hence, this song is Moses' testament and guidance for the future.

Parashat Haazinu contains a veil of sadness. Although Moses fully accepts the divine judgment, he is not happy with it; as it says earlier in Deuteronomy, he would have wanted to finish his life in the Land of Israel.

In addition, almost all of the Song of Moses speaks of the future, not only of upcoming events but also of the course of history.

This song is both a prophecy and the appointment of witnesses – heaven and earth – who attest to its words forever. Since the song constitutes words of prophecy, by its very nature it is the appeal of the lonely prophet to the people. The prophet does not speak "in the name of all of Israel" but in the name of God. The prophet places a partition between himself and the people; he does not speak for them, but to them.

A SONG OF CHALLENGE

But these differences between the songs, differences in tone and in context, are nothing compared with the main difference, the difference in content. The Song of the Sea is praise, and like every song of praise, it is essentially a recitation of good things. By contrast, the Song of Moses is a song of challenge: It has a vision that is based upon an assumption that the people will not be able to remain steadily on the path of tranquil progress. There are too many factors, from various angles, that can lead to failures and falls. Although the Jewish people possess a sense of national memory more than any other nation, nevertheless, there is forgetfulness that results from distance in time and from engaging in other things. In times of success, there is a tendency toward self-satisfaction.

The inclination of the individual, and certainly of an entire nation, is to achieve normalization, an ordinary life without special demands and requirements. The Song of Moses speaks not only of the possibility of such an inclination taking hold, but also, and primarily, of the fact that God will not allow Israel to become merely one of the nations.

Here we see the very same idea that appears in the book of Ezekiel, where the prophet speaks of the people's desire to be like the nations of the lands, and of God's harsh words in response: "As I live, declares Lord God, with a strong hand, with an outstretched arm and with outpoured fury will I reign over you" (20:33). All of the Song of Moses is a repetition, in various forms, of this motif: the fall and the descent, the suffering and punishments, but also the fact that God will lead His people on a path fraught with suffering and pain, in the "wilderness of the peoples" (20:35), and in the end will also save and redeem them. It not only promises redemption but also, more than once, mentions vengeance.

Moses transmits this song to Israel and instructs them to remember it and to memorize it. Indeed, some today maintain that it is a special mitzva to learn this song and teach it to children.

To be sure, the entire Torah communicates the idea of this song in many diverse ways. The main content of the song is stated in great detail in Moses' two reproofs, which also contain prophecies of wrath for the future. Nevertheless, the advantage of the song is precisely that it is a song. Prose is perhaps stored in our memory, and from time to time even rises in our consciousness. Song, however, is not only remembered from the text but from recitation and singing as well.

Although Moses communicates this message in several forms, here he gives an explicit command: "Now therefore write down this song and teach it to the People of Israel; put it in their mouth, so that this song may be a witness for Me against the People of Israel" (Deut. 31:19). This song must not only be written in a scroll, which one opens from time to time; it must be in their mouths, so that these words – precisely because of their poetic and sometimes obscure language – should echo and be remembered.

Vezot HaBerakha

MOSES' BLESSING AND JACOB'S BLESSING

Parashat Vezot HaBerakha has two focuses: the blessing that Moses bestows on Israel before his death and the account of his death.

Moses' blessing to Israel almost forces a comparison to the corresponding blessing in Genesis 49, the blessing that Jacob bestows on his sons before his death. These two blessings are not just a leader's parting words before his death; they also contain an aspect of guidance and prophecy.

The main difference between the blessings is that Jacob's blessing relates to all the tribes, whereas Moses' blessing skips at least one tribe – the tribe of Simeon.

The reason for this is that Jacob's blessing is primarily directed to his sons, and since he has twelve sons, each one merits attention. In Moses' blessing, however, this is not the case. Although he relates to the existing units that are still based on the tribal division, he has before him another significant structure: the People of Israel. Indeed, a considerable part of Moses' blessing – both its beginning and its end – relates not at all to individual tribes but to the People of Israel as a nation, in which the division into tribes, despite their significance, is becoming increasingly blurred.

Another difference between the blessings is their tone. Although Jacob's blessing is a father's parting blessing to his sons, Jacob tells his

430

sons from the outset that he will not only relate to them as they are now, but will also prophesy future events. By contrast, in Moses' blessing, although it, too, certainly contains allusions and references to future events, the main focus is on the tribes as they are in the present, not in the future. In short, Moses' blessing is composed only of words of blessing, whereas Jacob's blessing contains words of reproof and prophecy as well.

Jacob, alongside the prophecies for the future and the words of praise for some of his sons, does not spare his first three sons harsh words of reproof for their past mistakes and sins. By contrast, in Moses' blessing, there are no words of condemnation at all.

The reason for this is that Moses is not the father of the tribes; he cannot act like Jacob, who, upon departing from this world, could address his sons' sins. Hence, Moses does not mention the sins themselves at all.

Although it is reasonable to assume that his omission of the tribe of Simeon is not accidental but is a value judgment of the tribe, Moses does not spell this out. Additionally, although the Torah does not spell out the matter entirely, most of the sinners involved in Israel's sin at Shittim were Simeonites. A hint of this can be detected in the killing of one of the tribe's princes by Pinḥas, and another hint emerges from the final census taken of Israel in the wilderness, in which the only tribe whose number has decreased drastically is Simeon (Num. 26:14). This numerical decrease corresponds more or less to the number of those who died or were killed after the sin at Shittim. Nevertheless, Moses does not censure the tribe, but merely ignores it, or, as several commentators suggest, subtly includes it within the tribe of Judah.

MOSES AND JOSHUA

Besides these contextual differences, whether in the nature of the one giving the blessing or in the purpose of the blessing, there are differences in the treatment of the tribes themselves.

Like Jacob's blessing, Moses' blessing features Judah and Joseph prominently. These two tribes serve important roles, not only in the present but also in the future of the Jewish people. However, whereas Jacob's prophetic blessing, which relates both to the individual personality and the distant future, gives almost equal treatment to Judah and Joseph, Moses' blessing of Joseph is greater and more detailed than that of Judah. Here, too, as in Jacob's blessing, Joseph's two sons Ephraim and Menashe are blessed independently.

Although the commentators have not discussed the matter comprehensively, the extraordinary emphasis on the tribes of Joseph in Moses' blessing is not a vision for distant generations. In fact, over the generations, the position and significance of the tribe of Judah has been much more central than any other tribe, including the tribes of Joseph. Here, in Moses' blessing, the focus is on the present and immediate future, and is probably connected with Joshua.

Joshua was not just a member of the tribe of Joseph; he had a direct familial connection to the tribe's leadership (1 Chr. 7:26–27). For this reason, Moses gives special attention to the tribe that is most closely connected to him, the tribe of his right-hand man Joshua.

Although in the blessing itself Joshua is not mentioned by name, in the final *parashot* his character grows in significance, for Joshua fulfills the complicated and difficult role of taking over the leadership of Israel after Moses.

Anyone who enters the shoes of a giant personality will inevitably suffer from the comparison, whether he is a disciple or a son. Indeed, in Jewish history throughout the generations, we see how people who, taken on their own merits, were supremely exalted individuals, yet did not attain the prominence they deserved because their predecessors were so great that no one could properly succeed them.

The Talmud's characterization of Joshua demonstrates this clearly: "Moses' countenance was like that of the sun; Joshua's countenance was like that of the moon" (Bava Batra 75a). Although the moon is a great luminary as well, its light and intensity cannot be compared to those of the sun.

A less ancient historical example is the case of Rabbi Abraham the son of Maimonides, whose achievements were overshadowed by those of his great father. If Rabbi Abraham had lived in another context, he certainly would have received greater attention as one of the outstanding Torah leaders of the generation.

In addition to replacing Moses, Joshua is also given the responsibility of conquering the Land of Israel. An almost direct reference to this important task appears in Moses' blessing to Joseph: "His firstling ox, majesty is his; and his horns are the horns of the wild ox. With them he will gore the peoples all of them, even the ends of the earth" (Deut. 33:17).

Many interpret that the special treatment accorded to the tribe of Gad, the length of whose blessing is disproportionate to the tribe's historical importance, is because the blessing contains an allusion to Moses' own personality. When Jacob blesses his sons, he is certainly aware that he is addressing the tribes of Israel, but his blessings still retain a personal aspect. Moses' blessing, however, is addressed to the entire people, and thus there is no room for a personal element. Nevertheless, Moses seems to grant the tribe of Gad a special blessing because he knows that his burial site will be within their allotted territory. As he says, "for that is where the plot of the Lawgiver is hidden" (see Rashi, Deut. 33:21).

SIMEON AND LEVI

The biggest difference between Jacob's blessing and Moses' blessing is how they relate to the tribe of Levi.

Levi the man, the son of Jacob, receives from his father both words of reproof and a dim prediction of his future as dispersed and scattered, without a hold in any specific point of settlement in the Land of Israel (Gen. 49:7).

By contrast, Moses' blessing sets forth for the tribe of Levi the possibility of redefinition and rectification. By changing their ways, the Levites have the ability to gain a new awareness, which can not only rectify past faults but can also transform them from evil to good.

In addition, the tribe of Levi receives a lengthy and detailed blessing that relates to the tribe's special status, which was granted to it not only by God's choice but also as a consequence of its deeds. During the wilderness years, the tribe of Levi distinguished itself as the tribe of loyalists, the personal guard of the Sanctuary and the sacred. In this regard, God's command and His choice of the tribe of Levi came as a result of the complete devotion and faithfulness of the tribe's members to God and His Torah.

The Midrash notes that Jacob's blessing to Simeon and Levi, "I will disperse them in Jacob and scatter them in Israel," took on different meanings over the generations (Genesis Rabba 99:6). The tribe of Simeon, along with its territory, was absorbed almost entirely by the neighboring tribes over the course of its history, and it is mentioned sparingly throughout Tanakh. Jacob's prophecy was fulfilled also in regard to Levi, only that it assumed a different form: Although Levi was not given any portion or inheritance, "God is his heritage" (Deut. 10:9).

The blessing here to Levi bears an important message, which becomes especially clear when compared to Jacob's blessing. Apparently, the destiny of a person or of a whole community is predetermined and cannot be changed. Even after numerous efforts and changes in direction, life's general outline remains unchanged. Nevertheless, there are ways in which inner changes, *teshuva*, and good deeds can give a new aspect to one's predetermined fate. Even though there is a certain outline that cannot be fundamentally changed, nevertheless, every person has the power to change the meaning of this outline.

Similarly, our sages say that every newborn infant already has, from the beginning of his existence, contours that determine his characteristics, his achievements, even the nature of his personal life, yet he nevertheless has the freedom to change all of these (Nidda 16b). This does not contradict what was preordained but, rather, changes its meaning.

MOSES' DEPARTURE

At end of the *parasha*, the Torah's description of Moses' death is quite obscure. On the one hand, God fulfills His promise to Moses and shows him the Land of Israel. Our sages explain that He shows Moses not only the geography of the Land of Israel but also everything that is destined to take place in it (*Mekhilta, Beshallaḥ* 2). Moses gazes and sees not only the mountains and the sea but also the history, its rises and its majesty as well as its pains and its desolation.

Nevertheless, since Moses dies alone, his death is, in many respects, a mystery. From Israel's point of view, Moses does not die; he returns to his own plane of existence. Moses is described as "a fish that leaves the sea and walks on dry land" (see Zohar, *Balak* 187–188), meaning that although he walked and lived his life within our reality, he belongs and exists in a different world entirely. For this reason, Maimonides, who was a great admirer of Moses, writes in the introduction to his *Commentary on the Mishna*, "This was his death for us, since he was lost to us, but [it was] life for him, in that he was elevated to Him.

As [our sages], peace be upon them, said, 'Moses our Master did not die; rather, he ascended and is serving on high' (Sota 13b)." Moses dies only from the standpoint of his absence from the world, the world of human beings, but not in the sense of coming to an end.

The Torah implies that Moses is buried by God Himself; hence, Moses' burial is itself a supernatural event. In addition, we read in *Pirkei Avot* that Moses' burial is one of the physical creations that do not fully belong to the material world (5:6).

We see, then, that Moses' death was not a consequence of bodily deterioration and ruin, for "his eyes had not dimmed and his vigor had not departed" (Deut. 34:7). Hence, Moses' death was merely a "departure" – *histalkut*, in the lexicon of Kabbala: an uplift, an ascent.

The grand summary regarding Moses and his life's work raises here what Maimonides counts among the major principles of our faith: that the prophecy of Moses is the highest prophecy of all; that there never was nor will there ever be anyone like Moses, whose prophecy is the last word, the final summation of God's word to the world.

It is certainly fitting to conclude the book with the following mysterious words, which we would not have believed had our sages not uttered them: "What is the meaning of 'Moses, man of God' (Deut. 33:1)? From the middle of his [body] downward, [he was] a man; from the middle upward, [he was] of God" (Deuteronomy Rabba 11:4).

The fonts used in this book are from the Arno family

Maggid Books
The best of contemporary Jewish thought from
Koren Publishers Jerusalem Ltd.